Creole Religions of the Caribbean

Creole Religions of the Caribbean

An Introduction from Vodou and Santería to Obeah and Espiritismo

SECOND EDITION

Margarite Fernández Olmos and
Lizabeth Paravisini-Gebert

FOREWORD BY
Joseph M. Murphy

NEW YORK UNIVERSITY PRESS
New York and London

NEW YORK UNIVERSITY PRESS
New York and London
www.nyupress.org

References to Internet websites (URLs) were accurate at the time of writing.
Neither the author nor New York University Press is responsible for URLs
that may have expired or changed since the manuscript was prepared.

Library of Congress Cataloging-in-Publication Data
Fernández Olmos, Margarite.
Creole religions of the Caribbean : an introduction from Vodou and Santería
to Obeah and Espiritismo / Margarite Fernández Olmos and Lizabeth Paravisini-Gebert ;
foreword by Joseph M. Murphy. — 2nd ed.
p. cm. — (Religion, race, and ethnicity)
Includes bibliographical references and index.
ISBN 978-0-8147-6227-1 (cl : alk. paper) — ISBN 978-0-8147-6228-8
(pb : alk. paper) — ISBN 978-0-8147-2825-3 (e-book : alk. paper)
1. Afro-Caribbean cults. I. Paravisini-Gebert, Lizabeth. II. Title. III. Series.
BL2565.F47   2011
299.6'897294—dc22   2011003688

New York University Press books are printed on acid-free paper,
and their binding materials are chosen for strength and durability.
We strive to use environmentally responsible suppliers and materials
to the greatest extent possible in publishing our books.

Manufactured in the United States of America

c   10 9 8 7 6 5 4 3 2 1
p   10 9 8 7 6 5 4 3 2 1

Contents

Acknowledgments

Grateful thanks to the Professional Staff Congress of the City University of New York for a research grant. At Brooklyn College my appreciation for a Tow Faculty Travel Grant and to the Wolfe Institute for the Humanities for a faculty fellowship, both of which were crucial to the successful completion of this project, to Sherry Warman of the Brooklyn College Interlibrary Loan Department, to José Salce for his generous and proficient computer assistance, and to Robert Scott for his abiding support. Thanks also to AnaLouise Keating for her generous and valuable assistance with Gloria Anzaldúa scholarship, and to my always understanding and patient family, Enrique and Gabriela Olmos, much loving gratitude.

M.F.O.

Support for the writing of this book was provided by the Faculty Research Program and the Dean of the Faculty at Vassar College. I am deeply grateful to Lucinda Dubinsky of the Inter-Library Loan Department at Vassar, the staff of the Schomburg Center of the New York Public Library, and those friends and colleagues—principally Colin Dayan, Anna Wexler, and Ivette Romero-Cesareo—whose knowledge and critical eye were so important to my writing. My research assistant, Luis Marcial, was extraordinarily resourceful and diligent in the preparation of the first edition of the book. For help with the second edition I am most grateful to research assistants Camille Paul and Katy Indvik. My family—Gordon, Carrie, D'Arcy, and Gordon Jr.—without whose love and support my work would not be possible, have my never-ending gratitude.

L.P.G.

Preface to the First Edition

The Creole religions at the center of this book have been the focus of our work for many years. In earlier publications—namely, *Sacred Possessions: Vodou, Santeria, Obeah, and the Caribbean* (1997) and *Healing Cultures: Art and Religion as Curative Practices in the Caribbean and Its Diaspora* (2001)—we had sought to bring together the work of scholars and artists working on various disciplinary aspects of Caribbean Creole religious practices, seeking to convey the richness and variety of these African-derived cultural expressions. As scholars teaching in the area of Latin American and Caribbean Studies, however, we had been aware for some time of the need for a more general, introductory text that could be used as a teaching tool and as a springboard for future research. We were therefore very pleased when New York University Press offered us the opportunity to prepare this introductory volume.

The introductory nature of this work offers wonderful opportunities for showcasing the common roots and comparative aspects of religious practices that are quite unique and dynamic. The task of examining the entire range of dynamic religions practiced in such a wide geographic and cultural area, which includes the Caribbean Diaspora communities, however, imposes some choices and restrictions on the text. As a result, we have limited the geographic area considered in the following pages to the islands of the Caribbean basin, and the religions to a limited number of practices, those best known and most pervasive in the region and its Diaspora: Vodou, Santería, Obeah, Espiritismo, Quimbois, and their various manifestations.

The practice of Creole religions in Diasporan communities also impacted the direction of our research and its presentation: we both grew up in Caribbean homes (in Puerto Rico and the United States), where we experienced firsthand the dynamism and centrality of these religious practices, and we have both personally experienced the Caribbean Diaspora to the United States and are a part of that community. But beyond personal considerations, the Diasporic condition—which is so fundamentally Caribbean—is today a global concern, linking, through the encounters of peoples and cultures engaged in transnational movement, the ongoing (re)construction of identities that is itself a form of global creolization. Religion is one of the crucial elements of that ongoing process for the peoples of the Caribbean.

In the elaboration of this introductory study, we have greatly benefited from the experiences and research of numerous experts in the field—ethnographers, anthropologists, historians, sociologists, religious scholars, linguists, literary authors, and critics, among others—whose scholarship and creative work, together with the testimonial narratives of devotees of these religions, have made this book possible. Our most difficult task has been that of gleaning from the complexity and deeply etched nuances of those materials our own authentic, candid, yet comprehensive account intended for nonexperts with an interest in these fascinating and significant, although frequently misrepresented, cultural and religious practices.

Preface to the Second Edition

The interest and scholarship in Creole religions is like the creolization process itself: always evolving. The prospect of publishing a second edition of *Creole Religions of the Caribbean* was a daunting one, particularly given the surge of scholarship in recent years in the fields of Diaspora Studies and Caribbean Studies. The term creolization has been a contentious one, an issue we address in this second edition, which brings up to date the scholarship on the religions themselves and also expands the regional considerations of the Diaspora to Mexican American and other U.S. Latinos who are influenced by Creole spiritual practices. The increased significance of material culture—art, music, literature—and the healing practices influenced by Creole religions are also taken into account.

Scholars and students have used our work and made helpful suggestions for the revisions included herein. We are grateful for their input and are also keenly aware of the continued need for this work and many others like it. We noted in the Preface to the first edition that Creole religions are "frequently misrepresented, cultural and religious practices" and agree ultimately with Aisha Khan that "[h]egemonic and abiding, prejudices, stereotypes, and presumptions are notoriously slow to become corrected—in either popular or scholarly imagination."[1] We hope our work contributes to a better informed perception, adding another voice to a crucial ongoing conversation.

Foreword

It is wonderful to see this new edition of *Creole Religions of the Caribbean*. Margarite Fernández Olmos and Lizabeth Paravisini-Gebert have expanded and updated their first offering to bring out the most comprehensive introduction to Caribbean religions available. The new volume does yet more to educate and delight its readers as it breaks down misunderstandings and presents the various traditions in their beauty and power. One of the signal contributions of the new volume is a careful consideration of the term "Creole" and its various meanings in the experience of the Americas. For me "Creole" means creative, and Creole religions are inspired constructions of symbols out of wide experience and often deep hardship. The men and women who built the Creole religions portrayed here were forced by terrible circumstance to create healing systems out of the fragments of cultural materials available to them. They responded with profound and effective medicines to survive and thrive in the brave new world of the Caribbean.

The authors take into full account the rapid growth of scholarship on Caribbean religions and bring it to bear on the entrenched popular misconceptions that surround them. *Creole Religions* is a major step forward in the slow work of enlightening readers to the historic struggles and cultural triumphs of Caribbean peoples. Their traditions have now become world religions, as we find Rastafarians in South Africa and *babalawos* in the Netherlands. All the religions featured here are in renaissance in the United States and are being reclaimed and reimagined by people of all backgrounds. More and more Americans are finding "a righteous place" in Creole religious communities, places of inclusion and empowerment. Their embrace of creativity in symbol building suggests a key to understanding the future of American religiosity as borders are crossed and new communities formed. *Creole Religions of the Caribbean* is a critical work in understanding and appreciating these vital spiritualities among us.

Joseph M. Murphy
Georgetown University

Caribbean map. With permission of Amelia Lau Carling © 1991.

Introduction

What piece of our soil was not saturated with secret African influences?

—Lydia Cabrera, *Yemayá y Ochún*

Luis is a young man who works in the stockroom of a tourist café in Havana. An inventory reveals five boxes of missing supplies and, despite his claims of innocence, the police consider him a suspect. In his distress, he seeks out Marín, his spiritual godfather or padrino, a lifelong friend whose spiritual work in Santería, Regla de Palo, and Espiritismo follows the practices of his African ancestors. Marín summons the spirit of Ma Pancha, an African slave with whom he has communicated on previous occasions. Marín sits before a home altar that contains, among other things, the statues of the Catholic saints San Juan Bosco and Santa Bárbara, and a glass of water. Uncorking a bottle of strong cane liquor, he pours a drink into a dry gourd, lights a homemade cigar, and chants a verse, calling upon Ma Pancha's spirit to respond "in the name of Jesus Christ and of Papá Changó." At this point Ma Pancha greets them in broken Spanish through Marín's voice with "Good morning, how are my children here on this earth?" and is informed of the problem. Stating that Luis's boss is responsible for the theft, Ma Pancha counsels the men to gather the bark of certain types of trees "to open the eyes of the police" and suggests that Marín prepare a *macuto* or magical pouch, and dedicate it to Ochosi, the deity of forests and herbs, patron of those with problems involving the law, to protect Luis and convince the authorities of his innocence. The macuto is assembled with the name of the guilty party placed inside and set at the base of a nganga or spiritual cauldron.

Paulette, a middle-aged Haitian woman living in Coral Gables, Miami, has been married to a lawyer and former politician for many years. When she discovers that her husband is having an affair with his young secretary, a friend suggests that she speak with Denizé, a houngan, or Vodou priest who does spiritual readings using cards for divination. During the reading Paulette discovers that her tutelary *lwa* (spirit) is Erzulie, spirit of femininity and sensuality, and Denizé advises her to make efforts to become more attractive to her husband. He recommends a purifying bath of white flowers, powdered egg shells, and perfume, during which Paulette would be released from all negativity. Afterwards, she is to leave the flowers at a crossroads. He instructs Paulette to cleanse her house with water composed of the same ingredients as the bath, adding a bit of honey. She is to make an offering to Erzulie of sweet fruit and honey to be placed on her home altar. After the reading, Denizé prepares a small bottle of perfume for Paulette to bring her *chans*, or luck. In it he inserts a small plant (*wont*) believed to have the power to open paths for the achievement of goals.

Desmond and Earl, young Jamaicans living in Toronto, have engaged in a series of robberies involving small suburban banks. They are assiduous clients of an Obeahman, from whom they seek the ritual cleansings and massages they believe will protect them from arrest and punishment. When they kill a young woman during a robbery, their Obeahman alerts the police to their possible involvement. Surveillance equipment is installed in his consultation room, and when his clients return—this time seeking protection that will allow them to return to Jamaica, where the woman's duppy or spirit will not follow them to do them harm—their sessions are recorded and the evidence leads to their arrest. The case against them centers on the admissibility of the evidence, an issue that itself revolves around the confidentiality—or sacredness—of the communications, or "confessions," between the Obeahman and his client. The sanctity of their interactions is rejected by the courts on the basis of Obeah being a healing practice and not a religion, and the two are convicted of robbery and murder.

These tales—based on the actual experiences of people living in the Caribbean and its Diaspora—speak to the continuing power of the Afro-Caribbean spiritual traditions that have sustained the peoples of the region and beyond for centuries. *Creole Religions of the Caribbean* is intended as a comprehensive introduction to the creolized, African-based religions that developed in the Caribbean in the wake of European colonization. It shows how Caribbean peoples fashioned a heterogeneous system of belief out of the cacophony of practices and traditions that came forcibly together in colonial society: the various religious and healing traditions represented by the extensive slave population brought to the New World through the Middle Passage; Spanish, French, and Portuguese variants of Catholicism; the myriad strands of Protestantism brought to the English and Dutch colonies; and remnants of Amerindian animistic practices.

Creolized religious systems, developed in secrecy, were frequently out-lawed by the colonizers because they posed a challenge to official Christian practices and were believed to be associated with magic and sorcery. They nonetheless allowed the most oppressed sectors of colonial Caribbean soci-eties to manifest their spirituality, express cultural and political practices suppressed by colonial force, and protect the health of the community. These complex systems developed in symbiotic relationships to the social, linguistic, religious, and natural environments of the various islands of the Caribbean, taking their form and characteristics from the subtle blends and clashes between different cultural, political, and spiritual practices. This book traces the historical-cultural origins of the major Creole religions and spiritual practices of the region—Vodou, Santería, Obeah, Espiritismo—and describes their current-day expression in the Caribbean and its Diaspora.[1]

Caribbean Creole religions developed as the result of cultural contact. The complex dynamics of encounters, adaptations, assimilation, and syncretism that we refer to as creolization are emblematic of the vibrant nature of Dias-pora cultures. They led to the development of a complex system of religious and healing practices that allowed enslaved African communities that had already suffered devastating cultural loss to preserve a sense of group and personal identity. Having lost the connection between the spirits and Africa during the Middle Passage, they strove to adapt their spiritual environment to suit their new Caribbean space. The flexibility, eclecticism, and mallea-bility of African religions allowed practitioners to adapt to their new envi-ronments, drawing spiritual power from wherever it originated. More than simply a strategy for survival, this dynamic, conscious, syncretic process demonstrates an appreciation for the intrinsic value of creativity, growth, and change as well as for the spiritual potential of other belief systems.

Transculturation, a term coined by Cuban anthropologist Fernando Ortiz to describe the ceaseless creation of new cultures, was intended to counter-balance the notion of acculturation, the term in vogue among anthropolo-gists during the 1940s. Ortiz understood the notion of acculturation as one that interpreted the development of Caribbean cultures as the one-way imposition of the culture of the dominant or conquering nation on the con-quered societies, an imposition that devalued and eventually supplanted the conquered cultures. Believing that colonization had initiated instead a cre-ative, ongoing process of appropriation, revision, and survival leading to the mutual transformation of two or more pre-existing cultures into a new one, Ortiz posited the notion of transculturation as a more accurate rendering of the processes that produced contemporary Caribbean cultures.

Religious practices were at the very center of the processes of transculturation. "Throughout the diaspora, African religions provided important
cultural resources for not only reconstructing ethnic ties and social relations
that had been disrupted by slavery, but also for forging new collective identities, institutions and belief systems which partook of the cultures of diverse
African peoples to meet the daunting challenges of new and oppressive social
contexts" (Gregory 1999: 12). The metaphor for the process of transculturation used by Fernando Ortiz is the *ajiaco*, a delicious soup made with very
diverse ingredients, in which the broth that stays at the bottom represents
an integrated nationality, the product of synthesis. This metaphor has found
an echo throughout the Caribbean region, finding its counterpart in the
Dominican *sancocho* and the West Indian *callaloo*. However, although rich
in metaphoric power, neither the ajiaco nor the callaloo are ideal formulas.
They have been challenged by Caribbean scholars and critics for failing to do
full justice to the "undissolved ingredients" represented by the magical, life-
affirming elements of Afro-Caribbean religions. Cuban art critic Gerardo
Mosquera, for example, has argued that "beside the broth of synthesis, there
are bones, gristle, and hard seeds that never fully dissolve, even after they
have contributed their substance to the broth. These undissolved ingredients
are the survivals and recreations of African traditions within religious-cul-
tural complexes" (1992: 30).

Creolization

Creolization—that is, the malleability and mutability of various beliefs and
practices as they adapt to new understandings of class, race, gender, power,
labor, and sexuality—is one of the most significant phenomena in Caribbean
religious history. Given the subtle negotiations necessary for the survival of
the cultural practices of the enslaved and colonized in the highly hierarchical
colonial societies of the Caribbean, the resulting religious systems are fundamentally complex, pluralistic, and integrationist. In our approach to the creolized religious systems that developed in the region in the wake of colonization, we seek to avoid essentialist definitions of religious experience, opting
instead for a practice- or experience-based presentation and analysis, rooted
in particular historical circumstances. Although the Creole religions vary in
their origins, beliefs, and rituals, all of them demonstrate the complexities
and the creative resourcefulness of the creolization process.

The term *creole* was first used in the Americas to refer to native-born
persons of European ancestry and evolved from a geographical to an ethnic

label: New World enslaved Africans were distinguished from African-born contemporaries by the label *criollos*. Hoetink notes the multiple contemporary nuances of the term.[2]

> I take the word *creole* to mean the opposite of foreign. Thus *creole culture* refers to those aspects of culture that evolved or were adapted in the Western Hemisphere and became part of a New World society's distinctive heritage. In Latin America, the term *criollo*, when used in reference to people, was originally reserved for native whites. In the Hispanic Caribbean nowadays, it often includes all those born and bred in a particular society. Elsewhere, as in Suriname, the term may be used to denote long-established population groups, such as the Afro-Americans, as opposed to more recent immigration groups. (1985: 82)

Melville Herskovits challenged prevailing assumptions regarding the survival of African influences in the New World in his *Myth of the Negro Past* (1941), demonstrating in great detail that African culture has survived and indeed thrived. In the 1970s, Edward Kamau Brathwaite in his essay, "The African Presence in Caribbean Literature" and in *Folk Cultures of the Slaves in Jamaica*, claimed that the Middle Passage "was not, as is popularly assumed, a traumatic, destructive experience, separating the blacks from Africa, disconnecting their sense of history and tradition, but a pathway or channel between this tradition and what is being evolved, on new soil, in the Caribbean" (Brathwaite 1974: 5).

Creolization thus describes the ongoing and ever-changing process (not the static result) of new forms born or developed from the interaction of peoples and forces due to "adaptive pressures omnipresent and irresistible" in the Americas (Buisseret 2000, "Introduction": 7). The concept of Creole and creolization has been extended to other "transplanted" categories of interchange: from linguistic speech variations (*Créole*, for example, refers to the national language of Haiti, developed as a result of Old and New World contact) and literary styles to a wide range of cultural contexts—religious, musical, curative, and culinary (Mintz and Price 1985: 6–7). "There is, then, a vast range of examples of the Creolizing process, even without taking into account such areas of human activity as art, law, material culture, military organization, politics, or social structures" (Buisseret 2000, "Introduction": 12).

Anthropologists, historians, and literary and social critics continue to expand the linguistic application of the term creolization to that of metaphor for a wide and diverse cross-cultural and transnational phenomena.

Aisha Khan's essay in *Creolization: History, Ethnography, Theory* describes our conception of the term as defined above and throughout this book as a "means of revealing the successful and creative agency of subaltern or deterritorialized peoples, and the subversiveness inhering in creolization, which contradicts earlier notions of cultural dissolution and disorganization" and considers it among several definitions used in creolist scholarship.[3] The editor of *Creolization*, Charles Stewart, acknowledges that the term "'creole' has itself creolized, which is what happens to all productive words with long histories."[4]

> [T]he concept of creolization is at once fascinating, fertile and potentially confusing. Those who approach it from one or another of the disciplinary approaches or literary currents . . . or with the normative meaning from a particular historical period in mind, are in for some surprises should they encounter it outside their own familiar territory. (2007: 3)

According to Silvio Torres-Saillant in *An Intellectual History of the Caribbean*, in the late 1980s the focus on postcolonial cultural studies and globalizing theoretical approaches in European and North American intellectual circles elicited globalized paradigms from Caribbeanists: "Perhaps sensing that the focus of Third World thought production had shifted away from their region, Caribbeanists gradually came to give in to the new academic world order. Thus marginalized, they began to assert the relevance of their studies by highlighting their link to the larger, grander, and more 'theoretical' postcolonial field" (2006: 43). The manner in which they secured their intellectual legitimacy, however, is problematic for Torres-Saillant: Caribbeanists relied on the pillars of Western tradition as they did prior to the rise of anticolonialism in the region, reaffirming the "centrality of Western critical theory" (44).[5] One example he cites among many is that of Antonio Benítez Rojo, who examined the notion of creolization utilizing the Western scientific branch of physics known as Chaos Theory in his influential work, *The Repeating Island: The Caribbean and the Postmodern Perspective* (1996), which describes creolization by means of three fundamental principles: plantation, rhythm, and performance.

> [C]reolization is not merely a process (a word that implies forward movement) but a discontinuous series of recurrences, of happenings, whose sole law is change. Where does this instability come from? It is the product of the plantation (the big bang of the Caribbean universe), whose slow explo-

sion throughout modern history threw out billions and billions of cultural fragments in all directions—fragments of diverse kinds that, in their endless voyage, come together in an instant to form a dance step, a linguistic trope, the line of a poem, and afterward repel each other to re-form and pull apart once more, and so on. (1996: 55)[6]

Cultural *bricolage*, from the French, meaning to improvise with whatever is at hand—a concept introduced by French structural anthropologist Claude Lévi-Strauss in *The Savage Mind* (1966) to describe a form of being in the world—is another Western model used to describe the creolization process. "Creolization can be seen enacted through bricolage as the art of the disparate and fragmentary; the art of adopting and adapting multiple concrete fragments or artifacts as well as elements of imaginative, ideological, cultural, social or religious practices, experiences, and beliefs" (Knepper 2006: 73). Wendy Knepper notes, however, that while Lévi-Strauss's use of the term bricolage may be politically neutral, the application of the word to describe the creolization process in the Caribbean is evasive; there, cultural bricolage was an uneven process, highly politicized, involving "selective, coerced, forced, and violent intermixtures in addition to spontaneous meldings, subversive appropriations, and processes of adaptation. The creolist appropriation of this structuralist term could be seen as instituting a kind of white-washing of bricolage rather than consciously embracing the ambivalent cultural and sociopolitical etymology of bricolage within the Caribbean" (73).

The concept of creolization has thus expanded to become synonymous with hybridity, syncretism, multiculturalism, créolité, métissage, mestizaje, postcolonialism, and diaspora.[7] In an age of mass migrations and globalization, creolization is employed to reframe notions of past and present transnational and diasporan cultures and communities. In the French West Indies, for example, the concept of *créolité* was formulated by authors Jean Bernabé, Patrick Chamoiseau and Raphaël Confiant in their *Eloge de la créolité* (*In Praise of Creoleness*, 1989) wherein creole identity is based on a multiethnic and multilingual Caribbean culture; it is also a response to the African-identified model of *négritude* and its defiant affirmation of black anticolonial identity.

Martinican author Edouard Glissant contributes to the discourse on cultural creolization by expanding the multiple metaphors of the creolization process and the language of Creole cultural identity. Responding to the notion of créolité, Glissant presented his influential concept of *antillanité* (Caribbeanness) creating a postcolonial "Archipelic" view: a Creole identity which is highly flexible and adaptable and "traces the path from an onto-logical model of being to an historically and geographically situated, hence changeable, existence" (Schwieger Hiepko 2003: 244). Indeed, Glissant speaks of the "archipelagoization" of the Caribbean in its interaction with Africa and the United States, and of the world.

> Europe is being "archipelagoized" in its turn and is splitting into regions. Florida is in the process of changing completely in response to its Cuban and Caribbean populations. It seems to me that these new dimensions of existence escape national realities which are trying to resist the forces of archipelagoization. . . . We must accustom our minds to these new world structures, in which the relationship between the center and the periphery will be completely different. Everything will be central and everything will be peripheral. (Glissant 2000)

Creolization as a concept can never be neutral; its very semantic origins force us to confront issues of power, race, and history. Stephan Palmié questions the "proliferating mangroves of metaphors" of Caribbean/creolization rhetoric beyond linguistic applications to other "kinds of discourses on 'culture,' local or global," creating a transglobal identity that may be empirically and theoretically ill advised (2006: 434, 443). Although scholars and critics are always eager for new analytical and descriptive tropes, more specificity in the construction of indigenously Caribbean analytical and political projects could avoid an imaginary reinvention of the region: "It is difficult to under-stand how—other than by retrospectively constructing a 'Caribbean' of the (nonregionalist) anthropological imagination—we could ever have regarded the region as a 'prototype' (in both temporal and evolutionary senses) of an allegedly global postmodern condition" (443). Palmié offers the example of Ulf Hannerz's 1987 article, "The World in Creolisation," regarded by Palmié as an essay that establishes a "creolization paradigm" in which Hannerz claims "we are all being creolised," yet does not refer to a "single intellectual (or social scientist) from the Caribbean" (443). The expediency of using creolization as a conceptual tool will undoubtedly continue to be controversial and prob-lematic. For Torres-Saillant, such authors as Glissant and Benítez-Rojo, while contributing impressive organizing metaphors that capture the complexity of Caribbean history and culture at a discursive level, fail, in his estimation, to take into account the region's extratextual reality and the "trauma of our cata-strophic history . . . postcolonial studies have seldom shed meaningful new light on historical, cultural, or political dynamics in the region" (2006: 238).

Syncretism

[handwritten: derogatory effect]

In current theories of globalization, Creole and creolization are often mentioned as synonyms of hybridity and syncretism. "All these terms, currently used in positive senses to describe the resilience, creativity, and inevitability of cultural mixture, had extremely pejorative meanings in the past. In the cases of syncretism and hybridity, various writers have examined these pasts and reappropriated the terms through a positive reevaluation of the political significance of mixture" (Stewart 2007: 4). The strategies of religious syncretism—the active transformation through renegotiation, reorganization, and redefinition of clashing belief systems—are consistent with the creolization process.

In *African Civilizations in the New World,* Roger Bastide differentiated between various categories of religious syncretism in the Caribbean, among them morphological or mosaic syncretism based on the juxtaposition and coexistence of African-derived elements and Catholic symbols—the Vodou *pé,* or altars, with stones, wax candles, crosses, the statues of saints, and pots containing souls of the dead, for example—and institutional syncretism, which combines prescribed religious observances by reconciling Christian and African liturgical calendars (1971: 154–156). The most common, however, is syncretism by correspondence, or what Leslie Desmangles calls a "symbiosis by identity," through which an African deity and a Catholic saint became one on the basis of mythical or symbolic similarities.[8]

[handwritten right margin: side by side, comparison]

Syncretism has been a polemical term for centuries. In the seventeenth century it was used to defend "true" religion against heresy and referred to the "illegitimate reconciliation of opposing theological views" (Droogers 1989: 9). The term was later applied by scholars to the early forms of Christianity that were perceived to be syncretic as well, and was later broadened to apply to all religions when a review of religious history revealed syncretic elements at the foundation of all major religions. However, syncretism is not a value-free concept. The identification of Creole religions as "syncretic" is problematical and disparaging: a Eurocentric bias limits the definition to non-European religions, negating their full legitimacy. Creole religions are frequently identified with and "legitimized" by accentuating their Roman Catholic elements, for example, but are not always afforded an equivalent status.

The term "syncretism" first appeared in Plutarch's *Moralia* in reference to the behavior of the Cretan peoples who "mixed together," came to agreement, or closed ranks when confronted by a mutual enemy; it was later used to describe the integration of two or more separate beliefs into a new religion. Thus, from its origins, the term presupposes encounter and confrontation between systems: "Syncretism is in the first place *contested* religious interpenetration" (Droogers 1989: 20).[9] Though all definitions of syncretism are thorny, Michael Pye recognizes the term's dynamism when he describes it as "the temporary ambiguous coexistence of elements from diverse religions and other contexts within a coherent religious pattern" and considers that the process should be understood as "a natural moving aspect of major religious traditions . . . a part of the dynamics of religion which works its way along in the ongoing transplantation of these religious traditions from one cultural context to another whether geographically or in time" (1971: 92). However, despite the existence of historical interactions, borrowings, and modifications based on contact and context that have occurred among all the major religions, the rhetorical division between so-called *pure* faiths and *illicit* or "contaminated" syncretic belief systems persists, often mentioned with the related concepts of "hybridization and creolization as a means of portraying the dynamics of global social developments" (Stewart 2007: 40). Syncretism in the Creole context is not the description of a static condition or result but of a dynamic process. Roman Catholic missionaries adopted a policy of "guided syncretism" during the conquest of the Americas and the colonial period, tolerating the existence of a polytheistic idolatry that could be identified with Catholic saints and considering it a necessary evil— a transitional state that would eventually lead the conquered peoples to the "true" faith and the elimination of such beliefs. However, the policy never fully realized its goals. The old gods refused to disappear (and still do).[10]

Whether to avoid further oppression in a type of "defensive syncretism"[11] or to gain legitimacy, the conquered peoples embraced Christian forms but with new meanings they themselves had refashioned, at times appropriating them as tools of resistance.[12] According to Mosquera, syncretism should designate "something that corresponds more to the concept of 'appropriation,' in the sense of taking over for one's own use and on one's own initiative the diverse and even the hegemonic or imposed elements, in contrast to assuming an attitude of passive eclecticism or synthesis," strategies that he claims are clearer now thanks to the evolution of a "postmodern" contemporary consciousness (1996: 227). The stress on syncretism and such terms as "syncretic cults" emphasizes the "accessory syncretic elements to the detriment of the essence: the truly effective evolutions of African religions in America" (Mosquera 1992: 30).

In an interesting example of the historical revision of the definition of cultural and religious "legitimacy," Stephen Palmié notes in "Against Syncretism: 'Africanizing' and 'Cubanizing' Discourses in North American *òrìsà* Worship," that the American Yoruba movement created in the United States in the 1960s, also known as Yoruba-Reversionism or the Oyotunji-Movement, has attempted to purge all European elements from Cuban and Cuban-American Santería/Regla de Ocha in order to regain a more "pure" form of worship and cultural "legitimacy." The re-Africanization of "syncretistically adulterated" Cuban beliefs and practices "runs counter to an understanding of 'tradition' still at the very heart of North American variants of Afro-Cuban religious practices" (1995: 77). A movement to eliminate any vestiges of European religions from Santería and other Creole religions, led by so-called "African revisionists," and return to a more "pure" and "authentic" African-centered religion has led to African-centered movements in Cuba as well where some advocate for a "religión Yoruba" to replace Regla de Ocha/Santería.

For Andrew Apter, religious syncretism is yet another form of empowerment, another modality of revision and popular resistance:

> The syncretic revision of dominant discourses sought to transform the authority that these discourses upheld . . . the power and violence mobilized by slave revolts and revolution were built into the logic of New World syncretism itself. The Catholicism of Vodou, Candomblé and Santería was not an ecumenical screen, hiding the worship of African deities from official persecution. It was the religion of the masters, revised, transformed, and appropriated by slaves to harness its power within their universes of discourse. In this way the slaves took possession of Catholicism and thereby repossessed themselves as active spiritual subjects. (1991: 254)[13]

And, according to Laura E. Pérez in "Hybrid Spiritualities and Chicana Altar-Based Art," U.S. Latina/o artists and intellectuals in the fields of religion and visual arts are radically redefining the understanding of religious and cultural syncretism beyond the Eurocentric notion "that vestiges of the precolonial survive as largely incoherent fragments within the engulfing colonial culture" and are replacing it with the realization that globalization has restructured religious beliefs and practices and given birth to "altogether new forms" (2008: 344–345).

Shared Characteristics of Creole Religions

Despite notable differences among African-based Caribbean Creole practices, a general overview of the Creole religions reveals that they share a number of fundamental features.[14]

1. The first of these is their characteristic combination of monotheism and polytheism. At the center of all Afro-Caribbean religions is a belief in a unique Supreme Being—creator of the universe. This belief is complemented by belief in a pantheon of deities (*orishas*, *lwas*, and the like) who are emanations of the Creator and who serve as intermediaries between mankind and the supreme god.

2. These religious practices are also linked by a cult of dead ancestors and/or deceased members of the religious community who watch over and influence events from beyond.

3. In addition, Creole religions share a belief in an active, supernatural, mysterious power that can be invested in objects (mineral, vegetable, animal, human), a force not intrinsic to the objects themselves.

4. This belief is in turn linked to animistic beliefs in other spirits (often found in nature), beyond the divinities and the ancestors, who can also be contacted and who can exert a positive or negative influence over a person's life. Plants and trees, for example, have a will and a soul, as do all things under the sun.

5. Afro-Caribbean religions are centered on the principle of contact or mediation between humans and the spirit world, which is achieved through such numerous and complex rituals as divinatory practices, initiation, sacrifice, spiritual possession, and healing.[15]

6. These contacts are mediated by a central symbol or focus, a fundament or philosophical foundation that serves as the dynamic organizing principle of spiritual worship: the sacred stones (*otanes*) of the Afro-Cuban Regla de Ocha and the *nganga* cauldron and sign tracings of Regla de Palo, the sacred Ekué drum of the Abakuá Secret Society, and the *poto-mitan* of the Vodou ritual space (the *hounfort*). These and other consecrated objects are not merely the symbols of the gods but are the material receptacles of divine power. The image of Catholic saints and the crucifix may appear to dominate altars or shrines, but, as William Bascom has noted regarding the Afro-Cuban religions, the stones, blood, and herbs of ritual offerings and sacrifice contain the "secrets" and are the real focus of religious power (1950, 1972).

7. Central to the ceremonies of Creole religions is music and dance: sound has the power to transmit action. Consecrated drums and the polyrhythmic percussion they produce, along with clapping, the spoken or sung word in

repeated chants, and dance (rhythms and dance are coded to the identities of the gods that are summoned in ceremonies and rituals), produce an altered state of consciousness that beckons the supernatural entities and communicates between worlds.[16]

8. Music and dance are also instrumental in strengthening the conscious sense of community and an institutionalized regrouping of Africans and their descendants, and the transference of African "space" into houses, temples, or rooms. Ritual communities are more than simply religious groups. Rather, they re-create the types of family ties and obligations to the deities and to each other that would have existed in Africa.

9. This re-creation relies on religious leaders responsible for the care of the religious space, sacred objects, and ritual implements and the general spiritual care of the community. The leaders represent "the depository of maximum mystical and initiatory powers and liturgical knowledge. The cult priest [priestess] distributes or 'plants' power by initiating novices and infusing them with the power of which he is the depository" (Dos Santos and Dos Santos 1984: 77). There is no central authority in Creole religions, however; worship is individualized and community-based. Devotees are members of a religion, but not of a specific institutionalized church.

10. In Caribbean Creole religions, spiritual power is internalized and mobilized in human beings who become, through the experience of possession, "a real live altar in which the presence of the supernatural beings can be invoked."[17] In possession, the deities—orishas, lwas—manifest themselves through the bodies of the initiated.[18] "During the experience of possession, the entire religious system, its theogony and mythology, are relived. Each participant is the protagonist of a ritualistic activity, in which Black historic, psychological, ethnic, and cosmic life is renewed" (Dos Santos and Dos Santos 1984: 78). Ritual dramatizes myth and promotes the magic that responds to life's problems.[19]

11. Given the complexity of the practice of magic in the form of spells, hexes, conjurations, and ethno-magical medicine-healing, it deserves more extensive examination here.

Magic, Witchcraft, and Healing

The logic, structure, and "technology" of magic in Creole religions follow the principles described by Sir James Frazer in his classic text *The Golden Bough (1922)*: "homeopathic" or "imitative" magic, following the law of similarity in which like produces like and an effect resembles its cause, so that one can produce any effect by imitating it (a photograph or doll in the likeness of the person one wishes to influence); and "contagious" magic, which follows the law of contact, namely, that things which have once been in contact continue to act upon each other at a distance, a "magical sympathy" that exists between a person and any severed portion of his or her person (human remains or dirt from a grave invested with the power of the deceased, for example). Anyone gaining possession of human hair, nails, or other portions of the body may work his or her will upon the person from whom they were obtained, at any distance.[20]

In *Spiritual Merchants: Religion, Magic and Commerce*, Carolyn Morrow Long uses the generic word "charm" to designate "any object, substance, or combination thereof believed to be capable of influencing physical, mental, and spiritual health; manipulating personal relationships and the actions of others; and invoking the aid of the deities, the dead, and the abstract concept of 'luck'" (2001: xvi). Although the objects themselves may be commonplace and ordinary, faith and belief invest them with their true "power":

> More important than the magical principles of imitation and contact is the spiritual presence that governs the charm. In the African traditional religions, European folk Christianity and popular magic, and the African-based New World belief systems, charms are often believed either to be endowed with an indwelling spirit or to enable the user to contact and direct an external spirit. An African deity, God the Father, Jesus, the Holy Ghost, one of the saints, a folk hero, or the dead might be summoned through the use of charms. In African American hoodoo practice the religious concept of an indwelling spirit has sometimes been lost, and the user may believe that the charm itself performs the desired act. The principles of imitative and contagious magic, plus the spiritual presence behind the charm, work to achieve the intention of the charm user through choice of ingredients, charm type, and related ritual actions. (xvii–xviii)

Bastide notes that Europeans brought their own varieties of medieval magic with them to the New World, often in the form of witches and magicians who were no longer burned at the stake but rather deported to the new Western territories. (Recall that the major phase of the European witch trials coincided with the colonization of the Americas and that the *Malleus Maleficarum,* the handbook for witch-hunters and Inquisitors throughout late Medieval Europe, was published in 1487, five years before Columbus's voyage.) "Of greatest importance was the folk Christianity and popular magic practiced by many Europeans of the sixteenth through the nineteenth centuries. Characterized by veneration of the saints as minor deities, belief in spirits, and the use of sacramental objects as charms, folk Christianity was remarkably similar to the traditional religions of Africa. European popular magic and healing were also compatible with African magical and medicinal practices" (Long 2001: 9).

European magic retained the advantage, however, of representing the practices of the ruling class and was perceived to be superior in one major aspect: it guaranteed European hegemony, while African magic had not prevented enslavement. "This is why, though they never rejected any of their own African practices which proved effective, the black population would reinforce the unsuccessful one with some European formula" in a process referred to as "magical accumulation" which serves to strengthen the operative force of a given spell or remedy (Bastide 1971: 16). He also observes, "It remains to be said that, while Negroes may borrow European magic to strengthen their own spells, the reverse is also true. Europeans tend to regard Negro magic as more effective, because of its 'weird' character and the old colonial terrors which it inspired" (161). According to Eugene Genovese,

> Magic, in the widest sense of the word, as Frazer, Tylor, and other pioneer anthropologists taught, is a false science with an erroneous idea of cause and effect, but it is akin to science nonetheless in its appeal to human devices for control of the world. . . . For peasantries magic, however petty many of its applications, has served the vital social function of providing some defense, no matter how futile in the end, against the natural disasters and forces beyond their control. (1976: 230–231)

Magic is typically associated with the religions and cultures of premodern societies. That notion, however, is contested by scholars who have noted the interconnectedness of cultures created by world economic systems and link the practices of magic and witchcraft in the Americas to modernity and to Western colonial and anticolonial processes. In *Wizards & Scientists: Explorations in Afro-Cuban Modernity & Tradition*, Palmié argues for the "modernity" of Afro-Cuban religious and cultural adaptation to the transatlantic experience, establishing that the modern structures of power in the transition from the colonial period to the modern were located not only in the New World of colonial power, but within the very structure of religion itself. Both, he claims, are linked to Western rationality, emerging out of the relations of inequality and oppression in colonization that created modernity's achievements, and, citing Swiss anthropologist Alfred Métraux's 1972 statement, "It is too often forgotten . . . that Voodoo, for all of its African heritage, belongs to the modern world and is part of our own civilization" (2002: 57). Magic and witchcraft have been linked to forms of political and cultural resistance but also, as in Raquel Romberg's *Witchcraft and Welfare: Spiritual Capital and the Business of Magic in Modern Puerto Rico,* to the consumerism and the global flow of products and ideas in a postcapitalist world where *brujos* become "spiritual entrepreneurs" providing for the spiritual, emotional, and at times economic needs of their clients (2003: 14).

Religious and cultural development follows many paths; a true understanding of magic and its place in a society requires an appreciation of cultural context, as we will observe in the chapters that follow. A complex and thorny issue, magic can be used as a form of resistance or retaliation, a means of redressing issues within a group, of defining self with regard to others, or a mode of gaining a sense of security and empowerment.[21] On some level, magical thinking is common to all societies, but magic as a religious and spiritual practice is a category that is perhaps the most misunderstood, maligned, feared, and sensationalized of all identified with African-derived religions. Value-laden assumptions have been assigned to the category and definitions of "miracles" and "magicoreligious" practices as well as their legitimacy and authenticity; indictments of superstition and witchcraft are common.

Of course, the expression "magicoreligious" itself is problematic, usually assigned to the religions and the spiritual practices of the "Other" that the modern Western world considers archaic. Where does one draw the line between magic and religion? A straightforward definition can be found in Keith Thomas's *Religion and the Decline of Magic:* "If magic is to be defined as the employment of ineffective techniques to allay anxiety when effective ones are not available, then we must recognize that no society will ever be free from it" (1971: 667). It is a question that Yvonne P. Chireau also examines in *Black Magic: Religion and the African American Conjuring Tradition,* a book concerning

> [t]he creations that black people have woven into their quest for spiritual empowerment and meaning. It is about magic, as that term refers to the beliefs and actions by which human beings interact with an invisible reality. But it is also about religion, which may be defined as a viable system of ideas and activities by which humans mediate the sacred realm. In some African American spiritual traditions, ideas about magic and

religious practice can enclose identical experiences. . . . Individuals may utilize the rhetoric of miracle to characterize this kind of spiritual efficacy, or they may adopt a lexicon that is associated with magic. Or they may choose both. A fixed dichotomy between these ideas is not always apparent. It is clear, then, that we are dealing with contested notions of belief. (2003: 2–3)

Diasporan Religions and Religion in the Diaspora

The "diasporan religions," a term coined by Joseph M. Murphy,[22] share significant traits, but perhaps the most characteristic is their dynamism. The globalization process has created an "intense intra-Caribbean circulation of ritual specialists—a free-flow of *espiritistas, santeros, brujos* [witches or sorcerers]. . . . These encounters and the availability of ritual commodities from distant parts of the world yield incomparable opportunities for mutual learning and exchange. . . . These interactions have broadened the pool of saints, deities, and spirits" (Romberg 2005: 141–142).

In the 2001 edition of Karen McCarthy Brown's ground-breaking ethnography *Mama Lola: A Vodou Priestess in Brooklyn,* we learn that cultural pluralism and transnational contacts have expanded religious options for Alourdes, the Haitian mambo whose story is the focus of the book. In addition to Haitian Vodou, Alourdes has added Santería and was initiated into the religion by a friend who was born in Puerto Rico and lives in Oakland, California, where she hopes that "bringing Vodou and Santeria together can help reduce the tensions between the Latino and black populations in Oakland" (399). Mama Lola observed the ritual similarities between the two religions and when asked why, if they are, in her words, "almost the same thing," she would go through the expense and responsibility of adding Santería to her religious practices, her response demonstrates a practical and religious intent: she wants to add more spirits to insure protection for herself, her family, and her support network, living and deceased. "I do it because my grandmother . . . she used to travel to Cuba …in her trade. That's how she get it. Now, I got Yemaya too" (400).

The religious and cultural influence of the Creole religions of the Caribbean and its diaspora has broadened its reach: to the African American and U.S. Latino population, and, interestingly, to the artists and writers of those communities who have demonstrated an affinity with and been inspired by the Creole spiritual traditions, an issue we will discuss further in subsequent chapters. Orishas and lwas have claimed such spiritual daughters in the African American feminist spirituality movement as writer, performer, and ritual priestess Luisah Teish in the Bay area of California, an initiated elder in the Ifa/Orisha tradition of the West African Diaspora and a devotee of Damballah Hwedo, the Haitian Rainbow Serpent, under the guidance of Mama Lola. In *African American Folk Healing*, Stephanie Y. Mitchem observes that Teish, "like many African-Americans who are searching for religious meaning, draws from multiple African traditions to construct and define a spiritual tradition" (2007: 124):

> For some, then, African religions reconcile seemingly disparate parts of the self—culturally, religiously, and socially. Part of the attraction is what theologian Joseph Murphy describes as "the reciprocity between community and spirit." For some, there is a sense of belonging and coming home. In a way, the participant constructs his or her core identity. (125)

One woman Mitchem interviewed, who was disillusioned with Roman Catholicism and found a spiritual home in Santería, claimed, "Thank God for the Cubans who saved it for us" (125).[23]

Mexican American muralists, writers, and poets have combined Creole spirituality with Native American and European influences in their art and their lives. Hailing from the Rio Grande Valley of South Texas, the acclaimed Chicana[24] author and cultural theorist Gloria Anzaldúa—who helped transform contemporary Chicana and border theories and whose works appear in class syllabi throughout the United States in courses on contemporary American women writers, Chicana/o and Latina/o literature, among others—considered herself a spiritual activist and daughter of Yemayá and included the orisha in her spiritual pantheon, according to AnaLouise Keating, editor of *The Gloria Anzaldúa Reader*.[25] In her influential work *Borderlands: The New Mestiza = La frontera/*, Anzaldúa crosses bridges and borders with illuminating analyses surrounding gender, class, and racial and ethnic identity.

In the bilingual opening poem of the first chapter of *Borderlands*, "The Homeland, Aztlán/El otro México," the author invokes Yemayá's name with that of the Catholic Virgin of Guadalupe, the patron saint of Mexico. Both spirits guide the inhabitants of the borderlands, "transgressors, aliens— whether they possess documents or not, whether they're Chicanos, Indians or Blacks," who populate the U.S.-Mexican border, an area Anzaldúa refers to as a third country or "border culture" (Anzaldúa 1987: 3).

[. . .]
But the skin of the earth is seamless.
The sea cannot be fenced,
el mar does not stop at borders.
To show the white man what she thought of his
arrogance,
Yemaya blew that wire fence down.
[. . .]

Anzaldúa invoked Yemayá in the years prior to her death in 2004 to summon the orisha, her "ocean mother," as protector spirit in the final years of the poet's life and we will see the artistic and spiritual significance of a "spirited identity" in our discussion of Creole religions and Mexican Americans.

The chapters that follow seek to elucidate how the various elements described above manifest themselves in the specific systems of belief and practice of the major Creole religions of the Caribbean and its Diaspora, as well as their influence on U.S. Latino cultures in contact with Creole diasporic cultures. As we trace their histories and characteristic elements we will seek to illustrate how, although at times severely restricted, controlled, penalized, ostracized, and devalued by the dominant cultures of the respective countries, they constitute practices of resistance that devotees have succeeded in maintaining for centuries, contesting the racialized inequalities in their societies, defining and shaping the everyday lives of individuals and communities. As such the Creole religions are at the very center of the process of transculturation that has defined Creole societies.

Historical Background

L'histoire d'un morceau de sucre est toute une leçon d'economie politique, de politique et aussi de morale. (The history of a cube of sugar
is an entire lesson in economy, politics, and also in morality.)
—Agustin Cochin (1823–1872)

The Sugar Islands and the Plantation (1492–1900)

The islands of the Caribbean—the focus of this book—were Europe's first colonies in the New World, and as such, the site of the first multicultural experi-
ment, the cradle of ethnic and cultural syncretism. Spain, the nation responsible for Columbus's momentous "discovery" of these new lands in 1492,
ruled unchallenged over the region for a century, but by the final decades of
the sixteenth century other aspiring European maritime powers—England,
France, Portugal, the Netherlands, and Denmark—had begun to contest its
hegemony over the area that would become known as the West Indies.

The diversity of the metropolitan powers vying for hegemony in the
Caribbean led to the fragmentation of cultural and linguistic patterns characteristic of the present-day West Indies. However, their collective focus on
the development of a plantation economy centered on the production of
sugarcane by African slaves provided a common link between the various
islands. During the early decades of the seventeenth century, the ever-threat-
ened enclaves of European-style farming communities that had struggled to
flourish throughout the Caribbean during the previous century were gradually replaced by large-scale plantations. The consolidation of sugar production through the plantations was the foundation of the Caribbean colonial
economy. By the middle of the seventeenth century, the sugar industry had
become so pervasive throughout the archipelago that Adam Smith, in his
Wealth of Nations, would refer to the entire area as "our sugar islands."

As the plantations of the Caribbean became the centerpiece of an international trade subordinated to the needs of European markets and often
financed from abroad, the region became the destination for thousands of
African slaves, themselves a valuable commodity central to the triangular

trade that fed upon the plantation system for centuries. According to Franklin Knight, African slaves became as a result "the most important single ingredient in the economic success of plantation society" (Knight 1978: 83). While it is true that millions of human beings of diverse racial, geographic, and cultural origins would be pressed into service in the sugar system, the brunt of the enterprise was undoubtedly borne by enslaved Africans, making the Caribbean archipelago "the historical and geographical core of Afro-America" (Hoetink 1985: 55).

The first African slaves arrived in the Caribbean at the very beginning of the "discovery" and conquest, and the region was among the last areas in which slavery was abolished in the Americas (Cuba in 1886, two years prior to its abolition in Brazil in 1888). Lasting nearly four centuries, African slavery would span nearly all of postcontact Caribbean history. Consequently it has been described as "the most massive acculturational event in human history" (Mintz 1974: 9). Upon arriving in the Americas, Africans experienced multiple levels of acculturation: an initial adaptation to new languages and customs in an interchange with slaves of other cultures, and later with the culture of their masters. The strategies of accommodation, transformation, and resistance of African peoples are exemplified in the syncretic, creolized religions described in the following chapters, practices that evolved from the experiences in which Africans were obliged to re-create their cultures and systems of belief within a very restrictive social structure in a new and unfamiliar environment.

Of the roughly five million Africans transported to the Americas, more than half were intended for the sugar plantations of the Caribbean. The plantations, which first proved their potential as producers of "white gold" in the English-held territories of Barbados, Antigua, and Surinam in the middle decades of the seventeenth century, consumed their greatest number of African slaves during the eighteenth. By 1750 Jamaica had superseded Barbados and Antigua as the region's leading producer of sugar, only to lose its dominance to the French colony of Saint Domingue by 1780. Cuba would surpass them all in the nineteenth century, but only after the Haitian Revolution brought an abrupt end to sugar production in Saint Domingue, and those planters who survived the violence fled the newly independent island to start anew in Cuba.

The importation of slaves and their ultimate destination within the Caribbean followed the uncertainties of these changing patterns of sugar production, with the highest concentrations of slaves to be found wherever production was highest and most technologically advanced. The shifting patterns of these concentrations are central to our discussion, as they were responsible for the intensity of cultural exchange that would bring about the development of the African-based religious practices commonly known today as Creole religions. The practice of Obeah, for example—the set of "hybrid" or "creolized" Caribbean beliefs "which includes such practices as ritual incantation and the use of fetishes or charms" (Richardson 1997: 173)—was perceived to be widespread throughout the late seventeenth and early to mid-eighteenth centuries in Barbados, Antigua, and Jamaica, then at their highest levels of sugar production. Even at that early stage in the history of slavery in the New World, Obeah could be traced to the concentrations of Ashanti and kindred tribes from the Gold Coast of Africa, heavily represented in the slave population of the British colonies of the Caribbean.

The practice of Obeah, seen by British colonial authorities as a threat to the stability of the plantation and the health of colonial institutions, had been outlawed in most British Caribbean islands early in the eighteenth century, after being perceived as one of the few means of retaliation open to the slave population. Moreover, Obeahmen were seen as potential leaders who could use their influence over the slaves to incite them to rebellion, as had been the case in the Jamaican rebellion of 1760. "The influence of the Professors of that art," wrote the authors of the *Report of the Lord of the Committee* . . . (1789) at the time, "was such as to induce many to enter into that rebellion on the assurance that they were invulnerable, and to render them so, the Obeah man gave them a powder with which to rub themselves." As Alan Richardson underscores, Edward Long had discussed the role of a "famous obeiah man or priest in the Tacky Rebellion in his *History of Jamaica* (1774), a work notorious for its virulent racism, and stated that among the 'Coromantyns' (slaves shipped from the Gold Coast) the '*obeiah-men*' were the 'chief oracles' behind conspiracies and would bind the conspirators with the 'fetish or oath.'"[1]

Likewise, the practice of Haitian Vodou—the array of practices that Michel Laguerre has called "the collective memory of the [African] slaves brought to the sugar plantations of Haiti"—grew in intensity as the colony's accelerated rate of production during the mid- to late-eighteenth century redoubled the massive migration of thousands of men and women to a new and unfamiliar world marked by their brutal exploitation and early deaths in the plantations of Saint Domingue. The French colony of Saint Domingue (as Haiti was named prior to independence), on the western half of the island of Hispaniola—the site of Spain's first colony in the new world—had achieved an unprecedented degree of economic prosperity during the eighteenth century, becoming the world's leading producer of sugar. French pirates, taking advantage of Spain's neglect of its Caribbean colonies after the discovery of the gold-rich territories of South America, had established sugar plantations on the western end of the island following the foundation of Port-de-Paix in 1664 and the establishment of the French West India Company. Haiti's aboriginal Arawak population having disappeared early in the colony's history as a result of conquest, warfare, excessive work, or disease, the island's sugar-based prosperity was built on a violent and systematic exploitation of labor unlike any known in early modern history. It represented the "epitome of the successful exploitation of slave society in tropical America" (Knight 1978: 149).

In 1791, the Haitian slaves—a population estimated at 452,000 in 1789— rebelled against the brutal conditions of the plantation and the denial of the most basic civil liberties, beginning the long process that became known as the Haitian Revolution, which would eventually lead to the establishment of the first independent republic in the Caribbean. Like the Obeah-inspired rebellions in the British West Indies, the Haitian Revolution was rooted in the commonality of religious and cultural practices centered on Vodou, and its beginnings were marked by a pact between the revolutionary leaders and the Vodou lwas or spirits at a ceremony held at Bois-Caïman (described by a captured slave during legal proceedings against him at Cap-Français). The links between religion and the uprising were established early through the slaves' belief in the powers of their legendary leader Makandal to predict the future and transform himself into various animals, attributes that served him well in his clandestine war against the French colonists. Makandal's chief strategy was sabotage by means of poison, but his reputation as a *houngan* or Vodou priest grew in proportion to the fear he instilled in the French settlers that his knowledge of the poisons, spells, and other subtle weapons he deployed against the white population had its source in magical powers linked to mysterious African practices.

The implications of the Haitian Revolution for the entire Caribbean were enormous, as the former slaves laid the country to waste, destroying its economic structure and severing their connection to international markets, to which they had been the leading supplier of sugar, coffee, and cacao. The vacuum opened a golden opportunity for Cuban sugar producers who had met with only limited success in their ability to compete against Saint Domingue's enormous production capacity. Thousands of French émigrés from Saint Domingue resettled in Cuba, bringing with them capital, slaves, and, most importantly, considerable skill and experience in sugar and coffee production. A surge in the price of sugar, new trading possibilities with the United States after the American Revolution, an industrial revolution that mechanized and greatly facilitated sugar production, and the successful independence movements of Spain's mainland colonies that eliminated Cuba's former strategic role set new priorities for Cuban growers, who dominated the industry throughout the nineteenth and twentieth centuries. As the burden of sugar production shifted to Cuba, so did the concentration of slaves, making of Cuba the crucible of syncretism in the nineteenth-century Caribbean.

The nineteenth century was a period of transition for the region. After the consolidation of the new Haitian Republic, the island's political leaders were hard-pressed to establish and maintain a stable regime. As a result, the country's history since independence has been marked by social turmoil, economic instability, frequent political coups, and the use of political assassination as an instrument of terror. Dessalines, who emerged from the Revolution as Emperor Jacques I, was killed in 1806 while trying to put down a mulatto revolt. Henri Christophe, heir to his kingdom, forced the newly freed slaves to return to the plantations in order to improve the country's economy, and committed suicide in 1820 at his citadel of Laferrière, with rebelling soldiers storming his gates. His successor, President Jean Pierre Boyer, invaded the Spanish half of the island, which had just declared its own independence from Spain, and was overthrown in 1842, a year before the Haitian army was expelled from the Dominican Republic. Between then and 1915 a succession of twenty heads of state tried to govern Haiti, sixteen of whom were overthrown by revolution or were assassinated. The resulting political instability, greed, and corruption, coupled with a systematic depletion of the country's resources, contributed to Haiti becoming the poorest nation in the Western hemisphere. At the dawn of the twentieth century, the once-promising young republic was poised for a lengthy American occupation and a tortuous struggle against poverty, corruption, despair, and environmental degradation.

Prior to the nineteenth century, the Spanish-held territories of Cuba, Puerto Rico, and Santo Domingo—on the eastern half of the island of Hispaniola—had failed to fulfill their early promise as major sources of colonial wealth. For the greater part of their histories they had been severely neglected by Spain, particularly following the discovery of the more valuable territories of Mexico and Peru. Unlike Cuba, whose main port of Havana had played a major role as a supply depot for the Spanish fleet on its way to and from Latin America, Puerto Rico and Santo Domingo had failed to establish themselves as important posts in the line of defense against Spain's European enemies—the French, British, and Dutch pirates intent on interdicting the gold and silver pouring out of the Americas and interrupting the empire's supply systems. Largely characterized by underpopulated small towns, tobacco farms, cattle ranches, coffee plantations, and a small number of sugar plantations whose production was geared to internal consumption, and few African slaves, the population of Santo Domingo (today the Dominican Republic) and Puerto Rico—mostly Creoles of mixed European, Amerindian, and African stock—had expanded slowly. Until the Haitian Revolution gave them an increased role in sugar production, they had found themselves subordinated to a peripheral role as way-stations for the Spanish *flota* transporting the wealth of South America to Spain. Their social and political lives had revolved around fortified garrisons for the armies protecting the naval routes between the new center of the empire and the metropolis, their economies dependent on the *situado,* a subsidy collected from the Mexican treasury. Their fates would be significantly altered by events in Haiti, although they would remain in Cuba's considerable shadow.

The Haitian Revolution truly transformed Cuba, turning it into the greatest of the Spanish "Sugar Islands." Among the numerous changes caused by the resulting economic upheaval was the concomitant increase in Cuba's general population and the tremendous new demand for African slave labor. Between 1512 and 1761 about sixty thousand slaves were imported into Cuba; from 1762 to 1838 the figure rose to four hundred thousand (an increase from two hundred and fifty per year to nearly five thousand).[2] Although one quarter of the slave population (mostly Creoles, or native-born) lived in urban centers, the majority of Africans toiled on the sugar plantations or in the coffee and tobacco fields where they worked under the most wretched conditions, not unlike those the slave population of Haiti had known during the heyday of that country's sugar production. The mortality rate was so high that new acquisitions were constantly required to replenish the population.[3] The response to such oppression, as in Jamaica and Haiti, was very often *marronage* (flight), suicide, or rebellion. Controlling the slave population soon became a dominant social and political issue in Cuba.[4] Slave revolts were frequent, ranging from spontaneous eruptions of violence on individual estates to large organized uprisings that included free persons of color and whites. Perceived as a serious threat to central authority, these organized revolts were brutally crushed by the Spanish colonial government, among them the famous conspiracy referred to as La Escalera (The Ladder, 1844), one of the best organized and most severely repressed. Thousands were tried in military tribunals and hundreds were condemned to death, imprisoned, or deported.

Within Cuba's restrictive colonial social and economic structure, the free population of African descent, which during certain periods represented a dominant percentage of the population, maneuvered a space for themselves in many occupations and trades, due in part to the policy of *coartación* (manumission), through which a number of Cuban slaves were permitted to purchase their freedom from their masters in installments. The system favored Creole or native-born over newly arrived slaves from Africa, and urban over rural slaves who generally lacked similar opportunities to save money to purchase their freedom. In rural agricultural areas, where conditions were harsher and emancipation more elusive, many disregarded the brutal punishments reserved for recaptured runaways and fled to the isolated interiors of the south and central-eastern Cuba's mountain range to establish fortified maroons settlements, *palenques*,[5] where they fashioned their own unique cultural traditions. The experience of culture building that took place in maroon societies is considered emblematic of the process that resulted in the syncretic African-based traditions (including religions) shaped by enslaved Africans in the Americas. The difficulties of creating and maintaining maroon societies in the colonial slave systems of the Americas required the full range of the collective experiences of Africans from a variety of cultures who had to adapt themselves not only to a challenging environment but also to a new social community that could range from newly arrived Africans to highly acculturated Creoles.[6] "What the majority of these people did share was a recently forged Afro-American culture and a strong ideological (or at least rhetorical) commitment to things 'African'" (Price 1973: 26).

Cuba remained a slave society until the abolition of slavery in 1886, and the tensions and alliances created during a long history of racialized labor exploitation featured prominently in the coalitions brought together to fight the Cuban War of Independence in 1895. Black and mulatto soldiers fought side by side with the most liberal sectors of Cuban Creole society, hoping to establish a new nation on democratic principles and greater class and race representation. The victory over Spanish forces—coming in the wake of the United States joining Cuban forces in what would be known as the Spanish-American War—would disappoint the broader social aspirations of the black and mulatto sectors of the Cuban population. Independence, when it finally came in 1903, came under restricted neocolonial conditions, with American sugar corporations taking over sugar plantations, and the United States throwing its considerable support behind the most conservative military-backed dictatorships. Renewed hopes would wait until the 1959 Cuban Revolution, which opened a new chapter in Afro-Cuban history.

Cuba's Spanish-speaking Caribbean neighbors—Puerto Rico and the Dominican Republic—followed significantly different paths during the nineteenth century. Both intensified their production of sugar in response to the opening of markets following the Haitian Revolution. Neither would rival Cuban production, although both would see their economies transformed by sugar production. The Spanish colony of Santo Domingo opened the decade by joining Haiti, the United States, and Spain's Latin American colonies in wars of independence against continued colonial rule. As the Dominican Republic, it gained its independence from Spain in 1821, only to be invaded by the Haitian army in 1822, in Haiti's bid for annexation of Santo Domingo and consolidation of the island's territory under one flag. The struggle against Haiti, and the humiliation of an almost twenty-two-year occupation, left deep emotional scars on the young Dominican nation, and frequent boundary disputes only consolidated the already existing animosity between the two nations. As a result, the consolidation of national independence was the salient political and economic intellectual focus of Dominican leaders throughout the nineteenth century.

The Dominican Republic, bound as the country had been throughout the century in a seemingly ceaseless struggle to solidify its independence, entered the twentieth century solidly in the orbit of the new neocolonial power in the region, the United States. Like Cuba, its sugar production, long neglected because of the internecine war against Haiti, and plagued by inefficiency and limited access to new technologies, fell into the hands of American sugar corporations. Its governments, corrupt and greedy for the most part, subordinated the country's independent economic development to serving American interests. As in Haiti, American occupation loomed ahead in the opening decades of the new century; like Cuba, it would see its full share of American-backed dictatorships and would have to defer dreams of racial justice and greater class equality.

Puerto Rico followed a different path during the nineteenth century. Although it intensified sugar production in the wake of the Haitian Revolution, it maintained a steady production of coffee throughout the century, with coffee surpassing sugar after 1850. As a result, it never reached the high percentages of slave population of other Caribbean islands. At the height of its slave-centered sugar production, only 11 percent of its total population was enslaved. The only one of Spain's possessions in the Caribbean and Latin America not to wage a war of independence against Spain, Puerto Rico, despite a strong separatist movement responsible for at least one serious attempt at rebellion—the 1868 Grito de Lares—would close the century having obtained an Autonomous Charter from Spain. Only months later it was ceded to the United States as a new American territory, following Spain's loss of the Spanish-American War in 1898. As a result of its idiosyncratic path—the result, perhaps, of having been the refuge of conservative Latin American Creoles fleeing the continent's wars of independence as well as the main garrison for the deployment of armies to fight the rebels of South America—Puerto Rico had the heaviest influx of European immigrants of any Caribbean island in the nineteenth century. The 1815 Decree of Thanks—granted by Spain in recognition of the island's loyalty during the Latin American wars of independence—ironically opened the island's doors to Catholic immigrants from all parts of Europe, bringing an influx of French, Corsican, German, Irish, and Scottish immigrants who would transform the island culture, opening it to a flow of new ideas. Chief among these was European *espiritismo* (Spiritism), a major ingredient in the creolized Afro-Hispanic Espiritismo widely practiced on the island today.

The British islands of the Caribbean—Jamaica, Trinidad, and the various islands of the Lesser Antilles, such as Barbados, Antigua, and St. Kitts—had experienced the heyday of their sugar production in the eighteenth century. Some of them, like Dominica, had never been efficient producers of sugar, and their economies had been sustained by smaller cash crops such as coffee, indigo, ginger, and limes. By the dawn of the nineteenth century, West Indian sugar production was becoming increasingly uncompetitive both on the international market and within the empire itself. As a result, planters were philosophical about the cessation of the slave trade and the declaration of Emancipation that followed in 1838. The remaining French colonies in the archipelago, Martinique and Guadeloupe, faced similar declining returns from the production of sugar by slave labor, and Emancipation was declared in the French colonies in 1848.

The second half of the nineteenth century, in both the British and French Caribbean islands, would be characterized by the dynamic growth of a free colored peasantry that followed Emancipation and the breakdown of the large formerly slave-run estates. Land became inexpensive, or readily available for occupation by squatters. A local economy based on the plot system of agriculture, independent from the remaining large sugar estates, began to impact the social, political, and cultural development of the various islands. Those estates which continued the large-scale production of sugar, had to rely on imported Asian laborers, mostly Chinese and Indian, who arrived in the Antilles in large numbers in the second half of the nineteenth century and brought new languages, cultures, and religious beliefs and practices to the amalgam of the region's Creole religions.

In both the British and French Caribbean islands, the social pressures brought about by a free colored peasantry pushing for greater participation in the political and economic processes led to strong attempts at controlling the peasant population through the prohibition of certain religious and cultural practices. As a result, many of the activities associated with Obeah and the related Quimbois practices of the Francophone Caribbean became illegal or were discouraged and persecuted. Throughout the nineteenth century—perhaps as a backlash against the renewed power given to the former slave population by freedom and access to land—there was widespread discrimination against believers and practitioners of Afro-Caribbean religious and healing practices, as well as relentless campaigns on the part of mainstream religions and civic organizations to eradicate all Obeah and Quimbois practices, which they deemed superstitious and pernicious. These efforts seriously limited Obeah and Quimbois practices from regaining their ancestral religious roots and reestablishing community-based rituals and priestly duties, although their healing aspects actually gained strength during this period. When syncretized with newly arrived Asian practices, already endowed with strong healing components, they would develop into a significant element of Afro-Caribbean cultures in the Lesser Antilles.

As the postslavery Caribbean looked ahead to the twentieth century, it faced a transformed social and political reality. The plantation, although not a thing of the past, had bowed to the pressures of the international markets and had lost its hegemony. Although the lives of many Caribbean laborers would continue to revolve around the cultivation of sugar, the diversification of the agricultural sector and the introduction of new industries—among them the growing tourist industry—would change forever the nature of work in the region. As the new century dawned, the seeds of the labor and independence movements that would control political development in the first half of the twentieth century had been planted. With the affirmation of the workers' power to define the terms of their relationships with the metropolis would come independent nations whose national identities would be bound with the affirmation of cultures rooted in African-derived cultures. Among the deepest of those roots would be those of the Afro-Caribbean religions that had sustained the Caribbean slave populations through the dark years of plantation America.

Throughout the twentieth century, the region's path to decolonization was to bring creolized religious practices into new focus as the islands of the Caribbean moved to root their identities as nations on recovered African practices and pan-African connections. This process took many forms, from the decriminalization of practices that had been forced underground by colonial governments to research by local scholars into half-forgotten or localized practices that gained new followers as Caribbean peoples sought to recover cultural markers that had been lost or repressed throughout a history of slavery and the plantation. The work of anthropologists (among them Fernando Ortiz and Lydia Cabrera) and musicologists (Alan Lomax's recordings of Caribbean music in the 1930s, for example) played a central role in this process of recovery that would make practices accessible to a population eager for a stronger connection to its African roots. The resurgence in the practice of Santería and Vodou in Cuba and Haiti, respectively, and the emergence of a creolized version of the French-derived Espiritismo in Puerto Rico became parts of an African-Caribbean revival that became a central element in religious practice as well as in artistic and literary renewal in the region.

One of the most salient developments associated with this resurgence was perhaps the birth of the new African-derived religion of Rastafarianism in 1930s Jamaica. Rastafarianism represents, in myriad ways, the epitome of the cultural transformations that marked the first half of the twentieth century and had cleared a path to a redefinition of religious and artistic practices in the region. Nurtured by Marcus Garvey's pan-Africanist movement, and rooted in the coronation of Haile Selassie as Emperor of Ethiopia in 1930 (and the hope for liberation from colonial control that it brought to African nations at the time), Rastafarianism sought to reconnect Africa and the Caribbean, provide an ethical path away from the evils that colonization and slavery had brought to the region, and offer new forms of social organization founded on emerging sustainable environmental principles. Its message spread worldwide through reggae and the popularity of Jamaica's musical stars. Rastafarianism has had both regional and international impact in redefining the ways in which creolized Caribbean religious practices are deployed and understood.

Of equal importance, perhaps, has been the Caribbean Diaspora that began with the building of the Panama Canal in the opening years of the century and has grown apace as Caribbean peoples have fled desperate economic conditions or political repression at home (as in the case of Haitian boat people and anti-Castro Cuban refugees) or sought greater opportunities and education abroad. The growing Caribbean enclaves in major cities throughout Europe and the United States have internationalized Caribbean religious and healing practices, bringing them into contact with other systems of belief and practice that has led in turn to new transformations and creolizations. This diasporic broadening of the contact zones of creolized Caribbean religious practices has been aided by artists and musicians who have found their artistic inspiration in their own paths to spiritual development. From Cuban salsa star Celia Cruz's call of "que viva Changó" (long live Changó) to Edouard Duval Carrié's depiction of a desolate Ezili Dantó in tears on the deck of a U. S. Coast Guard ship, music and the arts have served as a conduit for the growth of Caribbean Creole religiosities around the world.

This globalization of the Caribbean's Creole religions, however, has developed on a par with the growth of evangelical Christianity in the region, which has brought new threats to the continued survival of some practices whose flowering in the twentieth century we have come to identify with the path to political and cultural independence of most of the region's island nations. Unlike Catholicism (with its often *laissez-faire* approach to religious coexistence) or local variations of Protestantism (like the Jamaican Baptist Union, with its roots in eighteenth-century slave society), the growth of evangelical Christianity throughout the region has come in part at the expense of creolized practices of African origins which have to be formally renounced by devotees before they can be received into their new churches. Whereas formerly it could be said of Haiti, for example, that it was 85 percent Catholic, 15 percent Protestant, and 100 percent Vodou, new forms of Christianity make such dualities impossible. Indeed, they are seen as threatening the survival of important material culture as new adherents must destroy their Vodou paraphernalia before their acceptance into new churches is formalized.

During the last decade of the Caribbean, however, the Creole religions of the Caribbean have found a new role in fostering the connection to the spirits of the ancestors and the land they inhabit through the growing environmental sustainability movements throughout the region. Faced with increased pollution, the threat of global warming, devastating deforestation and coastal deterioration due to tourism development, epidemic rises in AIDS infection, and the resurgence of tuberculosis and malaria in some Caribbean regions, Caribbean peoples have been slowly rediscovering the sustainable roots of Caribbean religiosities. The notion that respect for nature and the land, the possible return to sustainable agricultural practices with roots in African culture, the rejection of mass-produced food that is at the basis of the *ital* practices of Rastafarianism, the reliance on African-derived healing practices for both body and spirit, and the defense of the national environment as repository of sacred spaces can be traced back to spiritual practices, forms the core of creolized Caribbean religiosities. There is in the history of the Creole religions of the Caribbean—in Santería, Obeah, Vodou, Rastafari-anism, and Espiritismo—a shared notion of the peoples of the region as *ti-ginea* (children of Guinea or Africa, to use the Haitian term) and therefore as belonging to one human family connected by history and shared experiences and responsibilities. As we move deeper into the twenty-first century, these spiritual connections, fostered and sustained by the region's Creole religions, have become the foundation for ethical and moral choices about community and the environment.

2

The Orisha Tradition in Cuba

Santería/Regla de Ocha

Forging Creole Religions in Cuba

Afro-Cuban religions were born and developed within three principal institutions of colonial Cuban slave society, which became "improvised temples" of profound cultural resistance (Castellanos and Castellanos 1992, 3:15): the urban *cabildo* or mutual aid society, the *batey* or slave barracks of the sugar plantations, and the mountain *palenques* or fortified cimarrón settlements. The three major religious practices of Santería or Regla de Ocha,[1] Regla de Palo, and the Abakuá Secret Society follow the traditional African approach of dynamic and flexible cultural borrowing and merging, a resourceful and creative strategy common in Africa where religious ideas travel frequently across ethnic and political boundaries. Thus the deities of the Cuban Creole world resulted from the "crossing" and mixing with those of other regions of Africa and the Catholic saints; individuals choose, or are chosen, to receive initiation into one or several traditions.[2]

Spanish colonies had a wider cultural array of African slaves than most Caribbean islands: Spain was the only colonial power not directly involved in the trade, purchasing slaves from a variety of countries in distinct areas of Africa. In the final stages of the slave trade (most of the slave population arrived after 1800), Yoruba-speaking groups dominated, primarily from the southwest of Nigeria and from Dahomey, Togo, and Benin. They contributed most directly to the tradition that would come to be known as "Lucumí" (the name given to Yoruba-speaking people in Cuba and to the religious practice of Regla de Ocha, the rule or religion of the orisha,[3] considered a variant of the Lucumí religious tradition).[4]

The Lucumí, from the southwestern part of Nigeria that includes the heterogeneous groups of tribes referred to as the "Yoruba" (a name that only came into general use in the nineteenth century)—the Oyo, Egba, Ijebu, Iyesá, and their neighbors—predominated in the nineteenth-century Cuban slave trade. Their preponderance accounts for their crucial role in the creation of the island's most widespread Afro-Cuban religion, Regla de Ocha, also known as Santería. The other major Afro-Cuban religions are from the Kongo tradition (Bantu-speaking peoples from the Congo Basin are referred to as "Congo" in Cuba) and the Carabalí (from southeast Nigeria [Calabar] and west Cameroon). While these are believed to be the most influential of the cultural groups transferred to the island, they were far from being the only ones.[5] In Cuban slave society people from all the African ethnic groups were divided into *naciones* (nations) upon their arrival, each assigned ethnic names which are frequently unreliable: inexact, erroneous, based on inconsistent criteria, the names would often refer to the slaves' ports of embarkation in the African slave trade rather than to their place of origin.

The religious traditions that resulted in Cuba emerged as much from the contact between cultures and traditions as from coercion. The indoctrination and instruction of slaves in Roman Catholicism in Cuba was in most cases sporadic and perfunctory. Attention to religious instruction in the countryside, where the great majority of slaves resided, was lax, restricted and/or corrupted by the pervasive and overwhelming interests of the plantations. The reasons for the Catholic Church's comparative weakness in Cuba and the relative absence of religiosity in the general population include the enormous influence throughout the country of the secular, cosmopolitan port city of Havana, Spain's indifference to her colony throughout most of the colonial period (matched by the Church's disinterest in religious organization and development), leading to a lack of resources in terms of clergy in urban and particularly rural areas; and the conflicts of the "sugarocracy" with the Church during the sugar boom of the late eighteenth to mid-nineteenth centuries. "In addition to refusing to economically support a religious presence at the mills, the owners were also unwilling to grant slaves the time to practice the sacraments, to receive religious indoctrination, and to observe Sundays and religious holidays" (L. Pérez 1994: 152).[6]

As a result, large numbers of arrivals from Africa were not effectively indoctrinated in the Catholic faith. As one nineteenth-century English traveler observed, "The state of religion in this island is most deplorable. Slavery, that contaminates everything it touches, has not spared even the Church, or its ministers, in Cuba."[7] With few churches and a clergy that for the most part preferred to remain in urban areas, the Church's influence declined among whites and blacks in rural areas. The long distances to be traveled to attend mass discouraged many, and wealthy planters, who resented the unproductive time slaves would expend in religious services, fought the efforts of the Church to retain their rural mission.[8]

As in other areas of the Caribbean under Spanish domination, Roman Catholicism was the only religion officially permitted on the island of Cuba. Although the rhetoric of the conquest of the Americas may have forged the image of dedicated missionaries spreading civilization with the word of God to primitive savages, a more accurate understanding of the process of Christianization and the development of Catholic practice would have to take into account the faith of the humble people who made up the majority of Spanish settlers to the New World. Their religion formed the basis of the Catholicism that would eventually contribute to the creation of a Cuban folk religion.[9] The Spanish settlers followed the local cults of their rural home villages and brought those traditions along with them to the New World; despite local variations, they shared a strong devotion to the Catholic saints who were believed to be intermediaries between men and an inaccessible God. Having lived on earth as virtuous human beings, saints were closer to men than the divine force that was beyond human comprehension.

As in the case of Greek and Roman deities, the saints were specialized. For every disease, for example, a different saint could be invoked for a cure. Some were associated with certain places and were considered the area's patron; some were the spiritual patrons of certain professions or trades. Attempts by the official Church to control or eliminate folk Catholic devotions to the saints met with little success. Two types of Catholicism resulted: the Catholicism of the priests and that of the people. The culture of the folk, which represented the majority of the people, evolved its own syncretic path, "maintained by the ongoing cultural, genetic, and social mixture among the groups. It was not so much a thing as a process of continuous and continuing definition and redefinition through encounters" (Brandon 1993: 43).

A combination of demographic and institutional factors created the conditions for the emergence of religious syncretism in nineteenth-century Cuba. In racialist Cuban colonial society white culture provided the means for social mobility and a possibility of escape from the intolerable conditions imposed on people of color. Acculturation as a means of survival in that society meant adopting Catholicism and to some extent espousing the values of the dominant culture, at least openly: "[T]he Negro knew very well that the only way in which he could get his foot on the social ladder was by acquiring 'a white soul'" (Bastide 1971: 153). However, in the less restricted environment of the city, African slaves and later *libertos* or freemen, a sizable component of Havana's population, discovered a refuge from the oppressive racism of the larger society in their clubs and fraternal organizations formed on the basis of ethnic origins, where they could maintain their religious values and sustain themselves through the remembrance of their cultures of origin.

The most important of these organizations, from a religious perspective, were the church-sponsored *cabildos de nación*,[10] societies organized by ethnic provenance (there are accounts of black cabildos that date to the colonial period as far back as 1598). Church-sponsored cabildos were based on the mutual aid confraternities or *cofradías* (religious brotherhoods) common throughout Europe in the Middle Ages in which groups gathered to assist one another in times of need and to worship their patron saint. While in Europe the Counter-Reformation limited the role of cofradías, their existence was prolonged in the Spanish and Portuguese colonies where they were perceived as a means of social control of the African population.[11] Excluded from white fraternities, blacks were permitted to govern and organize their own in institutions that were a combination of a mutual aid society and a social confraternity to plan the communal feasts, dances, and carnival processions, and help members in need. Each cabildo had a house, frequently owned by the members, and the money they collected helped to finance their activities, assist members in need, pay for burials, and occasionally purchase a member's freedom. The Cuban Catholic Church sponsored religious cabildos for the purpose of evangelization through a policy of "guided change," tolerating those African values that could be reinterpreted within Catholicism and radically opposing those that could not (Brandon 1993: 71).

Borrowing their titles from political and church institutions, elected cabildo leaders were called king (usually a respected elder), queen (women held positions of influence and prestige in the cabildo), and captain, among other designated positions. As official church associations, they were required to conform to certain laws and customs regarding their roles in religious processions and festivities, laws that shifted over the years from prohibition of certain days for dances and processions to restrictions on the display of African images or drumming in public festivals. African dances in the paraded processions or *comparsas* were permitted at certain times on limited days, usually devoted to the patron saint of the cofradía. Cabildo leaders wore the costumes and uniforms of the monarchy and the military, and all rallied under an identifying flag. Among the most popular street celebrations was that of the Epiphany, "el Día de Reyes,"[12] on January 6, when naciones with their king (considered a type of accredited ambassador of his ethnic group before the authority of the Spanish Captain General), and other members would parade through the streets in costumes and masks, dancing to their own music:

> The cofradías, cabildos and other institutions created within Afrocuban society were centers of cultural and social creativity and improvisation where African peoples and their descendants not only affirmed their humanity, but also mobilized social, economic and cultural resources to oppose the colonial and later post-colonial system. Through public festivals and processions, Afrocubans challenged elite control over public space and over the iconography of the nation, while creating unifying symbols of their own ethnic and political identity. Through economic cooperation that enabled the purchase of property and the freeing of their enslaved members, the cofradías and cabildos challenged the ideology and political economy of the "chattel slavery" system. And through rituals and everyday religious practices, Afrocubans forged and sharpened the solidarity and sense of purpose that catalyzed countless acts of covert and overt resistance to the system of racial domination. (Gregory 1999: 98)

During the nineteenth century the functions of the cabildo expanded, as did their membership, which began to include, in addition to slaves born in Africa, Creole slaves, and free men and women of African descent. Thus, although the associations were encouraged by colonial authorities as a method of controlling slave beliefs and maintaining internal divisions among the different ethnic groups (taking advantage of resentments based on past histories of intertribal warfare, and so on), cabildos eventually helped to replace families and institutions that had been lost in slavery.[13] In addition, they provided a structure for enslaved Africans to evolve their alternative religious systems:

> Behind the Christian, European façade an entire world of the remnants of African culture throbbed. Behind the king was a priest (*babalao* or *mayombero*) who on many ceremonial occasions wore the sacred robes that the Cuban populace mistook for carnival devils. This duality led inevitably to acculturation, perhaps best symbolized in the double names assigned to things. . . . The patron saint, if it was San Lázaro or Santa Bárbara, outside, was called Babalú Ayé or Changó, within. (Castellanos and Castellanos 1988, 1: 113)[14]

Restrictions and the interference of the state in the affairs of the cabildos began in 1790 and increased steadily: in 1882 each cabildo was forced to obtain a license, renewable on an annual basis, and in 1884 a government proclamation prohibited the cabildos from practicing on Christmas Eve and January 6. "The African saturnalia passed into history. That of 1884 was the last: the 6th of January of 1885 was the first silent Epiphany that Cuba had" (Ortiz 1984: 22).

After the abolition of slavery in 1886 the interference intensified and in 1888 a law was passed forbidding the creation of "old style" cabildos. Many disappeared under this pressure, went underground, or became the *orisha ilé, casas de santo* or house-temples, heirs to the legacy of the cabildo. The cabildos were in decline, but the social and cultural consolidation of the Lucumí was already established; the response was to group together the worship of many orishas or deities into one individual *ilé*, the house-temples that are the modern descendants of the cabildo.[15]

It is not difficult to imagine how the syncretism between Catholicism and the African traditions that would give rise to Afro-Cuban religions took place in the cabildos, where African worship continued under the façade of Roman Catholicism. According to Roger Bastide, while the ethnic cabildos helped to promote the process of Catholic-African syncretism, they were also instrumental in maintaining diverse African values and beliefs: "[W]herever black brotherhoods existed, African religion survived" (1978: 54). The cabildos were the site where Africans and their descendants transformed the institutional structures available to them to support their own African cultural and religious practices; they borrowed from Catholic discourse and reinterpreted it in terms of African religions under the guise of an alternative form of folk Catholicism.

The saints, Jesus Christ, and the Virgin Mary were identified with African gods or ancestors who, in return for sacrifices, would protect or assist blacks in their daily lives. Debate exists regarding the actual degree of syncretism between Catholicism and African worship, as most devotees clearly distinguish between the two; though the slaves danced before a Catholic altar, "and though their masters found this somewhat bizarre, it never occurred to them that these Negro dances, with their prominently displayed lithographs and statuettes of the saints, were in fact addressed to African divinities" (Bastide 1971: 156). Though the condition of slavery obscured or eliminated certain African rituals that were replaced or combined with Catholic ceremonies, African religious traditions survived nevertheless and predominate in practices that thrive to the present day.

Of the three major Afro-Cuban religious practices in Cuba today, Regla de Ocha, commonly known as Santería, is the most widespread. Its worshipers are called *santeros*[16] as they venerate the Yoruba deities called *orishas* or *santos,* syncretized with Catholic saints. While each religion reflects a different tradition in beliefs and practices, practitioners do not perceive them as mutually exclusive: "In Cuba it is common to find someone . . . who worships the African deity of metals and of war in both its Lucumí (Ogún) and its Congo (Sarabanda) incarnation, celebrating the 'feast' of these deities on June 24, the date assigned in the Roman Catholic Church for the feast of Saint John the Baptist, with whom these deities have been syncretized in Matanzas" (Vélez 2000: 12). "Religion," in fact, is not an adequate word to describe these comprehensive practices in Cuba and elsewhere: "'religion' in the normative Western sense of the term does not do justice to the complex system of systems that is Afro-Cuban religion, a comprehensive system that syncretizes, articulates, and reproduces extensive orders of knowledge in the areas of psychotherapy, pharmacology, art, music, magic, and narrative" (Matibag 1996: 7).

Santería/Regla de Ocha is based on the religion of the peoples of the ancient Yoruba city-states, a conglomeration of numerous and diverse tribal groups united by a common language and a belief system linked to those of the neighboring kingdoms of Benin and Dahomey (today the Republic of Benin),[17] who shared with the Yoruba the claim of descent from Oduduwa, the founder of the sacred city of Ile Ife, the cradle of their civilization. At the apex of the hierarchical organization of Yoruba worship was the earth's creator, Olodumare (also named Olorun and Olofi in Cuba), a remote being and supreme deity who is the ultimate embodiment of *aché,* a spiritual-mystical energy or power found in varying degrees and in many forms throughout the universe. Olodumare is considered an inaccessible and omnipotent god who abdicates his powers to divine intermediaries.[18]

Beneath the supreme creator in the Yoruba hierarchy are the pantheon of deities known as the orishas, spirits created in some cases prior to the creation of human beings and others who were human at one time and evolved into deities because of some remarkable quality. The orishas intercede in the daily lives of humans and, if appeased, can help mankind. "The Yoruba religion, the worship of various spirits under God, presents a limitless horizon of vivid moral beings, generous yet intimidating. They are messengers and embodiments of àshe, spiritual command, the power-to-make-things-happen, God's own enabling light rendered accessible to men and women" (Thompson 1984: 5). This vital force permeates all aspects of life; the propagation of aché in rituals and ceremonies is believed to bring balance, well-being, and harmony.

Worshipers of a particular orisha in Africa, considered "children" of that spirit, passed the tradition down through generations of their kin. While some orisha worship was strictly local in origin and practice, other orishas evolved from a combination of beliefs with those of neighboring groups, the result of contact throughout the area through trade and/or conquest. The influence of the Yoruba city-states in West Africa was considerable, given the power and extension of the Oyo Empire. Internal political turbulence, however, and increasing attacks in the Bight of Benin by warring neighbors in slave-producing imperial warfare combined with the growing pressures of the Atlantic slave trade to weaken the resistance of the Yoruba peoples. Taken captive in slave-hunting raids, they would be forced to confront the terrifying Middle Passage, joining with the millions of other Africans who had been facing a similar fate since the fifteenth century onward.

The persistence and predominance of Yoruba worship in Cuban Santería/Regla de Ocha, the best preserved practice and the most influential, is observable in the worship of the orishas, styles of divination practices, ritual relationships, sacrifice and possession, as well as conservation of the ritual language. Its success is due to the creation of a complex Yoruba religious structure prior to their arrival in the New World, and to their having been the most recent and most massive of all African groups, which allowed them to replenish and strengthen African transplanted culture. They were also aided by the fact that many of the Yoruba prisoners of war who had been taken as slaves were from the priestly class and thus possessed a firm knowledge of their religious beliefs and practices.[19]

Among these practices is the noteworthy Ifá divination practice, the Yoruba corpus of wisdom in the form of parables and proverbs that codified the wisdom of an entire culture and kept it alive so far from its source: "The Ifá itself is a vast information-retrieval system that preserves, accesses, and processes the texts of mythological, naturalist, medicinal, and spiritual knowledge. At the heart of the Ifá system lie the thousands of narratives that the babalao has memorized as part of his training and that he recites to clients in consultations" (Matibag 1997: 153). (In Cuba these Yoruba narratives or ese Ifá would become the pataki myths recited in Regla de Ocha divination, discussed below.)

The eventual pattern of Yoruba religious practices in Cuba and elsewhere in the Americas was based on the form of local worship practiced in the slaves' respective cities of origin; the destruction of the traditional family

kinship structure in slavery disrupted or eliminated kin-based orisha worship as well as that which had been based on religious societies in Africa. As
a result, from among the hundreds of different orishas worshiped in Africa,
fewer than twenty survived to play a significant role in Cuba. Others were
completely lost or were fused with the deities of peoples from other African
cultural groups. Orishas are worshiped in other Afro-Cuban cults, overlapping with Kongo or Arará deities, for example. "New World Yoruba emerged
from all this strife. . . . A remarkable fusion of orisha, long separated by civil
war and intra-Yoruba migrations, took place in the New World" (Thompson
1984: 17).[20]

The religion of Regla de Ocha views the world, both sacred and profane,
as motivated by *aché*: "growth, the force toward completeness and divinity" (Murphy 1993: 130). All that one perceives are forces of aché that can be
awakened in objects and people: "Ashe is a current or flow, a 'groove' that initiates can channel so that it carries them along their road in life. The prayers,
rhythms, offerings, tabus of santería tune initiates into this flow. They are
lifted out of the self-absorption and frustration of ordinary life into the world
of power where everything is easy because all is ashe, all is destiny" (Murphy
1993: 131). The ultimate object of aché is God, Olodumare, and the orishas are
the numerous forms of his expression. Murphy observes that there are four
major avenues for humans to approach the orishas' world: divination, sacrifice, possession trance, and initiation (1993: 134). These are elaborated below.

Regla de Ocha/Santería, the most complex and structured of the Afro-
Cuban religions, can be broadly defined therefore as the veneration of the
orishas of the Yoruba pantheon as identified with their corresponding Catholic saints. It is a religion that integrates human concerns with spiritual force
and has been described as an "earth religion, a magico-religious system that
has its roots in nature and natural forces . . . a system that seeks to find the
divine in the most common, ordinary things. . . . All that Santería wants to
do is to embrace nature, but in so doing it embraces the soul of all things"
(González-Wippler 1989: 4, 23).

"Regla de Ocha" is translated as the religion, order, or rule of the orisha
(ocha). As the orishas in Cuba were referred to by the Spanish word *santos*
the practice came to be named Santería, the worship or way of the saints. The
orishas are spiritual entities that have been anthropomorphized and identified with a force of nature and an aspect of human character or personality, the representation of multiple spiritual metaphors. To obtain their aché,
however, the orishas must be propitiated through an *ebó*—sacrifice, offering,
spell—which has the double purpose of honoring the deities and commu-

nicating aché from spiritual being to human. The sacrifice can range from a simple offering of fruit, candles, food, or flowers appropriate to the attributes of a particular orisha to a blood sacrifice involving a specific sacrificial animal for a serious problem, if so indicated by divination. The offering is then transformed into aché to carry out the needs of the petitioner.

The *egún* (the dead) must also be honored with small offerings. Ancestor worship, although not an evolved or distinct cult, is a central tenet of the religion: "[T]he dead come before the saints." The concepts of ancestor and family extend to the religious community: initiated devotees are called *omo-orisha* or "child of an orisha," the *santero* or *santera* who initiates them is their *padrino* or *madrina*, "godfather" or "godmother," and the ancestors who are honored at all ceremonies include one's ritual family in worship, the lineage of the *ilé* house-temple. A "here and now," crisis-oriented religion, the herbs, stones, amulets, necklaces, and other ritual objects used in worship are vital to achieving its magical or healing purposes. As in the Yoruba worldview, Regla de Ocha does not polarize goodness and evil; they are perceived as complementary and relative. Bad things will happen, but humans can find holistic balance and peace by maintaining personal, social, and cosmic harmony, living in accord with their destiny (discovered through divination), proper character, appropriate behavior, and a relationship with and worship of the orishas.

The Orishas

Occasionally compared to the gods of Greek and Roman antiquity, the orishas have been defined as "archetypes, primordial beings, magical agents, the receivers of prayer and sacrifice." They are the "axis of worship in Regla de Ocha" (Matibag 1996: 46).[21] Neither gods nor deities in the Western sense, orishas are personified natural forces that interact with human beings. Whereas in Africa each orisha had his or her own priests, fraternities, and sanctuaries, in Cuba the dispersion caused by slavery precluded this specialization. However, the "generic" orishas of agriculture, the seas, thunder, iron, and the like persisted, resulting in a reduced Afro-Cuban pantheon (Cros Sandoval 1995: 84–85). As Bastide has observed, a process of selection occurred in which the collective representations brought over from Africa were reoriented. Gods who protected agriculture were discarded or forgotten, for example. Why sacrifice for a bountiful harvest to benefit an exploitative slave master? Slaves worshiped Ogún, the protector of blacksmiths in Africa, as a deity of war; Changó, the warrior orisha, became identified with exacting justice. In like fashion others would reflect qualities of self-identity and legitimacy valued by people living in oppression (Bastide 1978: 66). Miguel Barnet describes this dynamic process within Cuba:

> Four hundred and five divinities have been identified in Nigeria, whereas in Cuba they do not exceed thirty. The passage of time has eroded the Yoruba pantheon, and many santos worshipped in the nineteenth century are almost unknown to practitioners today. However, ongoing syncretism has atomized elements of old deities and incorporated others from religions of Bantu origin or from Catholicism itself. Divinities who occupied an important place in the Yoruba pantheon of Nigeria, like Odduá, for example, have been nearly lost in Cuba; some who had not been tutelary [protector] gods gained primacy and are today the object of preferential worship. The process of accrual and loss typifies the transfer of elements from one culture to another and gives evidence of the permeability of a religion when, forced not so much by sociological as by ecological circumstances, it has to adjust to a new environment. (Barnet 1997: 87–88)

For nearly every orisha there is a correlating Catholic saint based on associations made by the slaves between the mythology of the orishas and attributes or qualities identified with Catholic saints, particularly as perceived in the iconographic representation of the latter in the statues and chromolithographs that were an important element of colonial popular Catholicism and religious instruction. The hagiography of the saints that described their lives and legacies would bring to mind characteristics that could be associated with a particular orisha. Thus, Changó, the Yoruba orisha of fire and thunder, for example, was identified with Santa Bárbara, the patroness of Spanish artillery, due to her iconographic representation in chromolithographs in which she is dressed in red—Changó's symbolic color—and her identification with the thundering artillery cannons.

An alternative explanation takes into account the legends surrounding Santa Bárbara's pagan father who, in order to separate her from the Christians, had her locked up in a tower. Upon discovering her Christian faith her father Dióscoro gave her up to the authorities who condemned her to death for her faith and beheaded her with a sword—one of Changó's attributes—which appears in many of her iconographic lithographs. Her association with Changó is made clearer in the version of the legend that states that her father was struck by lightning (Cros Sandoval 1995: 85; Bolívar Aróstegui 1990: 112).

Santa Bárbara

The Regla de Ocha/Santería system reflects the creolization process: the orishas were syncretized with divinities from other African traditions and with Roman Catholic santos,[22] a process of accommodation to social realities and a way for Africans to incorporate native culture into their spirituality. Whether adding the Christian gods to their pantheon was a pragmatic choice of incorporating the potent "magic" of Catholic rites, or was based upon a desire for upward mobility, one ought not ignore the fact that Catholicism was superimposed on African beliefs and that "at first the saints were no more than white masks covering the black faces of the ancestral divinities" (Bastide 1978: 162).

If their specific origins are varied and complex, so too are the Christianized representations which vary from one locale to the next within a particular country, and from country to country in the African Diaspora.[23] These variations are based on historical and environmental factors; orishas changed as a result of their transplantation to the New World and in their adjustment to the various regions of the Diaspora. As a result they have numerous *caminos*—avatar, aspect, path or road, identity, form, or manifestation. Changó's aspects include both the male and female, Eleguá is young and old, and so on. And orishas are protean and multifaceted in character. While their principal forms can have a Catholic equivalent, there may be several for the same orisha, which helps to explain the variety of Christianized representations in Cuban Santería and other creolized practices. The process of merging deities begun in Africa continued in Cuba where, for example, the Yoruba Shango merged with the Kongo Kanbaranguanje, a blending that, when added to the syncretization with the Catholic saints, "presents no distortion of their 'true' identities but rather successive variations on the same theme of the caminos, paths, or avatars that the orisha takes up in certain life stages or incarnations" (Matibag 1996: 57).

The caminos of the orisha, while multiple and varied, comprise a specific theme identified by qualities and objects (*atributos* or attributes) associated with a specific orisha's "universe."[24] Ogún's universe, for example, is that of the forge and the mountain, and includes iron tools and implements, miniature representations of keys that signal the orisha's syncretization with Saint Peter. The attributes—qualities, traits, aspects, characteristics, domains, or powers—are central to the ritual operations that summon the orishas or represent them in devotion.

The primary representation of the orishas, however, is found in the *otanes* or sacred stones that are kept in a soup tureen and "fed" with the blood of sacrificed animals and the ritual liquid *omiero*, "so that in and through the otanes the orisha can drink up nourishment in the form of *aché*. As transmitters of aché, the sacred stones call to the gods, inviting them to come down and take possession of their omos [children], to give the sign that they accept the sacrifice and feel strengthened by it" (Matibag 1996: 48). Along with the otanes in the tureen go the orisha's own set of twenty-one cowrie shells that will be used in divination rituals (see below) in order to communicate with a specific orisha.

Orisha Profiles

First among the gods in Regla de Ocha, the Creator and Supreme Being, is Olorun/Olodumare/Olofi, a single Ultimate, ranked above the lesser divinities, the orishas. His triplicate form in Cuba, different aspects of the supernatural being, liken him to the Christian God: Olorun, the origin and Creator of beings; Olodumare, the Almighty, the divine essence of all there is; Olofi, the creation itself, he who dwells in all creation. Julia Cuervo Hewitt observes that Olodumare is a "cosmological replica" of the sociopolitical structure of Oyo; analogous to an earthly king, the heavenly counterpart does not rule personally: "In the cosmological realm the orishas, as Oyo's elders, carry out the governing duties. Otherwise, Olodumare follows the archetypal characteristics of all universal Sky Gods equivalent to Zeus, Yaweh or Alá" (Cuervo Hewitt 1984: 67). In one of the many origin myths of the orishas it is said that they left the sacred land of Ile Ife one day and descended to earth where their presence remains in stones that resonate with their aché: "Devotees can find these orisha stones among ordinary ones if they can learn to listen carefully enough. For the orisha stones are alive with the orisha's ashe. They are most likely to be found in the element most expressive of their force—ocean stones for Yemaya, river pebbles for Oshun, meteorites for the thunder king Shango" (Murphy 1993: 41).

Orishas are identified with specific numbers, foods, and plants used in their worship, and explicit chants, drum rhythms, dance movements, and sacred narratives of their lives and relationships. Thus spiritual work to venerate Ochún, for example, would be done using her number and attributes: five yellow candles and cakes, amber beads, and the like, in order to obtain Ochún's aché. In the following profiles, we present a brief overview of the more familiar *caminos* or avatars[25] of several of the principal orishas favored in Cuba and in the Diaspora, those more commonly consecrated ritually or spiritually invested in a devotee in initiation.[26]

The myths surrounding the orishas—their family ties, adventures, affairs, problems, arguments, loves—referred to as *patakí,* are the explanatory stories of Regla de Ocha. In Cuba, as in all societies generally, these stories contribute to the formation of a social, moral, and even political consciousness, essential for an understanding of Cuban culture: "[M]yth here functions as a powerful cultural homogenizing factor" (Barnet 1983: 158–159). The mythology of the orishas changed in the course of their travels to Cuba: the family of orishas was transformed in the syncretic process which created kinship relationships among them—father, mother, sister, husbands, wives, children— that did not exist in African mythology. "In Santería there is a tendency to create relationships among the gods in the most diverse fashion, due to the desire to establish order and a hierarchy in the mismatched celestial family" (Cros Sandoval 1975: 159). These narratives, which are part of Cuban popular culture, also inform the divinatory practices of Regla de Ocha (and other Afro-Cuban practices). An example of the Cuban mythical narratives or patakís associated with the orishas and the natural world are included in the brief profiles below to demonstrate the concept.[27]

Eleguá

It is fitting to begin with Eleguá, as all Santería ceremonies must be initiated with a request for permission from this powerful deity, the ruler of the roads, crossroads, and thresholds. Messenger between humans and the orishas, he reports the actions of humans to Olodumare. Eleguá, also called Echú-Eleguá, opens or closes paths, and indicates the crossroads—the future. Eleguá must be propitiated before any other orisha and must be consulted before embarking on any important step in life. Characterized as a mischievous trickster, he can be severe in his punishment of those who ignore his commands, and is always justified in his actions.

Eleguá is frequently anthropomorphized in an artifact of cement with eyes, ears, and mouth made of cowrie shells and placed behind the street entrance door, guarding the homes of santeros with Ogún's cauldron containing Ochosi (the orisha of justice whose representation is a metal bow pierced by three arrows; usually stored all together in a small cabinet or in a *velador,* an appropriately named night table which in Spanish means "vigil-keeper").

Called the "divine enforcer," Eleguá visits misfortune upon those who fail to heed Olodumare's commands as expressed through divination. "Fate, the unexpected, forgetfulness, tragedy, good or bad luck, any sort of triumph, and even our own actions and hopes depend on Elegguá and Echú. He is indisputably the most influential of the Lucumí santos who have exerted their authority over Cuba" (Barnet 1997: 89). Eleguá has twenty-one very different paths. He is often syncretized with the Christ Child of Atocha, San Antonio de Padua, the *Anima Sola* or Wandering Soul in Pain. In the guise of Echú he is the Christian Devil, closing paths and doors. In Vodou he is syncretized with Papa Legba or Papa LaBas. His attributes and symbols include a cement or clay head with cowrie shells, a coconut, or a large stone, among other things. Eleguá's colors are red and black, his day is Monday, his sacred number three, and the offerings appropriate to him include pastries, sweets, rum, tobacco, a rooster, or a male goat.

A story that demonstrates Eleguá's role in enforcing justice concerns the coconut, which represents Prince Obi, one of the orisha Obatalá's children.[28] Prince Obi lived in a beautiful castle high up in the palm trees where he held court in impeccable white robes of exquisite beauty and saw important visitors from the world over. But his brother Eleguá noticed that Obi was becoming vain and snobbish, neglecting his poor subjects, and receiving only the rich and powerful. One day at a feast in Obi's castle, to which only the richest kings were invited, Eleguá arrived disguised as a pauper. Obi had the guards remove him, indignant that someone should attempt to enter in such ragged clothes. Eleguá told their father Obatalá what had happened, so Obatalá also disguised himself and returned with Eleguá to the castle. Now Obi was even more furious. "Two good-for-nothings in my castle! To the dungeon!" But then Obi heard a familiar voice say, "I think you are mistaken, son," at which he fell to his knees begging his father's forgiveness. Obatalá cursed Obi for his vanity and pride, saying, "Henceforth your exquisite white clothing will be worn inside and you will always wear filthy brown rags without, you will fall from the palm tree and roll on the ground and be kicked about by children in the dirt, and your brother orishas and humans will cut you into pieces and use you as the simplest of oracles." And thus Obi, the coconut, became the most commonly used of all the divination systems.

Ogún

Ogún, the orisha of war, of iron, the instruments of work, minerals, the mountain, and the forge, is a warrior and blacksmith, an important figure in African mythology with all that the technology of iron represented in the development of African societies. Ogún's cult spread far beyond the Yoruba culture; as with Eleguá, Ogún is one of the most important *lwas* in

Eleguá. Photo courtesy of the artist Héctor Delgado.

the Fon culture of Dahomey and in Haitian Vodou. Frequently portrayed as his brother Changó's competition for the love of Ochún, astute and bellicose in war as in work, he has many avatars and is the protector not only of blacksmiths but also of all who drive vehicles made of iron or steel or work with the same—surgeons, butchers, carpenters, mechanics, farmers, policemen.

Though he protects people against criminals, Ogún is also responsible for railroad and auto accidents and violent crimes that employ metal weapons. A symbol of war and violence, he is the orisha of the sacrificial knife and the force in bloodletting, of conflict as an element of human nature, "the archetype of the violent occurrences that result from man's weaknesses and lack of control" (González-Wippler 1989: 45).[29] Ogún is syncretized with Saint Peter, who carries the keys of heaven; also with Santiago or Saint James the Elder. In Vodou he is Papa Ogoun. His attributes and symbols include all types of iron objects—keys, cutlasses, shovels, hammers, chains, and machetes are symbolic of Ogún, who is represented in the Ocha temple by an iron pot containing miniature implements, or simply a horseshoe or railroad spike. Ogún's colors are black and green, his day is Tuesday, his sacred numbers seven and three, and fitting offerings include palm wine, salt, roasted yams, tortoises, and dogs.

In one well-known tale Obatalá was troubled; he noticed that his son Ogún was acting strangely toward his mother, Yemmu, who treated Ogún not like a son but as would a woman in love. The enchanted rooster Osún was supposed to inform him of the goings-on at home in his absence, but had not reported anything unusual. But Eleguá, his other son, was sad and emaciated. "What is the matter, Eleguá? Tell me, why are you so sad?" "Baba-mi, it pains me to tell you this, but Ogún has been doing a terrible deed with my mother; he gives all my food to Osún to make him sleepy and then locks me out of the house so that I don't see what is happening, but I know." That evening Obatalá told Yemmu he was leaving for several days and hid. He returned to find Ogún and Yemmu together. Ogún then cried out in fear and shame. "Do not curse me for I curse myself. I will never again know the meaning of peace, and will work night and day and teach men the secrets of making iron." And as Ogún left, Obatalá turned to Yemmu and declared, "The next male child you bear I will bury alive." The baby boy Changó was sent to live with his sister Dada on top of the palm tree, and when Yemmu's new son, Orula, was born, he suffered the fate Obatalá had determined.

Changó

Changó is perhaps the most venerated and popular of the Cuban orishas, one of the tutelary or protector-guardian gods; many consider him the
strongest and most important. "He is a womanizer and drinker, quarrelsome,
courageous, and daring; made for challenges and dares, proud of his masculine virtues, boastful of his strength and manly beauty, castigador (a heart-
breaker)" (Barnet 1997: 91). Of great importance in the New World, Sango
in Yoruba, Shango in English, Xangô in Portuguese, Changó in Spanish and
French, "when his name is pronounced, believers rise from their seats making a drinking gesture and thus salute and revere him" (Barnet 1997: 91).[30]
Both feared and venerated, his domain is music and he rules over the sacred
batá drums, fire, thunder, and lightning. He is the protector of warriors, fishermen, and hunters.

Changó is believed to have been a historical figure, the fourth Alafín
(another name for Changó in Santería) or king of Oyo, a victorious ruler
who had earned a foremost place among the mythical founders and heroes
of the Yoruba kingdom. All Changó's legends, which are numerous, concern
some form of power—"procreative, authoritative, destructive, medicinal,
or moral" (González-Wippler 1989: 40). Changó's most widely recognized
Catholic syncretic form in Santería is with Santa Bárbara, but Changó has
many paths and in other aspects is syncretized with Saint Patrick, Saint
Mark, and Saint George. His attributes and symbols are the double-bladed
axe or hatchet, *piedras de rayo,* thunderstones or flintstones collected after
lightning storms, a mortar, a castle, the sword, and the cup. Changó has his
own type of tureen for his thunderstones, a wooden *batea* (pan) elevated on
a mortar stool. His colors are bright red and white; his day is Santa Bárbara's
feast day, December 4. His sacred numbers are four and six, and offerings to
Changó might include a ram, tortoise, okra, bean fritters, and cornmeal with
okra.

As one of the most popular of the orishas, Changó also has a great number of myths ascribed to him. One tells of his fabulous gift of divining which
he traded with his brother Orula. Although he had spent years studying all
types of divination, hoping to be the best in creation, Orula did not have
Changó's talent. However, Orula was a talented dancer and drummer,
something Changó envied. One day at a party the god of thunder told his
brother, "I would happily trade my powers of divination for your musical
talent." Orula was stunned that his brother would give up such a great gift

and warned him against making a hasty decision, but Changó's mind was made up. "If I could dance and play the drums like you I would feel perfectly happy." So the two exchanged gifts and Changó became an even better dancer and drummer than Orula, whose powers of divination have no equal.

Yemayá

Yemayá is the great universal mother. The deity of maternity, the sea, and of salt water, Yemayá gave birth to all the orishas as well as to the sun and the moon, with which she is associated. Yemayá represents fertility and is portrayed occasionally as a dark-skinned mermaid. In some versions she is the adopted mother of Changó, who was given to her by Obatalá, his mother, and in one of her many avatars she is Yemayá Olokun who is found at the bottom of the ocean (although some categorize Olokun as a distinct deity). Yemayá is the orisha of intelligence and rationality. "Sister of Ochún . . . she is judgment and reason, but she can also be inflexible when she punishes. Majestic queen of the oceans, she is presumptuous and haughty. She protects her children in her skirt, feeds them, and raises them with absolute motherly rigor" (Barnet 1997: 92). Multiple myths and legends surround Yemayá and she has many avatars, but, according to some, "there is no more than one Yemayá. A single one with seven paths" (Cabrera 1980: 30). When she takes possession of her children she swirls around quickly, swaying like the waves of the sea.

In her Catholic syncretization, Yemayá is La Virgen de Regla, a black saint and patron of the Bay of Havana, who also looks to the sea. Her attributes and symbols include seashells or stones found near the sea and she is symbolized by a sword, fan, the half-moon, a seashell, an anchor, and a silver or white-metal sun. Yemayá's colors are navy blue and white, her day is Saturday, her sacred number is seven, and suitable offerings made to her include maize, pigeons, ducks, rams, and cocks.

In one of many versions of a story that explains why women are excluded from the use of the oracles or divination systems of Ifá (the system reserved for the babalao priests, the sons of Orula, also known as Ifá), it is said that Yemayá was Orula's wife, but the marriage was rocky. One day while he was away he heard rumors of a famous female seer from his town who was earning a fortune with her prophecies. Orula disguised himself and returned home to find the house full of people. He waited his turn, paid the *derecho* (fee) for the consultation, and Yemayá said, "You are my husband, but I wasn't going to die here of hunger." Orula made her leave his house but

Yemayá continued until Orula found that she had used his divining board or *Tabla*. Now Orula was truly furious that she, a woman, had dared touch what he had prohibited. "A woman cannot know more than I! In this home I can be the only seer!" which is why women are barred from the use of Orula's divining chain or *tabla*.

Obatalá

Obatalá is the god of purity and justice whose name means "King of the White Cloth." Always dressed in his characteristic white color Obatalá represents truth, purity, peace, and compassion. Obatalá has several male and female paths and is the archetypal spirit of creativity: he was sent down by Olodumare to create the earth and to mold the human race and is therefore of great importance in Regla de Ocha as the owner of all heads (*orí*) where the spirit, thoughts, and dreams dwell. "In the liturgy of Santería he is the head, birth, that which stands high, pure, and clean. . . . [I]n the rites of initiation the color white is used as a symbol of what is born pure in life . . . an extremely rigorous santo. His devotees must behave well; they must not utter blasphemies, drink, argue, undress before anyone" (Barnet 1997: 93–94). As noted above, though Olofi created the world, Obatalá created man and governs a person's thoughts and ideas. Oduduwa is believed to be Obatalá's wife by some, but is considered by others to be the oldest Obatalá and his female aspect. The first orisha and owner of the world, Obatalá's tureen (*sopera*) is located in the highest spot of the *canastillero* or shelved cabinet where the orishas' soperas are traditionally stored in a worshiper's home, above all others.

Obatalá is syncretized with Our Lady of Mercy and his/her attributes and symbols include the white *iruka* (horsetail switch), *agogós* (chimes) of white metal, crowns of silver or white metal, and holy water. Obatalá's color is white and he/she is celebrated on September 4, the Catholic feast day of Our Lady of Mercy. The sacred numbers for Obatalá are eight, sixteen, and twenty-four, and appropriate offerings include coconut, cotton, cocoa butter, powdered eggshell (*cascarilla*), doves, pigeons, and snails (all offerings should be covered with cotton and be immaculately clean).

In a famous creation story Olofi, the supreme deity, decided to create the firmament and assigned the task to the pure and peaceful Obatalá, who would be assisted by Orúnmila, wisdom itself. After Orúnmila consulted the oracle and told him what he would require, Obatalá descended through a gold chain to the swampy ground beneath the sky and trickled some earth onto the marshy terrain; he then let loose a hen that dug into the spilled earth and dispersed it in all directions, creating solid land over the water. Olofi then showed Obatalá how to mold males and females out of clay. When the figures dried Olofi would come down and breathe life into them. One day, Obatalá became thirsty and drank palm wine to quench his thirst. The liquor made his hands clumsy and the figures were twisted and malformed. Olofi trusted Obatalá and gave them life without examining them, which is why deformed people exist and why their patron orisha is Obatalá, who has protected them ever since, and never touched liquor again.

Ochún

Ochún-Kolé (one of many names and avatars for the orisha, including Panchágara, Iyammu, Yeyé-Karí, and the nickname Yeyé) is the deity of rivers, fresh waters, and gold, and she represents female sensuality, love, beauty, and sexual desire. Ochún is the Lucumí Aphrodite and is identified with Cuba's patron saint, the Virgen de la Caridad del Cobre. She is the protector of pregnant women and in Haitian Vodou Ochún is identified with the lwa Erzulie. Indeed, the deity's significance extends to a worldwide devotion, referred to as "Ósun religion" in *Ósun across the Waters: A Yoruba Goddess in Africa and the Americas*, a collection of essays that documents the centrality and authority of Ochún in Yoruba religious thought and practice in Africa and the Americas. Most representations of the deity, according to the work's editors Joseph M. Murphy and Mei-Mei Sanford, are ethnocentric and reductive and "fail to reflect the multidimensionality of her power: political, economic, divinatory, maternal, natural, therapeutic" (1).

In Cuba popular anecdotes of Ochún's turbulent love affairs with Changó and other orishas abound, and in her avatar as Panchágara she is an irrepressible and capricious seducer of all men. She is usually represented as a beautiful, light-skinned *mulata*, who charms and attracts like her favorite food—honey. "Among the orishas she is one of the most venerated, perhaps the most easily and naturally adapted to Cuba, not only because of the syncretism of the patroness of Cuba . . . but because she is thought to represent many Cuban women in her sensual grace and Creole mischievousness" (Barnet 1997: 95). In her Cuban Catholic syncretization, Ochún is, as noted above, the Virgen de la Caridad del Cobre. Her attributes and symbols include a chime (*agogó*) of yellow metal, gold, copper, the peacock, mirrors, fans, canoes, and coral; pumpkins are sacred to her. Her color is yellow and she is celebrated on September 8, Our Lady of Charity's feast day. Ochún's sacred number is five, and fitting offerings to her include a female goat, fish, hen, beans, honey, pastries, and a dish made of shrimp and almonds.

Clearly a New World creation, one story of the deity tells about the sadness of the goddess of love as she watched her children forced from their home to be taken to a new land named Cuba. Ochún visited her sister, Yemayá, to ask her advice. "It must be this way, Ochún. Our children will now go through the world spreading our wonders and millions will remember us and worship once again." But Ochún wanted to be with her children and asked Yemayá, who had traveled the world over, to describe Cuba to her. "It is much like here: hot days, long nights, calm rivers, abundant vegetation, but not everyone is black like us; there are also many whites." Ochún decided to join her suffering children in Cuba and asked her sister to grant her two favors before leaving: "Please make my hair straighter and my skin lighter so that all Cubans can see some of themselves in me." Her wish was granted and Ochún became Cuba's beloved patron saint.[31]

Oyá

Oyá is a female warrior deity who often fights at the side of Changó, mistress of lightning, the wind, and gatekeeper of the cemetery. She is the protector of the dead, owner of the rainbow, and, like Changó, she inherited fire which she shoots from her mouth when angered. Sister to Yemayá, Ochún, and Oba, she competes with all for Changó. "In some Lucumí ceremonies, like that of *Itutu,* meant to appease and refresh the dead, Oyá fulfils an important role. On the day a person dies, Oyá 'descends' and shakes the iruke over the deceased's face as a signal of welcome to the cemetery. The dead must enter clean into the kingdom of Oyá (Yanza)" (Barnet 1997: 94). In Cuba Oyá is represented by the black horsetail switch (*iruke*), and her personality is likened to that of the Greek Medusa and Hecate and the Hindu Kali in her fierceness, as well as to the Greek Hera in her relentless battles for Changó's affection (Cuervo Hewitt 1988: 173). Oyá is syncretized with the Catholic Virgen de la Candelaria (*candelaria* means "conflagration" in Spanish) and Santa Teresa. Her attributes and symbols include the black iruke. Oyá's colors are deep maroon and white, her day is Friday, and sacred number nine. Suitable offerings to Oyá include hens and goats.

In Cuba, as in Africa, Oyá is identified with death. Among her avatars are Yansa Oriri, the streak of lightning, and Oyá Dumi, the owner of the cemetery. In one legend Osain gave Changó a small gourd and told him to stick his fingers into it every morning and trace the sign of the cross on his tongue to shoot fire from his mouth when he spoke. Oyá became curious about her husband's strange ritual and one day attempted the same, observing in horror the fire that blasted from her mouth each time she spoke. Horror-stricken, she hid in a palm tree until Changó discovered her hiding place and began to chastise her. But Oyá quickly explained, "But now, husband, I can go by your side to make war with Ogún," which accounts for the beginning of warfare in the world and is the reason why Oyá is usually portrayed as a fierce female warrior next to Changó.

Orula

Also called Orunla, Orúnmila, or Ifá, Orula is the tutelary divinity in the Lucumí pantheon, the master of divination, owner of the *Opon-Ifá* or *Tablero de Ifá,* the divining board that is the domain of the babalao priest, of whom he is also the patron. As he was present during the creation of mankind, Orula knows everyone's destiny and can give proper guidance, communicating through his *ekuelé* divining chain and the Tablero or divining board; his prophecies are always fulfilled. Respected and venerated, Orula is the true secretary of Olofi, mediator between humans and the gods, the orisha who must be consulted before all major events in life to seek guidance and instruction for proper procedure, including those related to such religious ceremonies as initiation, sacrifice, and possession. "Wise, old, cantankerous, he exerts limitless power over the lives of the babalao and his clients. With a will of iron, tending to drastic decisions, this santo is one of the most beloved of Cuban Santería" (Barnet 1997: 91). He is syncretized with Saint Francis of Assisi (perhaps because Orula's divining chain recalls the beads of the rosary); his attributes and symbols are the Tablero, which is a symbol of the world, and the ekuelé chain. Orula's colors are green and yellow, he is celebrated on October 4, the feast day of Saint Francis, and his sacred number is sixteen. Offerings to Orula include chickens and doves.

To demonstrate the origins of Orula's talent for divination it is told that Yemmu became pregnant after Ogún was banished from the home by Obatalá and gave birth to a baby boy. Given his earlier command, Obatalá ordered that Yemmu bury him alive. So the suffering Yemmu buried the child—whom she named Orula—from the neck down under the sacred Iroko (*ceiba* or silk-cotton) tree. From Iroko, Orula learned the secrets of divination and became the greatest seer of them all, the father of the mysteries. People came from all over to hear their fortunes and fed him in exchange. Orula became famous and one day Eleguá came to see him and recognized his brother, assuring him that he would ask their father to forgive Orula. Eleguá was very persuasive and Obatalá finally relented, crying when he saw his young son buried in the earth. He then lifted his arms, asking the earth to release Orula. When he told Orula to come home the young man was reluctant to leave the shadow of the Iroko that had been his mother for so long. So Obatalá turned the ceiba tree into a round tray that Orula could take with him to keep his Iroko by his side as he cast his fortunes.

Babalú Ayé

Of Dahomeyan origin (where he was named Chankpana or Shonpona),[32] Saint Lazarus for the Christians and nicknamed Babá, Babalú Ayé[33] is the crippled orisha who preaches good habits, receiving the veneration of all. Like his Catholic counterpart in the parable of the rich man and the leper in the New Testament, he limps about covered with sores, dressed in sackcloth, and with a shoulder bag (*alforja*) filled with toasted corn crisscrossed on his chest, accompanied by loyal dogs that lick his wounds.[34] He is the god of illness, owner of epidemics and diseases—especially leprosy and skin diseases, and at present, also AIDS.[35] His messengers are mosquitoes and flies, and he both cures and infects, punishing through leprosy, syphilis, gangrene, and smallpox. He is fierce and implacable toward those who forget to fulfill their promises or who disobey him. He is the owner of grains and women, whom he counsels in matters of love. His devotees flagellate themselves; every seventeenth of the month they dress in sackcloth like the orisha and on December 17 they lead a procession that is traditional in Havana each year: on foot, on their knees, pulling stones on chains, they crawl from distant places to the sanctuary and leprosy hospital of Lazareto in the village of Rincón where San Lázaro is worshiped.

"Arará or Yoruba, his origin is no longer of much concern. A transculturated divinity, he has become Cuban more by sustained modifications in his worship than by preserving those characteristics that he brought to Cuba during slavery. Model of hybridity and fusion, Babalú Ayé maintains to this day a certain allure throughout the country" (Barnet 1997: 96). He is syncretized with the Lazarus described in a parable by Jesus Christ as a leprous beggar followed by faithful dogs, and with Saint Lazarus, Bishop of Marseilles. His attributes and symbols include the *ajá,* a whisk of palm fronds, the *tablillas de San Pedro,* three pieces of wood tied together to sound a warning of his arrival; his colors are royal purple, white, and blue. December 17, Saint Lazarus's feast day, is Babalú Ayé's day as well; his sacred number is seventeen, and fitting offerings include bread soaked in olive oil or spread with palm oil, toasted corn, and different grains.

Babalú Ayé dresses in sackcloth like a beggar and the shoulder bag he crosses on his chest contains toasted corn, his favorite food. It is said that he was originally from Yorubaland but had to leave when his disrespect for the elders caused him to contract smallpox. All the others threw water behind him in contempt but Eleguá took pity on him and took him to Ife for a consultation with Orula. Orula informed him that he would be venerated again some day in Dahomey if he cleansed himself with grains first and kept a dog by his side. Babalú Ayé cleansed himself and traveled to Dahomey where Olofi sent rains down to wash away his ailment in forgiveness. There Babalú Ayé established his kingdom and became a powerful king who was venerated and well loved.

Ochosi

Ochosi is the orisha of hunters and belongs to the triumvirate grouping of orishas, with Eleguá and Ogún, known as the orisha *guerreros* (warriors). The protector of prisoners, transgressors, political dissidents, and of those who seek justice, in slang the expression to "have the letter of Ochosi" means to be on the way to jail or in trouble with the law. Ochosi and Ogún "eat" and "live" together: "That is, their implements are kept together inside a small cauldron, and when one receives a sacrifice, the other usually partakes of it. But Ochosi is for the most part a solitary who shuns others" (González-Wippler 1989: 51). Ochosi's Catholic syncretization is San Norberto, his attributes and symbols include a metal bow pierced by three arrows, kept in Ogún's cauldron. His color is violet, Tuesday is his day, three and seven are his sacred numbers, and offerings to Ochosi include male fowl, a drink of milk, honey, and cornmeal.

The close relationship between Ochosi and Ogún is explained in a myth in which both combine their talents to solve a problem: hunger. All the animals used to run away from the sound of Ogún's machete in the forest and the density of the trees caused them to be blocked from the great hunter Ochosi's view. One day the two orishas decided to combine their talents: Ogún cleared the field for Ochosi's sure arrows to reach their mark, and thus both orishas were able to appease their hunger together.

Osain

Osain is the patron of *curanderos* (folk and herbal healers, often referred to in Osain's honor as *osainistas*). The deity of *el monte*,[36] the forests, the bush, and of medicine, Osain is herbalist, healer, and master of the healing secrets of plant life. Portrayed as lame, one-eyed, and one-armed, Osain has one overlarge ear that is deaf and one small ear that hears extraordinarily well. He was never born: he simply sprang from the earth. Osain is represented by a *güiro* (gourd) that hangs in the Santería *ilé* or house-temple, and he must be propitiated before any of his plants and herbs (*ewe*) are used in the ceremonies, spells, or cures of Regla de Ocha. "The woods have everything the santero needs to preserve his health and to defend himself against evil. But he must always remember to ask the woods' permission before removing a stone or a leaf from a tree. . . . All the ewe is the property of Osain, and without enlisting his aid beforehand, it is not possible to do any work in Santería" (González-Wippler 1989: 55). Osain is syncretized with Saint Joseph, Saint Benito, or Saint Jerome (also Saint Anthony Abad or Saint Sylvester). His attributes and symbols include the gourd in which he lives (a good luck talisman) and a twisted tree branch; his color is green, reminiscent of vegetation.

Initiation

Afro-Cuban religious practices focus on the relationship of devotees with the deities and the spirits. Followers celebrate the spiritual entities, offer sacrifices, consult their will in divination, follow their advice, attempt to control them, and, if possible, incarnate them in their bodies in possession— the ultimate communion with the divine—in quest of assistance in coping with human problems and the challenges of everyday life. Spiritual growth is manifested by stages of initiation, complex and symbolic ceremonies of death and rebirth that are the source of ritual knowledge, development, and evolution. Those who require balance and harmony in their lives due to a physical or emotional illness or a life crisis seek out the help of a priest of Ocha who will undoubtedly consult the oracle to hear the spiritual solution proffered by the deities. The remedies can range from a spiritual cleansing, a *resguardo* or protective charm, to more advanced initiatory steps. Divination will determine whether the individual needs to undergo a series of rituals culminating in the seven-day ceremony called *asiento* or *kariocha*, "making Ocha," comparable to an ordination: it will also determine the correct identity of that person's Guardian Angel or "Orisha of the Head."

However, religious participation does not demand this ultimate stage. Those who have passed through one or several of the initiation rituals that precede the asiento may participate actively in most of the religious activities of the house-temple. Those who ultimately "make Ocha," however, will establish bonds with several godparents and will acquire a number of orishas whom they will serve. Simultaneously they will also acquire spiritual kinship in an *ilé-orisha* (*casa de santo* or house-temple of Ocha), an extended ritual family which is at once a dwelling place, a place of worship, a family, and a community founded by an initiate called to the priesthood who has dedicated his or her life to worship and the initiation of others. The members of the family of brothers and sisters *en santo*, in the spirit, respect each other and show deference appropriate to the seniority of initiation, the birth order of the family member in ocha. The head of the family, the senior priest or priestess, presides over the ceremonies of initiation and guides the family's spiritual growth.[37]

A series of initiation rituals mark the stages in the religious life of the practitioner and create different roles and/or ranks within the religious community:

1. The *iyawó*. For the year following the asiento or initiation a man or woman is an iyawó. He or she can decide after this period whether he or she wishes to exercise the functions of a priest or attend to the orishas privately.

2. The *babalocha* and *iyalocha* (baba=father and iya=mother). Those who have passed the novitiate period, dedicate themselves to the priestly role. They are sometimes called *santero* and *santera*.[38]

3. The *oriaté* (the head "ori" of everything taking place on the mat, "até"). This is a specialized priest; in some houses the oriaté performs all tasks without deferring to the babalao. The oriaté is a highly trained diviner and ritual specialist, an orisha priest also called the *italero* after the Itá divination reading he performs on the third day of initiation. This figure of the Lucumí religion developed in Cuba as part of the transformation process that took place at the turn of the twentieth century. The oriaté officiates in initiations and is the chief authority of the asiento initiation, with a complete knowledge of procedure, songs, herbs, plants, and divination—the secrets of making all the different orishas.

4. The *babalao*. A priest of the cult of the orisha Orula or Ifá. The babalao priests belong to a distinct cult called la *Regla de Ifá*. Their ritual roles are complementary with the babalocha and iyalocha of la Regla de Ocha, although rivalry occasionally emerges regarding jurisdiction. Some explain

the differences between the cults as varying *caminos* or roads: *el camino del santo* or the road of the saints, and *el camino de Orula* or the road of Orula—in other words, the priesthood of the orishas and the priesthood of Orula/Ifá (Murphy 1993: 140–141).

The babalao is the ultimate authority in divination and the most highly regarded of all priests. While many women hold important positions as priests in Regla de Ocha with their own house-temple, the babalao priesthood is only open to men, the "sons of Orula." They are the exclusive holders of two systems of divination: the ekuelé chain and the Table of Ifá (both discussed below). They also preside over most initiation rites to authorize the process at certain points, contribute Orula's aché, conduct the sacrifices of animals, and hold funeral rites. Other duties of the babalao include the annual "Reading of the Year" predictions divined from the Ifá oracle determining the identities of the two orishas who will govern the coming year (king and queen) and the design and color of the banner which represents them, which will hang in the house of Ocha. Babalaos are initiated, "make Ifá," in a highly secretive and complex ceremony.[39]

Among the origin myths that explain the development of the two roads or branches in Afro-Cuban orisha worship—Regla de Ocha and Regla de Ifá—it is told that with the creation of the world at Ile Ife the first sixteen orishas descended from the sky to establish their respective domains; Orula, however, had preceded them in Creation. Therefore the sixteen original houses grew and propagated in the cabildos and house-temples dedicated to the orishas separately from the cult of Orula.

A series of initiatory passages give the individual increased spiritual powers and new ritual obligations that eventually culminate for some in the ultimate consecration or "coronation." In the first step an initiate receives the *ilekes* or *collares,* beaded color-coded necklaces from a padrino or madrina in Ocha, usually of the five principal deities—Eleguá, Obatalá, Changó, Ochún, and Yemayá—in a solemn ritual preceded by a *rogación de cabeza* or ritual cleansing of the head. With the necklaces the initiate obtains the spiritual force of the orishas and their protection.

In a subsequent initiation an individual receives or is granted, usually by a babalao who becomes the person's padrino in Ifá, the power and protection of the guerreros or warrior orishas Eleguá, Ochosi, Ogún, and Osún representing the *eledá,* the spiritual essence of the person initiated. (Osún is not a warrior but an orisha who guards the home, advising when danger is near.)

The initiate obtains a variety of artifacts that are a material representation of the orishas' protection and the strength of the spiritual bond between the initiate and the deity. The Eleguá received is a little, conical, cement head with cowry shells representing the eyes, nose, mouth, and ears, and a steel spike protruding from its head placed atop a terracotta dish. (The Eleguá made by babalaos are distinguished from those created by santeros by yellow and green beads embedded in the head; babalaos will usually give Orulá's necklace and his bracelet of green and yellow beads—the idé—together with the warrior orishas.) The representations of Ogún (iron implements) and Ochosi (metal bow and arrows) reside in a small, black iron cauldron; Osún is received in the form of a tiny rooster surrounded by bells atop a small, silver colored, metal cup. Depending on the result of divination, the receiving of the warriors from a babalao could be followed by another step, the receiving of the Mano de Orula ("hand of Orula"), called the Kofá for women and Abofacá for men. For males this can represent a calling to the babalao priesthood in Ifá; for women, who cannot become babalaos, it could be a calling to the service of Orula, perhaps working with a babalao.

The ultimate step is the coronation, asiento (seating), or formal consecration of an initiate (see description below). Although the majority of devotees are not initiated—it is costly and is also the first step toward priesthood— once it has been determined through divination that a client should be initiated, whether in response to a life-threatening illness or a family or personal crisis, and that the solution can be found in a commitment of service to the spirit, they must follow a complex one-year process of spiritual transformation called kariocha.

The Kariocha Initiation

Joseph M. Murphy observes that the language of the initiation ritual is highly illustrative. One "makes the saint" (hacer santo) in initiation, an active construction by humans using plants, animals, songs, and movements, to create the presence of the deity in the body and spirit of the novice; the initiation is a "crowning" (coronación), likened to that of African kings and cabildo leaders, where a novice is crowned with the orishas; the process is also called an asiento, "seating," and "agreement" or "pact" connoting the seating on a throne and simultaneously a binding relationship established between the novice and the spirit who is "seated" on the head/throne of the novice, who in turn has made a commitment to the orisha. Kariocha literally means to place the orisha over one's head, a description of the literal and spiritual act that occurs during the ceremony, as we shall see (Murphy 1994: 93–95). But the orisha is also consecrated *in* the novice.

> By a variety of symbolic actions . . . by ingestion, anointing, and incision, the sacred ingredients which "make" the *orisha* are literally placed inside the body of the initiate. She or he eats and drinks *orisha*-consecrated foods, is soaked in *orisha*-valent poultices, is infused with *orisha*-active herbs and preparations. The spirit, now dwelling "in" the initiate, can be shown or manifested through her or his actions in public ceremony and in ordinary acts of generosity and power. (Murphy 1994: 95)

The godchild who will be crowned acquires or "makes" a single major "orisha of the head" and "receives" the rest, a group of some four to seven auxiliary deities, in a concurrent ceremony. The Guardian Angel, who is "seated," and one other orisha, who is "received" (of the opposite sex from the Guardian Angel), are the initiate's "parents"—spiritual father and mother. If Yemayá is seated or crowned and Changó is received, for example, the *omo-orisha*, child of the orisha, will declare, "Yemayá is my mother and Changó is my father." The omo is ruled by the orisha he or she serves; newly born in Ocha, the omo serves the spiritual parents, who are also newly "born" in the process. The godparents who made Ocha for others are considered babalo-cha, babalorisha (father of the orisha) and iyalorisha or iyalocha (mother of the orisha) to the extent that the orishas on the godparents' heads are the progenitors or parents of the new ocha or santo on the head of the iyawó or novice. They are priests who "have" the saint and "make" the saint; their ori-shas have given birth to other orishas.

The formal coronation ceremony[40] lasts seven days, although the most solemn rituals occur during the first three. The initiation, "expressed by a rich variety of symbols in the many societies that ritualize social and cultural transitions," reflects the transformative nature of the ritual process, the "liminal" states analyzed by Victor Turner based on what Arnold van Gennep identified as the three phases of all rites of passage. In the first phase the individual or group is detached from an earlier point in the social structure or from a set of cultural conditions; in the second, the liminal (from *limen* or "threshold" in Latin), the ritual subject enters into an ambiguous condition, at the interstices of structure, transgressing or dissolving social norms. In the third phase the passage is complete and the ritual subject returns and is reincorporated into the social structure, with clearly defined rights and obligations (V. Turner 1969: 94–95).

The "symbolic behavior" is manifested in the steps the Regla de Ocha initiate must follow. Several days before the initiation ceremony a *Misa Espiritual* (spiritual mass) based on Espiritismo practice takes place in most, though not all, house-temples where the initiation is to be carried out (see chapter 7 on Espiritismo). The Spiritist session combines the recitation of Catholic prayers around an altar with a crucifix and other items and invokes the ancestors and other spirits through a medium, identifying and insuring the protection of one's guardian spirits and the orishas. It is an example of the way borrowings from Catholicism and Spiritism have transformed Regla de Ocha rituals: "The old Kari-Ocha has been transformed from an African rite into an Afro-Cuban celebration. The original *ashé* of the Yoruba religion is enriched with the *aché* of the Catholic Church and the forces of spiritism" (I. Castellanos 1996: 48).

The first ceremony of initiation, the *Ebó de Entrada,* a consultation with the orisha Orula, prescribes the proper prior sacrifice and cleansing to be performed. On the first actual day of the initiation the *oyugbona,* assistant to the madrina or padrino, and other priests typically take the initiate to a river to greet Ochún, the owner of the rivers, to be purified symbolically. The initiate's clothing, considered contaminated and impure, is ripped off and discarded in the river, and the initiate is told to select a stone that will be used to receive the attributes of Eleguá, Ochún, or their tutelary orisha. Other stones and plants are also selected, all of which will be questioned by means of coconut divination to deem their suitability as ritual objects. The novice is isolated from the world and instructed in the faith, the doctrines, myths, and rituals, and undergoes a spiritual and physical preparation for the trance state of possession in which he will incarnate the deity.

After this preparation, the coronation commences in an inner sanctuary of the ilé house-temple, the *igbodu* ("sacred grove of the festival"), a sacred room, a secret, purified, and guarded space in which the most important ritual, the "making" and "receiving" of orishas takes place. The room, which is normally a regular part of the house, is an inner sanctum for the more esoteric rites (the *eyá aránla* or *sala,* often the living room, is reserved for semiprivate rituals and public ceremonies if a patio is not available; the patio, or *iban balo,* is for public occasions, plant cultivation, holding animals to be sacrificed, and the like). The igbodu is ritually purified and transformed: palm fronds are hung from the room's door frame to keep out undesirable spiritual influences, and a white sheet, representing Obatalá's immaculate white cloth, is stretched out over the threshold, "cooling" the space—a concept that accompanies many ritual ceremonies in Regla de Ocha. The spirits of the dead had been asked the prior week to step back. The uninitiated and those not directly involved in the ceremony are excluded: the "secrets" must be guarded to protect the divine from defilement and knowledge falling into untrained hands.[41]

On this first day of the asiento ceremony the iyawo will have thrust upon him or her the *collar de mazo,* a heavy and elaborately beaded necklace-collar often weighing some five pounds, a giant version of the single stringed necklaces worn every day. The ceremony is called the *prendición* or pinning. It takes place without warning and begins a symbolic process of transition which many initiates claim creates a feeling of anticipation and confusion about the event to take place. At this point the initiate is a "child" who has lost his or her status in the outside world and must observe strict silence, speaking only if spoken to by his or her elders. He or she must sleep for seven days on a straw mat on the floor, eat with a spoon, and be supervised constantly by the oyugbona who will bathe him or her and accompany the initiate everywhere. In a concurrent ceremony, invited priests are called in to contribute their orishas' aché when the new santo is born during the preparation of the *omiero* or sacred purifying liquid. This is the liquid with which the neophyte is purified during the ordination, a process in which songs, chants, and prayers summon the orishas. (See similarities in the Vodou initiation ceremonies in chapter 4.)

All is now ready for the actual kariocha, the placing of the sacred stones on the head of the iyawó. Wrapped in a white cloth, with eyes closed, the iyawó is taken toward a door of the igbodu where the padrino or madrina are waiting to ask him or her a series of ritual questions ("Why have you come?" "To find orisha," "Which orisha?" and so on). When he or she answers, the iyawó gains access to the sacred space where the coronation will take place. Once inside, the priests wash the iyawo's head, remove the initiate's clothing, and bathe him or her with the omiero. Dressed now in a simple sack, the iyawo's hair is cut off and saved. It will be buried with the novice after his or her death. The oriaté proceeds to shave the head of the iyawó, draw concentric circles in red, white, blue, and yellow dye on the scalp to invite the orisha to enter, and anoint the head with a special paste made of a combination of herbal and animal substances. Fabrics of different colors are placed on the iyawo's head and finally the padrino holds the sacred stones representing the santos on the head of the initiate.

This is done in rigorous order, beginning, as always, with Eleguá and ending with the stones of the iyawo's tutelary orisha whose identity had been determined earlier in divination. The placement of the tutelary orisha ushers in the ultimate moment of the true "seating" on the head or coronation. Iyawós will frequently go into a trance, possessed by their orisha, at this time. Small incisions are made on the initiate's tongue to insure that the orisha will descend with the "gift of speech," and an elaborate animal sacrifice ceremony follows as an offering to the orishas. The meat is cooked and saved for the banquet that will occur on the following day, *el Día del Medio* (the middle day), an occasion of public acknowledgment and celebration.

After having slept on the mat next to the sacred stones, the iyawó dresses for the Día del Medio in an elaborate costume in the ritual colors of his or her tutelary orisha (clothing that will be worn twice in the novice's lifetime: on the day of his or her presentation to the public, and at the end of life for the burial ceremony, the *Itutu*), as well as the sacred necklaces, including the collar de mazo, and a crown.[42] The novice is seated on a stool covered with cloth on an ornate throne of colorfully beaded and sequined fabrics, described here by Marta Moreno Vega in a personal account of her initiation in Cuba in 1981:

> They escorted me to the front room, where I saw an elaborately deco-
> rated altar in honor of Obatalá. Constructed in the corner of the room
> and draped in the ceremonial cloths lent by the elders, the throne was
> magnificent. Like a nineteenth-century parasol, it was covered with lace,
> intricately embroidered materials, and decorative doves, creating an envi-
> ronment of dignity and elegance. . . . In place of the porcelain bowl with
> the sacred stones at the center of the altar, I would sit on a stool covered
> with white satin cloth, in my ritual dress, and the altar would become
> my throne. The throne radiated pride and pulsated with an energy that
> engulfed the room. (Vega 2000: 246)

Along the sides of the throne are the tureens containing the initiate's sacred stones and those of his or her godmother or godfather, and the temple is open to friends and family who will honor the new member of the Ocha family. The fiesta begins with a drumming ceremony—*toque de güiro, tambor, bembé*—in the igbodu with the otanes stones and the iyawó. The drummers then proceed to the living room or patio of the house to continue the celebration with the guests, who sing and dance in honor of the orishas. The iyawó does not participate in the festivities but sits on the throne and receives the guests who come to pay homage. In the afternoon the music stops and all participate in the communal banquet prepared with the flesh of the animals sacrificed the day earlier, food considered filled with aché and blessings.

The dilogún divination shells are consulted on the third day of the asiento ceremony. This ceremony, called the *Itá*, charts the iyawo's past and future, and advises of potential dangers to be avoided. The iyawo's rebirth in the faith is designated by the sacred name in the Lucumí language which is revealed during the Itá when the new santo is consulted. The predictions are transcribed in a notebook (*la libreta de itá*), which the iyawó will keep for the rest of his or her life. After the Itá, the iyawó remains in the house of his or her padrino or madrina for several days with the soperas. On the seventh day, which is a market and church day, dressed in white with a covered head, he or she is accompanied to the marketplace by his or her oyugbona. While in Cuba this would be the traditional open-air market or Plaza de Mercado, in the Diaspora the iyawó would be taken to a store whose owner is probably an initiate familiar with the proceedings. The oyugbona makes small offerings of food to Eleguá in the four corners controlled by the orisha and, after buying some fruit and other items to prepare sweets for the orishas, the iyawó furtively steals a small gift—a transgression typical of liminal rites—probably a fruit of some kind for Eleguá. Before returning to the house-temple the group stops at a Catholic church and lights a candle for the iyawó.

The novitiate can now return home to place the tureens in a sacred spot and begin the daily worship of the faith following a series of prescriptions and taboos that will last a year and vary according to the orisha received.[43] Within the year (or as part of the kariocha ceremony) the initiate is presented to the sacred batá drums, authorizing him or her to dance in front of the consecrated instruments in a toque or fiesta de santo. This establishes a special link between the initiate and the particular drum ensemble used in the ceremony. One year and seven days after the asiento, the *libreta*[44] or notebook containing information essential to religious practice is passed down to the novice by the sponsoring padrino or madrina.

The Spirit World

The alliance between humans and the orishas, firmly established and consecrated in the initiation process described above, as well as that between humans and the spirit world in general, relies on the concept of the eledá (explained below), the idea that the essence of the human being is located in the person's head. The head is the physical vessel that was molded by Obatalá and then filled with the breath of life or consciousness by Olodumare, a sharing of God's essence. "That primordial life force or essential 'character' seen also as a 'primal ancestral spirit' (egun) which has reincarnated itself into

Santería altar. Photo courtesy of the artist Héctor Delgado.

each new human being, makes up the spiritual 'inner dead' (*orí inú*), called eledá, that part of the Creator in each person" (D. Brown 1989: 225).

In Cuba the Yoruba concept of the spiritual double or eledá merged with the Catholic belief in the "Guardian Angel" and the *protecciones* or protector spirits of Kardec Spiritism. However, the concept is interpreted differently by different santeros, reflecting the variations of a practice which is not governed by a strict orthodoxy. "Thus some say that the *eleda*/guardian spirit is the protector god of the individual; others claim that it is a spiritual force in the individual; and still others believe that it is the spirit of a dead person who protects the individual" (Cros Sandoval 1995: 90). One's destiny, it is believed, is chosen before birth and forgotten once born; humans must take care not to allow other persons, events, or their own improper behavior to cause them to deviate from their proper path.

The cult of the dead (the egún or the ancestors) is distinct in Regla de Ocha from that of the orishas. Highly respected, the dead must be ritually invoked and propitiated before Eleguá himself and before anything else can be done, and their ritual space must be separate from that of the orishas. Ritual forebears are honored in regular veneration. The priests responsible for the establishment of the house-temple, who are therefore the ritual ancestors of the children of today, are gratefully acknowledged in worship. The dead sanction the rituals of the living and must be appeased in prayer and "cooling" libations poured upon the earth to prevent them from acting wrathfully. The prayers (*Moyuba*) include a list of ancestors' names that are recited together with petitions for the house and the ritual family members.

The ancestors therefore play an essential role in sanctioning everything that is done in the Ocha house. However, the spirits of the dead do not comprise a single category; in addition to the ritual family ancestors, they include deceased spirits who appear in dreams or through divination and mediumship, and who are part of a person's "spiritual picture" or protective spirit cadre. These spirit guides, who can form an extensive group, range from deceased members of one's biological family to Gypsies, Indians, and old Congo slaves, often represented in paintings, photographs, lithographs, and statues of saints, figurines, or dolls.[45] Part of one's spiritual personality, they may "work" with an individual as a medium. Whereas the ritual ancestors who are addressed through prayer and sacrifices do not manifest themselves in possession, other spirits can possess their mediums in the spiritual mass. This mass is an Espiritismo rite that has been syncretized in Regla de Ocha practices and is a part of many initiation rituals and funeral rites. In a belief system in which death is simply one more step toward spiritual development, spirits and humans empower each other in Espiritismo rituals with the assistance of the medium.

While the orishas will reside in the assigned cabinets or shelves within a room, ritual family ancestors are typically enshrined on the floor of the bathroom under the sink (the vertical pipes allow them to "travel" between worlds via their favorite medium, water) and other spirits of one's *cuadro espiritual* or spiritual cadre may be located on a table referred to as a *bóveda*—literally, vault or crypt—an altar based on the Kardecian Spiritist White Table. Typically such a table has, among other things, an odd number of goblets filled with water (representing a particular ancestor or spirit guide), flowers, cigars, candles (all to appease the spirits), statues, photographs of deceased family members, rosary beads, bibles, and prayer books by the Spiritist leader Alan Kardec (see chapter 7 on Espiritismo).

At the end of one's life, spirits are appeased with spiritual rites for the dead. Special funerary rituals (Itutu) include a funeral mass in the Catholic church nine days after death to properly "send off" the soul of the dead santero or santera to the world of the spirits. These rituals set in motion a year of funeral rites that include the breaking of the warriors received during initiation, which are among the artifacts buried with the body. At the end of the year, the ritual *levantamiento de platos* or breaking of a dish symbolizes the final departure of the deceased.

Divination

All the major rituals of Regla de Ocha/Santería require prior divination: initiation, sacrifice, and other practices seek the mediation of Orula/Orúnmila/Ifá for an interpretation of the divine will. Central to Afro-Cuban religions, devotees consult the oracle for guidance and counsel at the beginning of every important transition in life and at critical moments. The three principal methods of divination—the coconut or Obi, the sixteen cowries or dilogún, and Ifá (in the form of the ekuelé chain or the *Tabla de Ifá*)—are practiced differently and by a sort of ranking in terms of difficulty and prestige. The Obi can be practiced by all believers; the dilogún by all priests and priestesses of Ocha; Ifá, considered by some the most complex and prestigious form requiring years of study, is only practiced by the babalao. Divination is not limited to the above, however: messages from the gods are also communicated in states of possession.

The coconut, Obi, or Biagué system, also used by the Regla de Palo religion, is the simplest of the four systems: only basic questions and answers are dealt with. Four pieces of a dried coconut that has been split in half are used; within each piece the symbolic number representing the orisha that is to be consulted is scratched out. Prayers are said to Olodumare, to the dead, to the ancestors, and to Biagué (the first Obi diviner), and water is sprinkled on the ground for Eleguá. The pattern or *letras* made by the four pieces when thrown on the floor, depending on whether they fall with the concave white pulp facing up or on the dark side, determines the answer, in five possible combinations. Each response is a reply from specific orishas: Alafia (Changó and Orula), four white pieces face up, means yes, and the coconut is usually cast again to confirm; Etawa (Changó, Ochún, and Yemayá), three white up and one dark, means a probable yes, but the process must be repeated to determine the final response; Eyefe (Eleguá, Ogún, Ochosi, and Ochún), two white and two dark, is an emphatic yes; one white and three dark is Ocana Sorde (Changó, Babalú Ayé, the Ikú [spirits of the dead]) and conveys difficulties and caution, requiring another throw to discover what is needed. When all four dark sides are visible, the letter or sign is called Oyekun (Changó, Oyá, and Ikú), a negative response that warns of death and tragedy. At that point the santero throws the coconuts once again to determine what can be done to *matar la letra* or offset the danger.

The divination practices of dilogún and Ifá utilize the patakís, narratives or stories discussed above, also referred to as *caminos* (paths or roads) in their diagnosis and prediction of a client's situation. The stories have been likened to fables or parables in their moral message or etiological explanations of nature (see examples above in the profiles of orishas). Esteban Montejo, the former slave interviewed by Miguel Barnet in his famous work, *Biography of a Runaway Slave,* describes the process he witnessed in the nineteenth-century slave barracks of Cuba as follows:

> The Lucumí are more allied to the Saints and to God. They like to get up early with the strength of the morning and look at the sky and pray and sprinkle water on the ground. When you least expect it, the Lucumí is doing his work. I have seen old blacks kneeling on the ground for more than three hours speaking in their tongue and telling the future. The difference between the Congo and the Lucumí is that the Congo does things, and the Lucumí tells the future. He knows everything through the diloggunes, which are snails from Africa. With mystery inside. (Barnet 1994: 35)

The patakís have been compared to the creation myths of the Bible and to the mythological tales of many cultures that explore the problems of life and the mysteries of the cosmos. The gifted diviner will decide which narratives best apply to the life and problems of the client as well as the ebó—the sacrifice or offering that must accompany every request—prescribed by the oracle. The interpretation of the oracle is based on the idea of the eledá, the client's ancestral soul; one's destiny is chosen before birth by the client and/or the client's ancestor and divination enables one to discover that destiny:

> In carrying out the sacrifice or ebbó prescribed in the recited narrative, the client cannot change his or her destiny in any fundamental way, but the client can make the best of the situation by increasing the probability of receiving possible benefits (such as long life, money, marriage, children, etc.) or by averting anticipated evils (such as fighting, sickness, death, want of money, etc.). (Matibag 1996: 77—78)

The patakís are recalled and recited by the diviner in whole or in part during the ceremony, as well as the accompanying proverbs and prayers, all interpreted within the context of the oracle. The verses or *odus* are divided into three parts: the presentation of the problem with an explanatory myth, clarification and interpretation for the client, and the required ebó sacrifice or offering.

The reading of the dilogún (a process which has many names, including *registrarse*, "register or search," or *echarse los caracoles*, "casting the shells"), summarized briefly here,[46] is the most popular divination practice in the Americas, perhaps due to its simplicity and to the fact that it can be used by both men and women (Ifá, as we have discussed, is limited to the babalao). The cowry shells (the dentated opening of the species used, *Cypraea moneta*, recalls the human mouth and is called the *boca de santo*, "mouth of the saint," or the orifice through which the orisha speaks) used in the ceremony are prepared in advance. They are opened and filed down on the back to lie flat so that their "mouths" are turned upward, then washed with the sacred herbal liquid *omiero*,[47] and fed with omiero and sacrificial blood. Of the twenty-one shells in a divination set, two are set aside to "watch over" the session and sixteen shells are cast for the *registro* or consultation; five additional auxiliary divination items, the *igbo*, are used as aids in the ceremony (a black stone, a long seashell, a piece of animal bone, the head of a tiny doll or a ball of *cascarilla* or powdered eggshell). As in all rituals, the santero first sprinkles or sprays water to "cool" the house and "refresh" the saints. He or she then prays

Reading of the shells. Photo courtesy of the artist Héctor Delgado.

to the dead and the orishas to bless the proceedings, touches the shells to the client, places the *derecho* or ritual tribute-fee (the orisha's money that accompanies all ritual work) on the straw mat with the cowries, and proceeds to cast the shells on the mat.

The number of shells with their "mouths" facing up determines the sign— *odu* or *letra*—of the cast, as well as the specific auxiliary igbo to be used in deciphering the sign. The igbo are handed to the client. He or she takes one in each hand, shakes them between each, and presents them with closed fist to the priest. The latter will choose the hand indicated by the pattern and determine if the answer to the question asked is yes or no, that is, if the sign or direction of the reading comes for "good" (*por buen camino*) or bad (*por mal camino*). The orisha might be asked which offering should be made—food, candles, purifying bath, and so on—when the oracle reveals a positive direction; if the answers are consistently negative, the diviner will continue to question the oracle until the client finally receives a response with instructions for an appropriate resolution.

The skillful santero will be familiar with the corresponding myth, proverb, ebó formula, and identity of the orisha who speaks through that odu. Ogún speaks through or in Ogunda, odu number three, for example, a forewarning to the client to beware of weapons of iron or other such perils; the diviner will select the appropriate proverb associated with the odu and prescribe the ebó the client must make to appease the divinities. "Diviners in the New World apply the myths as paradigms for the diagnosis and solution of human problems much as their African counterparts do. Through the stories they hold up contemporary problems to mythical comparisons and prescribe rituals according to mythical precedent" (Brandon 1993: 140).

In Cuba the dilogún process has been made more complex, likening it to Ifá divination: two hands of shells are thrown, making a new odu from the combination of the two letras. Thus if the first time odu number five Oche comes out, and the second number is two Eyioko, the sign would be Oche-Eyioko and would be read in pairs of odu, requiring their narratives to be combined in interpretation (the first odu of the pair carries more weight). The possibilities are now more complex: 16 x 16 or 256 letras or odus. Each odu or letra has a specific name, as in the following list with the related proverb:[48]

1. Ocana—"If there is nothing good, there is nothing bad."
2. Eyioko—"An arrow between brothers."
3. Ogunda—"A family argument causes tragedy."
4. Eyorosun—"No one knows what lies at the bottom of the sea."
5. Oche—"Blood flows through the veins."
6. Obara—"A king does not lie."
7. Odi—"Where the grave was first dug."
8. Eyeunle—"The head rules the body."
9. Osa—"Your best friend is your worst enemy."
10. Ofun——"Where the curse was born."
11. Ojuani—"Water cannot be carried in a basket."
12. Eyila chebora—"In war the soldiers never sleep."
13. Metanla—"Where illness is born, blood is bad."

14. Merinla—"Envy surrounds you."
15. Manunla—"As it moves you, so does it paralyze you."
16. Meridilogun—"You were born to be wise, but you don't heed advice."

The correct ebó or sacrifice is the motivating element of the pataki and of divination itself, and the oracle must be obeyed and respected: "[N]othing is gained if it is not offered" (Matibag 1996: 84).

An example of a typical reading will help to illustrate. The letra number five, Oche (five shells facing up, through which Ochún, Olofi, Orúnmila, and Eleguá speak) might receive the following response:

You are a son of Ochún and are lucky, but things don't always turn out well for you. Your plans fall through and your personality is unstable; you can be in a good mood and suddenly you feel like crying. You believe you have been betrayed but that isn't the case. These are trials sent to you by Ochún. There is a deceased member of your family awaiting a mass. If you have promised something to Ochún, fulfill your promise, and you will have to make the saint sooner or later.

The story that would complete Oche's message might be the anecdote of the man who owned a large number of pigs and who took great pains over their care. Each day the man would feed them well, then take the fattest one home for dinner. One of the pigs realized what was happening and refused to eat the man's food, eating only the tender shoots of the garlic plant. While the other pigs feasted, he would dig into the dirt to distract himself, not realizing that over time he had dug a hole. Eventually he escaped through this hole one day, as did the other pigs. The moral of the story? "The needle guides the thread; one makes the opening and the rest find an opportunity through the same space. Did one of your ancestors make the saint? You and the rest of your family should be initiated as well." The ebó for Oche is five fish, five hens, five squash, five peanuts, and five parrot feathers; a bath with yellow flowers, an offering to Eleguá of a mouse and smoked fish; play the lottery.[49]

Although empowered to read all sixteen signs, most people consider numbers thirteen to sixteen the province of the babalao, the children of Orula/Ifá; a client will be told to consult an Ifá priest so that his divining tools—the ekulé chain and the ikin nuts—can be employed on the client's behalf. Ifá divination derives its name from the orisha that speaks through the oracle. He is Orula or Orunmila, also called Ifá, the name for both the orisha and the divination process. The orisha speaks through this oracle as interpreted by the babalao, who must have at his command the thousands of divination verses that are the language of Ifá. The two interchangeable instruments of the Ifá divination system share the same corpus of odu mythology. The origin of the system, as in the dilogún divination system described above, is the belief in reincarnation: before birth every individual receives his or her destiny from Olofi. The only orisha witness to the event is Orula, the owner of secrets. Through divination one's destiny can be discovered and modified negatively or positively, depending upon one's conduct and the influences of one's environment:

> In the Yoruba cosmos, as in the Bible's, the objective manifestation of man's salvation is also in the word made flesh, in the verb. But in contrast to the latter, Yoruba logocentrism is purely oral . . . writing has a wider connotation than the Western one. The letters [*letras*], or positions in which the seeds fall, are written by the orisha, the reading is done by man, the babalao. (Cuervo Hewitt 1988: 76)

Divination systems share the sacred atmosphere created by the sprinkling of water and the prayers, the required derecho or fee, and auxiliary divination items to determine the direction of the reading. But the Ifá system uses the ekuele chain for day-to-day consultations, or the *ikin* (palm nuts/seeds) and the Tablero de Ifá or divining table for more extensive, final decisions. The ekuele chain is based on the same principle as the ikin; the numbers obtained in the casting can result in up to 256 possible combinations. The ekuelé, three to four feet long, is composed of eight disks of gourd, tortoise shell, mango seeds, or brass inserted between sections of a chain. After having touched it to the body of the client, the babalao holds the chain in the middle and tosses it so that it will fall in two parallel lines of four seeds each with the concave side of the disk up or down. The chain is cast several times to determine the principal sign and the combinations are written from right to left on paper (or, if using the ikin, marked upon the divining Tablero which had been previously covered with white powder). The resulting odu is indicated in a configuration of eight vertical markings set in two parallel columns of four. In the following example, lines indicate the concave side of the disk, and circles the convex:

Sixteen possible forms (letra or odu) for each half of the chain (likewise for each half of the figure marked on the Tablero tray) are read, each one with its own name and with a compound name for the figure as a whole (the combination of the left side with the right). The figures are read from right to left and the names of paired figures (both sides are the same) have the word "two" (*melli* or "twins") added. As each side may arrive at any of sixteen possible forms, the number of possible figures is 256. The sixteen compound odus can also be subdivided into sixteen "subjects" for a total of 4,096, which in turn can be subdivided for a total of thousands of patakís. Clearly, the more verses and prayers familiar to a babalao, the more complete his predictions. An important source of Afro-Caribbean knowledge, the Ifá oracle is "a system of specified obligations between humans and the orisha cast as propitiations, exchanges, atonements, thanks offerings, purifications, and protective measures" (Brandon 1993: 141).[50]

Music and Dance

Drum and vocal melodies and phrases, executed exactly as prescribed, are integral to all ritual activity; they will bring the orishas down from the heavens to possess their children and commune with their devotees. In religious ceremonies music plays a central role and drumming occasions (*güemilere*, *bembé*, or *tambor*) provide an opportunity for initiates to communicate with the orishas. These frequently "come down" and "mount" or possess their devotee, who in turn becomes the orisha's "horse." A great number of different kinds of drums (tambores) are utilized in the liturgy, though the drums which are most sacred in Regla de Ocha worship are the consecrated *batá*. While unconsecrated drums are frequently used to praise the orishas in most ceremonies, the rare, fundamental batá drums must be employed whenever possible in the most important rites, and must be played in specific drumming patterns based on Yoruba ritual practice.

The batá is a set of three instruments that produce varying sounds and levels of pitch. Wooden drums with an hourglass shape, the two heads of each drum, one on each end, are of different size and tone, covered with goatskins tightly laced together with leather strips wrapped firmly against the body of the drum with more strips, to which are attached small iron bells. The batá ensemble is of varying sizes: the largest and most important is the *Iyá* (the "mother"), the middle-sized the *Itótele*, and the smallest the *Okónolo*; they can be sacred (*tambores de fundamento, de Añá*), or profane, unbaptized (*tambores judíos*). Sacred drumming is a complex form of playing in which each drum plays a particular phrase that contrasts with the others to produce a polyrhythmic "symphonic synthesis of rhythms, tonalities, and chords. The batá drums are said to be able to 'speak'; Iyá and Itótele usually carry on a complex conversation, while Okónolo maintains a basic rhythm" (Canizares 1993: 70). Consecrated batá drums are more than musical instruments: they are the powerful materializations of the spirit Añá.

The consecration of the drums is a combination of complex ceremonies over several days, briefly summarized here, that involve the construction of the bodies, the preparation of the goatskins, and the "blessing" of the drums with the ritual "secret" they will bear inside.[51] The ceremonies involve the use of a specific omiero, the sacred herbal liquid, to instill sacred magic into those objects washed in its blessing, propitiation, and sacrifices to Osain, the orisha of herbs and plants; the marking of ritual signs and the installation of the spirit called Añá into the drums; divination rituals to assess the responses of the orishas to the various steps in the process and to offer specific instruction; the participation of three babalaos; an established *alaña* or consecrated drummer who is an initiated priest in the cult of Añá; an oriaté and other Santería priests; a consecrated set of drums from which the new ones will be "born"; and the future alaña for whom the drums are built. All must participate in the rites to legitimately consecrate the batá. Animals are sacrificed to the spirits that will possess the individual drums. These drums are presented to the older ensemble of instruments that serve as "godparent," fortifying the new set with ingredients from that of the established alaña.

The new drums receive a collective name discovered in divination and the *afoubo* or secret—a small leather bag containing a parrot feather, glass beads, and other objects where Añá is believed to reside—is nailed inside the largest drum, followed by the other two. More sacrifices follow in a ceremony in which the men will cook and partake of the sacrificed animals. (Women and homosexual[52] men do not participate in batá consecrations nor are they permitted to play the sacred drums. While women and homosexual men play an important role as heads of their own Santería house-temples, they are barred from certain ceremonies and from initiation as babalaos.[53] The same restrictions apply in the Abakuá Secret Society, as discussed in chapter 3.) After the goatskins are secured to the drums, the final ceremony takes place to enhance their aché with offerings of cane spirit, roosters, candles, coconut, and the important ritual tribute, the *derecho*. Established drummers begin by playing their own batás, then pass them to the new drummers to play without stopping, while they in turn play the new set to impart their aché to them. The new alaña (consecrated drummer) can now return to his set and play his sacred drums for the first time.

Batá drummers invoke Ochún. Photo courtesy of the artist Héctor Delgado.

As Canizares observes, "an enormous amount of psychic energy goes into its manufacture. It is little wonder, then, that santeros consider the sounds made by such drums to be magical" (1993: 72). Little wonder too that the sacred drums have been so rare in the Diaspora. Mastery of the drumming technique is a long process, akin to learning to speak a language; but it is the drums and not the drummer who "speak." Isabel Castellanos observes that the drums imitate the sound and tone of the Lucumí language and communicate with the orishas in the *oro*, a sequence of liturgical rhythms and chants, musical phrases that serve as a nonverbal means of communication to honor, greet, and entice the orishas and their children, as during the presentation of the iyawó or neophyte to the batá in the initiation ritual and in celebrations where the orishas are invited to transform a secular space into a sacred one (1976: 47–50).[54]

From "Divine Utterances" to "Rap's Diasporic Dialogues"

Sacred forms of music and dance have long been translated into secular settings in Cuba in a complex historical relationship between religion and secular art forms. Given the Cuban Revolution's emphasis on the nation's African roots, African-based religious rites (considered "fetishistic" magic in the early stages of the Revolution) were gradually embraced as examples of Cuban popular and folk culture and included in artistic venues, overlooking their religious context. The performance group Conjunto Folklórico Nacional de Cuba (Cuban National Folklore Troupe) was founded in 1962 with the idea of recovering and maintaining Cuba's dance and musical roots, and creating art while maintaining what was described as folkloric "essence." The self-described style developed by the Conjunto over the years is "Theater-Folklore."

Critics of the Conjunto perceive the effort as an attempt to relegate Afro-Cuban religious practices to anthropological folklore, "Santurismo," for the benefit of the vital tourist industry. In *Divine Utterances: The Performance of Afro-Cuban Santería*, Katherine J. Hagedorn provides a personal account of her initiation into the religion after numerous visits to the island. As a tourist, Hagedorn had attended staged events where the lines dividing the sacred and the secular, the touristic and the authentic, were blurred in performances where religious possession occurred at times and in settings the author felt were "inappropriate" for public consumption. Her fieldwork and study with the Conjunto Folklorico eventually provided a deeper perspective.

> It has been through the lens of folkloric performances that I have framed *lo religioso*, the religious, and now it is through the lens of religious performance that I frame *lo folklórico*, the folkloric.
>
> These dual perspectives have clarified for me the interplay between religious and folkloric Afro-Cuban performance. Both involve and invoke aspects of the sacred. What is sacred in Afro-Cuban performance is the connection of utterances—created and received, gestural and musical— to constructs of the divine. This relationship is determined by intent, which in turn is negotiated among all the participants in the performance, whether they are the audience members and musicians at a folkloric performance or the ritual assistants and priests at a religious ceremony. Sacred and secular inform each other, use each other, and in fact inhabit the same sphere of sacred intent. [55] (2001: 5–6)

Religion and spectacle overlap at times; musicians use the same *batá* songs and rhythms in folkloric performances as they would in a *toque de santo* where the intent is to summon the deity. Troupe members who are religious do their best to "guard the secrets" during performances by providing a mimetic representation of the *toque* without effecting the arrival of the *santo* and an "inappropriate" possession, an attempt to "convey sacred memory through secular manifestation" (238).

Despite strained political relations with the United States, U.S. music has always made its way into Cuban popular culture; Cuban music has also penetrated the U.S. market with performances and artists cherished by such authors as Marta Moreno Vega, whose spirited memoir, *When the Spirits Dance Mambo: Growing Up Nuyorican in El Barrio,* is both a spiritual *and* a musical journey. The narrator's experience of music in the era of such performers as Tito Puente and Celia Cruz in the mid-twentieth century at New York City's Palladium nightclub affirmed her ethnic-religious identity with a repertoire that "honored those warrior spirits that had traveled from Africa to Harlem" and "a beat that penetrated our hearts, calling spirits down and elevating or souls. Our *clave* rippled through our blood, creating kings and queens that soared beyond the limited borders of our neighborhoods" (2004: 242; 251).

In more recent cultural exchanges, U.S. rap music has been embraced by Cuban rappers' "transnational curiosity and use of African American and Caribbean idioms," as described in Alan West-Durán's essay, "Rap's Diasporic Dialogues: Cuba's Redefinition of Blackness" (2005: 146). An important element of that redefinition is, of course, spiritual. Inspired by U.S. rappers, Cuban rappers adopt elements that define their culture and reject what is considered irrelevant. Thus, while there is an absence of so-called "gangsta rap" and what West-Durán refers to as its "ghetto-centric warriors," Cuban rap comprises what West-Durán proposes as a possible equivalent, namely,

> the orisha warriors of Regla de Ocha: Ochosi, Ogún, Elegguá, and Changó. Indeed the expressions of Afrocentric ideas in Cuba need not hark back to the real (or imagined) glories of an African past; they are a living, palpitating presence through the practice of religion, music, and culture. Practicing *santeros,* particularly the younger ones, are now more inclined to worship the orishas as African and play down the Catholic side of the religion. The growth of Rastafarianism also points to this re-Africanization of Cuban life, but within the parameters of *cubanía* [Cubanness]. (144)

Earlier music in Cuba included references to Afro-Cuban religious practices as "exotic citations of afrocubanía"; for many Cuban rappers, however, it is a reaffirmation of the centrality of these practices in their own lives as African-Cubans (131).

Possession

Music and dance in liturgical ceremonies—initiations and anniversary celebrations of the same, feast day of the orisha, and the like—are, as stated above, essential elements of the worship of the deities and of the appeal to them to unite with their children on earth. Ritual styles vary according to such factors as the nature of the ritual, the preferences of the santero celebrating the occasion, as well as the economic resources of the community, and can range from a simple display of the soperas and emblems of the orishas to an elaborate and costly installation of exquisitely constructed ritual objects and generous amounts of prepared foods. However, the order of the drumming is fixed. It starts with the *oro seco*, dry drumming without singing, performed in the igbodú during which time no dancing or possession takes place. As in any ceremony, Eleguá must be saluted first. This is followed by the drumming with song performed in the area of the house-temple where the uninitiated are permitted to enter. Here the *oro cantado* or sung oro calls to the orishas in precise rhythms with specific meanings. Singing and dance are now incorporated into the ritual and the increase in energy summons different orishas, who respond to their specific musical themes and possess or "mount" their "horses."

The identity of the orisha is evident to all, as indicated by his or her particular representative, stereotypical gestures, and movements that are culturally constructed: novitiates learn the attributes, personality, and behavior of their tutelary orisha as part of the initiation process and participation in ceremonies. Thus, Changó's "horse" will manifest the eroticism of the deity conveyed in accentuated hip movements, Yemayá will toss and sway like the waves of the ocean, and Ochún will be flirtatious and coquettish with the men present in the room, often provoked to descend when her agogó or copper bell is rung in the ear of the "horse" who ceases to exist, replaced by the incarnated orisha.

Orishas will manifest themselves differently according to the specific avatar or path of "descent." Thus, for example, when Obatalá manifests himself as the avatar Obalufón, the horse will dance in the fashion of an old woman who nevertheless moves with grace and rhythm; Obamoro, another avatar of Obatalá, is a decrepit old man who falls to the floor, unable to rise (Cros Sandoval 1975: 139–140). Once possession occurs, the "horse" is moved to a separate room and dressed in the ritual clothing pertaining to his or her orisha before being returned to the ritual area where the orisha participates with the rest of the community and the other orishas present, offering advice, responding to questions, and dancing.

Though possession has been classified by some as a type of hysteria or madness, a control vehicle for repressed personalities, Eugene Genovese notes that contemporary anthropologists are skeptical of psychoanalytic explanations: "[N]o genuine schizophrenic could possibly adjust to the firm system of control that the rituals demand. No matter how wild and disorderly they look to the uninitiated, they are in fact tightly controlled; certain things must be done and others not done. . . . [A]s Max Weber says, ecstasy may become an instrument of salvation or self-deification" (Genovese 1976: 239).

The Cuban Revolution and Religion

In the years following the Cuban Revolution in 1959, tensions grew between the government and the Catholic Church, particularly after 1961 when Fidel Castro declared the commitment of the Revolution to the creation of a Marxist-Leninist state and eliminated all forms of religious schooling. While the Catholic Church regarded the Revolution with distrust, the practitioners of Afro-Cuban religions celebrated the change and generally supported the new government. In so doing they legitimized the government among the black and popular classes of the population, the sectors that felt they had the most to gain by the reforms promised by the regime. A silencing and discouragement of religion took place at the institutional level in Cuban society after its radicalization; considered backward or primitive by the state, religion was practiced privately or secretly. Those who openly practiced their religion were not admitted to the Communist Party or allowed to train for or practice certain professions.

However, given the Afro-Cuban religions' lack of an institutional or structural base, they were not considered a threat to the Revolution, which tolerated and on occasion even courted their favor. Since the late 1980s changes have taken place that affect the religiosity of the population, or at least their ability to engage in these practices openly: Fidel Castro's interest in Liberation Theology, expressed in his published interview with Frei Betto (*Fidel and Religion,* 1987), relaxed tensions somewhat between church and state; in 1991 the Fourth Party Congress of the Cuban Communist Party approved membership for persons who admitted to professing a religious practice; in 1992 the Constitution of Cuba was reformed, declaring Cuba a secular rather than an atheist state; and in 1998 Pope John Paul II visited the island in a much-publicized event.

A revival of African-based religious practices has also been observed. In 1992 the Fourth International Congress of Orisha Tradition and Culture took place in Havana, and numerous scholarly works on Afro-Cuban religions began to be published, contributing to a more literate and institutional approach to the religions. However, given the history of the island, Cuban religion has always been unorthodox and syncretic, more personal than institutional, an expression of popular religiosity. What does exist on the island, therefore, is not an orthodox form of Catholicism, Yoruba or Congo religion, or Spiritism, but practices that contain elements of all of these, more "unofficial" than orthodox, as well as idiosyncratic and creative.

The Pressures of Diaspora

The various waves of Cuban exiles to the United States after the Cuban Revolution in 1959, called by some the "second diaspora" of Yoruba religion, has created challenges and served to inspire and create a "pan-diaspora tradition of the orishas" beyond the borders of Cuba and beyond the Cuban exiles themselves: "[T]here are hundreds of thousands of Americans who participate in the tradition, ranging from relatively fewer committed 'godchildren' of a particular line of *orisha* initiation, to numberless 'clients' seeking consultations with priestesses and priests for help with critical problems. Nearly everyone of Caribbean background living in North American cities is touched by santería in some way" (Murphy 1994: 82). The preservation, maintenance, and revelation of the religion's secrets and mysteries (highly guarded for years so as to protect the practice from unsympathetic and openly hostile forces, and even from those considered nominally sympathetic) has been the task of courageous and devoted priests and priestesses who have handed down the knowledge of the religion's mysteries orally for generations.

However, according to Joseph M. Murphy and others, the oral tradition is under great pressure today, particularly in light of the religion's diasporan journeys in the twentieth century, "a second journey, one which if less terrible than the passage of the slave ships, is no less important for the survival of the way of the orishas" (Murphy 1987: 248). Cubans have arrived in the United States in several waves in the twentieth century: while there were a substantial number of Cubans in the United States prior to the Cuban Revolution of 1959, between that year and 1962 some 280,000 Cubans arrived. There was another wave of 273,000 between 1965 and 1973; the Mariel Exodus in 1980 brought an additional 125,000, followed by the so-called *balsero* or raft exodus of 1994. Those from the first group were predominantly white and middle class; the Mariel group saw a substantial number of Cuban blacks and, compared to the former, more priests of Afro-Cuban religions. It is claimed that the first babalao to arrive in the United States—Francisco "Pancho" Mora—came in 1946. Prior to the Cuban Revolution godparents took their godchildren to Cuba to be initiated; the first initiations in the United States took place in the 1960s. The lack of "ritual infrastructure"—difficulties in obtaining the necessary ritual resources, especially the herbs which were purchased in the "botanical gardens" of New York City's barrio, precursors to the *botánicas* seen in major cities today; the lack of ritual specialists of initiation, the oriaté or italero; and the lack of sacred batá drums and initiated drummers—determined the reconstitution of Afro-Cuban religious practice in the United States.[56]

Exile and the displacement of the devotees of the orishas to a new foreign culture have once again tested the adaptability of an old tradition in a new environment. Murphy observes that the particular challenges of North American society, including "its emphasis on time, its values on individualism, mobility and profit, its traditions of religious pluralism and secularism," ethics, and attitudes will affect a culture which, as in the case of other immigrant traditions, will have to accommodate to the "Americanizing" process. Among the accommodations the religion is being forced to confront is the increased need for literacy and accurate texts, which can lead to the development of an orthodoxy: whereas in the past the process of hierarchical initiation sustained the spiritual knowledge of the religion and provided the means for the continuity of the prayers, ceremonies, and ritual practices so vital for its existence, the spread of the religion far from its cultural roots has led to the need for authoritative texts for its preservation. Although many elders resist the trend, fearing that publication of the information might dissipate the spiritual power of the religion, others, according to Murphy, recognize the need for the construction of an authentic Ocha canon: "[T]he dangers of losing the religion to indiscipline and misinformation outweigh the risks of revealing secrets. . . . While the form of the rites can be known to all, their meaning can still be revealed by the laborious process of maturation in la regla de ocha. The mystery remains in the midst of open secrets" (1987: 253).[57]

In its transplantation outside Cuba, and particularly to the United States, Santería blended with Puerto Rican Espiritismo in such areas as New York and New Jersey, begetting what some have called a "Santerismo" adopted by a significant non-Cuban population in the United States and Europe (see chapter 7 on Espiritismo). Some segments of the African American population perceive in the religion a link to Africa and a more genuine form of religious practice that affirms their ethnic and racial identity and cultural heritage and links them to peoples of the wider African Diaspora. Rejecting the Cuban Catholic influence in Regla de Ocha, some followers have attempted to return the religion to its African roots and "purify" it of European influences. This attempt is exemplified in the case of the Yoruba Temple, Oyotunyi Village in South Carolina, reflecting what Steven Gregory refers to as Santería's importance as a cultural "space of resistance," and its practitioners' cultivation of "alternative and often oppositional forms of consciousness and social structures" (1999: 12).[58]

In recent years Santería/Regla de Ocha has become identified by many who study African Diasporic cultures as the "Orisha Tradition," a term that encompasses the diverse approaches to Orisha worship in Africa and throughout the world today, and the "multiethnic cosmopolitanism" of the social composition and ritual practices of contemporary Ocha houses:

> Most houses of Ocha today are multiethnic and include a mosaic of people from Latin America, North America, the English and French-speaking Caribbean and, in some cases, West Africa. Transnational relations of ritual kinship link African-American and Latino houses of Ocha in New York City to Havana and San Juan, as well as to Caracas, Mexico City, Madrid, Paris and other centers of the Afrocaribbean cultural diaspora. Moreover, practitioners of Santería or Yoruba religion in the United States have forged religious and social ties to devotees and scholars of African religions in other areas of the African diaspora, such as Brazil, Haiti and the Dominican Republic and, increasingly, in Nigeria, Ghana and other African nations. (Gregory 1999: 100)

The "globalization" of Santería, Gregory notes, has extended to its promotion within the new information technologies: multiple websites ("Orishanet," "Afrocubaweb," and others) offer religious, organizational, and on-line shopping information for "transnational cultural circulation and exchange" (1999: 101). [59]

For Cuban exiles Santería has taken on a special meaning: an alternative medical system, a support system, and a coping mechanism for dealing with the stress of exile and immigration, eliminating the feelings of guilt resulting from such dramatic life changes, and a way of expressing cultural identity in a foreign society without the socioeconomic and racial restrictions they might have encountered in their homeland.[60] "Outside of Cuba, Santería's function, as a social and economic network and as a supportive complementary health system, has been enhanced during the last thirty years. The people who frequent the house of a *santero* constitute a fictive extended family, who share economic and affection bonds" (Cros Sandoval 1995: 94). Once again, the religion serves to substitute for lost kin, severed ties, and a missing sense of belonging. Always flexible, the Afro-Cuban religions change with their travels, adapting to a new population and new environment, winning a new legitimacy for ancient practices that have not simply survived but are flourishing in the modern world.[61]

The Afro-Cuban Religious Traditions of Regla de Palo and the Abakuá Secret Society

While Regla de Ocha is commonly compared to a marriage with a santo or orisha, a dedicated, daily commitment to render worship in offerings, prayers, and ritual ceremonies to keep the orisha contented and appeased, Regla de Palo can be more accurately understood as a binding but more occasional and intermittent sacred pact with a spirit. The spirit is summoned when needed, being a reliable magical enforcer who carries out one's will. Esteban Montejo described the Congo rituals he observed as a slave in Cuba as follows:

> All the powers, the saints, were in that cazuela. . . . They brought things for the ngangas. . . . They did enkangues which were hexes made with dirt from the cemetery. With that dirt you made four corners in little mounds to resemble the points of the universe. They put star-shake, which was an herb, in the pot with corn straw to hold human beings. When the master punished a slave, all the others picked up a little dirt and put it in the pot. With that dirt they vowed to bring about what they wanted to do. And the master fell ill or some harm came to his family because while the dirt was in the pot, the master was prisoner in there, and not even the devil could get him out. That was the Congo people's revenge on the master. (Barnet 1994: 27–28)

The magical aspects of Palo are the best-known features of a larger practice that is less familiar to many inside and outside Cuba, although it plays an important role in Afro-Cuban religious culture. Originally predominant in the eastern end of Cuba, the *Reglas Congas,* commonly called "Palo Monte" in Cuba, derive from the Kongo religion of the Bakongo people. The Bakongo inhabit a broad area of sub-Saharan Africa stretching from the southern part of Cameroon through northern Angola all the way to Mozambique in the southeastern coast of Africa. As Robert F. Thompson explains, the Kongo language and beliefs combined with those of other peoples taken in slavery from the region to create the Kongo-based culture called "Conga" or "Bantu" in Cuba and the Cuban Congo religion (Thompson 1984: 103).[1]

More accurately, one should speak of Congo *religions* in Cuba, as several branches are subsumed under the general rubric of "Regla de Palo Monte Mayombe," including the Regla Biyumba, Regla Musunde, Regla Quirimbaya, Regla Vrillumba, and the Regla Kimbisa del Santo Cristo del Buen Viaje ("of the Holy Christ of the Good Journey").[2] Considered the most syncretized of Afro-Cuban practices, Congo religions in Cuba derive elements from Yoruba and other African practices and Roman Catholicism, particularly in terms of religious structural organization. This has caused them to be referred to as *religiones cruzadas* or "crossed." The tendency to "syncretizing assimilation" is demonstrated in the fact that, for example, "believers chant to the orishas of the Yoruba pantheon, identified either by Bantu, Catholic or Yoruba names: Insancio is Changó or Santa Bárbara; Nsambi, Sambia, or Asambia is Almightly God or Olodumare; Kisimba is St. Francis of Assisi or Orúnmila" (Matibag 1996: 156).[3]

Regla de Ocha/Santería and the Congo practices, although different, are nevertheless complementary. Many persons follow both religions and are both *santeros* and *paleros* or *mayomberos,* as followers of Regla de Palo are called: "The tower of Babel that was the slave plantation and the sugar mill in the nineteenth century favored this type of back and forth flow of values" (Barnet 1983: 207).

Congo traditions observe a different interaction with the spirits than Yoruba-based religions; focused less on a pantheon of deities, the Reglas Congas emphasize control of the spirits of the dead and healing with the use of charms (*prendas*), formulas, and spells, as exemplified by the remarks of Esteban Montejo cited above. "Congolese magicians and sorcerers developed a powerful role. . . . The ability to communicate with the dead and to use medicine [*minkisi*] to cure and harm made them major figures in maintaining social harmony but also in disrupting the social order" (Morales 1990: 107–108). However, the most carefully preserved, and the most respected and feared Congo element is that of magic. The main source of this magical power is the palero's ability to make contact with the spirit of a dead person and to control it and make it work for him. The spirit inhabits the *prenda* or *nganga,* a word that designates not only a spirit or supernatural force but also the object in which the spirit dwells—an iron pot or cauldron and its contents, the *fundamento* or centering focus of Palo religious practice. Those used for good purposes are *cristiana* (Christian), that is, baptized; those used for evil ends are unbaptized or *judía (Jewish)*. The spirit protects the palero and is his source of power and support. It bears names such as *Paso Largo* (Long Steps), *Viento Malo* (Bad Wind), *Remolino* (Whirlwind), or *Rompe Monte* (Forest Breaker) (Vélez 2000: 16), which identify both it and its owner. Congo traditions are a reflection of African practices and beliefs regarding the spirit world and the use of "fetishes":

> Africans, in their traditional religious practices, did not worship those material objects we call fetishes. Their belief, rather, rested on an idea of God as intruding Himself everywhere. Those "fetishes" supposedly held a particular spirit temporarily; the material and spiritual elements of life penetrated each other, with the former becoming a vehicle for the latter. . . . The most important positive application of the charms came in slave medical practice, which illustrated the way in which black folk religion permeated every part of the slaves' lives and served their daily interests. (Genovese 1976: 224)

The making of a nganga is a complex, magical, and at times macabre process that has been well documented.[4] It is an involved procedure that must take place at certain times of the day and month, and it uses the spirits of nature in plants, insects, animal and human bones (if possible the *kiyumba* or human skull), blood, graveyard dirt, cane alcohol, and spices; the sticks and branches of special trees ("palos") designate the sect and are a key ingredient in the nganga-making process. The owner enters into a pact with the spirit inside the cauldron (or alternatively the *macuto* sack) during a ceremony wherein the spirit is contacted through divination with gunpowder and trance. The receptacle is then buried for a period of time in the cemetery and in the *monte,* in nature; it is returned to its owner, for whom the nganga is "a small world that is entirely dominated by him. The kiyumba rules over all the herbs and the animals that live inside the nganga with it. The mayombero in turn rules the kiyumba, who obeys his orders like a faithful dog. The kiyumba is the slave for the mayombero and it is always waiting inside the cauldron or the macuto to carry out his commands" (González-Wippler 1989: 246).

We include below a fictional description of the process from a Cuban detective novel (*Adiós Hemingway y La cola de la serpiente,* 2001) for several reasons: the acclaimed author Leonardo Padura Fuentes bases the character of the palero and his remarks on an actual individual in Cuba who is known

A nganga. Photo courtesy of the artist Héctor Delgado.

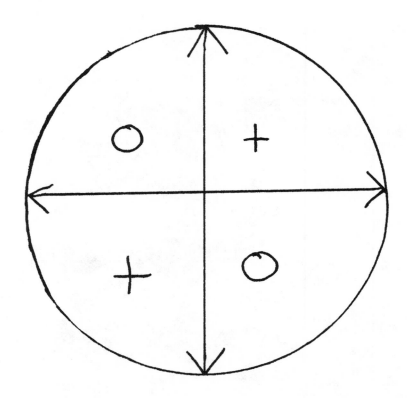

Zarabanda.

for his spiritual work;[5] the description, although it appears extreme, is, in fact, akin to those recorded by ethnographers and others; and the observations of the main character, the detective Mario Conde, on the unfamiliar nature of a world so closely identified with Cuban culture yet so distant from his everyday experiences as a Cuban, reflect the comments of many in Cuba who see these religions as belonging to a world apart. It is also an example of the significance of the theme of Afro-Cuban religions in contemporary Cuban literature.

The protagonist, Mario Conde, is involved in a murder investigation in which one of the only clues is a symbol scratched on the victim's chest which the detective is told is the sign of *Zarabanda*. A missing finger from the victim, possibly to be used in the making of a nganga, is one of the other clues. Zarabanda, in fact, is one of the Congo sacred drawings which are important elements of African Kongo religions, similar to the *vèvè* drawings of Haitian Vodou and the *anaforuana* of the Abakúa: "Like these other graphic emblems, the nucleating lines in the Palo Monte ground-designs represent the pulling of spiritual forces inward to the center while extending outward toward the four cardinal points of the universe" (Matibag 1996: 161). Zarabanda in Cuba is a Congo mystic ground drawing that, Thompson reminds us, attracts spiritual power, "*singing and drawing points of contact between worlds*" (Thompson 1984: 110; emphasis in original), invoked with the Congo chants referred to as *mambos* in Cuba. The Zarabanda sign and the spirit conjured by it in Cuba is syncretic, identified with Ogún, who in turn is identified with Saint Peter, combining the powers of Ocha and Congo practices.

In the novel the detective, who is not intimately familiar with the Afro-Cuban religions, is told to visit a respected old man in the town of Regla near Havana, the "Mecca of Cuban sorcery." The man is described as ancient, with eyes almost as black as his wrinkled skin. The grandson of African slaves, he was initiated into Palo and became a mayombero, but "as if that weren't enough," he is also a babalao, a member and leader of an Abakúa chapter, and a Mason. "Speaking with him was like consulting an old tribal guru who guards all of the history and the traditions of his clan in his memory." The old man goes on to explain the construction of a nganga cauldron.

"The sign, Zarabanda, is traced on the bottom of the cauldron, which is the base for everything. Look here, the circle is the earth and the two arrows in a cross are the winds. The other crosses are the corners of the world, which are always four. . . . Nowadays they use more arrows and adornments. But that's an old one from the colonial times. . . ."

"Is it true that they use human bones in a nganga?"

"Of course, if not, how are you going to control the dead person? The nganga has a thousand things, but it always has to have a man's bones, and better yet, the head, the *kiyumba,* where the bad thoughts lie. Then you add sticks from the forest, but not just any sticks, but those from powerful trees; then flint celts that have tasted blood, animal bones, the fiercer the better, cemetery dirt, quicksilver so that it will never be still, and holy water if you want it to do good. If not, it is unbaptized and remains Jewish. . . . But if the nganga is Zarabanda, since he is the owner of all iron, a chain is placed around the pot and inside you have to put a key, a lock, a magnet, a hammer and on top of it all Ogún's machete. . . . All of this you feed with the blood of a rooster and a goat, and then decorate it with many-colored feathers."

El Conde felt that he was losing himself in a world in which he had always lived but from which he had been infinitely remote. Those religions, eternally stigmatized by slave owners that considered them heretical and barbarous, then by the bourgeoisie who called them the stuff of brutish, dirty blacks, and lately marginalized by dialectical materialists who went so far as to categorize them scientifically and politically as remnants of a past that atheism had to overcome, held for Mario Conde the lure of resistance. . . .

"Does the owner of the nganga have to know the dead man he puts in the cauldron?"

The old man puffed on his cigar twice and smiled.

"That almost never happens, because people nowadays use any dead person. . . . But if you know him, much better, because that way you can choose. Look, if you want to make a nganga judía to do evil, you should look for someone who had been very wicked in life . . . because his spirit will continue to be as bad as the live man was on earth. And sometimes worse. . . . That's why the best bones come from crazy men, and better yet, Chinese men who are the angriest and most vengeful on the face of the earth. . . . Mine I inherited from my father and it has the head of a Chinese man who committed suicide out of rage because he didn't want to be a slave, and you cannot imagine the things I have done with that nganga . . . may God forgive me."[6] (Padura Fuentes 2001: 174–176)

The Palo reputation for *brujería* or witchcraft is based on these magical creations and on their supposed efficacy in magic, for beneficial or evil purposes; their spells or *bilongos* are considered powerful problem solvers.[7] The secrecy of Palo rituals adds to the mystery of a religious practice that believes its priests (*Tata* or father *Nganga,* or *Mama Nganga,* suggesting, as in Regla Ocha, that priests are the spiritual parents of the initiate) control the spirit residing in the nganga magic receptacle, which is also referred to as a *prenda,* meaning a "jewel" or valued article. Paleros, like santeros, communicate with the spirits or *mpungus* through trance in which initiates, called *perros* (dogs) or *criados* (servants) of the nganga, become possessed. Communication with the spirits is also attained during divination practices, two of which are borrowed from the Lukumí—the coconut (*ndungui*) and the shells (*chamalongos*)—and two Congo systems—*fula* (gunpowder) and the *vititi mensu* (small mirror).

Fula consultation and divination is accomplished by placing a certain number of small piles of gunpowder over a board or on the floor and, after formulating a question, setting one of the piles on fire. If all the piles explode at once the response is affirmative; if not, more questions must be posed or interpreted in the response. For the vititi mensu, a small mirror is placed in the opening of a magically prepared animal horn (*mpaka*) embellished with elaborate beadwork. The palero interprets the oracle by filling the mirror with smoke soot from a candle and reading the various shapes that form.

Palero initiation is also different from Regla de Ocha as it involves a series of rituals known as *rayamientos* (markings), a name derived from the cutting made during the rite with a knife or sharp object on the body of the neophyte.[8] The supreme creator, Nsambi or Sambia, among other names, is similar to the Regla de Ocha Supreme Being, as he too is remote and no prayers or sacrifices are offered to him. The idea that Nsambi created the first man and woman himself rather than through intermediaries is believed to be based on the influence of Portuguese Catholic missionaries, who converted Bakongos in Africa in the fifteenth century. Thus scholars surmise that Congo slaves arrived in Cuba having already had prior contact with Christianity (Castellanos and Castellanos 1992, 3: 130–131).[9] After Nsambi, the followers of Regla Conga venerate the souls of the ancestors, the dead, and the spirits of nature that exist in the trees and the rivers.

Congo beliefs from Africa syncretized in Cuba with Catholicism and with Spiritualism, which shares the Congo focus on communicating with the dead. For the Congo, men and women are beings composed of a material or biological life in the body and by varying categories of spirit or *sombra* (shade), a force that has the capacity to separate itself and leave the physical entity, as in the dream state. Such ideas reflect the traditional African perspective of the soul and the spirit world in which

> Man's Soul is one spirit among many, for all things are infused with spirits. Man himself is one of many material hosts. For traditional Africans, like many non-Christian peoples everywhere, the Soul came to mean the inner life—the quintessential experience of which matter was merely the form. Thus the Soul, crystallized in a man's shadow, could be detached from his person. Hence, spirits wandered in this world. (Genovese 1976: 247–248)[10]

For the Cuban Congo, however, the spiritual and material elements of the human being always maintain contact by means of a "silver cord," the *cordón de plata* after which the popular form of Espiritismo in Cuba, *Espiritismo de Cordón* (see chapter 7 on Espiritismo), is named. The Congo notion of the spirit "shadow" merged in Cuba with similar Spiritist beliefs in a kind of spirit-vapor that surrounds the body (the "perisperm" idea of Allan Kardec), affirming the concept that death does not deny a spirit intelligence, will, language, or the capacity to go from one level of reality to another. The ancestors and the dead can therefore communicate with and guide the living.

People who practice both Palo and orisha religions keep the Palo spirits, considered "fierce" and "unruly," at a significant distance from the orishas. Generally a person will be initiated into Regla de Ocha after Regla de Palo, as the reverse is not usually permitted; it is not uncommon, however, to find a priest who works in both Palo and Ocha whose rituals complement each other (analogous to the Rada and Petro systems in Vodou). The orishas are considered more benign spirits and will be kept near a bedroom or in some other part of the house; the Palo prenda, independent and associated with nature, their natural habitat, are set into the earth in a cellar or in a backyard shed. "The Kongo's chosen position 'outside civilization' gives it a unique sanctuary from which to perform spiritual work which most of the *orichas* cannot, or do not deign to, perform. The spirits of the *prenda* are seen as pragmatic, shrewd, and unhampered by many of the 'moral' strictures of the *oricha*" (D. Brown 1989: 372).[11]

In *Wizards and Scientists: Explorations in Afro-Cuban Modernity and Tradition,* Stephan Palmié focuses on the contemporary practices of Afro-Cuban religions in order to more fully address their complexity and the "role of representations of difference," in particular the "universe of discourse and practice" of Regla de Ocha and Palo Monte (25). The differences relate to contrasting conceptions of morality with regard to relationships between humans and the spiritual or cosmic sphere—what Palmié refers to as "non-human agents." In Regla de Ocha humans and the orisha are believed to exist in a reciprocal interchange, usually initiated by the divine (an orisha will call a human, in divination, to be initiated and incorporate the orisha into the body of the practitioner, "claiming their heads"); in Palo Monte, the spirit of the dead is called upon at human initiative to work for the human as his/her slave, bound by "mystical" capture to achieve a certain end (168). The resulting image of Palo Monte practice resembles what is conventionally referred to as witchcraft.

Palmié reminds us, however, that this perception derives from the vantage point of Regla de Ocha, one in which the practices associated with Palo Monte and the nganga "complex" are conceived of as evil and brutish.[12] And he would have us recall that, despite their ritual differences and the fact that clear-cut distinctions are maintained between the practices, both religions emerged from the same experience of Cuban slavery and its aftermath.

What we are facing, then, is not a mere New World juxtaposition of "essentially" different African traditions—one inherently instrumental, the other expressively oriented. Rather, we are dealing with an aggregate formation in which notions deriving from western Central African minkisi cults and Yoruba-derived forms of worship of divine beings known as òrìsà were jointly conjugated through a single New World history of enslavement, abuse, and depersonalization. In the course of this process, Yoruba-derived patterns of *oricha* worship and western Central African forms of manipulating minkisi objects, not only underwent parallel changes, but also became morally recalibrated in relation to each other . . . . [R]ather than tracing such contemporary constructions back to any putatively essential features of the different African traditions that came to exist in Cuba, a more fruitful way of tackling this problem seems to lie in focusing on the way in which practitioners of the Yoruba-derived oricha cults emerging in nineteenth-century Cuba came to assimilate the nganga complex and the violent imagery surrounding its practices of dealing with spirits of the dead into their own conceptual universe. They did so, it appears, by assigning to the cult of nganga objects a strictly mercenary ethos, thereby ideologically purifying their own practices of moral ambiguity. In the course of this process, the two traditions not only merged into a larger complex of partly overlapping conceptions and practices, but came to offer functionally differentiated ritual idioms that spoke—and continue to speak—to fundamentally different forms of historical experience in contemporary sociality. . . . Yoruba-Cuban and Bantu-Cuban traditions nowadays form part of a spectrum of religious forms that intersect in the religious lives of many, if not most, practitioners of Afro-Cuban religion. (2002: 26–27, 163)

Of all the different branches of the Palo religions in Cuba, the sect with the most pronounced form of syncretism is the Regla Kimbisa founded in the nineteenth century by Andrés Facundo Cristo de los Dolores Petit, a fascinating figure who founded one of the most interpenetrated of the Creole religions in Cuba—a symbiosis of Cuban Conga and Lukumí religions with Catholicism, Espiritismo, and elements of a Masonic rite—and was the first to perform a controversial initiation of white men into the Abakuá Secret Society in 1863. The stories surrounding Andrés Petit are as compelling as the man himself.

Born in the first half of the nineteenth century in Guanabacoa, Petit was a secular Franciscan monk of the Third Order (a tertiary), an *Isué* leader of the Abakuá Secret Society, padre nganga of the Conga religion, and babalocha in the Lukumí religion. A tall, handsome man of Haitian origin, Petit spoke several languages, lived in a Franciscan monastery, and begged for alms for its support. He was always well dressed, bearing a frock coat and cane—although, as a monk, he went around the city of Havana in sandals. Petit performed frequent acts of charity. Numerous legends surrounded his life, including an alleged visit to the Pope to obtain acceptance of his syncretic practice (Cabrera 1977: 1–3).

The sect he founded is strongly based on Palo traditions, including the nganga cauldron, which in this case is always "cristiana," as his Regla was dedicated to the ideals of Christian charity. In the Kimbisa temples, Virgins, saints, orishas, and a crucifix are also integrated, as well as an altar to the patron saint of the Regla Kimbisa, San Luis Beltrán. As a mulatto, and with the combination of beliefs he practiced and fashioned, both a "fervent Catholic and powerful sorcerer," Petit embodies the creolization process. In fact, Lydia Cabrera's informants described the practice of Kimbisa that he founded in terms of the classic transculturation metaphor: an "*ajiaco, un revoltillo*" (a stew, a scramble) that combines the most powerful elements of all the popular beliefs to *vencer* (conquer). "Petit, in order to protect and defend his followers from reprisals and evil spells, decided to found the Regla Kimbisa del Santo Cristo del Buen Viaje, leaving us the most perfect example of religious syncretism created in Cuba" (Cabrera 1977: 3). His decision to sell the Abakuá secrets to a group of young whites and initiate them into the Abakuá Secret Society, highly controversial at the time, was criticized for "whitening" the African Reglas (although simultaneously, of course, he was also Africanizing Catholicism).

According to Tato Quiñones, Petit's reforms of the Abakuá association were based on socioeconomic factors: with the abolition of slavery in 1886, the Cuban colonial society desirous of independence in the late nineteenth century was composed of an embryonic proletariat of blacks, mulattoes, and whites who had gained nothing from the racial segregation of the past. Petit's reforms "contributed in some measure to the arduous and complex process of Cuban national integration, linking blacks, whites and mulattoes in a joint group of beliefs, rites, interests and solidarities, as a result of which the *Abakuá* (also called disparagingly *ñáñigos)*, up to that point only a *cosa de negros* [Black or "n" word thing], became what it has been ever since: a Cuban thing"[13] (Quiñones 1994: 42). Strategically, the initiation of whites took into account the fact that the patronage of wealthy white members could buy Abakuá brethren out of slavery and serve to defend the association against persecution, an idea that many believe to have later proved prudent.

Palmié observes that the historical importance of Petit's decision had wider consequences than that of simply integrating individuals of African and European descent into a common pattern of identification and solidarity. Colonial Cuba was now joined, through the Abakuá, with the powerful commercial and political network of the African *Ékpè* Leopard societies, what some have referred to as an authentically African capitalist institution,[14] "transforming Cuban *abakuá* into an enduring part of a transcontinentally dispersed, indeed virtually rhizomatic, system of knowledge and ritual practice capable of rendering the forces of global capitalism locally coextensive with an awesome African power" (2007: 295). The initiation of whites, started in 1863, continued to grow throughout the first decades of the twentieth century, a cause for concern to the Cuban authorities, for whom "[t]he 'white *ñáñigos* became as fearsome, or more so, because they seemed to presage the slippage of the nation in general into the vortex of contagion, atavism, and Africanness'" (D. Brown 2003: 137).

The Abakuá Secret Society

One of the most original of New World African religions, only found in Cuba, the Abakuá[15] society, is a confraternity and magicoreligious esoteric society, exclusively for men.[16] It is, like other societies of initiation, one in which an oath is taken to maintain discretion and guard the group's "secrets," ritual knowledge taught to members incrementally as they rise in status in the society.

In the eighteenth and nineteenth centuries, settlements of the multilingual Cross River basin of present-day Nigeria and Cameroon, in lieu of a kingdom, had lodges of the initiation society called *Ékpè* or "leopard" (a sign of royalty in Central West Africa and the Calabar zone) that served as the highest indigenous authority, ruling local communities and maintaining regional and distant trade. Ékpè societies originated in the eighteenth century with the Efik people in order to transcend family and ethnic boundaries and form intercommunity business relationships for the sale of slaves and palm oil to Europeans. Each village had its own lodge in which members were afforded access to an extensive commercial network. Mystical secrets, sacred rituals, and commercial interests united members, all of whom were male (women were believed incapable of guarding a secret, no doubt due to their founding myths, described below); revealing secrets to outsiders could be punishable by death. Membership was not limited to Africans, however; during the slave trade era Europeans found it advantageous to be initiated into the powerful traffic and commercial network of the Ékpè.

Enslaved in battles and forcibly brought to Cuba in this period, Cross River Africans, or the "Carabalí" (the name given in Cuba to the peoples of the Cross River region, referred to as "Old Calabar" in colonial records), were grouped into ethnic Carabalí *cabildos*, officially condoned organizations of Africans based on ethnic identification,[17] joining with earlier enslaved Africans who had been identified as Carabalí (for a discussion of the cabildos, see chapter 2). Among these were Ékpè members who carried their traditions to the Caribbean. In the mid-nineteenth century free urban black workers in Havana acquired the tradition.[18]

> Using Cross River language, symbols, and philosophies, West Africans created an institution that existed parallel to the Spanish regime and was largely undetected by it.
>
> Abakuá expanded its urban networks through the interactions of many communities, including African nation-groups, free black artisans, the black and mulatto militias, urban fugitives, and African descendants from Spain. Abakuá secret codes of communication, based upon Ékpè codes called nsìbìdì, were useful in nineteenth-century anticolonial movements, where secret oaths in the manner of Freemasonry and Abakuá were operative. (Miller 2009: 176)

The first chapters of the society (called *juegos, potencias, tierras,* or *partidos*) appeared in the port town of Regla in 1836 and later spread through Havana, Matanzas, and Cárdenas.

On the eastern shores of the bay of Havana, Regla had grown to become an important warehouse district of the capital's rapidly developing and increasingly globalized industrial harbor complex. As an organization of mutual aid and advancement, and self-protection against a repressive colonial society, Abakuá chapters became unofficial guilds for dockworkers and those in other important labor sectors even before the abolition of slavery, despite the fact that their associations were officially prohibited by the Spanish authorities.

> Combining mystically sanctioned ritual authority with the power to grant access to, or withhold, steady labor, they built up tightly organized political structures among the members of their *potencias* or tierras (as individual abakuá chapters are known). These cult associations became visible to the uninitiated not only in lavishly exotic public ceremonies that recalled the discovery in a mythical Africa of the secret of a mystical voice belong-

ing to a being or force known as *ecue* and celebrated an ideal of agonistic manhood, virile elegance, and fraternal solidarity. Their presence also became palpable in the form of relations of patronage and clientelism at the various worksites abakuá had come to control. As a saying popular in the first half of the twentieth century went, at least at the dockside of Havana's extensive harbor, abakuá initiates decided "who would eat and who would not". . .When the colonial government outlawed the association as seditious and criminal in 1876, perhaps as many as fifty individual chapters of abakuá were operating in Havana, Regla, and Guanabacoa, where they repeatedly clashed with the police in violent confrontations over the control of neighborhoods and sources of employment. (Palmié and Pérez 2005:219–220)

Permission of the elders and collective consensus had to be obtained before establishing a new lodge, thereby limiting the number of lodges and controlling the orthodoxy of the tradition. "Unlike the fundamentos (core ritual objects) of other Cuban religions of African derivation, those of Abakuá have not left the Havana-Matanzas region, despite some documented attempts" (Miller 2009: 178).

Although not regarded exclusively as a religion, many of the Abakuá society describe it as such, with a deep spiritual base sharing many of the practices and beliefs of the Afro-Cuban Reglas analyzed above: a formal initiation, sacred ritual ceremonies accompanied by drumming, dancing, and music, and a belief in a hierarchy of deities and spirits. The Abakuá have a single ritual lingua franca—Brícamo—obtained from various linguistic varieties which is used for their chants, a form of oral historical memory. There is also a type of writing called *anaforuana*, based on the Ejagham *nsibidi* ideographs, sacred signs and tracings that are among the most complex form of symbolic African-based writing in the Americas (illustrated above and below). The pictograms are used to convey messages and serve as a form of identification, hence their alternative name of *firmas* (signatures). They are described by Thompson as

hypnotic variants of a leitmotif of mystic vision: four eyes, two worlds, God the Father—the fish, the king—and the Efut princess who in death became his bride. These signs are written and rewritten with mantraic power and pulsations. Mediatory forces, the sacred signs of the *anaforuana* corpus, indicate a realm beyond ordinary discourse. They are calligraphic gestures of erudition and black grandeur, spiritual presences traced in yellow

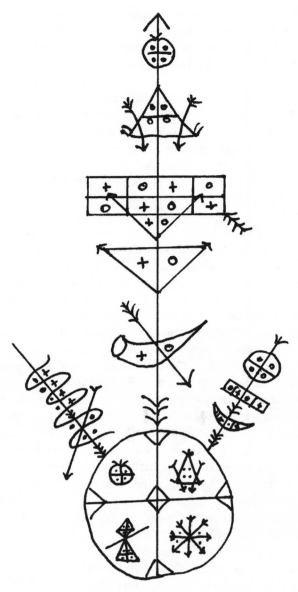

Emblem of the Bakokó Abakuá chapter that initiated the
first whites into the Abakuá Secret Society.

or white chalk (yellow for life, white for death) on the ground of inner patios or on the floor of sacred rooms, bringing back the spirit of departed ancestors, describing the proprieties of initiation and funeral leave-taking. (Thompson 1984: 229)[19]

Abakuá dancers—*íremes or diablitos (devils)*—are famous in Cuban colonial history for their performances on January 6 (the Day of the Three Kings) and for their elaborate ceremonial outfits: a multicolored checkerboard costume (perhaps to honor the ancient leopard cult), with a conical headpiece topped with tassels based on the ritual costuming traditions of the Ejagham.

The complex origin myth of the society plays a central and pervasive role in the rituals and the hierarchical organization of the Abakuá chapters (and also explains the exclusion of women from the society). The myth—of which there are numerous and sometimes contradictory versions—basically revolves around two hostile tribes from Calabar, the Efor and the Efik, who lived separately by the sacred river Oddán. In one version of the tale, Abasi (God) was to deliver the secret to the chosen ones (the Efor) in the river where the thundering voice of the Sacred, in the form of a fish, had been heard. Riches and honor would come to the tribe that could discover the fish. One day Sikán (or Sikanekue), the daughter of Mokongo, an Efor elder, went to the river to fetch water but, after placing the calabash on her head, she was frightened by a roaring sound. Her father warned her not to talk about her experience, fearing the reaction of Nasakó, the sorcerer of the tribe, but he took his daughter to Nasakó's cave nevertheless. There the calabash with the fish was hidden away while important elders spent days deciding what to do, and whether or not Sikán had seen the sacred fish Tanze, which became gradually weaker and finally died.

To recover the sacred voice they built a drum, the *Ekué*, covered with the skin of Tanze, but the voice refused to speak. Believing that only the blood of Sikán who had discovered the secret might bring it back to life, she was sacrificed. But the silence continued until the sorcerer guaranteed the *fundamento* or power of the drum with the blood of animal sacrifices and other ceremonies. Thereafter the drum regained the voice. The Efik pressured their rivals to share the secret with them and seven members of each tribe met to sign an agreement, with the exception of Nasakó, who did not sign. This is why there are thirteen major posts or *plazas* within the society—the thirteen plazas recalling the original signatories to the pact. In other versions of the myth Sikán reveals the secret of the fish to her lover, the son of the chief of the rival tribe, and is condemned to death for her betrayal.

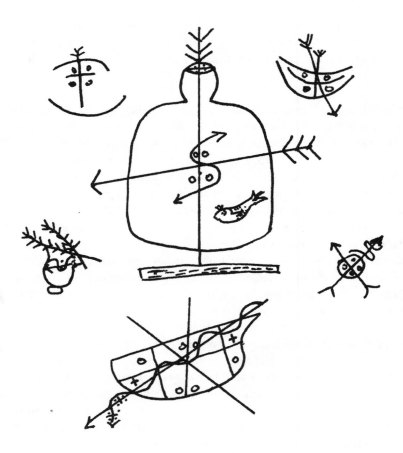

Emblems of Sikán.

Sikán, it is believed, replaced the mother of the leopard Ebongó, a figure representing the matriarchal period when women knew the "secrets" forbidden to men; the salvation of society depended on the sacrifice of the female body (Cuervo Hewitt 1988: 48). The myth can thus be interpreted as symbolic of the structural changes in societies that evolve from matriarchal to patriarchal systems:

> Matriarchy (Sikán), a more primitive socio-economic formation and, therefore more diffuse, is surpassed (killed) by patriarchy that neverthe-

less recognizes, and in some manner, reveres the role of women, even within the new social scheme, as a source of life and, as a result, of perpetuation. And, since her presence and incorporation into this society is at once indispensable and unavoidable, she is consecrated to the service of Ekue, that is, to unity, to the sole god, and to the perpetuation of the social model represented by him. (Bolívar Aróstegui and González Díaz de Villegas 1993: 12)

As in the Regla Conga, ñáñigos place much emphasis on magic in their rituals, many of which are based on a reenactment of the origin myth of Sikán and Tanze. Although they have underscored the secular elements of their sect (the mutual aid, for example), the religious dimension predominates. Sacred rites are hidden from others in order to protect their mystery and preserve the sanctity of the ñáñigos' liturgy (Castellanos and Castellanos 1992, 3: 222). Ceremonies are celebrated in a closed, intimate, secret space (the *fambá*, "the room of mysteries") and in public where observers can witness the ñáñigos' famous and spectacular ceremonies and their intricate dances.

The Abakuá have a highly organized and disciplined structure.[20] While there are numerous dignitaries or plazas who govern the lodges and celebrate rites in the organization, the four major plazas in ñáñigo ceremonies—*Isué, Iyamba, Mokongo,* and *Isunekue*—assume the roles of the protagonists in the pervasive origin myth. The Isué, who is the supreme chief in some lodges (in others it is the Iyamba), and is also referred to as the "high priest" because of his role in the ñáñigo initiation, is in charge of the feathered drum called *Sese* or *Seseribó* (illustrated below) which contains the magical fundament of the religion ("an instrument of display, not for use, an instrument of significant silence . . . an incarnation of Sikán" [Thompson 1984: 237]).[21] The Iyamba presides over the initiation ceremonies and has the principal task of extracting the sacred thundering voice (recalling the original leopard cult on which the sacred fish mythology was based) from the Ekué drum in a process referred to as *fragallar*. In this process the drummer wets his hands with water or with blood from the sacrifices and rubs a cane shoot in the center of the magic drum (Castellanos and Castellanos 1992, 3: 224). The sound produced by the friction is considered sacred, the voice of the divine, and is never reproduced outside of religious practices.[22] The Mokongo officiates over ceremonies in the open part of the temple. The Isunekue, the "Guardian of the Voice," is the custodian of the concealed chamber where the sacred Ekué drum is kept.

Sese drum.

Abakúa rituals and ceremonies (*plantes*) have been compared to theatrical dramas. Initiations of new members, funerals, the naming of dignitaries, the annual homage to Ekué, take place in the sacred chambers of their temple-lodges in the *fambá,* which has been ritually prepared with the drawings of their mystical *anaforuanas* or *firmas* (signatures). Music and particularly, as has been noted, the drums, play a central role, as they do in all Afro-Cuban religious practices:

> Abakuá, the secret, exclusively male society—auto financed by means of
> fees and dues collected from among its members, with a complex hierar-

chical organization of dignitaries, (*plazas*) and assistants, the presence of otherworldly beings, a dark ritual whose secret, jealously guarded, is materialized in a drum called the *ekwé*, ceremonies of initiation, renovation, purification and death, temporal and eternal benefits, mandatory laws and in-house punishments which must be accepted and implemented, a hermetic, esoteric language and a complementary graphic language of sign, seals and sacred tracings—comprises, to this day an unparalleled cultural phenomenon in Cuba and in America, of great importance in the understanding of our cultural traditions and institutions, of our folklore. (Sosa Rodriguez 1982: 124)

The Carabalís were located geographically between the Yoruba and the Congo in Africa and their religious system demonstrates the influence of both. Their god (Abasí) is similar to Olodumare and Sambi: an old detached god who lacks a particular cult dedicated to him. Intermediate deities, influenced by the Yoruba orishas, were also syncretized with the Catholic saints. Thus the Abakuá Obandío is identified with the Yoruba Obatalá and the Catholic La Virgen de las Mercedes, and the Abakuá Okún is syncretized with Changó and Santa Bárbara, among others.[23] The ancestors are also central to ñáñigo rituals; the spirits of the deceased and/or of supernatural beings, personified in the íremes or "little devils," are summoned by one of the symbolic drums of the Abakuá ensemble, the *enkríkamo* (Vélez 2000: 18–20). The dead return to the earth, it is believed, during their rituals when, as all members or *ecobios* have the right to do, they don the sacred vestments. What to many may appear to be a choreographed dance for the Abakuá is a religious language (Castellanos and Castellanos 1992, 3: 233). In *El monte*, Lydia Cabrera notes the artistry of Cuban spiritual practices in her description of the dance of an Abakuá liturgical procession:

It is an incredible spectacle—disconcerting and deplorable for many who consider *ñañigismo* a national disgrace—those parades of shabby-looking whites and blacks in which an African drum appears alongside a crucified Christ, the pagan head of a decapitated goat and an old earthen jar. Primitive and barbarous in nature, one need not stress its extraordinary interest to observers.

The gait, the rigorously stylized gestures—each one is a statement—of the *ñáñigos* dressed as devils representing initiates of the distant past, the immemorial mask, in its religious function and beyond, transform them into abstractions, sacred and unreal beings; their mime and dance contemplated in the light of a magical Cuban evening is a spectacle of strange beauty, so out of time, so remote and mysterious that it cannot help but fascinate anyone who watches it.

I remember the terror that the Iremes with their white cyclops eyes, inspired in Federico García Lorca, and the delirious poetic description he made for me the day after having witnessed a celebration.

If a Diaghilev had been born on this island, he undoubtedly would have paraded these *ñáñigo* devils throughout Europe's stages. (Cabrera 1983: 216–217)

In the nineteenth and early twentieth centuries, the Abakuá Society was the focus of harassment and persecution by the authorities.[24] As an all-male secret society they were believed to be harboring antisocial and criminal elements, and the word *ñáñigo* became the equivalent of "sorcerer" or "delinquent" in Cuban culture. Intergroup rivalries between lodges often led to violent confrontations and the machismo of some of the legendary figures of the society contributed to the stereotype (Castellanos and Castellanos 1992, 3: 261). Sensational press reports added to the effects of racism, bias, and ignorance suffered by *ñáñigos*; they continued to be repressed by the post-revolutionary government into the 1970s. Viewed as a potential center for political resistance, "[t]he threat these societies were perceived to pose to the 'establishment' may explain in part the prejudice, persecutions, and misrepresentation these societies have suffered" (Vélez 2000: 23).

Many claim, on the other hand, that the Abakuá Society has made the greatest and most original contributions of all the Afro-Cuban religious practices to the country's language, arts, and music; their relationship with Cuba's tourist industry has gained the Abakuá guarded appreciation.

The revolution's applied folklore program, with its nation-and culture-building goals, has had wide-ranging effects. . . . Clearly, *lo afrocubano* and its practitioners gained a kind of visibility and legitimacy as of the early 1960s, which they had never before experienced. . . . In the scholarly context, Afro-Cuban traditions were redefined in ways that contradicted age-old social stigma and persecution, but also attempted to "transculturate" them of perceived atavisms for the greater good of the national *ajiaco* [stew] and the taste of the middle class. As of 1964, *El Ñáñigo* was well on his way to becoming an icon of Cuban national folklore. However, as during the prerevolutionary period that Cubans call the "pseudo-Republic," state and society would remain highly ambivalent about Abakuá practice.

Abakuá *ireme*. Photo courtesy of the artist Héctor Delgado.

Museums would fill with Abakuá attributes and dollar stores with *ñáñigo* tourist souvenirs, while the gates of Abakuá lodges still remained subject to police vigilance. (D. Brown 2003: 210)

In his ground-breaking work, *Voice of the Leopard: African Secret Societies and Cuba* (2009), Ivor L. Miller describes his fieldwork tracing the Ékpè societies in West Africa and their Cuban incarnation, the Abakuá. After years of fieldwork with Abakuá initiates in Cuba and in the United States, and noting a similarity between Abakuá and Ékpè societies in Africa, Miller underwent initiation himself in Nigeria in order to gain an access denied to outsiders and a deeper understanding of the African rites. *Voice of the Leopard* attempts to link the Abakuá in Cuba with their Ékpè African counterparts.

When I presented twenty-first-century Ékpè members in Calabar with recordings of Abakuá music and when they actually met Abakuá members in a cultural festival, their response was a detailed recognition of its language and rhythmic structures. That Abakuá terms could be understood by contemporary Nigerian Ékpè members indicates an unusually orthodox practice of cultural transmission that has been sustained to the present. (178)[25]

As in David H. Brown's work (2003), Miller's book makes clear the profound and pervasive creative influence of the Abakuá on Cuban music, art, language, and popular consciousness to this day.

The Healing Traditions of Afro-Cuban Religions

As with other Creole religions, Afro-Cuban practices are wide-ranging, influencing the arts, language, and virtually every aspect of Cuban culture. Healing, both physical and emotional, is no exception. Cuban anthropologist Lydia Cabrera and her Haitian counterpart Michel Laguerre,[26] among others, have written of the syncretic medical traditions of their respective cultures, folk practices not usually addressed in research anchored in exclusively Western scientific conceptual categories. Although all healing practices originated in spiritual practices, boundaries gradually began to be erected between scientific medicine (symbolized by the germ theory of disease) and the supernatural. Although by the nineteenth century the process of desacralizing medicine appeared to be complete, in truth it was not. Faith healing and similar religious practices that consider faith a more effective cure than biomedicine experienced a revival in the 1980s as part of a search for spiritual approaches to wellness: "It was Hippocrates who first banished spirits from the healing arts, and for the past 2,500 years the faithful have struggled to force them back in" (Sides 1997: 94).

In the Caribbean the spirits never left. An intrinsic part of the Amerindian world that later blended with the saints of the Roman Catholic colonist and the orishas and lwas of the African slave, they are a part of a syncretic healing system that is inclusive, pluralistic, local, and, in many cases, magical. The elements of Caribbean folk healing most rejected by mainstream culture—those that cannot withstand the scrutiny of scientific empirical investigation—are precisely the ones that claim the most tenacious hold on the Caribbean cultural imagination, namely, the magical, spiritual, religious methodologies of Santería, Espiritismo, Vodou, Obeah, and the myriad other spiritual practices in the region and its Diaspora. ("Root" and "hoodoo" doctors studied by Zora Neale Hurston and others in the southeastern United States are an example of the herbal-magical ethnomedical practices transplanted to the area from the Caribbean.)[27]

Lydia Cabrera's brand of ethnobotany in her seminal work *El monte* is a case in point. The first half of the ethnographic work transcribes the belief systems of the Afro-Cuban peoples in the words of their followers—rituals, customs, and the magical causes of illness, legends, and traditions. In the second half Cabrera presents an extensive list of medicinal plants utilized by *curanderos* (faith-folk healers) classified by their local colloquial name in Cuba, the official Latin botanical nomenclature, and their spiritual name according to the appropriate Afro-Cuban religion: ("L") for the Lukumí-Regla de Ocha classification, and ("C") for the Congo or Palo name, succeeded by the plant's *dueño* or lord, that is, deity associated with it.

Some entries are brief, with descriptions of their medical use, alternative names, and suggested medicinal recommendations, followed by a popular expression or anecdotal story related to Cabrera by one of her many informants. However, other entries are much more complex and detailed, with intricate rituals, historical background, and occasionally extensive stories surrounding the experiences of an informant or the retelling of a Santería pataki of the Ifá divination system. Cabrera's brand of ethnobotany reflects the creolization process: established Western authoritative codes and hierarchies fuse in a fantastic synthesis and on equal footing with popular belief, personal anecdote, religion, spirituality, indigenous and folk healing traditions, official and oral history, testimony, fiction, and fantasy. Not limited to one religion or knowledge tradition, Cabrera presents several (Lukumí, Palo,

Abakuá-Ñáñigo, and derivations of the same) from within the Afro-Cuban context that complement rather than compete with the Euro-Western elements of Cuban culture.

Cabrera's 1984 study of Cuban healing systems, *La medicina popular en Cuba* (Popular Medicine in Cuba), particularly chapter 4, "Black Folk Healers," documents the resilience of these belief-healing practices.[28] Their "divinely-inspired science" was based on fulfilling the required sacrifices or *ebó* to cure a malady. Each of the Afro-Cuban religions arrives at a diagnosis in its own fashion: Regla de Ocha practitioners determine the origin of a problem by questioning an orisha through possession or by means of one of the divination methods described in chapter 2; the Congo practitioner will communicate with the *fumbi* (the spirit of a deceased person) or a *mpungu* (a supernatural force) in his or her nganga who will speak and diagnose through trance.

> Anyone who has been around practitioners of the African religions in Cuba can appreciate the fact that sickness and death are not always attributable to natural causes . . . a curse can cut our lives short, as can the ire of an oricha when carelessness, disobedience, or unfulfilled promises incur its anger. Neglecting the deceased is yet another cause for suffering and death. . . . Despite their severity, the orishas ultimately come to the aid of their children and the faithful who beg them and offer gifts. A generous and timely ebbó will appease them. (Fernández Olmos, "Black Arts," 2001: 33).

Afro-Cuban ethnomedical therapeutics is essentially plant-based: decoctions, infusions, aromatics, and/or baths are prescribed to cleanse an evil spell or attract beneficent healing spirits. Some evil spells—*bilongos, wembas, murumbas*—are so powerful, however, that another sorcerer cannot undo them without risk to his own life. One of the more fascinating procedures used by practitioners of the Palo tradition is that of "switching lives," a practice that reflects the Congo belief in the ability to control a person's life spirit, tricking death. After consulting spiritually with the spirit of the dead of his or her nganga, the palero will dispense the treatment:

> We have heard of the mayombero seated on the floor next to the patient administering the brew he has prepared to "extract the witchcraft," and of the latter who drinks it and vomits feathers, stones, and hair. At that moment the sorcerer "switches lives" [*cambia vida*]: he uses chalk, twine,

Preparing herbs for a spiritual cleansing. Photo courtesy of the artist Héctor Delgado.

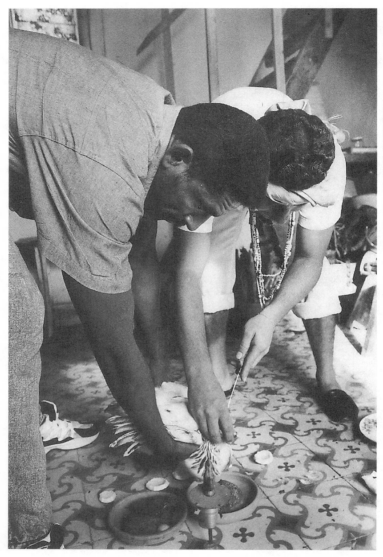

Sacrifice of a hen for an ebó. Photo courtesy of the artist Héctor Delgado.

a doll, or the stump of a plantain tree. He measures the patient and ties the doll or the stump with seven knots. With this procedure the evil that attacks the patient is transferred by the curandero onto the doll or stump, which is given the sick person's name, and thus death is tricked into believing that the buried stump or doll is the patient's cadaver. . . . A doll, we are told, properly baptized, is placed to sleep beside the sick person in his bed. The following day it is placed in a box, as if dead, and buried. The patient is cleansed three times with a rooster that is passed over the entire body. The rooster dies because it has absorbed the illness and is taken to a crossroad. The patient then rests and undergoes a treatment of infusions. (Fernández Olmos, "Black Arts," 2001: 37–39)

Folk healing modalities in the Caribbean region continue to become even more varied and complex due to migrations within the region and throughout the world, giving rise to new medical syncretisms and to a U.S. medical subculture. In Miami, Puerto Ricans can be found buying folk spiritual remedies from Cubans, and Bahamians consult root doctors, for example, while in New York, Puerto Rican Spiritist healers treat Cuban patients, and Puerto Ricans in turn consult Haitian folk healers (Laguerre 1984: 108–140). The alternative and integrative strategies of adaptation and reinvention are emblematic of Creole healing modalities and have been and will continue to be the tools of survival in resourceful Caribbean societies.

Haitian Vodou

Forging a Creole Religion in Haiti

Before the 1791 slave rebellion that laid its complex network of sugar plantations to waste, the colony of Saint Domingue, which occupied the western third of the island of Hispaniola, was the most valuable possession in the French colonial empire. A small territory, it had been nonetheless the destination of hundreds of thousands of African slaves, captives from west Central Africa and the Bight of Benin, home to such groups as the Yoruba, the Fon, and the Ewe. In the plantations of Saint Domingue they lived and died under a system of ruthless exploitation unlike any previously known, a system that took its death toll with unprecedented speed.

Slaves were brought to Haiti—the original Arawak name to which the Saint Domingue slaves would revert after the success of their revolution—from numerous different ethnic groups, and were systematically intermixed in an effort to destroy, whenever possible, all recollection of language, culture, ties of kinship, and connection to the motherland, 'Nan Guinée. However, the Haitian slaves' need to reestablish a connection to their culture and their gods, to seek the spirits' aid in their desperate plight, clashed against the violence and repression of the plantation and the imposition of French Catholic culture. The result of this clash was the system of beliefs and rituals we know as Vodou, a term that encompasses a variety of Haiti's African-derived religious traditions and practices. As Colin (Joan) Dayan writes in *Haiti, History, and the Gods*,

> In spite of this instability, or what some argue to be the capriciousness of spirits and terminologies, something incontrovertible remains: the heritage of Guinea maintained in Haiti by serving the gods. Those who live are reclaimed by their ancestors who do not die—who return as vengeful revenants if not properly served—and by the gods who cajole, demand, and sometimes oppress the mere mortals, the *chrétiens-vivants* who forget their ancestral origins. The gods are not only in your blood but in the land. (1998: 33)

The term Vodou, which meant "spirit" or "sacred energy" in the Adja-Tado group of languages spoken in Arada, was brought to Haiti from Ouida (or Whydah), on the west coast of Africa, at the height of the eighteenth-century slave trade. The word—and indeed most of the lexicon associated with the Vodou temple (*ounfo, oungan, manbo,* and *ounsi,* as we will see below)—is a legacy of the Fon kingdom of what is now Benin and was once Dahomey. So are the names of the African-born Rada spirits served by Vodou devotees: Danbala, Ayida Wedo, Ezili Freda, Legba, Azaka, Ghédé (Gede), and the names of the sacred drums that summon them to join congregants at ritual dances. Although in its most restricted sense it refers only to Arada rites, the word Vodou has over the years come to stand for all African-derived religious practices in Haiti. These include the traditions of the other African group to have a major impact on the development of Vodou, namely, the Yoruba-speaking people known as Nago, who held the territory east of the Fon nation and who were well-represented among the slaves brought to Haiti.

Harold Courlander, addressing the multiplicity of meanings conveyed by the term Vodou, differentiates between three interlocking sets of usages. Thus: "(1) vodou as only the rites derived from the Arada and Nago; (2) vodou as a complex of rites including others clustered around the Arada and Nago, such as the Ibo; and (3) vodou as all Afro-Haitian rites including those of the Congo and Petro" (Murphy 1994: 15). For the purposes of this chapter we will adhere to the last, most encompassing definition, since it is the one most commonly used.

Vodou, the most maligned and misunderstood of all African-inspired religions in the Americas, is also one of its most complex. Its liturgy and rituals revolve around a pantheon of spirits known as *lwa* or *loa* who represent a fusion of African and Creole gods, the spirits of deified ancestors, and syncretized manifestations of Catholic saints. The relationship between the lwa and the spirits is one of reciprocity. The lwa offer help, protection, and counsel; their devotees offer ritual service in return, which includes a variety of individual and communal rituals. Privately, the believer will wear the lwa's colors, feed the spirits, and make all necessary sacrifices when instructed. In group ceremonies, devotees congregate at an *ounfo* (*hounfort* or temple), where the *oungan* (*houngan* or priest) leads the celebrants in ceremonies that revolve around song, sacred drumming, dance, prayer, spirit possession, food preparation, and the ritual sacrifice of animals. The lwa communicate with individuals and the congregation through spirit possession, a trancelike state in which the devotee is "mounted" by the spirit and becomes the lwa's vehicle. As the incarnation of the lwa, the "horse" communicates with the congregation through words and stylized dances, offering advice, becoming a conduit for healing, and relishing the opportunity to be among its devotees.

Vodou is intricately connected to the twelve-year war of independence that we know as the Haitian Revolution (1791–1803). The Revolution's early leaders—Boukman and Makandal—were reputed to be powerful oungans whose knowledge of the powers and poisonous properties of herbs had helped mount a campaign of terror and death among French planters in Saint Domingue. It was with the blessing of the lwa that slaves gathered in the Bois-Caïman, in the north of Haiti, on the night of August 14, 1791. In a Vodou ceremony that included the sacrifice of a wild boar, they swore a sacred oath to overthrow their French slave masters. The ceremony represented the consolidation of the connection between Vodou and the Haitian spirit of resistance which, together with the appropriation of Catholic ritual that became part of the rites of liberation, remains a powerful repository of subversion today. As Leslie Desmangles has explained:

> This syncretistic nature of Voudou was disturbing to the church. Voudou assemblies were a cause for alarm among the colonists, for not only were they profane in their use of objects stolen from the church, but the planters feared that they would serve as catalysts for slave insurrections. . . . Voudou meetings had often been converted into offensive mechanisms for violent raids against the planters, some costly in human lives and materials. (Desmangles 1992: 27)

The destruction of Saint Domingue's plantation economy had momentous repercussions for the development of Haitian Vodou. The consolidation of the Revolution, and the land grants to former slaves it made possible, transformed Haiti into a rural nation of subsistence farmers working their small plots. This new peasantry organized itself around small villages that functioned as extended family compounds. Known as *lakous*, they opened a new space for the preservation of African-derived Creole religions (Murphy 1994: 12).

The connection between the lakous and the preservation of Vodou had important repercussions, as it meant that its rituals and practices grew out of the needs and concerns of specific communities. There is no central liturgical authority in Vodou, only a set of foundational principles and traditional rites that were allowed to adapt to the idiosyncrasies of various groups, merging and separating to accommodate the flow of peoples across the Haitian landscape. So while there are many informal ties among various communities of Vodou practitioners, each ounfo follows its own preferences and guidelines in matters of ritual and belief. As a result, practices vary (sometimes greatly) from one congregation to another, as do the nature and attributes of the lwa.

Vodou flourished in the lakous throughout the nineteenth century, unobstructed by competing religious forces, since the Catholic Church had left Haiti in 1805 in protest, refusing to work within the parameters set by the new Haitian masters, and did not return until the Concordat of 1860.[1] Given free rein to flourish, Vodou became the true religion of the Haitian folk. This did not mean, however, that Catholicism was lost as a basic component of Haitian Vodou. Prior to the Revolution slaves had been forced into Catholic baptism, as mandated by colonial codes. As in many other areas of the Caribbean, forced conversions had opened the way for the development of intricate correspondences between African religious practices and Catholic rituals and beliefs, especially between the lwa and Catholic saints. Chromolithographs and statues of the Catholic saints were appropriated to venerate African deities, a fusion that actually intensified after the French left Haiti and their abandoned churches became liminal spaces for religious synthesis (these forms of Catholic representation are still a central component of religious art in Haiti). As Alfred Métraux explains in *Voodoo in Haiti*,

> [W]henever there was a shortage of priests, some Blacks took it upon themselves to catechize or preach to the others and thus "the truths and dogmas of the religion were altered." Here, straight away, we hit upon the root of that "blending" which, two centuries later, was to provoke the indignant wrath of the Catholic clergy of Haiti against Voodoo. (1972: 35)

The return of Catholicism to Haiti in 1860 brought in a new phase of correspondences, this despite attempts by the Catholic Church to repress Vodou. These attempts increased as priests organized antisuperstition campaigns and sought to work closely with the government to stamp out what they saw as sorcery and sacrilege. The history of persecution of Vodou practitioners included antisuperstition campaigns in 1896, 1913, and 1941, during which temples were destroyed and hundreds of people who admitted to being practitioners of Vodou were massacred. The decades of American occupation (1915–1934) and the post-Duvalier era (1986–1993) witnessed particularly intensive persecution of Vodouists. Despite the persistence of Vodou, which claims 80 percent of the population of the island as adherents, Catholicism remained Haiti's official religion until the Constitution of 1987 recognized freedom of religion. Since the 1990s evangelical Protestantism has made significant inroads among Haitians.

Ironically, as Vodou was forced to the margins and became increasingly identified with superstition and ignorance, the use of Catholic beliefs, imagery, and rituals came to be regarded as special elements in Vodou rites, necessary to the invocation of the lwas. Vodou and Catholicism still coexist in Haiti, both practiced by the overwhelming majority of the population, flowing in and out of each other as the spiritual and healing needs of the Haitian people demand. For practitioners there is no conflict between Vodou and Roman Catholicism. (There is, however, growing conflict between evangelical Protestants and Vodou practitioners, as those who join evangelical Christian churches are expected to renounce Vodou.)

The Belief System of Vodou

Vodou is essentially a monotheistic religion, and practitioners recognize a single and supreme spiritual entity or God—Mawu-Lisa among the Fon, Olorun among the Yoruba, and Bondié, Bondyé, or Gran Met (the Good God) in Haiti. But the foundation of their religiosity is the service of a pantheon of powerful spirits called the lwa. The lwa, also known as mystères, anges, saints, or les invisibles, provide the link between humans and the divine. Their protean nature and the multiplicity of their possible avatars or manifestations can be disconcerting to those unfamiliar with the religion and its practices. As Colin Dayan has observed, any lwa "can have multiple emanations, depending on locale, on a particular ritual, on the composition of the hounfort . . . or on their association with particular individuals or family groups" (1997: 16). Each lwa has its own personality, favorite objects and colors, particular strengths and weaknesses, attributes and powers. They can be changing and capricious, loyal and stalwart, or unforgiving and demanding in their relationship with their devotees or serviteurs (those who serve the lwa).

In Haiti, as in Cuba, slaves arriving in the new world were divided into "nations" upon their arrival. Ethnic names, often inexact and linked to the slaves' port of embarkation, were assigned to various groups. This concept of "nation" has survived in Vodou, serving to categorize the lwas and the rituals based on their origin. According to Joseph M. Murphy, the idea of "'nation' . . . is not an ethnic, geographical, or political concept, but rather a means of classifying the variety of spirits by the kind of rites that are offered to them" (1994: 16). Each lwa is identified with one of these nations, and is bound to his or her "nation" just as humans in Haitian society are linked by ties of family and kinship. Murphy identifies eight nations as the most significant in Haitian Vodou: Rada, Petwo (or Petro), Nago (Yoruba), Ibo (Igbo), Wangol (Angola), Siniga (Senegal), Ginen (Guinée), and Kongo. The two most inclusive or largest nations are Rada, home to the wise and benevolent spirits that accompanied the slaves to the new world from ancestral Africa, and Petwo, the fierce and tempestuous spirits drawn from Central Africa and creolized in Haiti, whose rites, born of the rage against the evil fate suffered by Africans transported into the New World, speak to the wrath against the brutality of displacement and enslavement (Deren 1953: 62). Folk tradition maintains that it was at a Petwo ceremony that the leaders of the Haitian Revolution swore their loyalty oath. As the different congregations have chosen from among the various rites and practices of these nations to elaborate their own particular forms of worship, they have formed what Murphy calls a "liturgical mosaic" characteristic of the mutability and variety of Vodou practices. However, as Dayan warns us, such division into " 'nations' … does not help us to understand the link formed between these tribes in the New World, the lwa's wandering from one tribe to another, or the endless transformations of lwa as they relate to their servitors" (1997: 21).

Communities of Vodou practitioners gather around an ounfo or temple under the tutelage of an oungan and a manbo (male and female ounfo leaders, respectively). Members of a community, particularly in rural settings, may be members of an extended family, brought together by ties of kinship and serving the lwa who have incarnated themselves in the family group. They will worship the lwa in ceremonies held at the family's own plot of land—the family's *heritage*—in celebrations that are closed to those not belonging to the family. The urban ounfo, on the other hand, becomes a family through the process of initiation, having been drawn to a particular temple by ties of friendship or the reputation for knowledge and piety of a particular oungan or manbo. The ounfo, whether urban or rural, is guided by the oungan (the "master of the gods") or manbo, whose role it is to organize the various liturgies, prepare practitioners for initiation, offer individual consultations for clients in need of divination or spiritual advice, and use his or her knowledge of herbs to prescribe and prepare remedies to improve health or potions, "packages," or bottles to bring luck or ensure protection.

The oungans and manbos, as heads of autonomous ounfos, are highly self-sufficient and are not part of a priestly hierarchy. Their authority, consequently, is limited to those who voluntarily submit to initiation in their ounfo and is dependent on individuals' trust in the oungan or manbo possessing the gift of second sight. This gift, a sign that the person has been chosen by God as a vessel for supernatural powers, is revealed through visions or dreams. Métraux describes how an oungan realized his call to service through a recurring dream in which he saw a gourd containing the beads and snake bones covering the asson, the sacred rattle used in summoning the lwa, which is the symbol of the oungan's sacred profession (1972: 66). The expression "taking the *asson*" means having assumed the duties and responsibilities of the Vodou priesthood.

The Vodou community is organized around the development of spiritual powers—of "supernatural insight and the power which is derived from it" (Métraux 1972: 64)—under the leadership and guidance of the oungan and manbo. This supernatural insight is marked by stages of initiation into a special quality of mind called *konesans* (connaissance or knowledge) that includes knowledge of rituals, openness to communication with the lwa, and spiritual wisdom. There are various levels of konesans, and upward movement through these stages requires different degrees of initiation. At the bottom of this hierarchy there are ordinary devotees, the *pitit-caye* (or children of the house) who are more or less active in the service of the lwa. They may or may not be initiated to become *ounsi* or spouses of the lwa, those who have made a lifelong commitment of service to the spirits and who are a step below the oungan and manbo in the spiritual hierarchy. The oungan, manbo, and ounsis form the core of the Vodou temple, the group responsible for the veneration of the lwa. The oungan and manbo have the power to initiate the ounsi and transmit the konesans.

The oungan or manbo's power to transmit the konesans is predicated on their own knowledge of the rites of the Vodou religion, the attributes of the lwa, and the tradition of worship and service that makes possible their communication with the spirit world. Mastery of the lore requires training, usually received through a more established and respected oungan, extensive training in herbalism, musical aptitude (as so much of the Vodou ritual is effected through music), and a talent for understanding psychological and emotional problems and addressing them in consultation. As leaders of communities that can be extensive depending on the locale and on his or her reputation for wisdom, the oungan or manbo can also function as a political leader. Many oungans and manbos have been associated closely with political figures, as were the many drawn into the Duvaliers' orbit and who were persecuted and sometimes killed in the backlash that followed the overthrow of Baby Doc Duvalier.

The role of the oungan in Vodou is modeled on that of the lwa or spirit known as Loco, the chief of Legba's escort, known as "he of the trees." He governs the tree or temple center-post that serves as channel for the lwa, the divine life forces of Vodou, to enter into communion with their human serviteurs through the phenomenon of possession. Loco and his consort Ayizan are, as Maya Deren describes them in *Divine Horsemen: The Living Gods of Haiti*, the moral parents of the race, the first oungan and manbo, whose chief responsibility is that of imparting to humans the knowledge of konnesans on which the future of the race depends. They are also Vodou's first healers, as it was Loco "who discovered how to draw their properties from the trees and to make the best herbal charms against disease," and Ayizan who protects against malevolent magic (Deren 1953: 148). Together they represent the belief in Vodou that spiritual maturity rests on the understanding of the necessary balance between cosmic forces and the natural world.[2]

One of the oungan or manbo's chief responsibilities in their service to the lwa is the care and training of the ounsi. They, in turn, are known for their zeal in service and devotion to the oungan or manbo. The ounsi's chief task is devotion to the lwa, which takes the form of dancing for hours during ceremonies, maintaining the *peristil* (or peristyle), a shed or covered area where dances and ceremonies are held, cooking the food to be offered to the lwa, caring for and preparing the sacred objects needed for ritual, and above all, being possessed by the spirits. The most devoted and zealous of the ounsi assumes the role of *hungenikon* (*reine-chanterelle* or mistress of the choir) and is in charge of the liturgical singing and of the shaking of the chacha rattle, which controls the rhythm and flow of the singing. She (ounsis can be male, but are predominantly female) identifies the lwa as they appear during ceremonies. She is aided in her work by the *hungenikon-la-place* (the *commandant general de la place* or quarter master), the master or mistress of ceremonies. He leads the procession of congregants, is in charge of the offerings, and keeps order during the ceremonies. The confidant (*le confiance*) is the ounsi who takes care of the administrative function of the ounfo.

In Vodou, most communal activities center around the temple, a religious center that looks like a house or compound shared by an extended family. Its size and décor reflect the resources of the oungan and manbo and can range from a very small and humble shack to quite lavish establishments (the latter more often to be found in Port au Prince than in rural areas). The ounfo is divided into a ceremonial space called the peristil, and adjacent altar rooms or sanctuaries that are used for private healings and devotions. Haitians usually refer to the entire temple as ounfo, though some reserve that word for the private sanctuaries. Ceremonies in the peristil move to the rhythm of the drum, perhaps the most sacred of all objects associated with the practice of

Vodou, for they speak with a divine voice and summon the lwa to join the ceremony. The roof of the peristil, thatched or covered with corrugated iron, is supported by brilliantly painted posts, at the center of which is the central pillar, the *poto mitan* (or *poteau mitan*). It serves as a pivot during ritual dances and acts as the "passage of the spirits" into the temple, where they may mount their "horses."

Around the post, offerings are made in the form of animal sacrifices and elaborate cornmeal drawings called *vèvè*. The adjacent rooms, or chambers of the gods, include the sanctuary or *caye-mystéres* (also known as the *bagi, badji,* or *sobadji*), where various stonework altars (or *pè*) stand against the wall or arranged in tiers:

> A *bagi* is a veritable junk shop: jars and jugs belonging to the spirits and the dead, platters sacred to twins, carrying-pots belonging to the *hunsi*, "thunder stones" or stones swimming in oil belonging to the *loa*, playing cards, rattles, holy emblems beside bottles of wine and liqueur—all for the gods. Amid the jumble one or more lamps may cast a feeble light, the sword of Ogu is driven into the earth and near it, in some *hunfo*, you see *assein*, the curious iron supports which may still be bought in the market of Abomey. (Métraux 1972: 80)

The *bagi* is also the space that holds the clothing and objects that the possessed will need to represent the lwa who dwell in them: Zaka's bag and hat, Lasiren's combs, Legba's crutch, Baron Samedi's top hat, the clusters of necklaces worn by the ounsi. Many pès contain a sink, which is sacred to the serpent god, Danbala-Wedo. Most ounfos have a room, known as the *djévo*, where the future *kanzo* (or initiates) are confined during initiation. Because of its function as a center for the community, additional rooms are set aside for consultations for those seeking medical help, personal counseling, or other forms of advice.

The Lwa

The spirits and the people that are at the center of the Vodou ounfo are bound together as a spiritual community. They are bound by their belief in a distant and somewhat impersonal power, which is superior to that of the lwa but not very involved or interested in human affairs. His will and power is channeled through the lwa, the focus of most Vodou ceremonies.

The rituals through which the lwa are called upon to communicate with humans conform to one of two major rites, Rada and Petwo, which although manifestly different, share many common elements. The Rada rite can be traced back to the kingdom of Dahomey, in what are now Nigeria, Benin, and Togo. This rite is generally considered to be the most faithful to ancient African traditions, and to many, the most genuine. The Rada spirits are invariably portrayed as *dous* (*doux* or sweet-tempered). The Rada pantheon boasts the great lwa, or *fle Ginen,* the first to be saluted in ceremonies: Atibon Legba, Marasa Dosou Dosa, Danbala and Ayida Wedo, Azaka Mede, Ogou Feray, Agwe Tawoyo, Ezili Freda Daome, Lasirenn and Labalenn, and Gede Nimbo. The Petwo rite does not lay claim to the same connection to the ancestral spirits. The Petwo spirits are recognized as Creole or Haitian-born lwa, born in the crucible of the plantation and often incorporating beliefs and ritual practices drawn from central and southwest African groups such as the Kongo and Angola—late arrivals in the New World. Whereas the Rada lwa are thought to be dous, Petwo lwas are considered to be *anme* (*amer* or bitter). They are associated with fire and said to be lwa *cho* (*lwa chaud* or hot lwa) who display forceful and violent behavior. The Petwo pantheon includes major lwa such as Met Kalfou, Simbi Andezo, Ezili Danto, and Bawon Samdi. Many of the lwa, however, exist *andezo (en deux eaux,* or in two waters *or* cosmic substances), and are served in both Rada and Petwo rituals.

Legba

The most important place in the Vodou pantheon belongs to Legba or Papa Legba, the god who "removes the barriers" and is the first lwa to be saluted during ceremonies, with the characteristic plea for the opening of the gates: *Atibô-Legba, l'uvri bayé pu mwê, agoé!* As the interpreter to the gods, Legba's permission must be asked for before any other lwa is summoned or makes an appearance, and care must be taken not to offend him, as it could result in a believer's being deprived of the protection of his or her own lwa. As the protector of the barrier separating humans from the spirits, he is also considered to be the protector of gates and fences surrounding the house, and therefore the gardian of the home or *Maît'bitasyon* (Master of the habitation). He is also master of the roads, paths, and especially of the crossroads, where offerings are often left for him. Legba is often represented as a feeble old man leaning on a crutch, dressed in rags with a pipe in his mouth and a knapsack slung over his shoulder. Ounfo and altars may display a crutch in honor of Legba. Because of this piteous appearance he is also known as Legba-pied-cassé or Legba of the Broken Foot.

This apparent fragility, however, conceals terrific strength, which is displayed during possession. Legba's "horses" are jolted as if struck by lightning and thrown to the ground, where they lie motionless. Legba's role as guardian of gates and master of the crossing between humans and the lwas has resulted in his identification with Saint Peter, keeper of the keys to heaven.

Agwé

Of all the lwa who preside over the elements, the most significant is Agwé or Agwé-taroyo, also known as Admiral Agwé. One of the primary Rada spirits, he is captain and protector of ships at sea, of all marine or aquatic life, and of fishermen. He rules the sea with his consort, Lasiren. His emblems are miniature boats with oars painted blue or green, which may be found suspended from the temple rafters, shells, small metal fish, or occasionally tridents reminiscent of the god Neptune. In the frescoes that often decorate the walls of ounfo, he is represented by steamboats with smoking funnels or warships. He may also appear in the uniform of a naval officer, with white gloves and a pith helmet, in presidential guise. Services for Agwé take place by the sea or at the edge of lakes and rivers, where his effigy (a miniature boat) is carried in a procession and loaded with his favorite drinks (often champagne) and set to float. If the boat floats to the shore it means that the offering has been refused and a new one must be made.

Occasionally members of an ounfo will hire a boat, which they will decorate with streamers, and set sail for Trois Ilets. They will play the sacred drums and dance on board until they reach their destination, at which point they will throw a white sheep into the sea as an offering to Agwé. They then depart as quickly as possible so as not to risk offending the lwa with their presence when he surfaces to seize the offering. Those possessed by Agwé have to be protected from jumping into the sea when seized by his marine nature. He is often represented by images of Saint Ulrich holding a fish.

Lasiren

Agwé's consort, Mistress Lasiren, is a mermaid. She is linked in worship and song to the whale, Labalenn, and the two are considered either to be manifestations of the same deity, or a fusion of mother and daughter. Lasiren is usually represented as a siren or mermaid, and is believed to bring good luck and wealth from the bottom of the sea. As a result, she is sometimes known as Ezili of the Waters. Like Ezili Freda or Ezili Danto, Lasiren is a seductress and those she possesses appear in the guise of a very vain young coquette. Her altar is decorated with combs, mirrors, conch shells, and bugles, and she is often represented by chromolithographs of Our Lady of Charity, the Cuban patroness (Nuestra Señora de la Caridad del Cobre).

Zaka

Zaka (or Azaka) is the patron lwa of crops, agriculture, and of those working the land. Known as the "minister of agricultures" of the world of the lwa, he is a good-natured peasant from the mountains addressed familiarly as "Papa" or "Cousin." Those possessed by Zaka during ceremonies dress in his characteristic peasant garb of straw hat, blue denim shirt and pants, cutlass slung across the back, raffia bag, and short clay pipe in his mouth. His "horses" speak in the rough manner of rustic peasants. He is offered typical peasant fare—boiled maize, *afibas* (stuffed pig intestines), and glasses of *clairin* (peasant-distilled white rum), and raw sugar. He is represented in chromolithographs through the image of Saint Isidore.

Danbala

Danbala, the patriarchal serpent divinity, is one of the most popular of the Vodou lwa. He is an ancient water spirit, linked in ritual and service to rain, lightning, wisdom, and fertility. He and his wife Ayida Wedo, the rainbow, are often represented as intertwined snakes. His vévé or ritual symbol, drawn in cornmeal near the poto mitan in preparation for ceremonies, is shown below. In many ounfos a permanent basin of water, or often a sink in the Pè, is offered to Danbala, as he is known to haunt rivers, springs, and marshes. Since his color is white (as in the case of most lwa associated with water), food offerings to him must be white (his chief sacrificial offering is an egg). Silver, as a white metal, is under his command, and he is believed to be able to grant riches or guide humans to treasure. Those possessed by Danbala during ceremonies dart out their tongues, snakelike, crawl on the ground with sinuous movements, climb trees of the posts of the peristil, and have been known to land head down from the rafters like snakes.

Danbala is often represented as Saint Patrick crushing the serpents of Ireland underfoot, and sometimes as the patriarchal Moses holding the Ten

Commandments. In another connection to Irish lore, it is believed that whoever can grasp Ayida-wedo's diadem (the rainbow) will be assured of wealth (as in the proverbial pot of gold at the end of the rainbow).

Bawon Samdi

Bawon Samdi (*Baron Samedi* or Baron Saturday) is the head of the Gede (or Ghédé) family of raucous spirits whose activities are confined to the world of the dead, whom they are said to personify. They are not the souls of the dead but mischievous, ambivalent spirits who arrive last at Vodou ceremonies and are greeted with joy because they often bring merriment and sometimes coarse, raunchy jokes. In *Tell My Horse*, Zora Neale Hurston describes Papa Guédé as "the deification of the common people of Haiti":

> The mulattoes give this spirit no food and pay it no attention at all. He belongs to the blacks and the uneducated blacks at that. He is a hilarious divinity full of the stuff of burlesque. This manifestation comes as near a social criticism of the classes by the masses in Haiti as anything in all Haiti. . . . [H]e bites with sarcasm and slashes with ridicule the class that despises him. (1990: 219–220)

Bawon Samdi is married to Grand Brigitte, mother of the Ghédé spirits. Their devotees dress in black and purple and surround themselves with graveyard imagery. They are known for wearing top hats, old funereal frock coats, mourning dresses, and black veils. They are also known for their passion for sunglasses, which they wear in acknowledgment of the fact that they belong to the world beyond the grave and find sunlight too bright. (It is said that François Duvalier exploited the common perception that he was a devotee of the Bawon by dressing in black clothing reminiscent of the Bawon and by having his personal army, the tonton macoutes, wear the dark sunglasses for which they were known, as a sign of belonging to the Ghédé.)

Devotions to Ghédé are particularly common around the Days of the Dead or the feast of All Saints (November 1) and All Souls (November 2). Those possessed by Ghédé sing a repertoire of obscene songs and dance his favorite dance, the *banda*, recognizable for the violent movement of the hips and lascivity. Many ounfo keep a large wooden phallus on the altar, used by Ghédés "horses" in their suggestive dancing.

The symbol (*vévé*) of the snake god, Damballah-wèdo

Ezili Freda

One of the most beloved of the Haitian lwa is Mistress Ezili (Erzuli) Freda, goddess of love and luxury, a flirtatious light-skinned Creole known as the personification of feminine beauty and grace. She has, as Métraux describes her, "all the characteristics of a pretty mulatto: she is coquettish, sensual, pleasure-loving, and extravagant" (1972: 110). Her *vèvè* invokes images of sensuality, luxury, and unrequited love.

The symbol (*vévé*) of the goddess Ezili-Freda-Dahomey

Every Haitian ounfo contains a room, or corner of a room, devoted to Ezili. She adores fine clothes (red and blue dresses particularly), jewels, perfumes, and lace, all of which are kept on her altar, together with the basin, towel, soap, comb, lipstick, and other articles indispensable to her toilette. Those mounted by Ezili, whether male or female, make their entrance into the peristil dressed to captivate, walking slowly, swinging hips, ogling men, or pausing for a kiss or caress. Ezili Freda's colors are white and pink, and in a rare instance of "product placement" in Haitian Vodou, her favorite brand of perfume is said to be Anaïs-Anaïs. Offerings to Ezili Freda include heavily sweetened drinks made with orange syrup or grenadine, rice cooked in cinnamon milk or bananas fried in sugar, and mild cigarettes. Ezili Freda, the dous lwa of the Rada rite of Dahomey, is unhappy in love and is often represented by the chromolithograph of the Mater Dolorosa in her familiar depiction with her heart pierced by a knife. In *Divine Horsemen,* Maya Deren describes how she herself was possessed by Ezili:

> As sometimes in dreams, so here I can observe myself, can note with plea-sure how the full hem of my white skirt plays with the rhythms, can watch, as if in a mirror, how the smile begins with the softening of lips, spreads imperceptibly into a radiance which, surely, is lovelier than any I have ever seen. It is when I turn, as if to a neighbor, to say "Look! See how lovely that is!" and see that the others are removed to a distance, withdrawn to a circle which is already watching, that I realize, like a shaft of terror struck through me, that it is no longer myself that I watch. (1953: 258–259)

Ezili Danto

The second most popular manifestation of Ezili is that of Ezili Danto, a dark-skinned, hardworking peasant woman habitually dressed in blue, red, or multicolored fabrics. Like Ezili Freda she has no husband, but has a daughter, Anaïs, to whom she is devoted. The scratches on her cheek are said to be a reminder of the bitter rivalry between the two Ezilis. Her alter ego is the knife-wielding Petwo lwa Ezili-ge-rouge (Ezili Red Eyes). Offerings to Ezili Danto include scents like Florida Water, clairin or raw rum, fried pork, and unfiltered Camels. As the more mundane, peasant incarnation of Ezili Freda as mother, she is associated, not with the Mater Dolorosa, but with madonnas with children, like Our Lady of Mount Carmel, or black madon-nas, like Mater Salvatoris.

Ogu

Ogu, a lwa from Dahomey of great importance in Cuban Santería, where he is the blacksmith of the mythical world, is in Haiti one of the warrior lwa, represented in ounfo by a saber stuck in the earth in front of the altar. He is also represented by the iron rod or *pince* stuck in a brazier, both symbolic of his ancient role as ironsmith. As a tutelary god whose worship dates back to mythical African wars and the Haitian Revolution, an "old veteran from the time of bayonets" (Métraux 1972: 108), people possessed by him dress in red dolman and French kepi, or simply in red scarves around head and arms, and wave a cutlass or machete. Their speech is that of a rough soldier, full of coarse oaths and violent imprecations. He is a great drinker of rum and is always depicted smoking a cigar.

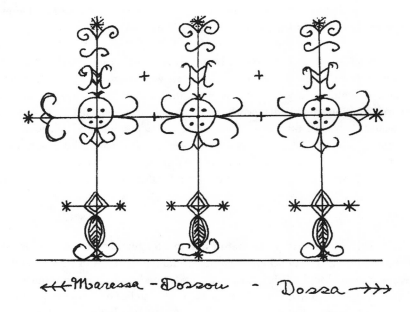

The symbol (*vévé*) of Twins (*marassa*)

Marasa Twins

In Vodou, twins are endowed with special powers and hold a privileged position in the pantheon alongside the tutelary spirits. As the Marasa, or Sacred Twins, they are invoked and greeted in ceremonies immediately after Legba. They are often depicted as three, as seen in the vévé below, because twins represent abundant life, and triplets mark exceptional fertility. They are interpreted as representing the sacredness of all children, and some of the ceremonies connected to them involve children in a special way. They rarely possess devotees, but when they do, they manifest themselves as tyrannical children who roll on the floor, whimper petulantly, walk uncertainly, and demand food. Special meals for the twins end in a rite during which the ounsi mixes the remnants of a meal in a huge calabash or wooden basin, goes around the peristil three times asking the children if they are pleased with it, and then leaves it for them. The children are expected to throw themselves at the bowl and fight for the contents.

Every "nation" of divinities has its Marasa, and as a result there are multiple manifestations of the twins in Vodou, some of them linked to the lwa Ghédé, who has special affection for children. In chromolithographs they are most commonly portrayed as the twin saints Cosmos and Damian, and with the Virtues, called the Three Egyptians. Saint Nicholas, who brought back to life the three children placed by the butcher in the salting tub, is represented as their father, Saint Claire as their mother (Métraux 1972: 146). To obtain the favor of the Marasa one must appeal to Saint Nicholas while facing the east.

Initiation

Initiation in Vodou requires great preparation as well as considerable financial sacrifice. Preparations for the ceremony assume the memorization of countless songs and elements of ritual, instruction in the characteristics and manifestations through possession of the various lwa, immense discipline (as the ceremony requires numerous hours spent motionless and some severe discomfort), and strict observance of a number of moral obligations. The ceremony involves the placing of the initiate under immediate contact and under the protection of a particular lwa, of which the *kanzo* will become the child. The kanzo, as both the ritual and the candidate are known, is both death and resurrection.

The first element of the initiation is the *kouche* (*coucher* or *huño*). It opens with the *chiré aizan* or ritualistic fraying of palm leaves that the initiates wear over their shoulders or in front of their faces. Although the ceremony varies in keeping with the preferences and practices of particular ounfo, this ceremony, sometimes replaced by the *bat ge* or *batter guerre*, literally "beating war," is meant to beat away the old, a symbolic death before the kanzos go into the retreat known as the kouche. In the kouche, the initiates enter the djèvo, where they remain for a week in a secret ritual from which they rise three days later and are presented to the community as *ounsi lave tèt*. In *Island Possessed*, Katherine Dunham offers a detailed description of her kouche as a period when the initiates are allowed only the most minimal movements and eat only unsalted sacrificial food:

> Perhaps it was the physical need for some change, if only to turn over on the dirt and bring momentary relief from the cramp of our awkward positions. Perhaps the fasting, the incessant subdued drumming, the intermittent ring of the bell and the rattle of the ason, the smell of burning char-

coal, fresh and dried blood and incense, the intoned instructions at our departing "selves" and entering "loa" were gradually effecting hounci out of bosalle. (1969: 78)

The kanzos also receive instruction on the attributes of their *mét tét* or tutelary lwa of which they will become children and to whose service they are committing themselves. It is the purpose of the uncomfortable kouche to accomplish a "head washing" or *lav tét* that will prepare the initiate's head to become a medium for the lwa. The head, which contains the two elements that comprise the soul—the *ti bònanj* or *ti bon ange* (the conscience that allows for self-reflection and self-criticism) and the *gwo bònanj* or *gros bon ange* (the psyche, source of memory, intelligence, and personhood)—must be prepared so that the gros bon ange can be separated from the initiate to allow the spirit to enter in its place. This part of the initiation process also involves the preparation of the *pot tèts,* as containers for the new selves, repositories for ingredients symbolic of the new union of spirit and human being: hair, sacrificial food, herbs, and oils. When the initiates join the community for their presentation as ounsis, they walk with these pots balanced on their heads and place them in the altar, as symbol of their entering the community as initiated ounsi. Their initiation is accomplished through their first experience of possession.

Music, Dance, and Possession

Vodou is first and foremost a dance, "a system of movements which brings people and lwa together in a progressive mutual relationship of knowledge and growth" (Murphy 1994: 17). Such knowledge is gathered during the process of initiation, but manifests itself most clearly in the communion of human and lwa achieved through possession. Possession may be a sign of the individual's call to initiation, since initiation regularizes the connection between lwa and devotee, affording protection and connection to the world of the spirits. Possession, an important dimension of Vodou worship, is among the least understood aspects of the religion.

Early observers of the possession trance, such as Moreau de St. Méry, saw the Vodou dance as an element of backwardness and savagery:

Faintings and raptures take over some of them, and a sort of fury some of the others, but for all there is a nervous trembling which they cannot master. They spin around ceaselessly. And there are some in this species of bacchanal who tear their clothing and even bite their flesh. (1958: 58)

Possession is, nonetheless, the most vital manifestation of the reciprocity that marks the relationship between Vodou devotees and the spirits that guide them. The *crise de lwa*, the mystic trance of possession, when the lwa communicate with their children by incarnating themselves in one of them, is the most fundamental element in the practice of Vodou. As Joan Dayan writes:

> The language of possession, or the *crise de loa*—that moment when the god inhabits the head of his or her servitor—articulates the reciprocal abiding of human and god. The "horse" is said to be mounted and ridden by the god. The event is not a matter of domination, but a kind of double movement of attenuation and expansion. For make no mistake about it, the loa cannot appear in epiphany, cannot be made manifest on earth without the person who becomes the temporary receptacle or mount. And the possessed gives herself up to become an instrument in a social and collective drama. (1997: 19)

This surrender of the "horse" to the lwa is induced by the rhythms of the sacred Vodou drums. Drums are the most sacred objects in the Vodou rites, so important that "beating the drum" has come to mean "celebrating the cult of the loa"—and the drummers are the lynchpins of the Vodou ceremony (Métraux 1972: 177). As they must have command of all the rhythmic combinations necessary for the various liturgies, as well as of a wide-ranging repertoire of Vodou songs, their task involves a long apprenticeship. The intensity of the dancers, and the current of energy that has to surge through them if the lwa are to manifest themselves through their serviteurs during a ceremony, is directly related to the abilities of the drummers to both lead and follow the pulse of the dance. They must be able, for example, to recognize the first bar of a song chanted by the hungenikon and follow at once with the appropriate rhythm. This is all the more difficult since Vodou orchestras are polyrhythmic, and the instruments are all of a different pitch and play different, if interwoven, themes. The work of the drummers also requires enormous physical and emotional stamina, as "for nights on end they make their instruments speak with a passionate violence which at times attains frenzy" (Métraux 1972: 178).

The various "nations" of Vodou have different drumming traditions; the composition of the orchestras varies from one tradition to another. The Rada drums can be traced back to the rites of Dahomey and have shells carved out of the trunks of trees in the shape of brightly painted truncated cones.

Their heads, made out of goatskin, are stretched by means of pegs braced with cords. They are always played in groups of three and are identical in shape but different in size: the largest is the *adjunto* or *manman,* the second is aptly called the *ségond,* and the smallest is the *bula.* The manman controls the rhythm and is credited with the true power to bring down the lwa. The Petwo drums are smaller and are played in pairs, with the larger one called the manman or *gros baka* and the smaller one known as *pititt* or *ti-baka.* In Petwo, it is the smaller drum that controls the beat. The large *assoto* drum, now extremely rare, is only played on the most solemn of occasions.

In Vodou the drums are considered to be sacred objects with a special relationship to the spirit that emanates from its *nam* or vital force (sometimes referred to as its *huntó,* a spirit that is said to inhabit both the drum and the man who beats it). The making of drums is a ritual process involving various ceremonies geared to making it worthy of being the repository of the lwa. Devotees entering the peristil for a ceremony customarily bow before the drums, and offerings are made to them in a ceremony called *bay manger tambour* or the feeding of the drum.

Maya Deren refers to the drummers as virtuosos, not so much for their technical ability as for their control of what she calls the "subtle fluctuations" of the rhythms that helps open the "horse's" head and allows the spirit to enter:

> I doubt that a profoundly informed musicologist could explain how it can be that, without any change in beat, tempo, pacing, tone or volume, it is possible for the drumming to become more or less intense, although this fluctuation is unanimously recognized and can be consciously controlled by the drummer. He may observe that a loa threatens to overcome the houngan who must execute some complex ritual detail, and he can relieve the situation by making the drumming less intense. On another occasion he may, by simply maintaining that intensity, make futile a serviteur's resistance to possession. (1953: 239)

The beat of the sacred drums is invariably accompanied by song. It is the hungenikon's task to lead the singing. In her role as choirmaster she uses her ceremonial rattle and sings the first bar of a new song when the flow of the ceremony calls for it. The lyrics of Vodou songs are characterized by their simplicity and repetitive nature. As such they function more as ritualized invocations, chants to summon or welcome the spirits, as in this song to Agwé, lwa of the seas, which asks him to bring the lwas to the ceremony:

We are announcing to you, Voodoo spirits
That a ceremony is about to begin,
We are inviting all the spirits of the Ville-aux-Camps,
We are asking Agouétaroio to bring them in his boat.
Please do use Agouétaroio's boat
And do come to the temple. (Murphy 1994: 31–32)

Métraux offers an example of a song intoned while the food is being prepared:

I am making ready a meal for the Twins of Guinea
O—may they come!
I am making ready a meal, it is for the dead, agoé
I am making ready a meal, it is for the Saints.
Come eat this food
Rada, Mondongue, Don Pedro, Mussondi, Ammine
Come, come and eat this food,
Motokolo, the earth is shaking, where are you? (1972: 186–187)

Moreau de St. Méry, writing with little understanding of the religious foundation of Vodou, could not distinguish the "danse vaudoux" from the ritual for which it opened a path. What escaped him was the vital link between the drums, songs, and dance: "The ritual orientation of the initiates, the rhythm of the drums, the songs of the ounsi, work together to create a kinesthetic medium for the lwa to manifest themselves in dance" (Murphy 1994: 27). Maya Deren called the Vodou dances "meditations of the body," arguing that they should not be seen as means to secular pleasure, but dances in which the physique projects to the psyche, leading to communication with the spirit.

The dances, like the songs, are marked by their apparent simplicity. There is no ritual choreography other than the general movement of the dancers counterclockwise around the poto mitan. Although specific movements may be used to indicate a dance dedicated to a particular lwa—such as swimming gestures to indicate Agwé, the lwa of the sea—the dances have a characteristically improvised quality: "The whole art of the dance is expressed less in the play of the feet than in the shoulders and hips. It is above all in *feints* that a dancer's virtuosity is revealed" as they follow the flow of the dance to its ultimate goal, that of throwing people into a state of paroxysm propitious to 'attacks' of loa" (Métraux 1972: 190).

The crise de lwa, the descent of the lwa into its mount brought about by drumming and dance, allows the *chwal* or horse to transcend his or her materiality by becoming one with the spirit. It also allows the spirit to renew itself by drawing upon the vitality of its living serviteurs, energized and invigorated by the music, dance, and feast. Most particularly, possession allows the lwa to communicate in a concrete and substantial way with their congregation, allowing them to ask pressing questions and receive guidance and advice.

The appearance of a lwa during possession is greeted with a burst of singing and drumming. Once the lwa is recognized, his attributes are brought out or he is escorted to the sanctuary to be dressed. (Lwa, whether male or female, have no regard for gender when selecting a chwal. Male lwa like Legba will possess female serviteurs as readily as Ezili can possess a male devotee.) As the lwa returns to the peristil, he is escorted with banners and the ground is kissed before him. He must, however, also bow to the oungan and manbo, pay homage to the drums, and prostrate himself before the poto mitan. He is then expected to make the rounds of the room, making personal connections with the assembled devotees. He can dispense small favors, clasp a hand, or offer a small caress or kiss in a gesture of recognition and support, touch a devotee's clothing to bring her luck, embrace or lift those to whom he wishes to show particular favor, or dance with anyone who strikes his fancy.[3]

These behaviors will vary according to the attributes and personalities of the particular lwa. Some can be entertaining and rejoice in the company of the congregants; others can be skittish or rough. As the communication with the lwa during possession also has a healing function, he is expected to listen to the physical complaints of the devotees and offer possible cures. He must also listen to the problems of the assembled serviteurs and offer advice on jobs, careers, family disputes, love affairs, and life decisions. Some of the advice may be to his mount, who will not have any memory of the possession after the crise de lwa has concluded, and must be conveyed to the chwal after the lwa has departed.

Thus the possessed benefits least of all men from his own possession. He may even suffer for it in material loss, in the sometimes painful, always exhausted physical aftermath. And to the degree that his consciousness persists into its first moments or becomes aware of the very end, he experiences an overwhelming fear. Never have I seen the face of such anguish, ordeal and blind terror as the moment when the loa comes. All this no man would ordinarily accept. But since the collective consists of ordinary men with a normal interest in their personal welfare, it is dependent upon its ability to induce in them a moment of extra-ordinary dedication if it is to have access to the revitalizing forces that flow from the center. It is towards the achievement of this—towards the forcing open of the door to the source—that the entire structure of Voudoun is directed. The serviteur must be induced to surrender his ego, that the archetype become manifest. In the growing control accomplished by the ordeals and instructions of initiation, and in the prospective vigilance of houngan and *societé,* he is reassured that the personal price need not be unpredictable or excessive. In the principle of collective participation is the guarantee that the burden shall, in turn, be distributed and shared. (Deren 1953: 250–251)

Offerings and Divination

If possession is the central collective ritual of Vodou, as filtered through the chwal's surrender to the lwa, feeding the lwa is the individual's foremost duty, a ritual of the greatest importance for adherents. Since the lwa's function is that of organizing the physical and spiritual world into patterns of knowledge and well-being for their devotees, their labor is cosmic and their energy must be replenished. It is the devotee's responsibility to provide the wherewithal from which that energy is to flow by feeding the lwa. Consequently, the feasting of the lwa, whether performed individually at home or through communal celebrations, is the most common ceremony in Vodou. Any ceremony that involves making requests of the lwa must open with offerings of food.

The lwa's ritual meals are prepared in accordance with time-honored traditions and must follow exact recipes and rules, since the lwa are often hard to please. The choice of foods and method of preparation are often determined by the lwa's attributes and personalities. The lwa have favorite foods and drinks which must be offered to them in specific ways. Meats, tubers, and vegetables prepared for Legba, for example, must always be grilled on a fire (*boucané*). A cock sacrificed to Legba must be cut in four quarters without removing the crest or feet. Foods prepared for lwa like Danbala, Agwé, or Ezili must be white or as near white as possible. Métraux describes the menu of a *manger* offered to Ezili as consisting of "rice cooked in milk, greengage jam, cinnamon milk, fried egg, bananas fried in sugar, maize biscuits, mangoes and a glass of water" (1972: 176). The Ogu and Nago families of lwa have a preference for raw rum or clairin. The various rituals of food preparation for the lwa are part of the process of initiation, being part of the konesans needed to move up in the ounfo's hierarchy. Food is placed in special calabashes (*assiettes de Guinée*) that rest on the altars dedicated to the specific lwa.

The lwa, being spirits, are not expected to consume the food offered to them, but to draw their essential energy. The food's material substance may be consumed by the individual or congregation during or after the ritual. Therefore, food may be left in a variety of places. It can be scattered on an altar, left at a crossroads, buried, or poured into the ground as a libation.

Feeding ceremonies abound in Vodou. Simple ceremonies can be preceded by a *mange sec,* an offering of grains, fruit, and vegetables. *Ceremony-yam,* a rare ritual offered to Cousin Zaka, lwa of agriculture, involves the presentation of the first produce gathered from the fields in a plea for the lwa's protection and assurance of a good crop for the following season. In annual feasts offered by the oungan to his congregation, elaborate meals can be offered to a multiplicity of lwas involving the sacrifice of numerous chickens, several goats, a pig for the Petwo lwas, or occasionally a bull, if the congregation's funds allow. During such celebrations, in addition to the specific foods desired by particular lwa, there are also offerings of food and drink believed to possess intrinsic virtues. These sacred foods—which include grilled maize, peanuts, and cassava—are often sprinkled over animals before they are sacrificed or piled on the *vèvès* drawn on the floor.

Service

The elaborate rituals involved in the feeding of the lwa remind us that the most fundamental premise of Vodou is the notion of service. The title of serviteur borne by devotees is a constant reminder that their relationship to the lwa is one of reciprocity. The devotee who remembers to make a libation to the lwa by pouring a few drops of his morning coffee on the ground is recognizing that service to the lwa is a form of discipline which can bring its own reward. His adherence to a moral code imposes certain obligations—some of them perhaps tedious and repetitive—but assures him of the possibility of divine intervention if he is ever in need.

> That action reaffirms first principles—destiny, strength, love, life, death; it recapitulates a man's relationship to his ancestors, his history, as well as his relationship to the contemporary community; it exercises and formalizes his own integrity and personality, tightens his disciplines, confirms his morale. In sum, he emerges with a strengthened and refreshed sense of his relationship to cosmic, social and personal elements. (Deren 1953: 198).

For Haitians, both in the island and throughout the world, Vodou's tra-dition of service—and the link to the spirit world and to the past it repre-sents—provides perhaps the clearest evidence of cultural and religious con-tinuity for a people whose history of struggle against poverty and oppression has known few victories since the Haitian Revolution simpered into dictator-ship and chaos. The connection to the lwa, rooted as it is in traditions con-nected to family and the land—to the ordinary peasant's *heritage*—seems at first hand threatened by migration to the United States, Canada, and beyond. One may indeed wonder if the lwa will follow their serviteurs across the waters to new peristils away from their native land. Will they cross the waters again, as they did when they left 'Nan Guinée behind to follow their devotees to the plantations of Saint Domingue?

The answers to these questions, if we are to judge by the proliferation of Vodou centers and the syncretization of practices in major metropolitan cen-ters and small towns across the United States, is that the vitality of this life of service, the concreteness of the reciprocity of the relationship between lwa and serviteur, continues to sustain individuals, communities, and the spirits that depend on them for their survival and renovation.

Sacred Works and Haitian Art

Central to Vodou practice is the notion of sacred works, and the concomi-tant need to follow prescribed ritual in re-creating sacred forms. As Maya Deren writes, "[I]n sacred works, where the acts will not, in themselves, result in anything, but may be rewarded if they please the divinity to whom they are addressed—where, therefore, there can be said to be no direct mate-rial purpose—the form is the total statement; and its distinctive quality is that reverent dedication which man brings only to divinity" (1953: 183). In her exploration of the work of Haitian flagmaker and Vodou priest Clotaire Bazile, Anna Wexler describes the "mastery of ritual detail" that character-izes his work as both oungan and artist as a skill that allows him to translate the "intense awareness of [his sacred work's] power to heal and to destroy into tangible forms" (Wexler 1997: 69).

This "mastery of ritual detail" encapsulates the aesthetic dimension of all sacred work in Vodou and guides the re-creation of those sacred forms which, in Deren's words, encompass the "distinctive quality" of "reverent dedication which man brings only to divinity" (227). In Vodou, mastery of the ritual forms is essential to the summoning of the spirits into the pres-ence of believers, and this mastery requires strict attention to the aesthetics of worship and representation. As Wexler explains, "[T]here is an edge to acts of beauty that not only represent but activate the transforming energy of the spirits" (Wexler 1997: 69).

Early historians of Haitian art found in the aesthetic foundations of Vodou a key to understanding the development of a painting tradition closely linked to religious practice. LeGrace Benson, writing about Wilson Bigaud, underscores the importance of "Haitian history, true and invented, and Haitian religion" as inspiration for the art created by the artists of his generation, born of "pride in the establishment of a sustained independent Black country by means of a revolution assisted by the *lwas* [and] despair that the promises made to the *lwas* were still unkept" (Benson 1992: 729).

Selden Rodman, in *The Miracle of Haitian Art*, argued that the artists of the first generation of the Centre d'Art in Port-au-Prince—many of them Vodou priests or practitioners—not only drew inspiration from religious beliefs and practices, thematically as well as formally, but also built the aesthetic bases of their visual language on the forms and objects familiar to them from ritual practice. Chief among these were the vèvè or ritual drawings sketched on the temple ground with cornmeal, ash, powdered eggshells, or coffee grounds as a means to summon the lwa to join believers during ceremonies. Vèvè, as Patricia Mohammed has argued, "consecrate the ground area they cover for the *loa* they represent" (2005: 124), turning the space of ritual into a canvas for the reproduction of intricate and ephemeral ritual designs that will be erased by dancers' feet during ceremonies. The masterful re-creation of these ritual designs, critics have argued, served as an introduction to artistic creativity for many Haitian painters and constitutes "the visual progenitor of Haiti's renaissance" (Kennedy 1991: 14).

Inspiration was also drawn from two other categories of religious art available to early Haitian painters, that of the Catholic chromolithographs and church frescoes depicting incidents in the lives of the saints, and the "richly ornamented" sequined ceremonial flags—such as those produced by Clotaire Bazile—which serve as "points of entry" (Martin 1977: 24) for the lwa during ceremonies. The chromolithographs offered a visual example of "an institutionalized religion's understanding . . . and . . . conceptual meditation of the sacred'" (290). The same could be argued for the flags, simultaneously objects of great beauty and potentially of great power, which, during ceremonies, "are unfurled and danced about . . . to signal the spirits represented by the vèvè . . . or the images of corresponding Catholic saints sewn on them" to join the ritual (Wexler 1997: 59). "Their reflective brilliance," Wexler argues, "is said to attract the spirits into the human gathering, mediating between two worlds" (59).

Toussaint Auguste's Papa Zaca en Possession (Possessed by Papa Zaca).
Image courtesy of Edwidge Danticat.

The ritual function of the vèvè and the *drapo* (flags) is not an abstraction, but rather the fulfillment of a ritualistic embodiment that invites the spirits to enter the realm of the living through physical manifestations of their presence, chief among them the phenomenon of possession. The achievement of beauty through ritual, which is vital to the success of the appeal to the spirits in Vodou, hinges on the "mastery of ritual detail" that Wexler observed in Bazile's work and which is realized primarily through manifestations of the lwa through the bodies of the serviteurs. The aim is to invite the spirits—les invisibles—to embody themselves in a chosen serviteur who in turn will give the spirit a voice. Success is predicated on mastering the forms, on reaching the high level of aesthetic practice that will satisfy the requirements of the lwa.

This close relationship between the spirits and the living—established through the body as a vehicle for sacred work in Vodou—is one of the most significant themes of Haitian art, particularly in the first and second generations of the Centre d'Art. Early Haitian painters turned the centrality of sacred work in Vodou practice into one of the guiding principles (and subject matters) of a bourgeoning artistic tradition. This close link between ritual practice, faith, and art has been repeatedly articulated through representations of bodies engaged in the masterful performance of sacred work, of ritual intended to breach the divide between living beings and the word of the lwa.

Toussaint Auguste's *Papa Zaca en Possession* (Possessed by Papa Zaca, 1953) depicts most vividly the breach of the divide between the living and the lwa that is the one common goal of all sacred work in Vodou. In the painting, Auguste has turned to the lwa most closely connected to the Haitian peasantry to depict Vodou's most significant embodiment ritual within the context of Haiti's most urgent historical crisis (the severe deforestation that has rapidly destroyed the land's productivity in the small island-nation). Papa Zaca, a peasant figure traced to Amerindian culture, is recognized by his blue denim jacket and the *makout* or sissal market sack he habitually carries. Those possessed by Papa Zaca usually don his characteristic peasant straw hat and go through the motions of sowing seeds. When he appears in a ceremony, he is typically offered peasant fare—boiled maize, *afibas* (stuffed pig intestines), and glasses of clairin (peasant-distilled white rum). His vèvè incorporates the elements of his agricultural role—his makout with its decorative tassels, the scythe and machete as instruments for clearing and sowing the land, the pipe that points to his enjoyment of simple pleasures, the grid-like patterns on the makout that recall seeded fields, and the bottle of clairin.

Auguste's painting articulates with great simplicity and acute clarity the reciprocity of the relationship between serviteur and lwa that marks the phenomenon of possession—the embodiment of a lwa in the body of a serviteur that is the cornerstone of Vodou as a belief system. During possession, the possessed—the "horse"—gives his or her voice to the spirit, articulating "the reciprocal abiding of human and god" and making communication between the world of the spirits and that of humans possible (Dayan 1997: 19). The horse must surrender his or her body temporarily to the needs of the lwa, allowing, through the process, the guiding wisdom and *ashé (aché* in Cuban Santería*)* to flow from the realm of the spirits into that of their serviteurs. In *Papa Zaca en Possession*, Auguste captures this ritualized reciprocity through the mirrorlike elements that articulate the link between the two figures—the lwa and the woman he has possessed.

The importance of the "embodiment" of the horse by the lwa is underscored in *Papa Zaca en Possession* by the prominence given to the possessed woman, who occupies the geometric center of the canvas. Dressed in the

Vévé for Papa Zaka

garb of the lwa—unadorned denim dress, makout, and straw hat—she is represented following the crise de lwa, the moment when the spirit occupies her head, just as she has completed the embodiment process and is ready to speak for the lwa. The reciprocity, evident in their mirroring positions, is underscored by the matching jugs, as Papa Zaca readies to pour the contents of his jug into hers. The exchange could be of seeds, water, the clairin or local rum favored by the lwa, or of the ashé or "power in the state of pure energy," as Miguel Barnet has defined it (Barnet 1997: 82). The prominence of the makout recalls the lwa's association with abundance and magic, attributes traditionally linked to the tassel decorations on Papa Zaka's straw bag (Thompson 1995: 124).

Auguste contextualizes his representation of possession, not by placing his reciprocal figures within the ceremonial space of the ounfó or temple, but by using the backdrop of the eroded and deforested Haitian landscape as the means of emphasizing the need for Papa Zaca's intervention to help the

Haitian land recover its fertility. The leafless and truncated trees in the foreground, the stump of a tree on the lower left corner, and the denuded and deforested hills in the background, all point to Haiti's devastating ecological dilemma. In Haiti, persistent and prolonged deforestation dating back to the clearing of the land for sugar cultivation in the early eighteenth century, and continuing into the present because of the lack of ready access to cooking fuel in the countryside, has left the island severely deforested, prone to catastrophic erosion and deadly mudslides (Diamond 2005: 329–333).

It is a situation exacerbated by the devastating loss of the sustaining connection between the people and the lwa who reside in the family's plot of land or *heritage* that many have been forced to abandon because of its decreasing productivity. The environmental contextualization underscores the "total integrity of cultural form" that characterizes Vodou as religious practice (Deren 1953: 10). Possession, as illustrated by Auguste, has the ultimate goal of practical intervention in solving Haiti's environmental dilemma. The painting underscores that the ultimate goal of successful sacred forms rests in the lwa's successful intervention in the resolution of the problems plaguing the mortals who serve them.

The placement of the possessed woman at the center of his painting also allows Auguste to use the space she occupies as a liminal space between the two realms—that of the spirits, occupied by the lwa, represented here in human form, and that of the serviteurs, toward which, in her state of possession, she has temporarily turned her back. His composition, which shows a fairly symmetrical allocation of space to the three realms depicted, balances the space occupied by the lwa on the left with the space to the right occupied by four elements: a truncated, branchless tree which reminds us of the barrenness and deforestation Papa Zaca is called upon to resolve; the cemetery cross usually found in the vèvè for Bawon (Baron) Samdi (the lwa who rules over death and the cemetery and who belongs to the family of spirits known as Ghédé); a lamb, Christian symbol of sacrifice, standing here for the animal sacrifices often offered to the lwa as a gesture of placation or thanks; and a red door on a white hut, combining the colors sacred to Papa Legba, keeper of the gates that divide the spirit and material worlds.

The allusions to the Bawon and the Ghédé and to Papa Legba underscore the liminality of the space occupied by the possessed. Legba stands at a spiritual crossroads between humans and the lwa they serve; his permission is required for such interactions to occur. Ghédé, as Maya Deren argues, straddles "the great divide between the living and the dead," being "naturally, not only the lord of both, but the lord of its interaction" (Deren 1953: 112). The allusion also emphasizes the link between Ghédé (who presides over fertility rites) and Papa Zaca (whose agricultural realm Ghédé is prone to invading). They are believed to be brothers whose relationship is marked by competition and uneasy truces.

Auguste's *Papa Zaka en Possession*, through the centrality of the lwa's horse (Papa Zaca's living manifestation) in its composition, underscores how the aesthetic quality of the ritual embodiment represented (the excellence of the correspondences between lwa and serviteur, in this case) allows for the precise representation of the straddling of "the great divide between the living and the dead" that is the ritualistic goal of possession. The precision of its representation—the naïve realism through which Auguste captures the ineffable quality of the horse's temporary transformation into the lwa— eschews needless metaphor, capturing the transformation instead through the literal *embodiment* of the lwa as a human *mirrored* by his horse. Auguste's aesthetic solution to the depiction of the transformation, resting as it does on an apparently simple device—that of showing the disembodied lwa both in its imagined bodily manifestation and as embodied by its horse—moves beyond mere representation of a particular religious phenomenon for the viewer. It suggests a symbiotic convergence of ritual and art through which the artists can convey the nature of belief and practice in Vodou within a context that establishes the ultimate function of these ritual practices.

Vodou and the Haitian Diaspora

Haitian migration, which had begun in 1957 with those fleeing the regime of François Duvalier, had intensified following 1971, when Duvalier's son Jean-Claude replaced his father as "President for Life" and "emigration had become the only hope of escaping the harsh political and economic realities of Haitian society" (Glick-Schiller and Fouron 1990: 336). Initially a migration of the upper and middle classes, after 1972 it became primarily an exodus of the hungry and persecuted who came to be known as *botpippel*—the Kreyol rendering of the term used to designate the undocumented Haitian immigrants who began attempting the treacherous voyage to the United States, the Bahamas, and other points in the Caribbean around 1972. Unable to afford exit visas or airplane tickets, the "boat people"—most of them rural Haitians—ventured on the seven hundred-mile crossing, financing their dangerous undertaking with the proceeds of the sale of their land and belongings, fleeing repressive political conditions, ecological devastation, and economic stagnation at home for freedom and opportunity abroad. Of the more than 100,000 Haitian refugees who arrived illegally in Florida during the 1970s and 1980s—more than 55,000 between 1972 and 1981 alone—many attempted the treacherous sea crossing to Miami in unsafe boats, often falling into the clutches of unscrupulous smugglers, risking their lives in the hope of a better life (Arthur 1999: 180).

With them came their lwa, as the growth and development of Vodou practices in the United States over the last three decades show. Their sea passage—undergone in solidarity with their worshipers—has been chronicled by Haitian writers like Edwidge Danticat, who, in her story "Children of the Sea" (from her 1995 collection *Krik? Krak!*) anchors the botpippel's narrative in culture and religion. In Haitian Vodou, the Africans who leapt to their deaths from the slave ships rather than accept slavery are said to reside under the water; upon death one follows the ancestors down to the depths of the ocean where the lwa or spirits reside (K. McCarthy Brown 2001: 223). The young man in Danticat's story understands his experience as a refugee through the prism of Haitian history and religion: "I feel like we are sailing for Africa. Maybe we will go to Guinin, to live with the spirits, to be with everyone who has come and has died before us" (1995: 14). This "walk back to Africa" across the water becomes a powerful metaphor when considering the risks of undertaking to cross the Atlantic on a frail boat or makeshift raft. Interestingly, the phrase used to describe the space where the lwas and ancestors reside, *lòt boa*, "on the other side," is also used in common speech to refer to relatives living in America. They are only lòt boa, able to return at any time from across and below the water to their families (Arthur 1999: 205).

In art, the passage of the Haitian people and their lwa across the sea has been chronicled by numerous artists. One of the most compelling images, showing the frequent confrontation of Haitian refugees with the U.S. Coast Guard, comes from Edouard Duval-Carrié's 1996 series, *Milocan, ou La migration des esprits*. Duval-Carrié, one of the best known Haitian American artists, evokes in his work "the magic and mystery of the Vaudou universe and comments on Haiti's history and socio-political realities with sharp, surreal wit" (Poupeye 1998: 89). In this series, now at the Bass Museum, the painter/sculptor addresses the departure of the Haitian lwa or spirits to follow the botpippel to their fate at sea. One of the paintings in the series (not pictured) shows the lwa in a dinghy arriving at U.S. shores. In *Le Monde Actuel ou Erzulie Interceptée*, Erzuli (Ezili), the Vodou spirit of sensuality and love, descends in tears from a Coast Guard ship, the stark steel and immutable expressions of the Guards contrasting with her coquettish Creole dress with its diaphanous sleeves and her bejeweled fingers. Tucked in the sash of her dress is the small figure of a refugee, symbolizing the failure to guide and protect, that explains her tears. The dagger piercing her halo recalls Cupid's love arrows (symbol of her powers to confer and withdraw love) but also the wounds inflicted on the Haitian people by the botpippel tragedy. The painting's composition, which places Erzulie in the very center of the canvas, uses the angularity of the boat's gangplank and the steely demeanor of the flanking guards to underscore the thematic contrast between the lwa's distress and the soldiers' (and, by definition, the American nation's) indifference to her and her people's anguish.

Erzulie's distressed arrival in the United States is countered by the growth of Vodou practice in major cities around the country. Major ounfo are to be found in cities like Miami, New York, Washington, and Boston, among others, and skilled oungan have brought their knowledge and skill to bear on their immigrant populations. In the Diaspora, moreover, the scope of participation has broadened, as non-Haitians (particularly African Americans and other immigrants from the Caribbean region) have begun to gravitate to oungan seeking solutions to their problems and alternative healing systems or as Vodou practices have begun to syncretize with other practices (Santería and Espiritismo among them) whose practitioners often recognize the greater power and closer connection to Africa of the Vodou lwa (see, for example, the work of Karen McCarthy Brown, Elizabeth McAlister, and Karen Richman).

Magic and Sorcery

The practice of magic and sorcery is peripheral to Haitian Vodou, so much so that practitioners often speak of it being the province only of oungans known as *bokor* who *sert des deux mains* (serve with both hands), those who in addition to their priestly functions in Vodou, also work with *lwa acheté* or "bought lwa." Many of the practices of sorcery and magic are linked with Petwo rites and are similar to those of Obeah, as described in chapter 5.

One of the most feared practices of sorcery in Haiti is the *envoi morts* or *expeditions,* the setting of dead people against someone, which is believed to lead to a sudden illness during which the victim grows thin, spits blood, and soon dies. (The practice is akin to that of setting a *duppy* on a person in Obeah.) The effects of this spell can be counteracted only by the quick actions of another oungan, and only through a complicated form of exorcism that includes invocations to protective lwa, massages, and baths. Evil effects

Edouard Duval-Carrié, Le Monde Actuel ou Erzulie Interceptée, 1996. Oil on canvas in artist's frame, 95 1/16 x 64 15/16 inches. Collection Bass Museum of Art, Miami Beach Gift of Sanford A. Rubenstein. Courtesy Bass Museum of Art.

and illness can also result from the use of *wanga,* a term used in Haiti for any object imbued with magical properties as a result of sorcery (of having been arranged or *rangé*) and are thus capable of inflicting harm or transforming situations. Poisoned powders prepared in small packets, mixed with other substances, which may include the hair or nails of the intended victim, are considered to be powerful forms of wanga. The effects of harmful wanga can be counteracted by the timely intervention of another oungan.

There are a number of superstitions in Haiti commonly associated with Vodou, but whose connection with the Vodou liturgy is tangential at best. They do not involve the intervention of the oungan, unless a Vodou priest is sought to provide protection or counteract their effects. These include a belief in the possibility of making deals with the devil or *diab* to forfeit one's soul after a specified term in return for prosperity (known as acquiring a "hot point"). *Zobops,* members of secret societies believed to roam the countryside at night, seeking victims for dark saturnalia, are believed to possess the *point loup-garou* or "werewolf point," which confers on them the power to transform into animals, most likely werewolves who go on night excursions seeking victims for their cannibalistic meals. These practices and superstitions, which as noted are only tangentially related to Vodou beliefs and religious practices, are conjured up by detractors of Vodou to prove the primitive and ignorant nature of this religious practice. Like the "voodoo dolls" of Hollywood films, or the figure of the zombie discussed below, they are often made to substitute for the complex liturgy and practice of true Vodou.

The Secret Societies and Zombification

Zombies are one of the most misunderstood phenomena linked to the practice of Vodou in Haiti. Transformed by the popularity of the worldwide Hollywood horror film into a titillating version of the Caribbean bogeyman, zombies have become one of the most sensationalized aspects of Haitian religiosity.

The popular conception of a zombie is that of a dead person's disembodied soul, captured and controlled by a sorcerer, or an actual corpse raised from the grave by mysterious means and used to work in the fields as a sort of automaton without any willpower. The reality is at once more simple and infinitely more complex.

African American novelist and anthropologist Zora Neale Hurston, in her book on Haitian Vodou, *Tell My Horse,* acknowledges the existence of zombies: in Haiti, she writes, "there is the quick, the dead, and then there are zombies," "the word which never fails to interest tourists" (1990: 179).

Katherine Dunham, the American dancer and Vodou initiate who made her home in Haiti for a number of years, describes zombies as either a truly dead creature brought back to life by black magic, "but by such a process that memory and will are gone and the resultant being is entirely subject to the will of the sorcerer who resuscitated him, in the service of good or evil"; or, what is "most likely," some person given a potion of herbs brought from 'Nan Guinée by a *bokor* (or sorcerer) who "falls into a coma resembling death in every pathological sense" and is later disinterred by the bokor, who administers an antidote and takes command of the traumatized victim (1969: 184). Zombies, Alfred Métraux argues, can be recognized "by their vague look, their dull almost glazed eyes, and above all by the nasality of their voice, a trait also characteristic of the 'Guédé,' the spirits of the dead. . . . The zombi remains in that grey area separating life and death" (1972: 250–251).

The phenomenon of zombification, long believed to be solely the result of sorcery and black magic, was demystified through anthropologist Wade Davis's research into the ethnobiology and pharmacopeia behind the zombification process. In his two books on the subject, *The Serpent and the Rainbow* (1985) and *Passage of Darkness* (1988), Davis has explained how, under very rare circumstances, the zombie poison (the formula for which appears in *Passage of Darkness*) can be administered to an individual, making him or her appear dead, leading consequently to the person being buried. Disinterred shortly thereafter by the bokor, who delivers an antidote, the traumatized victim remains under the control of his or her victimizer. Davis contends that zombification is far from being the result of arbitrary sorcery performed by the bokor for his own personal gain. It is instead a "social sanction" administered by the Bizango, a secret Vodou society, to those who have violated its codes. The Bizango function as "an important arbiter of social life among the peasantry," a force "that protects community resources, particularly land, as they define the power boundaries of the village" (1988: 8–10).

The Bizango, as Michel Laguerre explains in *Voodoo and Politics in Haiti*, is a remnant of Haiti's colonial past, when Bizango, the violent spirit of a warrior, functioned as the protective spirit of the Bissagot slaves. Individuals enter such secret societies—which are widespread throughout the island—through a ritual of rebirth or initiation that involves an oath of allegiance to the group, and by sharing secret handshakes and passwords. The society stands "as the conscience of certain districts in Haiti in that it protects the residents against exploitation by outsiders" (1989: 81).

Sorcery and poison have long been the Bizango's traditional weapons. Disclosure by Western researchers of the secret formula and of the local institutions in whose service it is administered has done very little to dispel the belief in Haiti that anyone whose death is the result of black magic may be claimed as a zombie. Zombification continues to be perceived as a magical process by which the sorcerer seizes the victim's *ti bon ange*—the component of the soul where personality, character, and volition reside—leaving behind an empty vessel subject to the commands of the bokor. It has done even less to allay the dread induced by the prospect of zombification. The various Western horror genres have made of the zombie a terrorizing, murdering creature.

Haitians will shun zombies, but they do not fear them. They may, however, live in fear of being zombified themselves. Katherine Dunham, in *Island Possessed,* tells of how she stubbornly insisted on an expedition to visit a bokor reputed to have seven zombie wives while a frantic hotel housekeeper tearfully urged her to reconsider. She catalogued for Dunham the dangers to which she was exposing herself: "Surely Mademoiselle would be made into a zombie wife or, worse still, sacrificed to one of the bloodthirsty gods and eaten by the priest and his chief hounci, all of whom were men. Some part of me would be left unsalted for the zombie wives, perhaps not even cooked" (1987: 184–185).

Death in Haiti, Maximilien Laroche has written, takes on "a menacing form in the character of the zombi[e]. . . the legendary, mythic symbol of alienation . . . the image of a fearful destiny . . . which is at once collective and individual" (1976: 47). The disastrous fate conjured up by the notion of the zombie is symbolic of the Haitian experience of slavery, of the separation of man from his will, his reduction to a beast of burden at the will of a master. Haitian writers and scholars stress this connection when the subject of zombies is raised. It is, in fact, at the core of many theories of Haiti's sociohistoric development. "It is not by chance that there exists in Haiti the myth of the zombi[e], that is, of the living-dead, the man whose mind and soul have been stolen and who has been left only the ability to work," Haitian novelist René Depestre has argued. "The history of colonisation is the process of man's general zombification. It is also the quest for a revitalising salt capable of restoring to man the use of his imagination and his culture" (1971: 20).

Vodou and the Pannkotis

"Gòn gè de relijyon annayiti" ("There's a war of religions in Haiti"), Melvin Butler writes in his study of the relationship between Pentecostalism, Catholicism, and Vodou in Haiti. In recent decades, as evangelical Christianity (Pentecostalism among other churches) has made deep inroads in Haiti,

there has been growing anxiety among former Vodou practitioners about their need to renounce Vodou practices that were never seen as incompatible with Catholicism but cannot be reconciled with these new forms of Christian worship. Leslie Demangles, in *The Faces of the Gods: Vodou and Roman Catholicism in Haiti*, describes how, although the "two belief systems differ on the surface, these differences do not prevent [Haitians] from practicing both religions simultaneously with no attempt to resolve whatever paradoxes may exist between them. Religiously, they venerate the saints of the church and the Vodou lwas simultaneously" (1992: 5).

The growing conversions to Pentecostalism have made the religious terrain of Haiti a more complex and problematic space while threatening the richness of the material culture associated with Vodou practice (Vodou flags, ritual sculpture, and sacred drums, among other items) which must often be destroyed as proof of true conversion. For *Pannkotis* (Pentecostal), Butler writes, this type of "cultural collision—an unwanted rendezvous between Vodou belief and biblical doctrine"—is the source of profound anxieties, as the lwa "must either be dismissed as the imaginary product of superstition or be relegated to a strict moral dichotomy with no obvious neutral ground" (2008: xx). As early as the 1970s, Frederick Conway, in "Pentecostalism in the Context of Haitian Religion and Health Practice," had documented how for many Haitians, conversion to Protestantism, with its concomitant abandonment of "backward" Vodou practices, was a sign that "the country is becoming more and more civilized," since embracing Protestantism was in and of itself a contribution to progress and development (Conway 1978: 172). Since then, scholars like Karen Richman have recorded a growing trend toward "the masses' abandonment of their peasant religion and identification as Protestants" (Richman 2008: 8). Butler, in his turn, argues that ultimately, despite Pentecostal pastors' vigilance in safeguarding the ritual boundaries between evangelical Christianity and Vodou, the lwa "occupy a space within Haiti's cultural sphere of practice" from which they may be impossible to dislodge.

Obeah, Myal, and Quimbois

Obeah

Obeah—a set of hybrid or creolized beliefs dependent on ritual invocation, fetishes, and charms—incorporates two very distinct categories of practice. The first involves "the casting of spells for various purposes, both good and evil: protecting oneself, property, family, or loved ones; harming real or perceived enemies; and bringing fortune in love, employment, personal or business pursuits" (Frye 1997: 198). The second incorporates traditional African-derived healing practices based on the application of considerable knowledge of herbal and animal medicinal properties. Obeah, thus conceived, is not a religion so much as a system of beliefs rooted in Creole notions of spirituality which acknowledges the existence and power of the supernatural world and incorporates into its practices witchcraft, sorcery, magic, spells, and healing (Frye 1997: 198). In the contemporary West Indies, the term has come to signify any African-derived practice with religious elements, and despite continued criminalization, has come to represent a meaningful and rich element in the Caribbean's ancestral cultural heritage that needs to be nurtured and preserved.

The etymology of the word has been traced to the Ashanti terms *Obayifo* or *obeye,* meaning, respectively, wizard or witch, or the spiritual beings that inhabit witches. The term was creolized in the Caribbean over the years as *Obeah, obi,* or *obia.* The Ashanti and kindred tribes, Tshi-speaking people brought to the Caribbean from the Gold Coast of Africa, formed the largest group of slaves in the British colonies. Considered to be too disposed to rebel—"more prompted to revenge and murder the instruments of their slavery" (McCartney 1976: 18)—they were shunned by planters in the French and Spanish colonies, who drew their chief supply from the Ewe-speaking slaves, exported from Whydah and Badogy (Ellis 1891: 651). Consequently, the Ashanti-derived practices known as Obeah are practiced primarily in the former British colonies of the West Indies, with the related practice of Quimbois prevalent in the neighboring French islands of Guadeloupe and Martinique. In recent decades, because of widespread migration of West Indians to metropolitan centers like New York, London, Toronto, and Miami (among others), Obeah practices have come into contact with other Caribbean belief systems like Vodou, Santería, and Espiritismo, contributing to the richness of healing and spiritual offerings available in the Diaspora.

Obeah practices had been identified in the British islands of the Caribbean—the Bahamas, Antigua, Barbados, Jamaica, and the colony of Surinam—as early as the seventeenth century, when the colonies became the first in the region to establish slave-dependent sugar plantations. Obeah, as a set of secret rituals intended to bring about desired effects or actions and promote healing, is thought to have provided the slave population with at least an illusion of autonomy as well as a familiar method of access to the world of the spirits, a measure of social control and medical care. According to Orlando Patterson, it was also used by the slaves as a system of intergroup justice in "preventing, detecting and punishing crimes among the slaves" (Patterson 1967: 190).

The practice of Obeah, seen by British colonial authorities as a threat to the stability of the plantation and the health of colonial institutions, was criminalized early in the history of the Caribbean plantation. The British perceived it as one of the few means of retribution open to the slave population and quickly set in motion a number of ultimately ineffective deterrents. Joseph Williams, in his study *Voodoos and Obeahs,* cites laws against the use of poisons (1684), the beating of drums, and the congregation of slaves for feasts (1699), and the beating of drums, horns, gourds, and boards (1717), all linked to religious practices focusing on building communities (1932: 159–161). In 1787, for example, the laws governing the slaves included a clause stating, "Any slave who shall pretend to any supernatural power, in order to affect the health or lives of others, or promote the purposes of rebellion shall upon conviction thereof suffer death, or such other punishment as the Court shall think proper to direct" (J. Campbell 1976: 39). Moreover, Obeahmen, as practitioners of Obeah are known, were seen as potential leaders who could use their influence over the slaves to incite them to rebellion, as had been the case in the Jamaican rebellion of 1760. "The influence of the Professors of that art," wrote the authors of the *Report of the Lord of the Committee of the Council Appointed for All Matters Relating to Trade and Foreign Plantations,* "was such as to induce many to enter into that rebellion on the assurance that they were invulnerable, and to render them so, the Obeah man gave them a powder with which to rub themselves." Tacky, the leader of the rebellion, claimed he had been "an African chief and that he had obtained the assistance of the obeah-man in battle. Tacky himself was invested with the power of catching any shots which were fired at him and of returning them to his opponent" (Morrish 1982: 41). Albert Edwards, in his study of Maroon warfare, writes of the persistence of the connection between Obeah and preparation for battle in the West Indies, citing ethnographic evidence focused on the incorporation of "music, dance and libations" traditionally associated with Obeah practices in Maroon warfare:

> The drums, which were used in the dance, were ideal for focusing one's attention on the task at hand. During the ceremony instructions could be easily passed on to persons preparing for battle. . . . The priest/priestess was no doubt a central part of the Maroon community. It was their role to justify to the fighters the reason and importance of the struggle they were waging. It was in the priest or priestess that the community looked for inspiration and morale building. (1994: 158–159)

From the Obeahmen, slaves had learned the usefulness of poison (particularly that of the manchenil tree) to bring about death of a broad variety of injuries and illnesses, the use of slivers of glass or ground glass in the master's food or drink, and the production of fetishes for luck and protection. William Cartwright describes how in the "slave era many slave masters were afflicted with incurable sores, and many died, as a result of deadly potions sprinkled in 'Massa's clothing or stirred into his food'" (Hedrick and Stephens 1977: 10). Richard Hart cites the following testimony regarding the link between Obeah and rebellion in the early history of the British colonies in the West Indies:

> Confirmation of the fact that the conspirators had received some guns was, however, provided by one of the last of their number to be arrested. This man answered to the name of Jack[,] and Corberand described him as "a Guinea negro" who "understood how to do everything and knew every sort of bush." He was accused, in addition to the charge of conspiracy, of practising [sic] obeah and using his pretended supernatural powers to bolster the courage of his fellow conspirators. He did this, it was alleged: "by rubbing the said Negroes and certain Slaves with certain Bushes at the same time saying that such rubbing . . . would give them Strength and cause them to be invulnerable." (1985: 236)

As the result of these perceived and actual threats, and the legal sanctions that followed, Obeah practices that had been part of community religious rituals incorporating song, dance, and offerings to the spirits (usually through animal sacrifice), went underground. Obeah, as a result, differs from Vodou and Santería in lacking the established liturgy and community rituals that mark the latter as recognized organized religions, although certain communities in Jamaica and Trinidad and Tobago are working on the recovery of communal practices in Obeah and practices in some islands demonstrate aspects of Afro-Caribbean community-based religiosity (veneration of the ancestors, spirit possession, animal sacrifice, and divination). The loss of the "codified, institutionalized, and consistent" elements of institutionalized religion, Diana Paton has argued, relegated Obeah to the proscribed realm of "witchcraft, magic, superstition and charlatanism," leaving it on the wrong side of the line separating "supposedly 'civilized' peoples (who practice religion) and 'primitive' peoples (who practice superstition or magic)" and thereby "blocking a key potential argument for the decriminalization of obeah on the basis of freedom of religion" (Paton 2009: 2–3).

As a result of the widespread criminalization of practices associated with it, Obeah—a protean term that encompasses a rich tradition of practices that vary regionally—has become synonymous with "iniquity," as Kenneth Bilby has argued. Its vilification has "formed an important part of the armament" organized religion has deployed "in the long struggle they waged against the understandings of the cosmos that Africans brought with them to the Caribbean" (Bilby 2008: 10). Despite efforts since the 1980s to decriminalize Obeah across the region, it remains illegal in most Caribbean territories, although enforcement is lax and the practices are tolerated unless the practitioners infringe other laws in the process. Most of the prosecutions against Obeah practitioners, as Claudette Anderson has demonstrated in her research on Obeah and the law in Jamaica,[1] center on accusations of charlatanism brought against individuals who have promised specific results in return for large fees and have not delivered on such promises. The movement to decriminalize Obeah has also run into opposition from Rastafarians across the region, since the Brethren strongly disapprove of Obeah practitioners, whom they associate with Babylon.

Unlike Haitian Vodou and Cuba's Regla de Ocha, Obeah is not generally centered around a community of deities or spirits who manifest themselves among humans through possession or divination or who protect their "children" in return for offerings, sacrifices, and other forms of devotion. It is, instead, a remarkably heterogeneous and protean grouping of African-derived practice that has benefitted from the circulation of people and ideas across the Caribbean region. As Lara Putnam has explained it:

> The centuries-long coexistence and cross-fertilization in the Greater Caribbean of multiple traditions of supernatural manipulation—including but not limited to those of western Africa and medieval Europe—in conjunction with the frequent similarities of symbolic logic in magical systems of utterly disparate origin, and combined with Caribbeans' ongoing engagement with North American and European commercial products offering knowledge and healing (from patent medicines to tarot cards), meant that magical practice could serve as a *lingua franca* in a region constantly on the move. (Putnam 2008: 13)

This heterogeneity and movement, however, has also meant that the practice of Obeah has flourished as one focused on individual practitioners who operate through consultations taking place on a one-on-one basis, the secrecy made historically necessary by the legal persecution to which they have been subjected. Since the practice of Obeah is limited to individual consultation, calculating the extent of the Obeahmen's client base is difficult. Practitioners are numerous across the Caribbean, the United States, England, and Canada, many of them working out of storefront consultation rooms in urban settings or discreetly out of their houses. In islands like Trinidad and Tobago, Obeahmen and women regularly advertise in the classified columns of newspapers like the *Trinidad Express*, where we can find numerous ads touting the talents and accomplishments of a variety of practitioners: "Lovers need uniting? Call Madame Theresa. Want to pass that exam? Prof Ali for immediate results. Sickness? Court cases? Casting out evil spirits? There is a St Flemin Healing School" (Kissoon 2009).

Practitioners of Obeah, who can be either male or female, are known principally as Obeah man or woman, or Myal man or woman. Other appellations across the Caribbean region include Bush man or Bush doctor in the Bahamas, Wanga man in Trinidad, the Scientists in Grenada, Professor, Madame, Pundit, Maraj, and work-man in Guyana. Generally, an Obeahman is believed to have the power "to propitiate or deceive strong spirits, and by his own secret knowledge and experience is able to make weak ones do his bidding. He also by certain rites and magical arts professes to have control over persons and things so that he is able to bring about what he wishes or engages to do" (Udal 1915: 282). Practitioners are believed to be born with special powers—to be "born with the gift"—normally revealed to them through visions or dreams in late childhood or early adolescence. Obeah powers are also believed to pass from one family member to another—most commonly from parent to elder child—as a family heritage. Some Obeahmen may acquire their powers through conversion, as a result of a radical change in beliefs or lifestyle or in response to a traumatic event. Maarit Forde, in her work on "The Moral Economy of Rituals in Early 20th Century Trinidad," describes how Mother Cleorita, a Trinidadian healer she worked closely with, "received her gift of healing during the prolonged rite of passage of *mourning*":

> Travelling in the Spiritual world, Mother Cleorita found herself walking down a road. Soon she saw two cobra snakes dancing in front of her, beckoning her to follow. Despite her fear she forced herself to follow the cobras down a long set of stairs into a cave. There she encountered a man, who told her he had been trying to call her for a long, long time. He led her into a room, where she saw a skeleton lying on a table. It was disjointing itself, pulling off bones joint by joint, all the way from one hand to the other, until it was completely shattered. Then it put the bones back to their places, deliberately, one by one. Once complete again, the skeleton greeted Mother Cleorita and said that it was her turn now! She had no choice but to try and disjoint the skeleton. Horrified, she managed to pull out the first finger with shaking hands, then the next one and so on, going all the way through. She then assembled the bones in the correct order. The man then led her to another place where a woman was about to give birth, and Mother Cleorita had to help to deliver the baby. After these lessons she found her way to the Zion Hospital, where she met the famous Chinese doctor, Dr. Lee. Dr. Lee told the exhausted Mother Cleorita that she was now qualified as a doctor herself and gave her a name tag and a chart; she also got a lilac dress. Her name on the tag was Dr. Su Ling. For forty years now she has been practicing her skills as a healer, including fixing dislocated ankles or knees just like the skeleton taught her. (Forde 2008: 14–15)

Once the powers are acknowledged, the youth is apprenticed to a seasoned practitioner whose role it is to teach him the specifics of herb knowledge and potion making, since Obeahmen are primarily skilled herbalists. Folk tradition speaks of a year of apprenticeship in the solitude of the forest—a version of apprenticeship with roots in African traditions and popular in Caribbean fiction. But in practice an apprenticeship can last as long as five to six years:

It is said that the whirlwind aja used to carry men away with it into the bush for one year or more. During this period the man thus carried away is fed and taught the art of making ju ju and prescriptions of various kinds by a supernatural being. When the man is discharged, he finds himself in his quarters without knowing where he has been and how he managed to get back to his quarters. Such a man is held in awe and respected, and is given a high title among the Olonasins (ju ju men), but such a case is very rare. (Ajisafe 1946: 42–43)

Modern-day prospective Obeahmen follow apprenticeships that differ little from traditional practices, as the experience of Nigel David Cobb, a young Jamaican training under a senior Obeahman in Balcarres, Portland, shows. Cobb, who began his five-year apprenticeship in 2004, "got a calling to seek the high physician" and explains that "The Lord sent me into the hills, He who has a clean hand and a pure heart" (Luton 2009). He has trained with a bush doctor known as "Mr. Murray," with whom he has learned enough in five years to consider starting to practice on his own: "Five years ago, before mi come here, mi neva believe inna it (obeah), but I have seen his work and I know that he is a high physician" (Luton 2009). On an average day, he explains, he "registers up to 25 clients" and "spends his days learning to read, bathe and cure persons around whose 'neck trouble hangs like an albatross'"; young and old come every day "in droves for deliverance at his 'teacher' and mentor's practice" (Luton 2009). For Cobb, his work as an Obeahman is not incompatible with his Christian faith, as from his point of view, "the *Bible* says seek the high physician and you have to find the highest knowledge," Cobb relates. "A lot of people do it (indulge in Obeah) because it can give them benefits in life, which is true. But some people do it for money. I want to use it to help people and to know more about the natural mystic of God's work" (Luton 2009).

Although there are no age limits placed on practitioners, older Obeahmen, perceived to have greater knowledge and experience, are usually more highly regarded than younger ones. As in the case of "Mr. Murray," one of their main roles is the transmission of their knowledge to a new generation. Sometimes the degree of trust in a practitioner is linked to his/her having a physical disability—an impediment such as a blind eye, club foot, or deformed hand—in the belief that nature has compensated the Obeahman for the physical disability with a higher degree of psychic ability. As a rule, Obeahmen do not wear any distinctive clothing or other marks of their trade, although in the past, particularly in the period immediately preceding and following slavery, Myalmen (closely identified with Obeahmen in Jamaica) were often portrayed as wearing waist belts from which hung a variety of knives, shears, and other weapons and instruments. Hart cites a description of an "obeah woman":

> Thicknesse described Quao's obeah woman as an "old Hagg" wearing "a girdle round her waste which (I speak within compass) nine or ten different knives hanging in sheaths to it. (1985: 113)

Obeah Healing and Protection

Accounts of Obeah practitioners, most of them by white visitors to the Caribbean in the nineteenth and early twentieth centuries, have emphasized the menacing nature of the practice and practitioners. Charles Rampini, in his *Letters from Jamaica* (1903), asserts that there is "something indescribably sinister about the appearance of an obeah man" (1983: 213), while Bessie Pullen-Burry, writing in 1903, describes Obeahmen as "generally a most forbidding-looking person, craftiness and cunning being stamped on his features" (1903: 31). Nineteenth-century descriptions of Obeahmen also point to the consistency of the practitioner's role through the years. Fowles, traveling through the Bahamas in the latter part of the century, speaks of Obeahmen as a "species of African magicians, who, for a trifling consideration, will bewitch your enemies and charm your friends, so that any one stealing from them will be punished by supernatural agency without the intervention of the policeman or the magistrate" (1999: 238). Bessie Pullen-Burry, in her *Jamaica As It Is, 1903*, describes the Obeahman's functions thus:

> He pretends to a medicinal knowledge of plants, and undoubtedly is well versed in the action of subtle poisons; his trade is to impose upon his simple compatriot. The negro consults him in case of illness, as well as to call down revenge upon his enemies for injuries sustained. . . . They always "set obi" at midnight. In the morning the stoutest-hearted negro gives himself up for lost when he sees the well-known, but much dreaded insignia of the Obeah man upon his doorstep, or under the thatch of his roof. This generally consists of a bottle with turkeys' or cocks' feathers stuck in it, with an accompaniment of parrots' beaks, drops of blood, coffin nails, and empty egg-shells. . . . The dread of supernatural evil, which he is powerless to combat, acts upon what nervous system he possesses, so that sleep

becomes an impossibility, his appetite fails him, his light-heartedness disappears as the ever-growing fear possesses his imagination more and more, and he generally dies. (1903: 135)

Hesketh Bell, a colonial official and later Governor of Dominica, in his *Obeah and Witchcraft in the West Indies* (1893), the first comprehensive study of West Indian Obeah available, describes an Obeahman's hut in some detail, pointing with particular interest to the paraphernalia of the practice:

The dirty little room was littered with the Obeah man's stock in trade. A number of vials containing some sort of unholy liquor were lying ready to be handed over to some foolish negro in exchange for their weight in silver. In every corner were found the implements of his trade, rags, feathers, bones of cat, parrots' beaks, dogs' teeth, broken bottles, grave dirt, rum and egg shells. Examining further, we found under the bed a large conarie or earthen jar containing an immense number of round balls of earth or clay of various dimensions, large and small, whitened on the outside and fearfully and wonderfully compounded. Some seemed to contain rags and were strongly bound round with twine; others were made with skulls of cats, stuck round with human or dogs' teeth and glad beads. There were also a lot of egg shells and numbers of little bags filled with a farrago of rubbish. In a little tin canister I found the most valuable of the sorcerer's stock, namely, seven bones belonging to a rattlesnake's tail—these I have known sell for five dollars each, so highly valued are they as amulets or charms—in the same box was about a yard of rope, no doubt intended to be sold for hangman's cord, which is highly prized by the Negroes, the owner of a piece being lucky. (1893: 9)

As in the past, contemporary interactions between an Obeahman or woman and the rest of society are primarily individual in nature. Unlike the group ceremonies and public initiation rituals of community-oriented practices such as Santería and Vodou, there are few group rituals, dancing, drum playing or singing connected to Obeah practices. The systematic repression of African cultural expressions on the part of the British had forced these practices underground, and they had ultimately been lost, except in some pockets of religious activity like Myalism in Jamaica (particularly the Convince-Bongo practices) or the Trinidadian Orisha tradition (also known as Shango), which retain African-derived rites, sacrifices, feasts, and musical traditions meant to establish spiritual contact with African gods. In Trinidad, locals remember fondly an Obeahman known as Papa Neza as an influential leader of the Shango movement. Papa Neza (Samuel Ebenezer Elliot, 1901–1969), a "Merikin or descendant of freed American slaves who arrived in Trinidad in 1812, was 32 years old when his powers as an Obehaman were revealed. He was particularly known for the ritual feasts he organized four times a year (June, August, September, and New Year's Eve), especially that of the Feast of St. Michael (Michaelmas or September 29), when his many followers would bring offerings of goats, fowl and cows which were cooked and distributed among the villagers after rituals were completed" (Kissoun 2009). His rituals, known particularly for their innovative use of drumming and singing, attracted people from as far away as Venezuela, while his popularity was such that at times "hundreds would line the street outside his home to get a dose of his infamous bush medicine" (Kissoon 2009). Lorna McDaniels, in her study of memory spirituals of former slave American soldiers in Trinidad, sees Papa Neza as "an essential musical link between the American black Baptists and the Orisha religion" for the role he played in bridging the world of Christian and Obeah practitioners in Trinidad (McDaniel 1994: 133).

Papa Neza's experiences as leader in Shango or Orisha practices find an echo in the Convince-Bongo practitioners of Jamaica. Convince, one of the oldest surviving forms of Myalism—although Creolized with Kumina and the teachings of nineteenth-century Protestant missionaries—retains nonetheless a pantheon of African spirits organized hierarchically according to their "degree of removal from the present generation, the more powerful being the Bongo spirits from Africans, Jamaican slaves and Maroons" (Payne-Jackson and Alleyne 2004: 62). The spirits, which are followed by recently-departed Obeahmen and the spirits of Convince believers, may possess or "mount" devotees, who, in turn, are expected to honor them with ceremonies that include the sacrifice of goats (Payne-Jackson and Alleyne 2004: 62). In return for animal sacrifices, the spirits will teach Bongomen the secrets needed to help humans, offer protection, and assist them in performing magic or Obeah. As an example of African spirituality in the Caribbean closely related to Obeah, Convince has shared in the vilification of its practices that has followed Euro-Christian cultural domination. In a conversation with Kenneth Bilby, a long-time practitioner of Convince acknowledges the need to defend Obeah practices as a positive force in Jamaican culture: "Obeah, it don't sound good in the English. But the work from it is pretty fine . . . We no rate it fe go out deh [in public], go seh [the word] "obeah." We just say it local [i.e. among ourselves]" (Bilby 2008: 5).[2]

Unlike practitioners of the Orisha tradition or Shango like Papa Neza, or Convince, however, a typical Obeah practitioner may chant or sing or go into a trance in the treatment of an individual client, but the practice bears little resemblance to the complex rituals of possession and summoning of the spirits through music and dance characteristic of other African-derived Creole practices. Typically, a consultation with an Obeahman comes as the result of an individual wishing to effect some change in his or her life: reach a specific goal, awaken someone's affection, seek revenge for an evil done, obtain protection from a "fix" by another Obeahman, attain success in a business deal or legal case, or change his luck. The practitioner listens to his client's description of the situation and recommends a remedy. Baths, massages, or healing prescriptions can be applied to physical maladies, while pouches or bottles made of various substances—herbs, earth, animal or human body matter (hair, nail clippings, blood, and other bodily fluids), articles of clothing (placed in strategic places or worn about the body)—are recommended for other problems. The desired results are usually linked to the client's faithful adherence to these recommendations. Among the most frequent prescriptions for physical maladies are "bush baths," regarded as particularly therapeutic in the treatment of fevers. Bessie Pullen-Burry describes bush baths as consisting of

equal proportions of the leaves of the following plants: akee, sour sop, jointwood, pimento, cowfoot, elder, lime-leaf and liquorice. The patient is plunged into the bath when it is very hot, and is covered with a sheet. When the steam has penetrated the skin, the patient is removed from the bath, and covered with warm blankets, leaving the skin undried. A refreshing sleep is invariably the consequence, and a very perceptible fall in temperature. (1903: 141)

The Obeahman's role as a herbalist or bush doctor has traditionally been considered his or her main social function. This function involves considerable skill and knowledge of the pharmaceutical qualities of the leaves, bark, seeds, and flowers of certain plants and herbs for the treatment of common ailments, the methods of preparation of particular medicines, and their administration, including dosages and potential side effects. Preparations include poultices, teas, and baths, used in the treatment of a full range of maladies, including heart and kidney disease, headaches, boils, sores, fevers, diabetes, tuberculosis, rheumatism, and AIDS. According to Joseph McCartney, Obeah practitioners subscribe to the idea that "plants absorb the cosmic properties of the sun, moon and planets and whether they are taken internally, used as a poultice or worn as a fetish or amulet, they convey to you the desired results" (1976: 98).

The modern practitioner's consultation room includes a broad variety of substances for the preparation of these remedies, although nowadays there is a preponderance of commercially produced items, especially as Obeahmen throughout the Caribbean have found the forests and savannahs that were their principal source of herbs and materials depleted by increasing development and the concomitant deforestation, particularly in the service of the tourist industry. A broad variety of substances aid in contemporary Obeah consultation. The eggs of white fowls are used to communicate with water spirits and help in divination. Uncooked grains of white rice and cloves are used with milk to feed the spirits. Brooms made from the manicole palm are placed over the threshold to ward off evil spirits. The bean caper known as beana is planted around the house to bring prosperity to the home. White lilies are used to appease the spirits. The tree of life is buried in a bottle near the doorstep to preserve the life of the owner (J. Campbell 1976: 18–19). Candles are used to "dress" or cleanse the consultation room of evil or harmful spirits. The commercial products used include imported herbs, processed soaps and lotions, and items manufactured especially for use in Creole practices, frequently found in herb shops or botánicas. Among these items are a variety of incenses and scented candles, and combinations of herbs and oils such as "Holy Spirit Bath," "Lucky Dream Remembering Oil," "Lucky Dream Incense," and "Fast Success Powder" (McCartney 1976: 122). In the practice of modern "literary Obeah"—which incorporates religious or mystical texts as an aid in advising or divination—a number of books on religion, astrology, the occult, and mysticism are used, particularly the Bible; The Sixth and Seventh Book of Moses: Or Moses' Magical Spirit Art Known as the Wonderful Arts of the Old Wise Hebrews, Taken from the Mosaic Books of the Cabala and the Talmud for the Good of Mankind; James Dillet Freeman's Prayer, the Master Key; Lewis de Claremont's Seven Steps to Power: A Study of Beliefs, of Customs, of Traditions of People in Various Ages; and Black Guard, the newspaper of the African Descendants Provisional Government, a black militant organization from San Francisco.

Many of these substances are used in the preparation of fetishes—inanimate objects that are supposed to have special powers and are carried as protection or revered. Parts of the human body (hair, fingernail clippings, blood, sometimes menstrual blood, or other body fluids) or parts of an animal (fur, feathers, bones), objects of clothing (underclothes, handkerchiefs, socks or stockings), and dirt (preferably graveyard dirt) are extensively used in the preparation of fetishes in Obeah. Hair, particularly, is thought to make "a very dangerous obeah" (Beckwith 1929: 115).

The practice of placing fetishes as objects of protection in homes and yards is of long standing. Clement Penrose, writing about the Bahamas in 1905, observed that "at some of the islands we found hanging to various trees, fantastically draped bottles and sticks, which, we were informed, were charms to frighten away thieves and evil spirits. It is believed by the negroes that if anyone but the rightful owners, should eat the fruit from a tree on which this spell has been placed, he will swell up and burst" (1905: 415). Likewise, Hesketh Bell speaks of having found many Caribbean gardens "dressed with obeah . . . to prevent the theft of their contents." In Jamaica Kincaid's collection of Antiguan vignettes, *At the Bottom of the River*, the mother instructs her daughter not to pick people's flowers because the daughter "might catch something" (1983: 5).

These substances and objects release their power when placed in strategic locations around the house, garden, or person. Substances can be sprinkled around the house or yard, buried in the walkways leading to the house, hung from trees, doorways, or windows, placed under pillows and beds, or sewn into clothing. An obeah flag, "a diagonal red cross on a black background," may be displayed in some Caribbean gardens as a guarantor of protection from thieves and Obeah spells (Hedrick and Stephens 1977: 22). Diane Stewart speaks of the practice of sacrificing a chicken or pigeon and pouring the blood on the perimeter of a building's foundation prior to construction to ensure success, protection, and blessing (Stewart 1997: 22).

When deployed according to the Obeahman's instructions, the measures involved in "setting Obeah" (placing a charm somewhere to do a person harm) and "work for me" (the use of Obeah charms to do a person good), are expected to lead to the desired results. Hedrick and Stephens, in their study of Obeah in the Bahamas, list the loss of hair, unexplained swelling of the stomach or limbs, headaches, ringing in the ears, unexplained boils and festering sores, deformity, blindness, and occasionally death as among the most common effects of Obeah spells. The effects of Obeah are also said to be capable of producing madness. Martha Beckwith, in her study of Jamaican folk life, reports an interview with a victim who described how under the effects of a spell, "You begin to creep . . . go naked. The spirit will argue with you in your mind" (1929: 140).

The problems upon which Obeahmen are called to bring their skills to bear are varied and involve goals that are often outside the client's direct control. Rupert Missick, in his study, *No Cure for Sure: Obeah Stories of the Bahamas* (1975), offers a comprehensive list of common goals that includes gaining the love of the opposite sex, finding lost articles, bending individuals to one's will, securing the love of an indifferent person, resolving legal issues, getting people out of prison, revenge, and obtaining luck in games or gambling (1975: 45). Obeah is frequently used to effect changes in male-female relationships. Joseph McCartney describes a practice to assure marital fidelity in which a client provides a lock and a key. The practitioner sets the lock and instructs the client to put the lock and key under his wife's pillow. During the sex act, the client should "close the lock and lock it with the key," thus assuring his partner's fidelity (1976: 160).

Numerous reports on the use of Obeah in the West Indies involve an individual's efforts to use fetishes to influence the outcome of trials and lawsuits and obtain favorable verdicts in court. Claudette Anderson, in her research, argues that in Jamaica "it is the Obeahman, as retained by Judge, Jury, defendant, lawyer and the host of other parties to the case, who uses dynamic power to control the power dynamics in the Jamaican House O'Law" (2008: 27). The following example, taken from an incident in Guyana, where (as in Trinidad) indentured servitude brought large numbers of East Indian immigrants in the nineteenth century, shows not only the link between Obeah and the manipulation of court cases, but also the ways in which Obeah practices have syncretized with Hindu mysticism. John Campbell, in his study of Obeah in Guyana, tells of a Hindu priest on the lower Corentyne region who moved back and forth between his Hindu temple and a home in the same compound where he held daily consultations with non-Hindu Obeah clients. He had gained a reputation for treating clients embroiled in criminal cases, using a mixture of Obeah and *dowtah,* as East Indian "witchcraft" is sometimes called. Once, when his consultation room was raided by the police,

> he was caught at a table filled with aerated drinks, roti and a brass pan with burning pitch pine-sticks and a lota (brass goblet), with mango leaves and hibiscus flowers. He passed the brass pan and lota alternately over the head of a man who had been charged with allegedly cutting out the tongues of six calves belonging to a village farmer and stealing and slaughtering a stud ram belonging to the Government. In the lota, emersed [*sic*] in water, was a slip of parchment on which was written in red ink, the names of the Policeman who instituted the charge, the Police officer in charge of the sub-division, a police key witness and the Magistrate who was due to preside over the preliminary inquiry into the matter. (1976: 8)

Other strategies for affecting the outcome of legal proceedings involve writing the prosecutor's name on a piece of paper wrapped around an egg and secured with a pin. The accused places the paper and egg under his armpit and presses on them as the prosecutor speaks. The rubbing of certain oils on the body of the accused is also said to affect the prosecutor's ability to build a successful case. Among the numerous cases cited by Anderson which involve the rubbing or application of various oils, is the following:

> A young man who had broken into a shop of a neighbouring village went to an Obeahman named Clarke to get him out of his trouble, and to prevent the police from catching him. Clarke told him not to fret at all, and that he would give him something so that the police shouldn't catch him. The young man then stated that "Clarke took down a paper parcel and threw something from it over my head. It was something like fine ashes. He was jumping about and speaking in a language I didn't understand. He told me to jump and while he jumped I jumped too. He then gave me a canister of water to put to my nose and say 'God Save the Queen.' I did so. He gave me then a black powder to put in the water I drank and the food I ate. He said it would carry away the policeman who caught me. I paid him two shillings. He also gave me a tin of water to throw away at the crossroads. (Anderson 2008: 14)

The Obeahman's services—whether medical, psychological, moral, or legal—are rendered in exchange for an agreed fee that is often connected to the client's ability to pay.[3] An Obeah practitioner's success is directly related to the reputation he has established as a herbalist, his skills as a listener, and his ability to achieve the expected results. These in turn establish his clients' belief and confidence in his magical powers. Prestige, and the influence he or she can wield in the community, is linked both to the practitioner's reputation for skill as well as his or her own economic position. The latter in turn is partly dependent on the clients' social class, since fees are determined by the client's available resources, but also on a "performance" of prosperity that can reassure clients in advance. In addition to fees for consultations, supplemental income is derived from the sale of prescribed drugs (either prepared especially for the client, pre-packaged by the Obeahman, or commercially prepared) and paraphernalia such as candles, soaps, or reading materials). Maarit Forde, in her study of contemporary Obeah practitioners in Trinidad, finds that although creole religions and healing in the Caribbean have developed in societies forged by and contributing to global capitalism and other facets of modernity, the ritual practice classified as obeah in the colonial Caribbean, or the spiritual work done by present-day ritual specialists does not align with the logic of commodification, short-term gain, anonymity and impersonality of exchange typical of capitalism. Money is a standard object of exchange in the ritual sphere of exchange, and moral debates of ritually earned money do not question the legitimacy of monetary transactions themselves. (Forde 2008: 16).

What we know about traditional practices confirms her conclusions. The popular Papa Neza, for example, was known never to take money as payment for his services. Whatever money was left by clients was reportedly invested in the feasts he organized periodically and, as such, returned to his community of followers. Cobb, the young apprentice learning with "Mr. Murray," explains that "a lot of people do it (indulge in obeah) because it can give them benefits in life, which is true. But some people do it for money. I want to use it to help people and to know more about the natural mystic of God's work" (Luton 2009).

The Spirit World

Central to the practice of Obeah is the relationship between humans and spirits. The Obeah concept of the spirit is different from that of the tutelary spirits of the ancestors found in Santería and Vodou, since spirits in Obeah manifest themselves primarily as ghosts—sperrids, spirits, or duppies—that can be "called" or summoned as helpers in the process of revealing mysteries, affording protection, or inflicting harm. A spirit or duppy can be "either the soul of a dead person, manifest in human form," "the soul of the dead manifest in a variety of fabulous beasts, and also in the forms of real animals like lizards and snakes," or "an order of supernatural beings only vaguely associated with the dead" (Leach 1961: 207–215). Linked to the notion of manipulating the spirits is the Obeah practitioner's reputed ability to control an individual through his shadow (Morrish 1982: 44). The practice of "catching shadows" involves capturing a dying person's last breath in a bottle or jar. Since the duppies are the conduits of numerous charms—particularly of evil spells—"working Obeah" is often synonymous with "setting a duppy for someone," while "pulling" (or "taking off") Obeah means "to extract the obeah set by another," usually by removing the duppy that had served as conduit (Beckwith 1929: 104, 107).

The world of the spirits includes belief in the sudden apparition of a variety of animal figures in the night sky. Among these the most feared is the lowing cow or rolling calf, a most dreadful harbinger of evil, who "keeps the secrets of the duppy world" (Beckwith 1929: 119). Bessie Pullen-Burry writes that "those who have witnessed the awful phantom describe it as a huge animal with fire issuing from its nostrils, and clanking chains as it rolls down the mountain-side, burning everything in its path" (1903: 138). In Herbert De Lisser's early Jamaican novel, *The White Witch of Rose Hall*, the eponymous sorceress displays her formidable powers by summoning a rolling calf to terrorize her slaves. Other frequent apparitions involve those of a cat as large as a goat with eyes like burning lamps.

Among the creolized variants of Obeah, the Shaker rituals of Guyana incorporate notions of exorcism of devils and spirits as part of their claim to heal chronic illnesses. The rituals usually take the form of beating the affected person and administering bush baths. In group ceremonies—which are not found among practitioners of Obeah in other Caribbean regions—practitioners dance frenetically to the rhythm of African drums until they are exhausted, then lie prostrate on the floor. The accompanying feasts include unsalted foods, milk, honey, and white rum, the remnants of which are gathered carefully along with a portion of white rum or high-wine and deposited on the seashore as an offering to a water spirit known as "fair maid" or "water mama" (J. Campbell 1976: 7–8). East Indians in Guyana, in a further syncretism, have added chiromancy or palm reading to the divination functions of Obeah.

Jamaican Myalism

Myal, a version of Obeah practiced only in Jamaica, retains aspects of African-derived religiosity that have been lost in other parts of the Anglophone Caribbean. Scholars working on Jamaican religious traditions have established a somewhat simplistic distinction between Obeah and Myal, which assumes a close connection between Obeah, poison, witchcraft, and the antithesis of Christianity—in short, bad or black magic—and a correlation between Myal, healing practices, ecstatic worship, and spirit possession—Myal as good magic. This distinction was initially established during the Myal Revival of the 1860s, when Myal practitioners engaged in a systematic anti-Obeah campaign.

However, this particular distinction between the two does not reflect the connections between the two practices established during the period of slavery in Jamaica, when both played a prominent role in resisting slavery and organizing rebellions, links that have been renewed since the 1860s. Throughout the history of Obeah and Myalism—the latter practiced chiefly in Jamaica—the two traditions have found themselves intricately linked. Bryan Edwards, in *The History, Civil, and Commercial, of the British Colonies in the West Indies* (1807), identified the two practices in the late eighteenth century through his description of the roles of Obeahmen and Myalmen:

> Obia-men or women . . . is now become in Jamaica the general term to denote those Africans who in that island (Jamaica) practise witchcraft and sorcery, comprehending also the class of what are called Myal-men, or those who, by means of a narcotick potion . . . which occasions a trance or profound sleep of a certain duration, endeavour to convince the deluded spectators of their power to re-animate dead bodies. (165–166)

George Blyth, however, in tracing the differences between the two practices in his *Reminiscences of Missionary Life. With Suggestions to Churches and Missionaries* (1851), establishes distinct dissimilarities between them that are worthy of attention. His description points to group practices in Myalism that are not characteristic of Obeah:

> The superstitions which prevail in Western and Central Africa have been brought to the West Indies and may be comprehended under the two systems of Obeahism and Myalism; the first of which is entirely mischievous, and the other professes to counteract it. The principal actors in the former are old men, generally Africans. These pretend to have power over others, even at a distance. . . . Latterly, however, baptism . . . has become so common, that it seems to have lost its charm, and the doctor, or Myal-man, is resorted to, so that he may neutralize the power of the Obeah-man. Sometimes his remedies are of a very simple character, particularly if his object is to cure some local disease. . . . Sometimes the Myalists meet in large companies, generally at night, and dance in rings, till they become excited and frenzied, singing Myal songs accusing others of being Myal men, and pretending to discover enchantments which have been made by them. . . . These Myal men also pretend to catch the shadow or spirit of persons who may have lost their lives by lightning or

accident. When the spirit is caught, it is put into a small coffin and buried, by which the ghost, as the superstitious of this country would call it, is laid to rest. The Myal men are resorted to in a great variety of cases, when disease is obstinate, or the nature of it is not understood: if a man's wife has forsaken him; if he thinks there is danger of losing the favour of his employers; if he supposes his horse has been bewitched; in all such cases the Myal men are consulted.[4]

The extensive quotation from Blyth points to the many similarities between Obeah—as practiced throughout the West Indies and Jamaica—and Myalism. Their practitioners' skill in herbalism, the healing aspects of both practices, their preparation of fetishes and other objects for the purpose of influencing behavior, assuring protection, and reaching one's goals—are all aspects in which the two practices are almost identical. It also highlights the two salient differences between the practices—the additional role of Myalmen as "charismatic leaders with identifiable groups of adherents" (Stewart 1997: 41) and the possibility of achieving the possession trance characteristic of more complex Creole religions like Vodou and Santería through music and dance. The ecstatic trance allows for the possibility of a direct interaction between ancestral spirits and the living, who in turn become the spirits' vehicles for prophecy, healing, advice, and revenge from those who harmed them while alive.

Myalism, as a group practice with a spiritual leader, brings a new dimension to the practice of Jamaican Obeah, one absent from the Obeah practiced in other Caribbean territories, which are characterized primarily by solo practitioners working with individual clients. This added component, which is characteristic of the Haitian and Cuban traditions, has been explained by scholars in those contexts through the specific patterns of syncretism between African and Catholic practices. The Jamaican slaves' exposure to both Spanish and British settlers—and consequently to Catholicism and Protestantism alike—may account for the Myal practices that bridge the apparent gulf between Obeah on the one hand and Santería and Vodou on the other. The religious gatherings involving singing, drumming, calling to the spirits, and possession thrived in Cuba and Haiti and became responsible for the creation and development of group relationships and clan loyalty, but were firmly prohibited throughout the British Isles. They succeeded nonetheless in sustaining, albeit in a limited fashion, some of the multifaceted elements that lend richness and depth to Santería and Vodou. In Jamaica, the three-day Christmas holiday was a testing time even for settled [Christianized] congregations. While rowdy heathenish processions with "revolting attitudes in their dances," filled the slave villages and the streets outside the chapels, the missionaries tried to encourage their congregations by contrasting their clean, dignified appearance with the "half-mad, half-naked" goombah dancers. . . . Even so, the festivities usually took their toll of converts; at best, Christian and African celebrations were juxtaposed and if the drums were silent on one estate, they were busy nearby. The missionary was fortunate if, drummed to sleep on Christmas Eve, he was roused by carol singing on Christmas morning. (M. Turner 1982: 71)

Myal Dance

The Myal dances linked the Jamaican slaves to the worship of a West African pantheon of gods from which they had been separated when transported to the New World, and which used drums, dancing, dreams, and spirit possession as part of organized veneration of both deities and ancestors. However, the survival of the ritual aspects of African worship, manifest through the Myal dance, did not necessarily mean that the pantheon itself had survived, although recent studies have indicated that more aspects of West African theology have survived than previously believed. Myalism, unlike Obeah, allowed for an initiation ritual involving the swallowing of a herbal mixture that would induce a deathlike state, akin to the process of zombification in Haitian Vodou, as well as a second potion to awaken the initiate from his false death. The ritual of the Myal dance, a hypnotic dancing in circles under the leader's direction, involved as well a mesmerizing opening for the entrance of the spirit in the body of the initiate, providing a bridge between the spirit possession characteristic of Afro-Creole practices and the filling with the Holy Spirit found in some variants of New World Christianity.

Myal dances are also organized around rituals designed to prevent duppies from doing harm, helping people recover their lost shadows (in a practice akin to the recovery of the *petit bon ange* in Haitian Vodou), and generally to propitiate the world of the spirits. Some Myal rituals combined dancing under the *ceiba* or silk-cotton tree, believed to be a favorite haunt of duppies, with animal sacrifices (mostly chickens, but occasionally goats as well) as the means of recovering spirits trapped by duppies. This version of spirit possession involved the use of marijuana and hallucinatory drugs to enhance the trance (Curtin 1955: 30), a practice that has survived in Rastafarianism. Moravian pastor J. H. Buchner, a witness to a Myal dance in the nineteenth century, described it thus:

As soon as the darkness of evening set in, they assembled in crowds in open pastures, most frequently under cotton trees, which they worshipped, and counted holy; after sacrificing some fowls, the leader began an extempore song in a wild strain, which was answered in chorus; the dance followed, grew wilder and wilder, until they were in a state of excitement bordering on madness. Some would perform incredible evolutions while in this state, until, nearly exhausted, they fell senseless to the ground, when every word they uttered was received as a divine revelation. (1854: 139–140)

Myalism went through a profound transformation in the wake of the virtual invasion of Jamaica by Christian missionaries in the late eighteenth and early nineteenth centuries. The Protestantism against which the slave population posited their dances and drumming was not the sedate Anglicanism of the established Church of England, but the more exuberant Christianity of English Methodists, Moravians, and African American Baptists accustomed to enthusiastic manifestations of the Holy Spirit through music and trance. These variants of Protestantism provided a theological style well suited to fill the vacuum left by the almost complete loss of an African pantheon among Jamaican slaves. Syncretized with newly introduced Christian practices, Myalism gave way to Revivalism.

The roots of Myal-inspired Revivalism date to the arrival in Jamaica of English Methodists, whose practices incorporated trances in which the Holy Spirit manifested itself through congregants, and Baptists, who, like the Methodists (and unlike the Anglicans), allowed for the ordination of black ministers and the autonomy of black congregations. With the arrival of African American Baptist missionary George Liles in Jamaica in 1783, Myalism took the first step toward transforming itself into the Native Baptist movement. Barry Chevannes, in *Rastafari and Other African-Caribbean Worldviews,* speaks of how "the Africans took rapidly and in large numbers to the new religion, but in doing so absorbed it into the Myal framework. African water rituals resurfaced in Christian baptism and missionaries had to wage theological battle to convince the people that John the Baptist was not greater than Jesus and should not be worshipped" (1998: 8). English missionaries attributed the centrality of dreams and visions in Native Baptist practices to the direct influence of Myalism:

Dreams and Visions constituted fundamental articles of their creed. Some supernatural revelations were regarded as indispensable to qualify for admission to the full privileges of their community. Candidates were required indeed, to dream a certain number of dreams before they were received to membership, the subjects of which were given them by their teachers. (Phillippo 1843: 273)

Native Baptists, working with Obeah practitioners, led the 1831–32 rebellion of slaves that paved the way for Emancipation in 1834, becoming in the process, in the eyes of most whites, "a new composition of the old hazardous 'black magic' and 'black art,' i.e.—Obeah Oaths, Myal traditions, visionary or prophetic insight, mystical power and the pursuit of temporal freedom" (Stewart 1997: 124). The Great Revival, the movement of religious enthusiasm that again swept Jamaica from 1860 to 1862, in turn spun two new versions of Christianized Afro-Caribbean Christianity out of Myalism and the Native Baptist movement: Zion and Pukkumina (known by its detractors as Pocomania).

Zion Revivalism

Zionist practices are "steeped in classical African ideas about Deity, Ancestors, and the relationship between forces, Spirits, elements and beings in the visible and invisible domains of the world" (Stewart 1997: 126). The Zionist movement inserts the familiar elements of the Christian faith—God, the angels, archangels, saints, apostles, and prophets—into the worship patterns characteristic of African religiosity. Spirits demand that they be fed regularly—as is the practice in the feeding of lwa and orishas in Vodou and Santería, respectively—with each spirit having specific preferences for certain foods, colors, and music, all of which are incorporated in the fundamentals of worship. Moreover, spirits act as personal guides to the worshipers they embrace or adopt, their loyalty, protection, and advice being contingent on the worshiper's ritualistic feeding and his or her wearing of specific colors as outward signs of devotion.

Worship moves from the church to the balmyard or healing center, in the leader's house, where a flagpole identifies the space as sacred. Zion Revivalism returns rituals of divination, visions, prophecy, animal sacrifice, ancestral veneration, ritual bathing, and healing, as well as the importance of the priest as herbalist and healer, to their original centrality in African devotion. Zion Revivalism's relationship to the spirit world, centered on a primary relationship with a spirit messenger, mark it as deeply connected to African theology:

Where Christianity is transfixed on Jesus as mediator, Myal was trans-fixed on the Spirit as possessor and sought it in dreams and secluded retreat. Whereas Christianity placed its emphasis on transmitted *knowledge* (doctrine, Bible, catechism) for conversion, Myal placed its emphasis on the *experience* of the Spirit. . . . Possession by the Spirit thus became the quintessential experience of the myalized Christianity. (Chevannes 1998: 18–19)

This connection with the spirits, achieved through possession, is induced through ring dances very similar to those of the eighteenth- and nineteenth-century Myalism which continue to be practiced today, albeit with some modifications. In Zion Revivalism, members of the congregation, or "bands," are led in rhythmic dancing and breathing toward a collective trance that opens the portals of the spirit world, allowing the angels or spirits to descend through the center pole (akin to the Vodou Poto mitan) into the waters of life at its base and enter the bodies of the congregation through the drinking of the water. Once in a trance, having entered Zion ("land of the ancestors, the golden past of Africa, lost by sin and oppression" [Murphy 1994: 142]) they speak and sing in an illogical language that becomes the source material for divination rituals that interpret the messages as positive or negative. As in Myal practices, marijuana and rum are used to induce trance. There is an elaborate chain of command in the bands—Captain, Shepherd, Mother, Cutter, Hunter, Sawyer, Planner, Nurse, River Maid, Bellringer—with specific responsibilities during journeys through the spirit world. Access to the spirit world allows members of bands who possess a spirit guide to perform both worthy and vindictive tasks.

Zionists maintain their closest connection to Christian Protestantism through the centrality of the Bible in their worship. It offers "the rules for Christian moral conduct, the techniques of healing by manipulating spiritual power, the ways to approach the spirits" (Guabo 1994: 521), while also offering "justification for African traditions such as animal sacrifice, veneration of Ancestral/Spirit messengers, erecting tables and altars (shrines), and other traditions that might be biblically-based but would be considered heretical practices in Orthodox Christian theology and piety" (Stewart 1997: 131). In this respect it is a profoundly Afro-Caribbean religious manifestation of Christianity, the hybrid product of a process of transculturation that allowed the remnants of practices believed lost during the devastation of slavery to be reconstructed through the incorporation of new theological content.

Pukkumina/Kumina (Pocomania)

Pukkumina or Kumina (also referred to pejoratively as Pocomania), is a tradition traced to African indentured laborers brought to Jamaica from the Kongo region of Central Africa after Emancipation. It represents another variation of Jamaican Revivalism linked, albeit tangentially, to the traditions of Myalism, with which it became syncretized during the second half of the nineteenth century. The specific characteristics that separate Zion Revivalism from Kumina are difficult to isolate as they are determined by the practices of particular groups. Joseph Murphy, in *Working the Spirit*, explains that

> There are no institutional structures connecting *pocomania* or revival churches: leaders are free to improvise upon the instruction and ceremonial patterns handed down to them by their elders in the tradition. There is often informal "fellowshipping" or mutual attendance at rites between likeminded churches, and leaders will often cooperate on these special and often spontaneous occasions, but there is no authority beyond the leader of the immediate congregation. (1994: 126)

Kumina can be differentiated from Zion primarily in its shunning of the Bible as the central textual authority behind faith and worship. Kumina, a more dynamic practice, is also more conspicuously African-derived. Like Zion, liturgy and theology are based on an understanding of the continuity between "visible and invisible domains of the human and ancestral world," but unlike Zion, practitioners worship one deity, known as Zambi or King Zambi[5] (Stewart 1997: 152) and pay homage to the fallen angels. Practitioners of Kumina share a deep African identity consciousness based on a constant awareness of a legacy of African persecution and suffering, akin to that embraced by Rastafarians.

Kumina practices are primarily focused on healing, and practitioners are known for their deep knowledge of bush medicine and the complex rituals involved in the gathering of plants, leaves, and flowers for use in curing rituals, and their preparation of various medicines. Healing ceremonies, which incorporate singing, drumming, dancing, spirit possession, and animal sacrifice—elements found in Myalism and Zion Revivalism—are intended to summon the spirits to descend and help restore the sick congregant to health.

The dynamic syncretism displayed by practices such as Myal, Zion, and Kumina showcases the enduring potential of African-derived religions in helping Caribbean peoples heal from the uprootedness and impoverishment imposed upon them by a history of dispossession—of land, culture, environment, language, and gods. The protean quality of these practices, their ability to transform the dominant colonial structures and bend them to their needs and functions, is a shared element in seemingly different practices like Obeah and Myal, and makes possible their revolutionary reconstruction of fundamentalist Christian practices. Monica Schuler summarizes this mutability thus:

> Myalists extracted and emphasized two central elements of the Baptist faith—the inspiration of the Holy Spirit, and Baptism, in the manner of John the Baptist, by immersion—because they seemed to correspond with beliefs or symbols already familiar to them. Some members actually referred to their church as John the Baptist's Church. The leaders developed a technique for attaining possession by the Holy Spirit and "dreams" experienced in this state were crucial to a candidate's acceptance for baptism. Without them they could not be born again, "either by water or the Spirit." The Myalist emphasis on ritual immersion by water may be understood better by a comparison with beliefs of twentieth-century Kumina adherents (descendants of nineteenth-century Central African immigrants) concerning baptism. Kumina members profess a special attachment to Baptists and Revivalists who practice baptism by immersion in the river because the river is the house of African spirits who they believe protect Baptists and Revivalists as they do Kumina devotees. In addition, Kumina members deliberately seek Christian baptism for their children because the ritual is believed to provide the protection of a powerful spirit—the one the Christians call the Holy Spirit. The Afro-Jamaican religious tradition, then, has consistently interpreted Christianity in African, not European, cultural terms. (Quoted by Stewart, 1997: 36)

Quimbois

When compared with these dynamic appropriations, the beliefs and practices of Quimbois, a variation of Obeah practiced in the French islands of Martinique and Guadeloupe, seems somewhat static. Akin to Obeah as practiced in the Anglophone islands of the Lesser Antilles, Quimbois is not a religion, but a set of practices related to magic and sorcery with roots in African religiosity. The chief function of the *quimboiseurs*—also known as *sorciers* and *gadé zaffés*—is to mediate between the living and the numerous spirits who come back from the land of the dead to threaten them. Herbalists by training, quimboiseurs are primarily healers and counselors with powers to call upon the supernatural, for good or evil, to help the living reach their goals and settle disputes. They can read the past, present, and future through divination practices such as interpreting the patterns of flames or the designs made by melting candlewax. They use magic to solve problems of the heart, help with business decisions, and prescribe treatments for physical maladies.

Although most practitioners use the terms interchangeably, some scholars differentiate between the gadé zaffés who work with secrets such as conjuring and treat chiefly psychological maladies, and the quimboiseur or *kenbwazé*, who uses Quimbois or *kenbwa*, material artifacts, to ensure positive or negative results or to cause someone harm (Romero Cesareo 1997: 256–257).[6] This Quimbois usually takes the form of small fetish cloth bags full of grain, feathers, and other magical substances placed on the threshold of houses to protect people from evil spirits. Protective practices also include the burning of candles at crossroads or the sacrifice of fowl to help assure a particular outcome.

The practice of Quimbois, like that of Obeah, has been outlawed through most of the islands' postencounter history. Like Obeah, the practice has prevailed despite its persecution, because it fulfills a vital social function through its healing capabilities and its contribution to the preservation of African culture, principally that of the cult of ancestors, and in offering protection from a number of supernatural beings that prey on the living. In Quimbois, the belief in the supernatural rests on animistic notions of spirits residing inside animals, and in some cases, within inanimate objects. A number of spirits are feared because of their capacity for violent harm toward the living: the *soucouyant* is a Caribbean version of the vampire, which sustains itself on human blood; the *dorlis* or *homme au bâton* can sexually abuse women as they sleep; the *morphoisé* can metamorphose into any animal and attack its unsuspecting prey; the *djablesse* is a beautiful woman who lures men away from safety into harm; the *zombi* is a tall headless and armless man condemned to wander through endless nights; the *bête a man Ibé* is a sorceress in chains with one human foot and one horse or donkey hoof who wanders neighborhoods at night shrieking.

Given the threats posed by these creatures, it is not surprising that the principal function of the quimboiseur is protective. In addition to the fetishes or small pouches filled with magical materials, quimboiseurs can prepare a series of talismans blessed through prayer that can be worn attached to clothing, principally underwear. Cars and other vehicles can be brought to the practitioner for a blessing, so as to protect drivers from car accidents.

Potions can be prepared not only as healing preparations but also as magic beverages that can empower individuals to reach certain goals or cause harm to someone from whom a client is seeking revenge. These can be made to order by the quimboiseur or, in the case of treatments for common problems or maladies, can be purchased ready-made. Catholic rosaries, worn around the neck or hung from the rear-view mirror of cars, are a common sort of protection, although they can also be used as conduits for spiritual forces in diverting harm to others.

The healing aspects of Quimbois are best manifested through two types of baths: the *bain démarré,* a special bath taken to rid oneself of problems; and the *bain de la chance,* which brings luck. The bain démarré is described by Guadeloupean novelist Myriam Warner Vieyra's *Le Quimboiseur l'avait dit* (1980) as taking place in "a big earthen pan . . . in the sun, full of water with all kinds of magic leaves—paoca, calaba balsam, bride's rose, and the power of Satan" in which her protagonist could steep, ritualistically ladling the contents nine times over her head, to "leave behind all the fatigues of the week" (quoted in Romero-Cesareo 1997: 255). The bain de la chance is usually taken in the ocean or at home with sea, river, or rainwater scented with various herbs.

Healing through baths, a ritual that restores balance, is linked in Quimbois practices to separation from one's home and the land. Traditional African-derived practices call for a newborn's umbilical chord and placenta to be buried in the yard, and for a tree to be planted on the spot. The ritual binds the newborn to the land and to the spirits of the ancestors who share the same plot of land. Separation from the land—particularly through the selling of the family plot or migration—leads to disconnections that have profound psychic and emotional consequences for which baths and other preparations of the quimboiseur are meant as remedies.

A powerful addition to the African-derived arsenal of weapons with which the quimboiseur battles the effects of evil spirits has come through immigrants who came to the region from India as indentured servants after the abolition of slavery. Of the several Indian deities that Guadeloupean practitioners have adopted into their practices, the most salient is Maliémen or Mariammam, a fierce mother figure whose cult has been Africanized and now includes offerings of her favorite foods and items (rice, coconut, milk, jewelry, embroidered fabric, and flowers) and animal sacrifices involving roosters or male goats. Ceremonies to appease Maliémen and seek her divine protection involve trancelike dances performed by Maldévilen, the war god who guards Maliémen.

Quimbois remains the most salient manifestation of a loosely conceived set of practices that are primarily of African origin but which have incorporated some aspects of Christian belief and worship (the rosary being one of them) and/or East Indian religiosity. Preoccupied primarily with protection and healing, it is not a belief system per se. It lacks the liturgy and elaborate rituals of practices like Myal, Zion, and Kumina, all of which involve theologies that seek to explain man's role in the world and his links to the world of the spirits and God.

Rastafarianism

Rastafarianism is an Afro-Jamaican religious movement that blends the Revivalist nature of Jamaican folk Christianity with the Pan-Africanist perspective promulgated by Marcus Garvey, and Ethiopianist[1] readings of the Old Testament. It is a twentieth-century religious and political phenomenon that originated in Jamaica and has gained international attention as a Pan-African approach to the problems of poverty, alienation, and spirituality. Founded in 1932, Rastafarianism was inspired by the crowning in 1930 of Ras, or Prince, Tafari Makonnen as Emperor of the Ethiopian Kingdom, at that time one of only two sovereign nations on the African continent.[2] The momentous event, which brought enormous international attention to the nation (see 1930 *Time* magazine cover below), ensured the new king's place at the symbolic center of the African world, and focused the hopes of blacks around the world on the possibility of a return to the fabulous African kingdoms of legend.

The link between the crowning of Ras Tafari, who took the name of Haile Selassie upon his coronation, and Jamaican religiosity was provided by fervent black nationalist leader Marcus Garvey (1887–1940), a native of Jamaica and founder of the Universal Negro Improvement Association (UNIA) in 1914, an organization devoted to promoting unity throughout the African Diaspora by underscoring common racial and cultural roots. At its heyday in the 1920s, Garvey's movement, known as Garveyism, had hundreds of chapters across the Caribbean, the United States, England, Europe, Africa, and Latin America. Its pan-Africanist message of black solidarity was founded on the recovery of black identity through an identification with Africa, or more precisely with Ethiopia, as the ancestral home of blacks of the Diaspora. The UNIA's anthem proclaimed the association's identification with Ethiopia: "Ethiopia, thou land of our fathers,/Thou land where the Gods love to be/As storm clouds at night suddenly gather/Our armies come rushing to thee./We must in the fight be victorious/When swords are thrust outward to gleam;/For us will the vict'ry be glorious/When led by the red, black, and green."

Emperor Haile Selassie and his court (1930)

In his writings and speeches, Garvey had repeatedly foretold the crowning of a black king in Africa as a sign of the deliverance of Africans around the world from the bonds of poverty, exploitation, and colonialism. The belief in the coming of a black Messiah was a basic principle of the UNIA, as written by Bishop George Alexander McGuire, which declared that blacks should worship a God in their own image: "If God is the father of all he must have had black blood in his veins. So it is proper for the dark race to conceive of their Spiritual Saviour as a Negro" (H. Campbell 1987: 134). Garvey had proclaimed that "We Negroes believe in the God of Ethiopia, the everlasting God—God the Father, God the Son and God the Holy Ghost, the one God of all ages. That is the God in which we believe, but we shall worship him through the spectacles of Ethiopia" (Garvey 1968: 120). He himself had written and staged a play in Kingston depicting the crowning of an African king as a great deliverer, and he greeted Haile Selassie's coronation in the *Blackman,* the journal of the UNIA, with promises that the new emperor and his people "are part of the great African race that is to rise from its handicaps, environments and difficulties to repossess the Imperial Authority that is promised by God himself in the inspiration: Princes coming out of Egypt and Ethiopia stretching forth her hands" (Garvey 1968: 3).

In Jamaica, news of Haile Selassie's coronation was interpreted widely as a fulfillment of Garvey's exhortation to "look to Africa for the crowning of a king to know that your redemption is near" (Chevannes 1994: 10). Haile Selassie, moreover, was not an upstart man-who-would-be-king, but one who claimed to descend from Israel's King Solomon and the Queen of Sheba and whose titles, which included Ras Tafari (Prince or Duke of the Tafari royal family), King of Kings, Lord of Lords, and Conquering Lion of the Tribe of Judah, implied a reaffirmation of the ancient roots of Ethiopian culture and of its claim to an autonomous niche in Judaeo-Christian history. Ethiopia, portrayed through Haile Selassie's solomonic symbolism as a black kingdom with an ancient biblical lineage, became the African Zion of the burgeoning Rastafarian movement.

Four members of Garvey's Association—Leonard Howell, his assistant Robert Hinds, Archibald Dunkley, and Joseph Hibbert—regarded Garvey as a prophet and concluded that the new emperor was an incarnation of Jah— the Rastafarian name for God—and consequently the messiah whose arrival Garvey had foretold. They began to preach the message of Haile Selassie's divinity in the streets of Kingston and to gatherings across Jamaica, proclaiming that black people could not have two kings (the English king and Haile Selassie) and that the only true king and redeemer was the Ethiopian emperor:

> The titles he bore, the homage paid by the White world through the heads and representatives of state, the antiquity of Ethiopia and its mention in both Old and New Testaments of the Bible, the Solomonic claim—like so many rivulets building up into a mighty river, all swept them away with the powerful conviction that Ras Tafari was none other than Jesus Christ. And he was Black. Now did the Song of Solomon make sense:
> I *am* Black, but comely, O ye daughters of Jerusalem.
> As the tents of Kedar, as the curtains of Solomon.
> Look not upon me, because I *am* Black, because the sun
> Hath looked upon me. (Chevannes 1994: 10–11)[3]

The Jamaican leaders' belief in Haile Selassie's divinity led to the elaboration of a complex West Indian–based theology that we now know as Rastafarianism. In the early years of the movement's development, its basic tenets were quite simple: Haile Selassie was the embodiment of Christian divinity (the Black Christ or Black Messiah) and the entire African race shared in his divinity; and there would be a mystic return to the African homeland (known as Repatriation) as a path to redemption. This Repatriation was not a call for massive migration to Africa—although a number of Jamaican Rastafarians ultimately resettled in Ethiopia—but was linked to notions of cultural recovery through a spiritual connection to the African homeland. The belief in the soul's return to Africa ('Nan Guinée) after death was widespread in the Caribbean. Rastafarians expanded on this belief, incorporating the idea of a future mystic exodus to Ethiopia, which is considered to be heaven on earth, gleaned from Protestant sects with millenarian approaches to the bodily transportation of the chosen to the New Zion. A broadsheet distributed by early adherents stated, "We interpret Heaven this way. The Heaven which is the uppermost part of man where God dwelleth in wisdom and understanding, declares the glory of God is the firmament, and the moon and the stars—Heaven to we is Africa" (quoted in Kitzinger 1969: 240).

At this early stage in the development of the movement, Rastafarians denied any connection between Repatriation and death, as it was believed that Rastas could not die. A taboo on discussing matters pertaining to death remains, despite the reconsideration of the matter forced upon the brethren by the deaths of the prophet, Marcus Garvey, and eventually of Haile Selassie himself. They fear that the world of the living will be contaminated by the spirits of the dead, for their conception of the spirit world is of a menacing realm similar to that in West Indian Obeah. Consequently, they will not engage in any of the customary West Indian rituals of death; they do not attend wakes and funerals, engage in any preparations, or mourn publicly. Although many Rastafarians believe in reincarnation, most are not concerned with the afterlife, as they believe that salvation happens on earth and its path is marked by Repatriation—the search for Africa—which they associate with heaven.

For all its Africa-centeredness, Rastafarianism is fundamentally a Bible-based religion that turned its back on Jamaican Zion Revivalism (with rituals inspired by Myalism) and Afro-derived magicoreligious practices such as Obeah. A new reading of the Christian Bible developed during the movement's formative years, which centered on the notion of blacks as the new Israelites sent by Jah (or God) into slavery to be subservient to white masters as punishment for their sins. Rastafarians became Israel's "Lost Tribe." The notion provided a link to a long tradition of Ethiopianism in Jamaica, where "African Christians had been identified by European missionaries as Ethiopians in accordance with references to Ethiopia in the Bible" (Taylor 2001: 71). In this new Ethiopianist interpretation of scripture, the very fabric of white Euro-American society, its social and political structures, responsible for centuries of black oppression and exploitation, emerges as a new Babylon from which the community must remain separate. As a result, Rastafarians tend not join unions or associations and the most traditional will not participate in the political process, as they see themselves as "only temporary sojourners in Jamaica" (Kitzinger 1969: 523).

The first phase of the movement, lasting from the declaration of Haile Selassie's divinity by Rastafarian founders in Jamaica in 1932 to the end of the 1950s, involved gaining adherents to the notion of a black living God whose divinity was shared by other blacks, both in Africa and the Diaspora. Chromolithographs of Haile Selassie as a full-bearded Black Christ were distributed widely at meetings and street corners. Howell was among the leading voices proclaiming that Christ had returned to restore the proper interpretation of biblical scriptures, which had been distorted by Jews and Christians, who had "appropriated the place of God's chosen people, guardians of the Ark of the Covenant, the black race" (Taylor 2001: 72).

The Rastafarians made numerous converts among the uprooted peasantry that had found refuge in the slums of Kingston. Their message of deliverance came at a time when Jamaican workers faced wretched conditions. With the world economy in the midst of its worst-ever depression, they faced massive unemployment and underemployment. (In 1938, for example, work in the cane fields was paid at the same rate of one shilling per day that had prevailed in 1838, two years after Emancipation.) Poor housing and the absence of political rights worsened the dismal economic outlook and provided fertile ground for a new politicoreligious movement. In Kingston, Rastas concentrated on a sprawling shantytown built on a former landfill site known locally as the Dungle, which came to represent their "active rejection on the part of dominant society" as well as their own rejection of the aspects of Jamaican society Rastas associated with Babylon (Kitzinger 1969: 242). Rastafarian leaders also made numerous recruits among Jamaica's sugar laborers just returning from Cuba, where, in the service of American sugar corporations they had learned first-hand of American-style racism and postcolonial exploitation. In Cuba, home to a number of chapters of Garvey's association, many were recruited into Rastafarianism. Depressed urban areas throughout the Caribbean, as Velma Pollard argues, became fertile ground for the Rastafari message as their inhabitants were "poor black people occupying underprivileged positions in societies with stark social and economic discrepancies" (2000: 54).

Rastafarianism's second stage of development was characterized by a radicalization of the movement's political ideology. This second generation of adherents, whose political convictions had developed amidst the racialized politics of the 1960s and early 1970s—the American civil rights movement, the Caribbean independence struggles, the black militant movement, and the Cuban Revolution—focused their attention on the mobilization of blacks in Jamaica and across the Diaspora in opposition to colonial rule and other forms of oppression. The political goals of the Rastafarian movement fitted well within the larger framework of Black Power or *Négritude*, and as a result this generation would bear the brunt of the Jamaican government's political repression. Their calls for recognition of Haile Selassie as the only true pan-African political and religious leader and for a sustained struggle against colonialism had led to attempts at repression and in some cases to open persecution. (At the time, Jamaica was still a British colony.)

Early Rastafarians, as Price, Nonini, and Tree have argued, used Jamaica's history of slavery and racial oppression as the cornerstone of their political philosophy. They envisioned instead a new society that would emerge out of an anticolonial, sustainable, antiracist, anticapitalistic, nonconsumerist moral stance: "[F]reedom from oppression and symbolic and literal pursuit of liberation, dignity, and justice. Ritual gathering focused on extinguishing evil, deep introspection and contemplation, spiritual discipline, discourses of communalism, and rejection of status quo trappings are primary tactics— not membership drives, fund raisers or analyses of political opportunities" (Price et al. 2008: 137). The resulting Rastafari state would be a "theocratic government guided by a constitution based on divine principles: a moral state" (Price et al. 2008: 138). Their political goals represented a clear threat to both British colonial power and to the local elites vying for independence, who unleashed waves of repression in their efforts to quash the movement.

Of the founding group of Rastafarians, Leonard Howell, the recognized leader of the new movement, had been arrested and indicted in Jamaica in 1932 on charges of sedition for advocating loyalty to Haile Selassie as the true king of Africans around the world. He and other adherents of the movement had defied the colonial authorities by selling images of Selassie for a shilling, advocating the nonpayment of taxes because the island belonged to them and not to the British crown, and looking upon Jamaica as an African nation that owed its loyalty to the Ethiopian emperor. Some were sentenced to years of forced labor; others had been branded insane and committed to lunatic asylums. As a result, the movement opted to operate without any central leadership, dispersing into smaller groups and communes so as not to provide the authorities with a clear target for repression. The strategy of consciously fragmenting the movement gave individual Rastafarian Houses (as communities of adherents became known) greater autonomy and left the development of Rastafarian theology to the various Assemblies of Elders that served as group leaders.

In the 1950s, as the movement became a political force in the struggle for black liberation and the end of black peoples' "sufferation," and would-be leaders engaged in Repatriation marches and other forms of agitation, repressive measures intensified. The 1960s were particularly turbulent. In 1958 the leader of one of Kingston's Rastafarian Houses, known as "Prince" Emmanuel Edwards, had called for a symbolic "capturing" of Kingston and its proclamation as a liberated city. Thousands marched through the capital to plant a ceremonial Rastafarian flag—three bands of red, black, and green with the Lion of Judah (Selassie's imperial emblem) in the center—in the city's central square. Edwards, imbued with millenarian hopes for redemption, had hoped the gathering would lead to a miraculous massive Repatriation to Africa. Thousands of Jamaicans answered his call, some selling their belongings and gathering to await the boats that would suddenly materialize to take them home to Africa, only to face disappointment as they waited in vain.[4] The repatriation movement had been given fresh impetus in 1955 when Selassie had set aside five hundred acres of land in Ethiopia for any "Black peoples from the West" wishing to return to Africa. There were renewed hopes of repatriation for believers in 1966, during Selassie's brief visit to Jamaica, when he was greeted by crowds of worshipers "waving red, green, and yellow banners with such inscriptions as 'Hail to the Lord Anointed' and 'Conquering Lion of Judah'" (*New York Times* 1966: 8).

Edwards's symbolic attempt at revolutionary political action was taken up in earnest by Claudius Henry, a Jamaican visionary who had trained as a religious leader in New York City, and who brought to Jamaica in 1957 the recruitment strategies of Harlem's store-front churches. In Kingston, he joined the Rastafarian movement, setting up his African Reform Church and calling himself Repairer of the Breach. He experienced his own failure when the boats again failed to materialize in response to another call for Repatriation—for which he had sold fifteen thousand tickets at one shilling apiece. But instead of retreating to the hills as Edwards did to organize a tight-knit Rastafarian community (the Bobo Rastas), Henry, who identified strongly with Fidel Castro's new socialist regime in Cuba, became involved in guerrilla activity (primarily by forming a guerrilla training camp in the Red Hills overlooking Kingston), amassing guns, and conspiring to invite Fidel Castro to invade Jamaica. His son Ronald, who had declared an armed struggle against the Jamaican government and was linked to the ambush and death of two policemen and an informant, was himself murdered by the police.

These developments had a profound effect on Jamaican society. After an initial middle-class backlash, the movement's ideas were more closely integrated into other nationalist movements and cultural manifestations. One result was the formation of a middle-class Rastafarian group, the Twelve Tribes of Israel. As Rastafarian ideas spread across the Caribbean, groups appeared in Dominica (where they are known as Dreads), Trinidad (where they are involved in Orisha worship), and in a number of other Anglophone Caribbean islands. They were responding primarily to the appeal of the movement's focus on "race consciousness" and incipient message of environmental sustainability, as expressed by one of the subjects interviewed by Sheila Kitzinger in 1968:

> We are people of God who like to worship in our own way as the Lord has commanded us through his inspiration, and we should be free to do such without any intimidation or force by anyone, whether police, soldier or anyone. We are not people who hate White people but we love our race more than other people and we are not preaching race hatred amongst people, but we are preaching race consciousness, because we can take an equal place in creation, as God did create us to do. We can assure you that no true Rastafari brethren want to hurt anyone. We love all people. In fact we would like all people—all races of people—to be Rastafari. Our aim is to see the hungry fed, the sick nourished, the healthy protected, the infant cared for, the shelterless be sheltered, those who desire to go back to Africa go back in love and peace. (Kitzinger 1969: 243)

However, it was the more radicalized "yard" Rastas, as the young adherents of the movement living in the slums of Kingston were known, who were responsible for the crystallization of a specific Rasta lifestyle that would become emblematic of their faith and beliefs. The Rastafarian public identity became recognizable through the wearing of hair in uncombed, coiled locks known as "dreadlocks," symbolizing the mane of the Lion of Judah (one of Haile Selassie's titles) and the strength of Samson. Dreadlocks are also believed to have been the hairstyle of ancient warriors. Red, black, green, and gold were instituted as the young religion's representative colors: red for the African blood that must be shed for their redemption and freedom; black for the race to which they belong; and green for the luxuriant vegetation of the Motherland. The smoking of ganja, or marijuana, as a ritual that opens a path to spiritual enlightenment, became a central, albeit controversial aspect of the movement's religious practice. Rastafarians defended marijuana consumption, an illegal practice in Jamaica and most nations throughout the Caribbean region, as a source of divine inspiration, healing, and strength.

This second stage of development also included the elaboration of Rasta talk or "I-talk," a distinctive form of speech that emerged through the brethren's "witnessing" or "reasonings." According to John Homiak, it was a "socially charged 'dialect'" which [Rastafarians] created by "substituting the morpheme 'I,' 'I-yah,' and/or 'Y' for the first syllable of the English form" of various words. Dread talk, or Iyaric language, is based on a combination of modifications on the lexical structures of the Jamaican Creole (see Pollard 2000) and old English forms found in the Bible. It may also have been drawn from an African-derived dialect, archaic in Jamaican speech. The speech was traced originally to a handful of young Dreadlocks who first came together at Paradise Street in Kingston and later established a camp at Wareika Hill:

We exile ourselves to the hills where there is no noise, no bus, no pollution. Is a different meditation reach you ther. Ya see, only a Bible and mi rod I tek to de hill. Eventually now, we guh into ourselves—into de "higher mountains" as wha Moses did do for his meditation—in search of de Creator. And de Creator speak to I-n-I through the spirit and fix a new tongue in de latter days which is de *I-tesvar I yound. See-knots-see-I, I-yah Kongo, I-yah-Yinghi-I. . . . One Yantifull I-yound!*—those art words dat Headful I-on and I create—even up to *I-rie I-tes.* We started dat at Wareika Hill . . . it never come from nowhere else. Well, after a time now we had to leave Wareika Hill to penetrate all them *I-tesvar I-ses I-Yasta Y-ool-I I yantifull-I* into Back-o-Wall to form a group. Dat was de *I-gelic House.* (Homiak 1998: 163)

Rastafarians do not proselytize, but the movement was able to disseminate its message globally during this stage of its development through its connection to reggae music (see O'Brien and Carter 2002–2003: 221). Reggae became closely associated with the Rastafarian movement, as Kingston musicians Bob Marley, Peter Tosh, Dennis Brown, Bunny Wailer, and others embraced the Rasta faith and lifestyle. Reggae, which derives from an earlier form of Jamaican popular music known as ska, is based on a pounding four-beat rhythm conveyed by drums, bass, and electric guitars, and the scraper, a corrugated stick that is rubbed by a plain stick. Through its connection to the Rastafarian pan-African philosophy, centered on the rejection of the white man's Babylon, Reggae's increasingly politicized lyrics addressed Rasta concerns with social and economic injustice, the rejection of white culture, and the pressures of life in the Kingston ghettos. Introduced to international audiences by Bob Marley, Reggae became widely identified with Rastafarian self-expression and was largely responsible for the spread of Rastafarianism in the 1970s. As a result, the movement has gained about one hundred thousand followers worldwide. However, Reggae emerged as a significant populist music tradition in Jamaica only in the late 1960s and 1970s, decades after the Rastafarians began to develop an African-oriented spiritual culture centered on a vision of Repatriation to the African homeland. In *Reggae Wisdom*, Anand Prahlad argues that Rastafarian music performers adopted the movements' masculine ideal of the "warrior/priest" and used their command of proverbs to convey their spiritual insight, "one of the most essential characteristics of the warrior/priest [as] no other genre connotes wisdom . . . as does the proverb" (Prahlad 2001: 58).

Belief System

Despite its prominent manifestations as a political movement, Rastafarianism is most fundamentally a Creole religion, rooted in African, European, and Indian practices and beliefs. It is said to draw on the mystical consciousness of Kumina, a Jamaican religious tradition that ritualized communication with the ancestors (see chapter 5). The fundamental principles of Rastafarian faith have not changed significantly since Leonard Howell proclaimed the six basic tenets of the movement: a rejection of the corrupting principles of the white race; a belief in the moral and religious superiority of the black race; a commitment to exacting revenge from whites for their wickedness and mistreatment of blacks throughout history; a rejection of the government and legal authorities of Jamaica as accomplices of the white oppressors; preparations for a return to Africa; and acknowledgment of Haile Selassie's position as supreme being and only true ruler of blacks in Africa and across the Diaspora. Central to Rastafarian theology is the notion of Repatriation, of a return to the land of Ethiopia, the new Zion. Repatriation is a theological rather than a political concept; few Jamaicans, in fact, have actually relocated to Ethiopia. As envisioned by Rastafarians, the term refers to relocation to the place where God dwells, a place of justice. Rastafarians, however, believe that the better life that Christianity relegates to the life of the soul after death is possible in this world. Rastafarianism, therefore, is focused on the here-and-now and not on a transcendental realm beyond death.

Becoming a Rastafarian involves a simple process of private affirmation of faith in Ras Tafari as a prophet or god and a personal commitment to adhere to the basic tenets of the faith and adopt the Rastafarian lifestyle. "A Rasta man born that way"—a believer explained to Sheila Kitzinger—"A Rasta man have an inborn conception. No Rasta man cannot change"; joining the Rastafari faith is the outward manifestation of "something he has always known within himself," a realization of the truth (an acknowledgment of Grace) to which his eyes had been blinded before "by the distractions of the world and its sins" (Kitzinger 1969: 246). It is also a recognition of being the possessor of "art," the Rastafarian term for "the ability to perceive the things of God and to be sensitively aware of the sacred in life; . . . man's inherent ability to see through the apparent to the real, to separate the false from the true . . . to discern the good and to communicate knowledge about mystical experience" (252). Rastafarians often change their names when they enter the faith, selecting an Old Testament or Ethiopian name to which they add the prefix "Ras." Rastafari life, as Chevannes explains, "is centered on Africa. Every Rasta home is adorned with photographs of Haile Selassie, sometimes referred to as 'King Alpha,' his wife, known as 'Queen Omega,' maps of Africa and posters with African themes and the Ethiopian colours. Every Rasta man possesses an array of decorative buttons with replicas of Emperor Haile Selassie or some other African leader, which he proudly wears in public" (Chevannes 1994: 18).

The theology of Rastafarianism was gleaned from a rereading of the King James Bible through the prism of the *Kebra Nagast* (or *Glory of the Kings*) of Ethiopia, a text that combines mythical history and allegory. Its central theme is the visit of Makeda, the Queen of Sheba, to Solomon and the birth of a son, Menilek, who became the legendary founder of the Ethiopian dynasty. (Recently, many Rastafarians have adopted *Holy Piby*, the "Black Man's Bible," compiled by Robert Athlyi Rogers of Anguilla between 1913 and 1917, as their main biblical text.) The result of this symbiotic reading was a new creolized interpretive process known as "reasonings," extended oral meditations on the scriptures and their significance to Rastafarian life and belief. One of the responsibilities of Rastafari leaders is that of guiding followers in analyses of the Old Testament, from which they can glean parallels between their lives and Hebrew history and prophecy.

Rastafarian "reasonings" are informal gatherings during which a small group of brethren sit in a circle to smoke marijuana (a sacred weed to the Rastafarians) and have "lofty discussions." The "reasonings" take place among groups of male practitioners in a process that Patrick Taylor sees as having "brought the oral into the written text to become the bearers of a Caribbean textuality at its fullest" (Taylor 2001: 74). These sessions of oral testimony constitute "the primary form of ritual encounter, spiritual communion, and sociability shared by the male members of the movement" (Homiak 1998: 129). Dependent on the composition of the assembled group, their relationships, and the degree of versatility of the various speakers, the practice of reasonings "den[ies] the existence of a reified domain of 'oral tradition' comprised of widely shared or constantly voiced narratives that can be isolated for separate study" (Homiak 1998: 129). There is, consequently, no Rastafarian dogma per se, but a series of basic principles that offer a foundation for meditation and scriptural interpretation. The belief system of Rastafarians remains vague and loosely defined since there is no single authoritative voice. Individual interpretation, shared through reasonings, is the basis for acceptable doctrine.

Barry Chevannes, in *Rastafari: Roots and Ideology*, offers several lengthy examples of "reasonings" he recorded during his research. The brief excerpt below gives some idea of how ideas evolve in these gatherings.

VOICE 1: Where is the capital of the whole world?

VOICE 2: Ancient . . . [*Here the tape was unclear, but the answer was one of the ancient kingdoms of Africa, probably Axum.*]

CHORUS: Jah! Blood bath and is there Black I come from!

SHAKA: Because they never tell me say in 1665 the pirate was being commanded under the influence of this English pirate, Oliver Cromwell, which commanded the pirate Admiral Penn and Venables, Cecil Rhodes, John Hawkins, Livingstone . . .

CHORUS: Burn them! Burn them! Power!

SHAKA: . . . to come on the shores of Ethiopia and take black people and pack them as sardines in tin and then come, rob and rape . . .

. . .

SHAKA: They try to tell the people that Jesus is in the sky, and the people look to the sky for Jesus, whereas I an I the Dreadlocks tell the people of such time that I an I can representatively present I an I chanting as a living monarch to the world as a representative to the world that the only monarch, the only creator, is the King of Kings. And up till this time—it going into the dispensation of another two thousand years, they cannot present their god!

VOICE: Their Jesus!

SHAKA: So I an I stand here this day to stamp away Lord God Jesus Christ and all of them. And unless the whole world, internationally Black, come to a realization of one Icord (accord) to know and to attain themselves to the fact that the only alternative solution to suffering humanity today and forIver is Black Supremacy . . .

CHORUS: Haile I Selassie I Jah Rastafari!

SHAKA: . . . out of that there is no alternative, or just like beast that must perish.

VOICE: Death! (1994: 215–216)

The Rastafarian relationship to the Bible, the focus of their "reasonings," is a complex one. Rastafarians' acceptance of the Bible is conditional, and the text is subject to interpretations that harmonize it with the Rastafarian principles and ways of life. Central to the Rastafarians' relationship to the Bible is the notion that much of the Bible's original content was distorted when it was translated into English, and that it needs to be subjected to minute critical readings so that elements of the existing narrative whose meaning and relevance have been altered or distorted can be recognized. Rastafarians prefer allegorical as opposed to literal readings of the Bible that explore its metaphoric and symbolic content and unveil hidden messages and directives. Linked to this interpretive position is the Rastafarian doctrine of avatar (the descent of a deity to the earth in an incarnate form), which owes as much to the influence of Hinduism (as brought to the West Indies by Indian indentured servants) as to the possession rituals of other Creole practices such as Santería and Vodou. Rastafarians believe that God revealed himself first through the person of Moses, the first avatar or savior, and later through the prophet Elijah. In this reading of the prophets as avatars, Christ emerges as the third avatar, who prepared the way for the climax of God's revelation, the advent of Haile Selassie as Ras Tafari. Rastafarian readings of the Bible find evidence of Jesus' predictions about the coming of Selassie.

The avatars are, in turn, linked to the importance of visions and dreams in the Rastafarian worldview. Both can be rich in symbolic meaning and open to readings and interpretations, particularly in formal discussions such as those that take place during the "reasonings." Unlike the practitioners of other Afro-Creole religions in the Caribbean, Rastafarians do not believe in spirits other than God—which explains the absence of rituals of spirit possession—but they believe that God communicates through human vessels. These can be avatars, in the case of the prophets, or humans through whose dreams and visions divine truth can be filtered.

The one exception to the Rastafarian lack of belief in spirits and spirit possession are certain Rastafarian groups in Trinidad, whose links to the island's Yoruba-derived Orisha practices bring them into the Orisha world of ritual possession (see chapter 1 for a discussion of the Orisha religion). It is not uncommon in Trinidad for the drummers participating in spirit possession rituals to be Rastafarians. Drummers hold a prestigious place in Orisha ceremonies since the possibility of an Orisha or spirit descending to possess a celebrant is directly linked to the drummers' skill in playing the sacred drums. Houk, in his study of the Orisha tradition in Trinidad, found that Orisha-practicing Rastafarians are attracted by "the heavy Yoruba influence on the Orisha religion in Trinidad and the opportunity to worship African gods" (1995: 134).

The unifying element in Rastafarian narrative is the notion of the self as a subject that comes to know itself only in relationship with others. The basic logic of Rastafarianism, the "I-and-I" that stands for the plurality, for "we," represents the most elementary connection to the deity—Rastafar-I, Selassie-I, the unifying one (Taylor 2001: 75). This concept represents the most important theoretical tool in Rastafarian thought, since it encapsulates the notion of the individual in oneness with others and with God. It rests on the notion of God being within us all, serving as the unifying force between people, making one people out of the group. "I-and-I" stands for an understanding that God is in all men and that the bond of Rastafari is the bond of God and man. This oneness acknowledges man's need for a head and posits Emperor Haile Selassie as the "head of man." The Rastafarian God, as Sheila Kitzinger gleaned from her early work on Rastafarian communities in Jamaica, is "the Jehovah of Israel 'returned as in former days, so terrible and dreadful amongst the wicked,' a God of vengeance who will 'break in pieces the horse and rider,' 'the return Messiah, almighty Jah,' made manifest upon earth in the form of the Emperor Haille Selassie" (Kitzinger 1969: 252). This Old Testament God, whose nature is ungraspable, encompasses the cosmic creative force and "the inner vitality of all created things, including man and the spirit of man—the Breath within the temple which is God himself'" (252).

Rastafarian Culture

The most significant model for Rastafarian culture is the world of the Maroon communities of pre-Emancipation Jamaica, highly organized enclaves reminiscent of African communalism. The survival of Jamaican Maroon settlements was predicated on particular modes of social organization based on the Maroons' voluntary exile from mainstream society and rules of behavior that guaranteed continued dialogue and conservation of resources, all oriented toward the good of the larger group. Rastafarian Houses seek to replicate these earlier communities, which were identified with the least creolized, most authentically African aspects of pre-twentieth-century Jamaican culture.

Central to the culture are communal meetings called Nyabinghi[5] or Binghi where Rastafarians engage in communal ganja smoking, drum dance, and "reasonings." The festivals—the only activities resembling an established communal ritual in Rastafarianism—take their name from the anticolonial movement of Kigezi, Uganda—the *Nyabingi*—which called for death to black and white oppressors.[6] Early Rastafarian leaders like Leonard Howell and Archibald Dunkley referred to themselves as Nya men. Horace Campbell, in his book *Rasta and Resistance,* sees the Rastafarians' identification with the Nyabinghi movement as showing an advanced level of ideological awareness: "Those Rastafarians who called themselves Nya men had understood, as the peasants of Uganda, that black agents of the colonialists, like the black slave drivers and the 'house niggers,' could be just as brutal as the whites" (H. Campbell 1987: 72).

Rastafarian Nyabinghis—also referred to as "groundings" or "grounations"—are usually held to commemorate important dates in the Rastafarian calendar, such as events in the life and death of Halie Selassie and Marcus Garvey, and Emancipation. The practice is linked to rituals aimed at bringing death to white oppressors, and the Binghi dances retain some vestiges of magic. Some Rastafarians will refer to "doing a Binghi" as a means of revenge or retaliation, but for the most part the connection with magic, which would link Binghis to Obeah spells, is vestigial or symbolic. Binghis, which may last for days, depending on the resources of the host, can bring together scores of Dreadlocks from all over Jamaica, who gather to dance to the rhythm of Rasta drums well into the night.

Amongst the Nyabinghis, Kitzinger reported, the drums form "the central focus of worship, and the primary means by which religious fervour is expressed" (247). The drums that produce the characteristic Rasta beat are three: the bass, which is struck on the first of four beats and muffled on the third; the *funde,* which plays a steady one-two beat; and the *akete* or *kete,* which plays the improvised syncopations (Chevannes 1994: 18). The first of these is struck with the padded end of a stick, while the other two are played with bare hands. Most of the songs played during the Binghi are adaptations of music taken from the Zion Revivalist movement (see chapter 5), and the drums themselves can be traced to syncretized variations of Buru, Kumina, and Zion Revival drumming traditions.

The Binghis aside, ritual is primarily confined to the domestic sphere, as service takes the form of personal devotion by living a Rastafarian life, which is regulated by "a number of personal taboos and practices" (Chevannes 1994:18). Rastafarianism is identified with closeness to nature and the land. Practitioners prefer to sit on the ground as it brings them into harmony with the forces of nature. The movement has a strong environmentalist component, with members opting, whenever possible, to live off the land by planting subsistence crops without artificial fertilizers or mechanical exploitation. In keeping with this respect for the land and its products, Rastafarians follow a strict dietary code known as *ital*, or natural living. The word derives from the English "vital" and signals the commitment to adhering to a diet that increases levity, the life energy that exists in all of us. The Rastafarian diet, therefore, should consist of natural or pure food, preferably organically grown vegetables and grains free of additives (colors, flavorings, or preservatives). Rastafarians also avoid the use of salt, a practice based on the belief that salt intake reduces the possibility of sharing in God's spirit, as salt repels the spirits.[7] (Sea or kosher salt is used by some.) Rastafarians also avoid the consumption of pork and crustaceans in their diet, a practice drawn from similar practices in Judaism, Islam, and Ethiopian Christianity. Many practitioners also avoid consumption of red meat and it is common to find strict vegetarians or vegans among followers of the religion.

Kitzinger, in her work among Rastafarians in Kingston in the 1960s, also found that Rastafarians would avoid eating food prepared by anyone outside the group, feeling that this food may poison them: "We don't eat from nobody at all. We cook all food with our own hands." For similar reasons, some Rastafarians will avoid food that has been preserved through canning or drying. Most Rastafarian communities avoid alcohol except for rather vaguely defined medicinal purposes because they are "waiting to drink the palm wine" (1969: 35). Rastafarians also avoid smoking tobacco (a proscription that does not extend to the smoking of marijuana).

Rastafarian dietary practices are linked to a perception that the Jamaican medical infrastructure is not sufficiently developed to ensure the health of the working and peasant classes from which the movement has gained most of its adherents. Consequently, rather than depending on consultations with Obeahmen when ill, the Rastafarian approach to health maintenance is based on consuming foods best suited to maintaining health, and learning as much as possible about the curative properties of Jamaican herbs and plants. These food choices also have a sustainable, political component. According to Horace Campbell, Rastafarians "embarked on a project to use the fruits, vegetables, and plants of the countryside so that they could break the dependence on imported food. Yams, boiled bananas, plantains, callaloo, chocho and a wide range of local foodstuffs, which had been the food of the slaves, were prepared meticulously by the Rastas" (H. Campbell 1987: 123). This ital diet does not differ greatly from that of most poor Jamaicans, except for the widespread avoidance of salt, processed condiments, and canned food.

Rastafarian healing practices are drawn from traditional Jamaican herbal medicine and place a lot of emphasis on individuals possessing the gift of healing. Since illness and death are seen as the result of unnatural meddling with the course of nature, remedies must be found in nature itself. Religious leadership is often associated with the ability to heal the sick, either through supernatural agency or knowledge of herbs and folk medicine, and Rasta leaders owe their authority in the community in part to their expertise in the healing arts. As with more generalized Jamaican healing practices, illnesses are treated primarily with bush teas or herb poultices. Rastafarians rely primarily on complex herb remedies based on thirteen healing herbs, used in proportions of three to five, seven to nine, or nine to thirteen and combined according to divine inspiration. Rastafarians, who normally avoid Western medicine, will use prescribed or over-the-counter remedies if they consist of herbal or other natural ingredients. Rastafarian remedies often include marijuana, which is used as a highly effective expectorant and aphrodisiac. (Ganja, according to Kitzinger, is also "cooked as a green vegetable like Jamaican "Callalu" which is similar to spinach, and often given to children in this form, in soup or stew, or as a bush tea" [255].) Ordinarily, Rastafarians will shun Western medicine—whether for the treatment of illness or childbirth—and will specifically avoid the piercing of the body by any means, including injections with hypodermic syringes, blood transfusions, or surgery. Western medicine is also associated with contraceptive drugs, of which Rastafarians strongly disapprove. Contraception interferes with women's true nature and constitutes "internal murder." Instead, Rastafarian women rely on an abortifacient bush tea to prevent pregnancy, a natural practice that is tolerated although not openly encouraged by the group.

Rastafarians in Jamaica have developed a culture based on a distinct set of Afrocentric communal values. Communities are loosely organized into Houses run by an Assembly of Elders, who oversee the affairs of the House, settle disputes, appoint delegations, plan liturgical events, and assign tasks when necessary. In theory the Assembly of Elders should number seventy-two, but they are in fact fewer. Other than the Elders, there is no formal membership in a House, which is open to any Rastafarian by virtue of being a Rastafarian. It is an open structure that allows a great measure of democracy, as there is no hierarchy of age, ability, income, or function.

There is, however, a hierarchy of gender. Rastafarian religion, a fundamentally patriarchal structure, has been slow to grant women a voice in the elaboration of theology and ritual or a specific role outside the domestic sphere. Women, inferior beings incapable of directly receiving "the fullness of divine knowledge," can only acquire it through their husbands or "king-men" (Chevannes 1994: 15). Constructed on the principle of women's submission to male authority, the movement has ritualized female inferiority through practices reminiscent of the most conservative Jewish or Islamic traditions. Gender relations are organized around institutionalized female subservience to men, since Rasta men are incapable of commanding their women to do anything unrighteous: "A good Queen obey her husband in all things that is righteous unto God" (Kitzinger 1969: 252).

Women, therefore, are not an integral part of the movement, as they are not only barred from positions of leadership but have no recognized role in ritual or healing practices. Although they are not excluded from attending rituals and can bear the title of "Queen" if they have a long-standing live-in arrangement with a Rasta man, they have no ritual function, and must keep their dreadlocks covered and show proper deference to males. They are not allowed to cook while menstruating, must obey dress and "household codes" that include wearing ankle-length dresses in public, and in some cases can be secluded from social contact. Marriage is not common, as it is a part of the institutions of Babylon Rastafarians reject, and women who leave the community are expected to leave their male children with their fathers to be raise in the Rastafari faith.

A challenge to this female subordination has been growing since the early 1980s, resulting in greater freedom of action for women within the movement but no significant increase in their religious role.[8] Alemseghed Kebede and J. David Knottnerus point to the emergence of Rasta women like Barbara Makeda Lee, a Rastafari intellectual, who, in her articles, "brilliantly articulates the philosophy of the movement," as signaling "significant changes in gender relations and various tensions among group members as established beliefs and behaviors are challenged" (1998: 504). Rastafarian thought has been slower to embrace homosexuality, which remains (mirroring homophobic attitudes in Jamaican culture) a most dreadful transgression.

The most distinctive mark of the members of the Rastafarian House is the growing and wearing of dreadlocks, uncombed and uncut hair which is allowed to knot and mat into distinctive locks that led to Rastafarians being described as "the menacing devils with snake nests for hair" (Sanders 1982: 59). Rastafarians regard these as a sign of their African identity and as a religious sign of their severance from the wider society they call Babylon. What has been called "hair culture" among the Rastafarians began when adherents of the movement adopted full beards in emulation of the Godhead Tafari, a practice sacralized through new interpretations of biblical texts. The origin of the dreadlocks themselves can be traced to a group of urban Rastas known as the Youth Black Faith in the late 1940s. These Rastas saw the locks as an instantly recognizable emblem of their difference from mainstream society: "Locks had a shock value, but they were also a way of witnessing to faith with the same kind of fanaticism for which the prophets and saints of old were famous, men gone mad with religion" (Chevannes 1994: 158). The length of the locks is also an indication of how long a person has been one of the brethren, proof of his or her commitment to the faith. Rastafarians cite Leviticus 21:5—"They shall not make baldness upon their head, neither shall they shave off the corner of their beard, nor make any cuttings in their flesh"—to explain the directive against cutting their hair.

Another familiar feature of Rastafarian culture is the emphasis on smoking marijuana or ganja, the "holy herb" mentioned in the Bible, the smoking of which is comparable to a sacrament. The large-scale smoking of ganja in Jamaica, which can be traced back to the importation of indentured East Indians into the island, became a working-class phenomenon in Jamaica. Barrett, in *The Rastafarians,* explains how, through the use of ganja, the Rastafarian reaches an altered state of consciousness: "The herb is the key to new understanding of the self, the universe, and God. It is the vehicle to cosmic consciousness" (1977: 254–255). Ganja is regarded as "wisdomweed," and from the beginning of the movement Rasta leaders had advocated its use as a religious rite. Belief that it was found growing on the grave of King Solomon and the interpretation of biblical passages such as Psalms 104:14—"He causeth the grass to grow for the cattle, and herb for the service of man, that he may bring forth food out of the earth" —have been cited as indications of its sacred properties.

Rastafarianism is practiced today in small Houses throughout the world, although it is often hard to ascertain to what extent these Houses are truly involved in the theology of the movement as opposed to its compelling lifestyle of sustainable approaches to agriculture, vegetarianism, and relative isolation from the more intrusive aspects of modern media and technology. The spread of the faith throughout the Caribbean region was occasionally marked by violence, especially in islands where significant efforts were made to persecute or repress the movement. In Dominica, a particularly violent period of repression against Dreads (when police were authorized to "shoot on sight") culminated in the kidnapping and murder of Ted Honychurch, a well-liked white farmer whose son Lennox was then press secretary for the Eugenia Charles government (see Paravisini-Gebert 1996: 266–267). On December 30, 2000, two Rastamen entered the Cathedral in Castries, St. Lucia, and doused the priest, a nun, and numerous parishioners with gasoline before setting them on fire (the priest and nun died). Quoting from the

Bob Marley/Peter Tosh song "Equal Rights," one of them claimed that "the reason why I did that is for equal rights and justice and for the freedom of my nation"; both of them, in subsequent testimony, linked their act to the region's history of *sufferation* and the resulting Babylon-resisting radicalism (Griffin 2006: 2). The killings, as Elmer Griffin argues, "attacked directly the symbols of an equivocal postcoloniality, and then reignited the awareness of Rastafari as a forceful resistance ideology and the problematic hope of West Indian militancy" (2).

As the movement enters its ninth decade and the unifying figure of the now-dead Haile Selassie as the embodiment of the God on Earth fades from memory, it remains to be seen how Rastafarianism will ultimately resolve the tensions between its appeal as a political movement and its status as a viable Caribbean religion. There is no doubt, however, that since the 1970s Rastafarianism has become a "global religion" with adherents throughout the Caribbean, the United States, the United Kingdom, and beyond (Yawney 1980: 75). Guyanese intellectual Walter Rodney underscored the importance of Rastafarianism to a growing pan-Caribbean African consciousness: "In our epoch the Rastafari have represented the leading force of this expression of black consciousness" (1969: 61). Echoing Rodney, Trinidadian Calypsonian the Mighty Stalin sings of the Rastafarians as the source of true pan-Caribbean hope:

> De federation done dead
> And Carifta going to dead,
> But de call of the Rastafari
> Spreading through the Caribbean.
> It have Rasta now in Grenada,
> It have Rasta now in St. Lucia,
> But to run Carifta, yes you getting pressure.
> If te Rastafarian movement spreading
> And Carifta dying slow
> Dem is something dem Rasta done
> That dem politicians don't know.
> So dey pushing one common intention
> For a better life in de region
> For de women and de children,
> That must be the ambition of the
> Caribbean Man.
>
> (quoted in H. Campbell 1987: 170)

────────────────────────────────────── 7 ──

Espiritismo

Creole Spiritism in Cuba, Puerto Rico, and the United States

Ese constante sabor por comunicarnos con el más allá. (That constant fondness for communicating with the other world.)
—Angel Suárez Rosado

In the mid-nineteenth century another component was added to Caribbean Creole religiosity. While African-based religions were undergoing a consolidation throughout the region, the Spiritualist and Spiritist practices of North America and Europe were making their way across the seas to the Caribbean. The enthusiasm for Spiritist philosophical, religious, and healing notions can be understood as a response to several important factors in nineteenth- and twentieth-century Caribbean societies, among them the social upheaval created by the quest for democracy and the diaspora of Caribbean peoples to the United States. In the Caribbean, the creolization process led to the creation of distinctly Cuban and Puerto Rican varieties of Spiritism—*Espiritismo*—and, in the diaspora to the United States, *Santerismo*. A Creole spiritual healing practice with roots in the United States, Europe, Africa, and the indigenous Taíno Caribbean, Espiritismo amplified and transformed European Spiritism in its travels back and forth from the Old World to the New.

In 1848, three young sisters from Hydesville, New York—Leah, Kate, and Margaret Fox—began hearing strange knocking sounds in their parents' small cottage. The knocks, which they took to be communications from the dead, slowly developed into a code—one rap for yes and two for no. Through these wall rappings the sisters came to believe that the spirit with whom they had been communicating was that of a murdered peddler whose body had been buried underneath their cellar (male remains were actually discovered years later). Spiritualism, the belief in the ability of the living to communi-

| 203

cate with the dead in and through such practices as table rappings, levitations, and trances by persons called "mediums" (mediators through whom communications are supposedly transmitted to the living from the spirits of the dead, a process also referred to as "channeling"), was born of these events and immediately became popular in the context of religious revivalist movements in the United States. It later captured the European imagination through such prominent Spiritualists as England's Queen Victoria and Sir Arthur Conan Doyle.

In France another philosophical movement developed at this time in response to North American Spiritualism, but with a more "scientific" and doctrinal approach: Spiritism. Based on the beliefs and philosophies of the French educator Hippolyte Léon Denizard Rivail (1804–1869), better known by his *nom de plume* Allan Kardec (a name supposedly based on previous reincarnations ascertained from mediumistic communications), Spiritism was a moral philosophy rather than a religion, incorporating the ideas of Romanticism and the scientific revolution to bridge the gap between the material and spiritual worlds. Having already published widely in the field of pedagogical reform, Kardec began to study spirit communication through mediumship. In 1857 he published *The Spirits' Book* and in 1859 *The Mediums' Book*. These were the first two books of several that explain the basic principles of Spiritism, an expansion of Spiritualism from a series of sporadic psychic experiences to an organized cult. (*The Spirits' Book* has been translated into numerous languages—in English it was translated as *Spiritualist Philosophy: The Spirits' Book*—and is still widely read today in Caribbean communities in the United States. Its widespread popularity is evident in the botánicas or herbal-religious shops in U.S. Latino neighborhoods.)

The Spirits' Book is the principal text of French Spiritist doctrine and was written with the assistance of two young mediums (Kardec himself was not a medium) using the method of automatic or slate writing to question numerous spirits, among them Saint Augustine, Socrates, Ben Franklin, and such Catholic reformers as Saint Vincent de Paul. Kardec's work as an educational reformer is clearly evident in the book as he interrogates his spirit interlocutors in a question and answer format with hundreds of answers organized by categories in what David Hess describes as an "otherworldly ethnography" (1991: 61), with lengthy recapitulations and elucidations of the spirits' replies. Thus one discovers such exchanges as the following under the categories of "Spirit and Matter" and "Progression of Spirits":

23. What is spirit?

"The intelligent principle of the universe."

_____What is the essential nature of spirit?

"It is not possible to explain the nature of spirit in your language. For you it is not *a thing*, because it is not palpable; but for us it is *a thing*.

24. Is spirit synonymous with intelligence?

"Intelligence is an essential attribute of spirit, but both merge in a unitary principle, so that, for you, they may be said to be the same thing.

25. Is spirit independent of matter, or is it only one of the properties of matter, as colours are a property of light, and as sound is a property of air?

"Sprit and matter are distinct from one another; but the union of spirit and matter is necessary to give intelligent activity to matter."

114. Are spirits good or bad by nature, or are they the same spirits made better through their own efforts?

"The same spirits made better through their own efforts. In growing better they pass from a lower to a higher order. . . . Spirits acquire knowledge by passing through the trials imposed on them by God. Some of them accept these trials with submission, and arrive more quickly at the aim of their destiny; others undergo them with murmuring, and thus remain, through their own fault, at a distance from the perfection and the felicity promised to them." (Kardec 1976: 8–9, 47)

The Spirits' Book describes the other world and offers moral guidelines for actions in this one; although it rejects such key Christian tenets as the divinity of Christ, it stresses charitable acts and embraces Christian morality, espousing the Christian golden rule of "doing unto others as you would have others do unto you." Given the scientific discoveries of the age that challenged traditional Christian theology (including Darwin's theory of evolution, published in the same period as *The Spirit's Book*), for Kardec Spiritism "bridged the gap between science and religion, provided a rational basis for faith, linked social progress to spiritual progress and equilibrated natural laws with moral laws. His doctrine spanned the gulf in ideology just as the spirit medium bridged the gap between this world and the other world" (Hess 1991: 61). Kardec defined a life in spirit in the above-mentioned works as well as in *The Gospel according to Spiritism* (1864), *Heaven and Hell* (1865), and in other books that struck a chord with Europeans and with many Latin American and Caribbean peoples of his time.

The nineteenth century was an age of scientific discovery, and one of its dominant doctrines was Positivism, developed by the French philosopher Auguste Comte (1798–1857). Positivism maintained that metaphysical questions are unanswerable and that the only true knowledge is scientific. Primarily a social reformer, Comte's goal, described in *The Course of Positive Philosophy* (1830–42), was a society in which nations and individuals would live in harmony and well-being. He considered religion the highest science, but it was a human-centered religion, lacking metaphysical implications. Earlier in the century, Claude Henri de Saint-Simon (1760–1825), one of the founders of modern socialism, had advocated a different Christianity in *The New Christianity* (1825). He conceived of Christianity as a spiritual force for progressive human development. But Kardec differs from Comte and the utopian socialists in emphasizing inward spiritual reform. Nineteenth-century European scientific concepts of philosophy and psychology combine in Spiritist goals for the moral and social development of mankind, accomplished through the evolution of the spirit.

Kardec departed from Anglo-American Spiritualism through his strong belief in reincarnation, preferring the term "Spiritism" to distinguish his ideas from the "trickery" of the Spiritualists. According to the tenets of Spiritism in *The Spirits' Book*, the primary purpose of life on earth is to master, through knowledge and participation, the lower nature and to be guided and influenced by the higher aspects of the divine spirit within. The universe, according to Kardec, was created by an eternal, all-powerful, just God who comprehends all beings "animate and inanimate, material and immaterial" (1976: xiv). The corporeal world is constituted by material beings, souls or "incarnated spirits" (the physical body is its "envelope"); the spirit world is the abode of "discarnate spirits." Man is composed of three things: "(1.) The body, or material being, analogous to the animals, and animated by the same vital principle; (2.) The soul, or immaterial being, a spirit incarnated in the body; (3.) The link which united the soul and the body, a principle intermediary between matter and spirit" (1976: xiv).

The link is the perispirit, a type of "semi-material envelope" or vital fluid that unites the body and the spirit (analogous with the "perisperm," the fleshy part of the seed of plants that surrounds the embryo); in dreams the soul, still connected to the body by the perispirit, journeys on earth and in space to communicate with other spirits while the body is asleep. Birth represents the reincarnation of a spirit. Upon death the soul, "the immaterial and individual being which resides in us, and survives the body . . . the vital fluid" leaves the body but the spirit remains encased in the perispirit and may be seen or heard by those in trance; it eventually abandons the earth to join other incorporeal or disincarnated spirits after a period of time (1976: iii).

Free will affords the spirit choices to create its own destiny and the possibility of spiritual evolution attained through knowledge and the experiences offered by repeated reincarnations in physical existences. The spirit can grow morally and achieve enlightenment to approach perfection and the ultimate goal of becoming a pure spirit, or remain backward, suffering and postponing evolution. One's "guardian angels" and "protector spirits" guide human beings through life's "tests"; communication with these spirits is therefore fundamental. Spirits are categorized in a hierarchy according to the degree of perfection they have attained: "pure spirits" have attained maximum perfection and love of goodness, and are the so-called "angels"; good spirits aspire toward goodness and support humans in their earthly trials, but have not yet achieved perfection; imperfect or ignorant spirits tend toward evil and the inferior passions and incite humans toward the same. A person's qualities are a reflection of those of the incarnate spirit. The soul's individuality is preserved after the body's death; in reincarnation it may recall the actions of its former lives.

As a consequence spirits exert an influence on the physical earth and interrelate with human beings: the good ones inspire and sustain one through life's trials; malevolent spirits take pleasure in creating suffering and in deceiving and causing harm. Advanced spirits, when contacted, are distinguished by their dignified, refined language and enlightened, high-minded ideas; less advanced spirits are distinguished by their coarse expression and ethically flawed arguments. Spiritism's goal, therefore, is the enlightenment of dark or "intranquil" spirits in need of light, redemption, and progress through reincarnation, and the advancement toward spiritual perfection. Reincarnation for Kardec is associated with the principles of choice and free will in the evolution of human beings across incarnations, and the law of cause and effect that governs the accumulation of karma according to the appropriateness of one's deeds.

Spiritism's belief in reincarnation appealed to Christians in Europe and in the Caribbean and to practitioners of African-based religions as well:

Kardec's doctrine includes beliefs that have historical origins in hermetic and esoteric traditions (the astral body, vital fluids, and spirit communications through mediums), Indic philosophy (reincarnation and karma), highly reformed Protestant theology (a unitarian doctrine and the interpretation of heaven and hell as psychological states), Catholicism (the emphasis on spiritual hierarchies and the mediating role of an extrabiblical doctrine), social reformism (the emphasis on equality, progress, freedom of thought, and education), as well as modern science (what Kardec called the "experimental" side of Spiritism which later became known as psychical research and still later as parapsychology). (Hess 1991: 2–3)

Although often identified as a popular religion, Spiritism was in fact a spiritual movement, an option for persons of various social classes. For French Catholics it was an alternative to the mainstream religious practice of Roman Catholicism, reflecting "a new pluralism of religious choice in nineteenth-century France" (Sharp 1999: 283). Enlightenment and revolutionary critiques of Christianity in the era led to attempts to find other spiritual explanations. French Spiritist challenges to the Catholic Church came from all sectors of French society, although Spiritists were generally found in the *petit bourgeois* and the urban working classes (rural Spiritists existed in smaller numbers), each group interpreting the messages from spirit guides according to its particular needs and perspectives: "Spiritism created alternative meanings that integrated 'tradition' and 'modernity' and continually created new forms of the marvellous" (Sharp 1999: 283–284).

Although Kardec believed that Spiritism was compatible with all religions, the relationship between Spiritists and the Roman Catholic Church in France was largely adversarial as Spiritists denied many of the Church's tenets, were anticlerical, and avoided the parish church. But they did not necessarily reject Christianity and their practices and beliefs generally followed Christian moral values. The Catholic Church condemned the practice as early as 1853 and, although it clearly could not deny the spiritual and supernatural aspect of Spiritism without threat to itself, denounced the manifestations of the spirits as the work of Satan, and Spiritists as profaners of the dead (Sharp 1999: 288–289). "Catholic dealings with spiritism illustrate the church's attempt to maintain control over the supernatural in the face of the materialist challenge of science as well as the spiritist challenge" (1999: 292).[1]

Spiritism's adaptations of popular tradition and belief to changing cultural values in Europe resonated in Latin America and the Caribbean where it became an urban spiritual philosophy for a middle class who also disavowed the Church's traditionalism in a protomodern world. The unorthodox doctrine of the evolution and enlightenment of the spirit allowed Cuban and Puerto Rican freethinkers to incorporate the Enlightenment values of reason and science into their spirituality as they turned their backs on a religious institution too closely identified with the oppressive colonial powers. The class and ideological division between an upper or middle class with a preference for a "scientific" approach and a lower or middle class with more religious tendencies was true of Anglo-Saxon Spiritualism, French Spiritism, and later the Latin American varieties that evolved in Brazil, Argentina, and other parts of the Americas. In Cuba and Puerto Rico, two islands under Spanish colonial rule until 1898, French Kardecian Spiritism also became one of the ideological factors facilitating the growth of a national consciousness. Such Puerto Rican political and social leaders as Rosendo Matienzo Cintrón and Luisa Capetillo, for example, discovered in Espiritismo a practice that reflected their break with conservative Roman Catholicism and their nationalist ideals. "At a time when all things French were revered among Latin American intellectuals, who were working through French-inspired revolutions to achieve national independence, Spiritism offered an anti-clerical, anti-catholic but profoundly christian religion" (Koss 1977: 32).

The ideas of Anglo-French Spiritualism, combined with Spanish Spiritism transported by persons returning to the region from study abroad, filtered beliefs proscribed by the Spanish colonial government into the islands. Although Spiritism initially had its greatest impact on the literate middle-class sectors in Cuba and Puerto Rico, other classes began practicing their own variety of Creole *Espiritismo* in a culture already prepared to absorb a doctrine that reinforced existing spiritual beliefs: the spirit-oriented popular and folk Catholicism of the rural peasant populations—the Cuban *guajiro* and the Puerto Rican *jíbaro* who had been largely ignored by institutional Roman Catholicism—and African-based religions. As a result, when "the literate classes represented by the incipient bourgeois, in their political protest against the Spanish Church and State invested energy and time in the diffusion of the spiritist belief system and with the Africans' ancestor worship present in Puerto Rico, its diffusion was not difficult" (Pérez y Mena 1991: 27).

Cuban Variants of Espiritismo

In chapter 2 we observed the influence of Espiritismo in certain Regla de Ocha/Santería rituals, in particular the *Misa Espiritual* or spiritual mass that precedes the important *Kariocha* initiation; Espiritismo has also influenced the Conga Regla Palo Monte, especially in the variant called Mayombe. According to José Millet and others, Espiritismo itself is among the most deeply rooted of "popular religions" in all sectors of Cuban culture. "The lack of an orthodox Catholicism, even in the loftier sectors of the Cuban society of the time, contributed to the emergence of a type of believer who mixed Catholicism with cults of African origin. This led to syncretism, the enriching exchange among systems of belief like Santería, Regla de Palo, Espiritismo, Vodú, and a distinctive type of Catholicism," which Millet refers to as "Espiritista-Catholicism" (1996: 9).

During the Ten Years' War of Insurrection, the first Cuban war of independence against the Spanish regime (1868–1878), the collaboration of the Church with the colonial government became evident. Consequently, Cubans in favor of independence began to consider Spiritism more liberal and progressive than Catholicism:

> Some progressive Creoles of that region, in favor of any tendency that was "contrary" to the colonial mindset, established that to be an overzealous churchgoer was to be in favor of the Spanish regime; to become a Protestant meant one was a party to United States annexation; becoming a believer in Regla de Ocha was to assume elements of slavery, and affiliation with Vodú was the same as calling oneself a foreigner. (Argüelles Mederos and Hodge Limonta 1991: 177–178)

The eastern rural zone of Cuba, an area harshly affected by the cruelty and bloodshed of the war, was described as undergoing a "spiritual epidemic," as people turned to Espiritismo and supernatural solutions to their suffering. By the 1880s Espiritismo had spread throughout the island, provoking its condemnation by the Cuban Catholic hierarchy. A vigorous Espiritista defense of the doctrine emerged in numerous publications from 1879 to 1890, as Espiritismo centers were established throughout the country (Argüelles Mederos and Hodge Limonta 1991: 178). The simplicity of its ritual and the possibility of direct communication with the spirits of the dead help explain Espiritismo's rapid diffusion, especially in a period of social crisis. Before long, however, this option, outside traditional Catholicism but also distinct from African-based creeds, began to incorporate elements of both in its rituals, expanding and creolizing the original Kardecian concepts with local nuances that evolved into three principal Cuban variants: "Scientific" or "Table" Espiritismo (sometimes referred to as "White Table"), *Espiritismo de Cordón* or "Cord Spiritism" (practitioners are called *cordoneros*), and *Espiritismo Cruzao (cruzado)*, "Crossed (Mixed) Spiritism."

"Scientific" or "Table" Espiritismo

"Scientific" or "Table" Espiritismo, originally an urban practice, closely follows Kardecian concepts; practitioners consider themselves scientists and study the writings of Kardec and others as part of their practice. The practice derives its name from the fact that believers are seated at a table, usually covered with a white cloth, from which they invoke and communicate with the spirits in a séance. Considered by practitioners to be a scientific philosophy rather than a religion and a more rigorous and elevated form of Spiritism than the others, the rituals are carried out by mediums who have demonstrated their "faculties" or abilities with respect to communication with the spirits. Those present, who do not share these faculties, nonetheless consult the spirits when they manifest themselves through the mediums, to ask questions and request solutions to different problems. Followers assume a meditative position and use music, hymns, readings of prayers from Kardec's works (typically from his *Selected Prayers* or his *Gospel according to Spiritism*, known as the *Evangelio*), and poetry during typical Table Espiritista sessions. Such sessions usually consist of small groups, although private consultations also exist. Spirits will manifest themselves differently depending on the level of the spirit: elevated spirits will communicate verbally in a refined and dignified manner, while the less evolved spirits' language will reflect their lower status. The abrupt or brusque movements generally associated with spirit possession are not usually evidenced in this type of spirit communication.

Espiritismo de Cordón

Espiritismo de Cordón derives its name from the form of its ritual: believers stand in a circle, hand in hand, then they turn and walk counterclockwise, chanting and praying, beating the floor forcefully with their feet, and swinging their arms intensely and rhythmically until they fall into a trance. While maintaining elements of Kardecian Spiritism, Espiritismo de Cordón also assimilates elements of folk Catholicism and to some extent trance aspects of African creeds. Healing is the principal focus of its practitioners; the prestige of a medium is generally based on the extent of his or her skill in solving problems. According to Joel James Figarola, the Cordón variant evolved in the provinces of Oriente and Camaguey from several sources. Among these were the Congo funeral rites in which the recently dead were invoked collectively by a group of people forming a circle to question if the deceased had left items to be resolved on earth (dead ances-

Kardec's *Evangelio* in a Boston botánica. Photo courtesy of the artist
Héctor Delgado.

tors of the recently dead were also invoked to assist the deceased in his or her first entry into the other world). Historical events originating during the Ten Years' War in which the insurgent civilian population was slaughtered ferociously by Spanish forces also inspired aspects of Espiritismo de Cordón. The terror created by the repeated massacres and the distance of the civilian population from the combating Cuban forces created a sense of peril, insecurity, and outbreaks of collective hysteria. Cordón ceremonies in which whites held hands under the guidance of their former Congo servants to invoke the spirits, hoping to discover the fate of family members or friends fighting in combat, or their own, offered solace to the besieged population (1999b: 136).[2]

Cordón Spiritism does not have a uniform or structured set of beliefs; cures are stressed over theory, and elements of possession analogous to those of the African-based religions combine with ideas considered scientific, distancing the practice from the "superstitions" and "fetishism" of the "blacks" and the authority and classist nature of the "whites" represented by Catholicism, uniting in one practice what Cubans are more likely to accept: "a Catholicism removed from the Church, a simplified system of spiritual beliefs, and a trance similar to that of the Africanized religions" (Millet 1996: 15–16). And, like all Espiritista practice, it is open: initiation rites are not required in order to actively participate in all the rituals, as distinct from the Afro-Cuban religions. There is no official clergy in Espiritismo. The principal or Head Medium directs the "temple," an informal ritual space, and conducts the spiritual work, although he or she is usually not included in the human "chain" during the session. Other levels of medium participation are the strong ("fuerte") mediums with specific faculties of development, and simple or ordinary mediums, with less developed faculties.

In a typical Espiritista center of the Cordón variety the altar occupies a large area, designed with the intervention of the spirits. The space has been ritually purified to dispel evil spirits; the entryway is protected by means of a large bowl of water. All who enter must wet their hands as a precaution, to avoid the spiritual contamination of the space with the entry of malevolent spirits. A table covered with a white cloth holds a large glass of water in the center directed toward the spirit guides of the temple. There are additional glasses of water as well; the mediums, apart from their individual spirit guides, make contact with the spirit guide or protector (discussed below) of the temple director as well. The spirits of the dead are usually grouped into so-called *comisiones* or commissions, a grouping based on race, origin, or similar cause of death.[3]

Underneath the table a bowl of water is placed to gather the harmful thoughts of those who arrive in search of cleansing or healing. Generally characterized by sobriety and economy, the Cordón centers will probably also include photos of deceased mediums, friends, and family members who were important in the work of the mediums in the temple, and lithographs of the Virgin Mary and of Catholic saints (in front of the photos of deceased mediums and of the saints one might find a glass of water and flowers, as it is believed that flowers strengthen the spirits and water offers clarity). Among the saints an image of Saint Lazarus might be included, for example, but not in the representation of Babalú Aye as in Regla de Ocha; believers energetically refute any connection to the Afro-Cuban religions in their Cordón practice.

The spiritual work is accomplished by contacting the spirits, which is begun at the table. At the beginning of the ritual sessions prayers are said to obtain God's permission to form the *cordón* and works by Allan Kardec are read to invoke the dead. After the prayers, the mediums rise and form a type of circular chain, holding hands and thus creating the circular cord that passes a "mediumistic fluid" (*fluido*) through the human chain.[4] The leader begins a chant and the rest respond with a rhythmic chorus, repeating it over and over again. Guttural sounds accompany the rhythm of the chants, deep breathing, and contrapuntal movements of the arms as the members of the group forcefully hit the floor with their feet. The Head Medium will guide the session, at times interrupting the cord to direct them to place their hand on the ground and lightly touch the floor with the tips of their fingers without breaking the chain and raise their hands to the heavens. According to Roger Bastide, the breathing and stamping sound patterns are akin to the sounds produced by the drumming and chanting in African cults, creating a hypnotic effect. And despite the denial of any African influences by *cordonero* practitioners, "It is clear that what we have here is a reinterpretation of the African ancestor-cult and cult of the dead through Allan Kardec's spiritualism" (1971: 168).[5] The work continues until the mediums go into trance and explain the source of a person's problems. Healing may take any one of several modalities, including a *despojo* (spiritual purification/cleansing), baths and/or *santiguación* (massage/blessing), discussed below.

El Espiritism Cruzao (Crossed)

As Joel James Figarola and others make clear, none of the Cuban religious systems can be considered in isolation, nor are they encountered in "pure" form; one must approach them with the intent of finding mutual mixed or overlapping tendencies, or both, and affinities. The name of the third major Cuban Espiritista variant, *El Espiritismo Cruzao* (Crossed), illustrates this concept. A combination of the other variants of Cuban Espiritismo and the traditional Afro-Cuban religions—especially the Regla de Palo Monte—and folk Catholicism, it is one of the most widespread Espiritismo practices on the island. In addition to the elements described above in the scientific and Cordón variants, Espiritismo Cruzao includes the Regla de Palo cauldron, Eleguá artifacts, the sacrifice of animals, the representation of Catholic saints, offerings of fruits and sweets, considerable use of tobacco smoke to invoke the spirits and elicit the trance state with the assistance of the medium's spirit guides, cologne (typically *Agua Florida* or Florida Water), candles and flame, all meant to attract and please the spirits exhibiting the "diverse forces that are part of the work" (Millet 1996: 27). Among the spirits received by a medium there will commonly be an African slave, generally a Congo, who speaks in the typical broken Spanish *bozal* that she or he might have used in life. The practice is not exclusivist: if during the ritual the proceedings are deemed too "weak," followers might form a cord in the *cordonero* fashion to strengthen the spiritual flow. Healing is an important element for the *Espiritista cruzao*; private spiritual consultations are also provided by esteemed and proven mediums.

One of the more important ceremonies is the syncretic *Misa Espiritual* (Spiritual Mass), the Espiritista ceremony that precedes the initiation of Regla de Ocha novices to invoke beneficent spirits and exclude maleficent or "intranquil" ones who may "contaminate" or impair the spiritual work (see chapter 2 on Santería/Regla de Ocha). The Mass for the Dead carried out by devotees of Espiritismo (and in many cases of Santería) is a crucial Espiritista ceremony that merges several religions.[6] A table called a *bóveda* (crypt or vault) dedicated to one's personal ancestors (found in the homes of most Afro-Cuban religious practitioners), covered with a white cloth symbolizing purity is located in a space that has already been ritually purified with herbs to alienate "perturbing" or negative spirits; all present must bless and cleanse themselves with water before the bóveda prior to the ceremony. Goblets of water, lit candles that "give light" or illuminate the path of the spirit toward a joyful afterlife, photos of the deceased, and cologne applied to family members and participants are all meant to attract the spirit of the dead who has made his or her desire to communicate with the living evident in dreams or visions. The dead continue to be seen as important family members who can intervene in the affairs of the living. Communication with deceased family members consoles those who believe that a connection is still possible and each can affect the other: spirits can be elevated, thanks to the mass, to a higher status in the otherworldly spirit hierarchy. After contacting the deceased through the medium, a meal is shared and a sense of peace and joy often animates family members who have celebrated the departed.

According to Jorge and Isabel Castellanos, the Misa Espiritual is a crucial part of Afro-Cuban religions nowadays; indeed, many practitioners and spiritual leaders of Regla de Ocha, Regla de Palo, and the other Cuban Reglas are also Spiritist mediums. As Lydia Cabrera's informants in *El monte* declared: "Ocha or Palo . . . doesn't it come to the same thing? Spirits all! Doesn't one fall into trance with the saint as with the dead? In religion everything is to do with the dead. The dead become saints." As Cabrera explains, "[S]aints and spirits are daily visitors in the houses of the Cuban people" (1983: 31). Honoring the dead has always been an essential element of Afro-Cuban practices. The dead (*egun*) play a fundamental role in the Congo Reglas and, as we observed in the discussion of Santería/Regla de Ocha in chapter 2, before the orishas are honored the ancestors must be propitiated, whether they are blood relations or of one's religious lineage. Egun shrines are located at ground level inside the house, in the bathroom or basement, or outside.[7] During a Misa Espiritual the spirits who speak are not necessarily one's ancestors; they may be any of a range of spirit guides and protectors. Food offerings on the bóveda reflect the syncretism of Egun veneration and Spiritism: "spiritual" items—incense, candles, tobacco smoke, cologne, and prayer—are offered to the spirits while food and other "material" offerings are made to the dead.

Given this history it is understandable that Espiritismo would exert such a powerful influence on Cuban society. As Castellanos and Castellanos observe, the Spiritual Mass is noteworthy because, while not a Spiritist session per se, it merges Espiritismo, Catholicism, and the Afro-Cuban religions in its ritual, fusing the diverse elements of the "Cuban cultural continuum":

> Of European origin, believers of orishas and ngangas celebrate it. It uses crucifixes, cane liquor and tobacco. Spanish and *bozal* are spoken. Our Fathers are prayed, hymns to the "beings" [spirits], and all during a ceremony that precedes the installation of the orisha Ochún in initiation. To the *ashé* of the Lukumí and Congo religions are added that of the Catholic Church and the occult forces of Espiritismo. That is Cuba or, at least, a part of Cuba. (1992, 3: 202)

The presence of Espiritista centers in Cuba grew throughout the country at the beginning of the twentieth century, with contacts established between Cuban and other Latin American Espiritistas. The Sociedad Espírita de Cuba (Cuban Spiritist Society) was founded in 1915 and held its first Congress in 1920, demonstrating a considerable presence on the island; in 1936 the societies of all the Cuban provinces were grouped under the Federación Nacional Espírita (National Spiritist Federation) to organize national meetings and events, especially in Bayamo, Camagüey, and Havana, where most of the societies existed at the time. Local and popular Espiritista centers, not usually formally affiliated with the organized "scientific" societies, also continued to flourish (Argüelles Mederos and Hodge Limonta 1991: 183–184). After the Cuban Revolution in 1959, Espiritistas continued to practice their beliefs in Cuba; with recent economic hardships, an increased religiosity has been noted in the country and Espiritismo maintains a presence in Cuban society, predominantly in terms of its healing and charitable work.

Puerto Rican Espiritismo

As in the case of nineteenth-century Cuban Espiritismo, educated Puerto Ricans opposed to the Spanish colonial regime perceived the Espiritismo doctrines of justice and charity to be inspirational in their quest to liberate the island from Spain and its oppressive institutions. Organized in secret— those who were discovered were arrested and prosecuted by the government for their affiliation with "revolutionary factions," and condemned and ostracized by the Catholic Church—the movement grew nevertheless. Espiritista ideas had entered Puerto Rico just as they had in Cuba: the sons of the middle class who returned home from study abroad in Europe imported Allan Kardec's ideas, which took root in the Puerto Rican intellectual community. Kardec's books entered the island clandestinely, as was the case with so much of the contraband that entered a colony living under the rigid, monopolistic control of the Spanish colonial regime.

The movement spread despite repression by government and Church authorities, creating Espiritista centers throughout the island. The earliest of these is believed to be "Luz del Progreso" (Light of Progress) founded in 1888 in Mayagüez. Espiritistas encouraged educational and health care reforms, organized libraries, established numerous newspapers and magazines, founded several health care facilities, including free hospitals (at a time when the public welfare system was neglected by the colonial government), children's homes, libraries, and courses of study. In short, Espiritista centers promoted progressive intellectual and moral standards as Puerto Ricans struggled for political reform.[8] When the Treaty of Paris ended the Cuban-Spanish-American War in 1898, giving the United States direct control of Cuba, Puerto Rico, Guam, and the Philippines (the United States invaded and took over the island of Puerto Rico just six months after Puerto Rican liberal politicians had finally wrested autonomy from Spain), Espiritistas were allowed to openly espouse their doctrine under the First Amendment guarantees. In 1903 the Spiritist Federation of Puerto Rico was founded to unite and organize Espiritismo centers and societies, and to develop the movement further.

While Puerto Rican Espiritismo in the Kardecian scientific mode began as a middle-class movement dedicated to the progressive moral and social development of the society as a whole, another variant of Puerto Rican Spiritism emerged among the urban and rural lower classes. Referred to by Mario Núñez Molina as "indigenous Espiritismo" (1987, 2001) and by others as "popular Spiritism"[9] (disparagingly referred to by the scientific Spiritists as *espiriteros*), this Espiritismo was centered on "a framework for understanding healing and treating illness" (Núñez Molina 2001: 117).[10] As Núñez Molina explains, this "indigenous Espiritismo" combines the native healing systems of the Taino (Arawak) Indians of the island—represented by the medicine man or shaman called the *bohique* who prayed to the spirits using massage, tobacco, herbs, and magic to effect cures—and the herbal medicine and folk healing practices of both the Spaniards and the enslaved Africans. All these were syncretized to create an indigenous, healing-oriented, popular Espiritismo which "integrates different healing systems and religious traditions that had evolved in Puerto Rico for hundreds of years," providing a coherent worldview (2001: 118). Koss-Chioino notes that the spread of Spiritism in the latter part of the nineteenth century was partly the result of the disenfranchisement of popular folk healers—*curanderos* (faith/folk healers), *sobadores* (massage healers), and *comadronas* (midwives)—by the new Spiritism supported by a "scientific" discourse, and by the harassment of the Catholic Church and the *protomedicates,* the licensing boards established by the Spanish colonial regime in 1844. "The Spiritist medium took over the social role of the *curandero* (or rather the latter became an Espiritista)" (Koss-Chioino 1992: 13).

"Indigenous Espiritismo" is therefore autochthonous to Puerto Rico and not a European import. It is also the most popular variant of Espiritismo on the island. Núñez Molina describes Espiritismo as a "community healing system" and like others regards it as an important mental health resource for Puerto Ricans, a healing alternative.

Certainly Kardec may have provided the intellectual aspect of Espiritismo through his books. . . . But one cannot ignore the fact that a linkage to this type of tradition of practices and visions existed since the early days of the island. It is in the space inhabited by Espiritista altars where resistance is maintained because this is the space of the people. That is where one perceives the mingling of the Indian, the Black and the *jíbaro* [peasant]. It is the space of constant germination, of fecundation that leads to thoughts of the new space that is America. (Suárez Rosado 1992: 125)

Puerto Rican "scientific" or White Table Espiritismo closely follows its Kardecian counterparts in Cuba and elsewhere in Latin America, seeking to communicate with the spirit world through intermediaries or mediums—a role that anyone with the necessary "faculties" can play—and protection and assistance in dealing with *pruebas,* life's tests or trials. The spiritual development of human beings and of spirits entails a reciprocal relationship: both elevated and ignorant spirits require the help of human beings to transcend their limitations, and incarnated beings cannot progress toward higher levels of spiritual development without the assistance of spirits. For White Table practitioners too Espiritismo is more a science than a religion: dogma and ritualistic cult practices are against Espiritismo's "true" principles. They gather for Espiritismo sessions in centers called "schools" and "institutes" lacking the paraphernalia found in indigenous Espiritismo—incense, candles, anthropomorphic representations of God and the saints, spiritually purified water—for they consider these to be elements of superstition that attract ignorant spirits. Study and moral development are essential; spirit possession is deemphasized.

However, as in Cuba, Espiritismo in Puerto Rico did not restrict itself to the middle classes; the popular classes identified aspects of Espiritismo beliefs with elements of Puerto Rican culture. Spirit belief was already present on the island and had been for a long time. Folk Catholic rituals were introduced into Espiritismo practice: given traditional Catholic teachings, the prospect of communicating directly with guardian angels and saints did not represent a leap of faith, and Espiritismo's philosophy of attaining moral perfection through trials and suffering appealed to those who could appreciate that worldview (Núñez-Molina 1987).

The religious atmosphere on the island was altered once again at the beginning of the twentieth century with the forceful reintroduction of North American Protestantism and a change within the Roman Catholic Church from Spanish domination to an Americanized Roman Catholicism. According to Eduardo Seda, Spiritism, "the psychiatry of the poor" (1973: 119), underwent a revival in Puerto Rico at this time as a result of Puerto Ricans' collective insecurity and the destruction of a sense of community created by the attempted Americanization of Puerto Rican culture and its colonial relationship with the United States (1973: 152).[11] For Andrés I. Pérez y Mena and Marta Moreno Vega, however, Espiritismo is not a result of social dysfunction but a continuation of Puerto Rican ancestor worship based on Taino and Afro-Puerto Rican cultures.[12] Their ideas largely correspond with Roger Bastide's assertions that for enslaved Africans Kardecism represented a means by which they could revive their ancestor cult on a "higher level" through a "fashionable theory" that was indulged in by their masters: "[I]f they had simply kept up their ancient customs, they would have been written off as unassimilable savages" (1971: 107). Nineteenth-century upper-class Puerto Ricans turned to French Spiritism to "whitewash" the African and jíbaro folk elements of their society with a European practice, although, according to Pérez y Mena, "by practicing Spiritism [they] provided legitimization of the ancestor worship already flourishing in Puerto Rico" (1991: 25).

In the twentieth century Puerto Rican Espiritismo continued to creolize further, giving rise to "new forms of the marvellous." Whereas in nineteenth-century Cuba White Table Kardecian doctrines had combined with African-based religions to produce such variations as Espiritismo de Cordón and Espiritismo Cruzao, and Espiritista practices, particularly the Misa Espiritual, became a standard element of Santería/Regla de Ocha ritual, in Puerto Rico this combination of Espiritismo with Santería or other African-based religions came about as a result of the immigration of Cuban exiles to the island subsequent to the Cuban Revolution of 1959. In his 1987 doctoral dissertation Núñez-Molina asserted that it was impossible for him to find Spiritist centers in Puerto Rico that integrated Santería into their practices; the indigenous Espiritistas he interviewed did not perceive Santería as representing a higher stage of development. Instead, they related Santería to sorcery and practices that attract ignorant spirits: "As Santeria becomes more popular among Puerto Ricans, the practice of indigenous Espiritismo will become more syncretized with Santeria" (1987: 132).[13] Indeed Santería did become popular in Puerto Rico after 1959, facilitating syncretism between popular Espiritismo and Santería.

The same phenomenon is observed among Espiritistas in Puerto Rican communities in the United States: the influence of Cuban exiles in the United States and a syncretized Spiritist practice from Puerto Rico influenced by Cubans in Puerto Rico resulted in the establishment of syncretized Spiritist temples or *centros* (centers) in U.S. Puerto Rican communities. According to Pérez y Mena, the emergence of this variant was tied to the search for ethnic and cultural identity in the Puerto Rican Diaspora; he describes it as one example of the "Afro-Latin" beliefs practiced in the United States, and identifies it as "Puerto Rican Spiritualism"[14] (also referred to by others as "Santerismo"[15] and "Puerto Rican Santería," different names for practices reminiscent of Espiritismo Cruzao in Cuba). African worship became more acceptable in the "mainland" environment than it had been on the island on account of several factors: the popularity in the 1950s of Cuban and Puerto Rican band music which was influenced by Santería chants and instruments and, more significantly, the social consciousness movements in the 1960s in the U.S. Puerto Rican community that identified with African American struggles, leading to a positive reassessment of African cultural identity.[16] As Migene González-Wippler makes clear, however, "[A]ll santeros are spiritist (*Espiritistas*), but not all spiritists are santeros" (1989: 274).

An additional observation by Alan Harwood with respect to the blurring of socioeconomic differences as migrants become a minority group in a new setting (observed in the Cuban exile community with regard to the participation of a range of races and classes in the Afro-Cuban religions outside Cuba) is also a key factor in explaining the syncretism of Mesa Blanca and Santería traditions outside the island: whereas in Puerto Rico Mesa Blanca and popular Espiritismo are divided along class lines, in New York City and other parts of the Puerto Rican Diaspora in the United States, the demographic composition of Espiritismo practitioners is more heterogeneous. This is consistent with the socioeconomic realities of the Puerto Rican migration, contributing toward the blending of several traditions:

> Since the extremes in class variation that obtain in Puerto Rico are by and large not present in New York, people in the narrower socioeconomic range in New York may, in the absence of the extremes, interact more readily and thus opt for either tradition. This homogenizing factor is further reinforced by the social organization of New York City, where the salient status for Puerto Ricans, regardless of class origin, is their ethnic identity, and sociocultural differences that are relevant on the island become much less important in this new context. . . . Whatever the specific reasons behind the growing syncretism between Mesa Blanca and Santería in New York, however, its effect is that many New York Puerto Ricans are competent in performing the rites of either tradition, and cults that go under the name of either Santería or Mesa Blanca (or *Espiritismo*) in New York are usually a blend of the two traditions. (Harwood 1977: 52)

GOD

PURE SPIRITS
or
ETERNAL ENTITIES OF SPACE
(angels, seraphim, others)

SAINTS/*ORICHAS*

HEROES AND LEADERS

SPIRITS OF ORDINARY PEOPLE

INTRANQUIL SPIRITS

INCARNATE SPIRITS

Harwood's Espiritismo pyramid.

Harwood conducted the fieldwork for his influential research on Espiritismo as a mental health resource for the Puerto Rican community in a low-income area of Manhattan called Washington Heights. There is an abundance here of botánicas[17] or herbal-religious shops and such folk healers as the *santiguadores,* who specialize in setting dislocated bones and in curing a type of indigestion called *empacho* with healing massages, usually in the form of a cross. Harwood participated as a member in the activities of three Espiritista centros, one of them Mesa Blanca and two influenced by Santería. They were located in storefronts and the basements of buildings with varying numbers of members ranging from six to forty. Harwood observed several other centros over a two-and-a-half-year period, identifying three fundamental aspects of the phenomenon of Spiritism: "(1) spiritism as an identity, a way in which people can classify and define themselves for others; (2) spiritism as a subculture, a set of standards for what it is (i.e., beliefs) and what one can do about it (i.e., ritual); and (3) spiritism as a cult, a religious group with a certain structure of social statuses and roles revolving around the central status of medium" (1977: 34–35).

Espiritismo is not exclusivist. Certain Spiritist beliefs are shared among the wider Puerto Rican and non–Puerto Rican cultures (the belief in spirits—*espíritus*—and in the possibility for harm resulting from feelings of envy—*envidia*—or hostility and competitiveness), and adherents are not prevented from practicing other religions. Espiritismo represents an alternative doctrine of beliefs and values, with widespread individual variations. Harwood discovered that the Spiritist centro contributed to the psychological and social well-being of its adherents by serving as a voluntary community organization, a religion, and a cultural identity. It provides for many of the needs of Puerto Ricans and other urban Latino migrants (centros in New York City are usually multiethnic in leadership and/or clientele) living in the midst of an alien urban metropolis like New York City.

Harwood's oft-reproduced pyramidal diagram of the spirit hierarchy in Spiritist cosmology is based on concepts generally accepted by all Espiritistas. Although Mesa Blanca and Santería worshipers differ in the number of ranks and the occupants residing in each of the spatial planes, Harwood's diagram portrays a generalized ranking representing "points of agreement" in the two traditions. Intranquil spirits at the lowest level of the spirit hierarchy, bound to the earth after a premature or violent death, or having failed to fulfill their spiritual potential in life—*espíritus poco elevados* or spirits of little enlightenment—are helped to advance to the next spiritual rank by the living—"incarnate spirits"—who recite prayers, light candles, and make offerings. They do so in order to *darle la luz al espíritu,* "give the spirit light" and to prevent sorcerers from employing restless spirits to harm their enemies.

A further division of the spirit world is that of the cadres (*cuadros*) by which each division of the higher-ranking spirits assists those below them in achieving the moral perfection that leads to advancement in spiritual rank. At birth each incarnate spirit receives a guardian angel which assists the person to make right decisions; the guardian angel is aided by lower-ranking incorporeal spirits from within the cadre into which the person was born, all acting as intermediaries to protect incarnate spirits and transmit their supplications to higher spiritual ranks (Harwood 1977: 41–42). This protection is attained through a bond realized in prayers and offerings; the ultimate connection, although less common, is achieved through development (*desarrollo*) as a medium, at which time one acquires an additional spirit guide.[18]

The identification of a spirit as either a protector or a *causa* (a spirit that creates problems or misfortune) is determined during trance, the focus of the Espiritista ritual (which is not limited to the mediums; everyone can join in calling the spirits). In a typical Mesa Blanca meeting the Head Medium

(*Presidente*), with his or her assistant mediums (*mediunidad*) and the *novicios* (developing mediums) sit around a table. Covering the table is a white cloth upon which are placed a goblet of water and a candle, in the presence of a number of *creyentes* (believers) who have attended to take part in the session (*velada*). Through prayers (usually from Kardec's books and the Apostle's Creed of the Catholic religion) and concentration, the Presidente and the mediums summon the spirits to the table to aid the assembled congregation in their trials and in their relationship to the spirit world.

After an invocation—typically "*Este centro se abre para el bien y se cierra para el mal*" ("This Center is open for goodness and closed for evil")—the spirits will manifest themselves in the mediums: the spirit guide will begin by opening the way for other spirits to manifest themselves with the guide's protection as the mediums are employed in spirit work. As the spirits manifest themselves in the mediums, the first stage of the healing process, *buscando la causa* (determining the cause of the problem), commences.[19] Mediums display the reception of a spirit by their facial expressions and at times by shuddering and jerky bodily movements; the individual thoughts and feelings of believers are ventilated (such terms as *evidencia,* evidence or proof, and vision are used to describe communication with a spirit); members of the centro and mediums relate to each other in a shared exchange of spirit communication. Once the cause of the illness or predicament is discovered, the Presidente will interrogate and persuade the malevolent spirits (*seres*) to depart from their suffering victim, a process referred to as *trabajando la causa,* "working the cause," to have the spirits lifted (*levantadas*).

Lifting or elevating the spirits is one of the principal healing objectives of Espiritismo. While an individual medium with the help of her or his spirit guides can discover the causas and cleanse the client spiritually, the working or elevation of spirits is generally carried out in a session with other mediums: one will "mount" the causa, another medium will interrogate it, and additional mediums present will assist the medium in trance in the event that a troublesome spirit is destructive or aggressive. In the final phase the spirit undergoes a *despojo* or purification wherein it is convinced that it is indeed a spirit and no longer a part of the world of the living, and is taught how to attain a more advanced level of spiritual evolution. The entire group generally participates in the cleansing ceremony.

Espiritismo cult groups vary widely: some are spontaneous, neighborhood-type community groups, meeting in the home of the leader, while others are organized as "churches" in which members pay dues to defray the cost of the center's meetings and celebrations, and occasionally to assist other members. Mediums may serve a healing role in the prescription of herbal and other spiritual remedies—candles, oils, perfumes, baths—available at the botánicas, where one discovers

> a seemingly unfathomable mélange of books, statues, herbs, candles, soaps, powders, spiritual lithographs and leaflets—few are aware of their cultural and functional diversity and complexity . . . shelves of multicolored "solutions" in a variety of forms claiming power to effect important changes in one's life—from a remedy for a problematic love life to the cure for a serious illness or relief from distress. . . . [W]ith a pluralistic and eclectic worldview, botánicas are a community enterprise, a heritage and a symbol of Caribbean cultural healing, a palpable representation of medical *mestizaje,* or syncretism.[20]

Seda notes that the curative herbs and potions purchased for baths and spiritual cures are compounds created by the folk "pharmacist." They frequently have captivating and intriguing descriptions, and are to be found on the shelves of botánicas: "follow me potion" (*esencia sígueme*), "good luck potion" (*esencia de la buena suerte*), "chain-breaking potion" (*esencia rompe cadenas*), "essence to tame tough guys" (*esencia amansa guapo*), "I-can-and-you-can't potion" (*esencia yo puedo y tú no puedes*), "essence of jealousy" (*esencia celitos*), "forget-me-not potion" (*esencia no me olvides*), "essence of mastery" (*esencia vencedor*), and "essence to subdue" (*esencia dominante*) (Seda 1973: 107). The Espiritismo centro does not comprise a ritual family in the sense of the *casa de santo* of Regla de Ocha worship, however. Although the Presidente retains control of all the major activities of the centro, clients and mediums who may defect to join other centros or form their own frequently challenge that authority.

Santerismo

Santerismo, as its name suggests, is a merging of Espiritismo and Santería; the African influence is clearly demonstrated in the connection to the spirit world via the *santos* or *orishas* of the Afro-Cuban religion, considered elevated spiritual beings, as well as to African spirit guides or *Congos*. Santerismo mediums communicate with lower-ranking spirits as well but are possessed by the orishas in a ceremony that varies in many respects from that of the Mesa Blanca.[21] One of the first differences one notes is the fact that in Santerismo centros the leader is referred to as the Godfather (*padrino*) or Godmother (*madrina*) as in the Santería religious kinship system (but lacking the lifelong bond established in the Afro-Cuban practice) and not as *presidente*. Pérez y Mena has observed a ceremony in which a Godfather stands in red Roman Catholic ecclesiastical vestments placed over white Santería garb (used in the latter part of the session), surrounded by "godchildren" dressed in white with colored scarves around their waists. The Godfather prays at the altar and later sits with the mediums at a table where a collective spirit possession session takes place in the midst of music varying from traditional conservative religious music to Afro-Cuban chants praising the orishas.

A ritual purification or *despojo* to remove evil influences occurs prior to the ceremony; after the customary invocations through prayer and readings that lead to the attraction of good spirits and possession, the causa or spiritual diagnosis takes place followed by the spiritualist cure of "working the spirit." The meeting may end with a ritual "exorcism" or despojo of the entire assembly, achieved through one or more of several methods: the area in which the session is to take place is purified with a type of fumigation called a *sahumerio* consisting of such items as burned charcoal with crushed garlic, incense, and pungent herbs to expel evil influences, and a washing (*riego*) with holy water, herbs, and cologne to attract beneficent ones. During the ceremony extensive use is made of cigar smoke and/or of fire burning in a flaming pail (a few drops of lit alcohol) to purify the session. The preliminary ritual would include prayers to Eleguá to protect the doorway or entrance from intranquil spirits.

A typical Santerismo altar is a paradigm of the creolization process; the Puerto Rican artist and devotee of Espiritismo Angel Suárez Rosado describes the space as a reflection of the "aesthetics of accumulation" (1992: 125).[22] The white tablecloth touches the floor to communicate with the higher beings; items used for the Espiritista session are placed on the table—a cross, a crucifix, goblets of water, pencil, paper, candles, rubbing alcohol, cologne, cigars, and Kardec's books of prayers. The chairs for the President (*Presidente de mesa*) and the mediums are situated at the table in front of an altar which may have several shelves behind it on the wall. A variety of objects are represented on these shelves: another crucifix, flowers, candles, numerous and varied effigies and chromolithographs (*estampas*) of Catholic saints (particularly of the patron saint of the centro). In addition one would probably find the stereotypic representations of various ethnic spirit protector guides of the centro mediums who offer advice, diagnose illnesses, and witness events in the spirit world: the *Madama* dolls, a Black "mammy" type, turbaned and rotund in a gingham dress, representing the *curandera* or faith healer, akin to the West Indian Obeah woman;[23] a North American Plains Indian, male and/or female, with typical headdress, representing a heightened warrior spirituality; the Hindu or Arab, a judicious philosopher spirit; the gypsy (*Gitana* or *Gitano*) who is in touch with the future; a Congo, a wise old African man or woman, familiar with nature, magic, and time-honored healing remedies. The mix of figures is undoubtedly based on healing cult practices from diverse earlier traditions, although one might also see representations of historical heroes.

In centros syncretized with the Orisha traditions the Seven African Powers (*Siete Potencias Africanas*)—Eleguá, Ogún, Changó, Yemayá, Obatalá, Ochún, and Orula[24]—in their Catholic representation and in the colors and attributes[25] that symbolize them are also represented at the altar. Santerismo centros vary in their degree of syncretism with Cuban Santería. The syncretic process of identifying orishas and Catholic saints is also individual and localized: the orisha Orula, for example, identified with Saint Francis of Assisi in Cuba, is celebrated as Saint John the Baptist, patron saint of the Puerto Rican capital city, among Puerto Ricans in New York City (Pérez y Mena 1991: 45).

Water is an essential component for all Espiritistas, to dispel intranquil spirits or petition elevated ones; flowers for the saints and Agua Florida cologne applied on those present serve the purpose of attracting the spirits. Clothing in Santerismo sessions ranges from a simple scarf around the neck or forehead to a complete vestment in the style and color attributed to a santo; shoes are removed to avoid interrupting the flow of spiritual *fluido* throughout the body. Music dedicated to each of the major orishas (the Seven African Powers, while not referred to as such in Afro-Cuban Santería in Cuba, are often the major saints propitiated in Santerismo ceremonies)[26] and the use of their representative *collares* (bead necklaces) in ceremonies prepare the way for the possession of the medium and the manifestation of a spirit. His or her spirit guide(s) will reveal the client's predicament, which is interpreted by the other mediums present. The client's causa can now be "worked" with such methods as *pases*, labeled by Harwood as "spirit-inducing movements" (1977: 66), gestures and strokes to the back of a client's head, neck, shoulders, and arms which are then raised above the client's head by the medium and abruptly thrown down so that the "magnetic influences" left by the spirits are removed. In another form of hand passes the medium moves his or her hands several inches from the client's body to come in contact with the client's "aura." He or she then performs a cleansing to rid the client of malevolent spirits and invoke the aid of the client's guardian angel.

Seven African Powers.

A water bowl nearby is tapped by the medium periodically during the proce-dure to release the negative effects of the cleansing into the water.

As we have seen, the principal method of Espiritista therapy is to discover the causa and convince the intranquil spirit to depart from its victim. Spir-itists are consulted when clients believe that the source of their problems is spiritual or if medical treatment has not proven satisfactory. Once it has been determined through trance that the sources of a client's problems are spiritual—a tormenting, intranquil spirit, difficulty with one's spiritual pro-tectors, human envy, sorcery, a trial or *prueba* sent by God to test one's moral strength—measures are taken to "give light" to spirits in need of elevation and strengthen the relationship with protective ones. The therapy may also include a number of tasks—baths, offerings, or ritual purifications of the home—that actively engage the client in the healing process.

It is generally believed that the two principal origins of spiritual misfortune that would bring a client to a practicing Spiritist are envy or *mala fé* (bad faith) and sorcery (*brujería*). Harwood distinguishes sorcery from witchcraft, the usual translation for brujería, because its properties as related to Santerismo are closer to the anthropological definition: [B]*rujería* involves the manipulation of material objects and spells to work harm, which is the defining property of sorcery, rather than a personal, psychic power which may be used to molest others (witchcraft). In the context of spiritism *envidia* is closer to the anthropological definition of witchcraft" (1977: 85). The language and techniques of brujería—charms made with something belonging to the intended victim and directed to its destination by the medium's spirit servant (*perro* or dog) summoned in spiritual rites—recall those used in Afro-Cuban Regla de Palo Monte ritual activities for creating harmful spells, following Frazer's concept of contagious magic. Harwood notes, however, that "Mediums who develop relationships with these 'dark spirits' are believed eventually to lose their beneficent spiritual guardians—a belief that deters some mediums from practicing sorcery entirely" (1977: 85).[27]

One of the more common causas among people who have problems with personal relationships is the *mala influencia* or evil influence of an attached spirit from a prior existence who impedes the client's involvement with living persons; the Spiritist must enlighten the spirit and convince it to depart. And another typical causa is the suffering of an untrained medium whose *facultades* or mediumistic abilities have not yet been determined. The uncontrolled possession of spirits can cause depression, seizures, and/or repetitive dreams (those focusing on a dead relative who had been a medium in life often confirm the diagnosis). Developing one's faculties as a medium is the usual recommendation.

Health and Healing

Spiritist "psychotherapy" as a form of indigenous and/or community healing among Puerto Ricans has been studied by Harwood, Koss, Garrison, and Núñez-Molina, among others; Koss has traced the history and evolution of Spiritism as therapy in comparison with Euro-American mental health sciences in the late nineteenth and early twentieth centuries:

[I]f Spiritism had not been arrested in its social evolution by Euro-American cultural imperialism in the medical sciences, it would have developed into a prestigious, more systematic and highly organized social movement instead of the cult religions and occult sciences of its present status in Latin America. Moreover, its better cultural fit as a treatment for many emotional disorders would have enhanced its potential function as a creative ideology and an organization supportive of healthy societal change. . . . [B] oth the psychological sciences and Spiritism share a common birthright and ultimately derive from parallel intellectual currents of the last half of the eighteenth century. (1977: 23)

The diagnosis of a Spiritist is similar to that of a psychiatric diagnosis in the search for a category to describe a client's state that would lead to a method of treatment, but it differs in one important respect: "In spiritism, clients do not play an active role in providing the diagnostician with information about their symptoms. It is the diagnostician's duty to uncover clients' symptoms" (Harwood 1977: 94). At this point the healer assigns a label (envidia, brujería, mala influencia, and the like) and a treatment procedure. Ignorant or malevolent spirits can cause controlling thoughts and actions called an *obsesión* (obsession), subjecting their victims to physical and psychological disturbances that can range from minor headaches to serious illnesses.

As mainstream psychotherapy has not always been found to be the most effective method in helping people from areas in which traditional and modern cultures coexist, Núñez-Molina stresses the need to recognize the value of indigenous healing systems such as Espiritismo to improve mental health services for Puerto Ricans on the island and in the United States (2001). Núñez-Molina and Harwood have studied the development of Spiritist mediums who, lacking any formal training in psychotherapy, have been found nevertheless to be effective in some cases, either alone or in collaboration with psychotherapists. Espiritista healers do not necessarily compete with mental health professionals, but offer complementary services that the community may be unable to receive from professional mental health systems.[28]

Most studies of Espiritismo as therapy deal with the practice as a form of short-term psychotherapeutic crisis intervention to deal with problems related to such interpersonal relationships as the death of a loved one or a life transition. Harwood observes that Spiritist ceremonies shift the locus of responsibility for a client's behavior outside the client within the spiritual realm, in contrast to mainstream psychiatric therapies that emphasize the client's responsibility for his or her condition (1977: 190–191). And, compared to psychotherapy, Spiritist therapy does not stigmatize a client as being *loco* (crazy); it is a culturally accepted method of treatment for many in the Puerto Rican community. The fact that the medium-healer shares the client's ethnicity and culture is another advantage: advice and treatments fall within the shared cultural premises and expectations of the client.

An example of the relationship of Espiritismo and psychotherapy is found in the treatment of a common psychiatric diagnosis from the 1950s through the 1980s, the so-called "Puerto Rican Syndrome," popularly referred to as *ataques de nervios* (nervous attacks), one of the supposedly "culture-bound" illnesses affecting the Puerto Rican community.[29] The malady varies in its description according to one's perspective, be it medical, anthropological, or political. It was first reported among Puerto Rican male patients in U.S. veterans' hospitals on the island in the 1950s and 1960s; their sudden hostile outbursts and partial loss of consciousness, among other symptoms, were attributed to an inability to adapt to the "highly competitive culture" of the U.S. military and to child-rearing practices that created "personality deficits" in Puerto Rican men (De La Cancela, Guarnaccia, and Carrillo 1986: 436–437). In the 1970s and early 1980s, Latino mental health professionals began to describe *ataques* as a social phenomenon, a culturally sanctioned response to stressful situations. Among medical anthropologists, connections were drawn during the same period that linked manifestations of the ataque—seizures, aggression, and dissociation at "inappropriate times," observed in some members of the Puerto Rican community (particularly women)—and Puerto Rican Espiritismo (linking spirit possession with the exhibited behavior).

From a feminist perspective, the ataques were considered a reaction to machismo, "the idiom by which further male violence is prevented or by which women attempt to extricate themselves from untenable situations and gain caring attention" (De La Cancela, Guarnaccia, and Carrillo 1986: 441). And within a wider historical framework that includes other U.S. Latinos, ataques de nervios have been viewed as a symptom of colonialism and dependence: "[T]he triggering of ataques, the behaviors manifested in them, and the impact they have on others is understood through socio-economic circumstances of colonialism experienced by *ataques* sufferers. *Ataques de nervios* provide Puerto Rican and other Latinos opportunities for displacement of anger, secondary gains, and direct rebellion against repressive conditions" (De La Cancela, Guarnaccia, and Carrillo 1986: 432). Spiritist therapy and rehabilitation for those who suffer such emotional illnesses have been successfully utilized in collaboration with mainstream mental health therapies: "[S]ince non-pharmacological psychotherapy depends heavily for its efficacy on the words, acts, and rituals of the participants, spiritist therapy has the particular merit of allowing both healer and sufferer to deal with the latter's problems within a shared symbolic framework" (Harwood 1977: 20).

Espiritista "healing dialogues" with tormenting spirits are used to deal with problems in personal relationships—the inability to form a lasting romantic attachment, for example—a recurring dream of a dead family member, or a chronic incapacitating malaise preventing one from leading a productive life, the types of problems that would precede a visit to an Espiritista healer. In his study of a Puerto Rican town in the early 1960s, Eduardo Seda observed the social functions of the practice in the community and noted the "psychodrama" of one type of Spiritist therapy in which "the spiritist session places the intrapsychic conflict of the patient in a drama in which the spirit demands reparations for offenses committed by the patient" (1973: 117). The following is an excerpt from one session included in Seda's study in which the temple president Don Perico, the second president Tulio Gerena, Doña Felipa, an eighty-year-old woman suffering from leg cramps she attributed to the actions of tormenting spirits, several middle-aged mediums, and a congregation of believers all participated. The session began with an invocation by Don Perico who read from Kardec's *Gospel according to Spiritism*. He asked God to open the temple for healings, and requested that "the spirits that come to this temple and take part in this table not be able to leave taking anyone who has come here. The spirits have to be admonished so that they never come back again." At this point Doña Felipa fell into trance.

> FELIPA: (shaking and lamenting bitterly): Forgive me, Father.
> TULIO: (to mediums): Come on now, come on, all right. Rub her hands real hard.
> PERICO: Now raise your hands up high, and don't bring them down till all those things have gone away. Ask God's forgiveness.
> FELIPA: (yelling): My God, forgive me! Oh Lord, forgive me! . . .
> TULIO: Go away! Go on, leave! . . .
> PERICO: May you find a happy future for yourself and for your children. I want you to do something for her, but she has many faults against her since she did not fulfill her obligations. (To mediums assisting him) Keep it up, go on till it has left. Let's go, keep it up, go away, put your hands on the table. . . . Detach yourself from her. Don't you hear me? . . . She's crying now. She

realizes that she's made a mistake, and she knows that she has to be good. It happens to us all.

FELIPA: Oh Lord, forgive me! My God, forgive me! (She continues, crying and sobbing in great despair.)

PERICO: You have to cure yourself, and you don't have to cry. Leave her now. I tell you, don't make her cry like that, more and more. Do as I say, come over here, so that you can find happiness for your children, as I've always encouraged. (The congregation joins him in the Our Father.) (1973: 120–121)

An excerpt from Pérez y Mena's report of a New York Espiritismo centro session describes a dialogue with the causa of a young woman who had been suffering from serious emotional problems. After having undergone the purification the young woman was unwilling to reply in either Spanish or English and the Godfather addressed her mother:

GODFATHER: When did you, after having this female child, think that she was crazy (*estaba loca*)? . . . You began to think this at about what age?

MOTHER: At about 10 years of age. (Mediums and congregation at this point in unison say "Proven!" "Comprobado!" Some gasping and marveling at the Godfather's pinpointing the problem via the spirits . . .

GODFATHER: To how many Spiritists (Spiritualists) did you take this young woman to have her cured?

MOTHER: Many.

GODFATHER: Then you were of the faith? You left the faith! (Here the audience gasped—"Proven!") . . . This daughter suffered a frightful experience; they tried to do her a harm. (*Un daño* means specifically rape or sexual abuse.)

MOTHER: Yes, that is the way it was. (Congregation responds dramatically with "Proven!" . . .

GODFATHER: You have to walk the streets looking for her.

MOTHER: Yes. (Mediums got frenzied and again demanded that the young woman not look at the Godfather and that the mother keep her hands on the water. Both mother and daughter had their hands atop water goblets. (1991: 90–91).

The mother left, hoping that the Godfather would help her deal with a troubled loved one whose life had been severely harmed by a childhood experience of sexual abuse.

Family influence often leads people to become followers or healers in a belief system such as Espiritismo.[30] The decision to develop one's faculties as a medium is usually preceded by a serious illness, an "initiatory illness," as described by Koss-Chioino (1992), or by some type of personal crisis; the advent of a life-threatening experience has been the route to initiation into the healer role in many cultures (Lewis 1971). Thus, for example, the Spiritist medium in New York City interviewed by Carolyn Prorok who leads Santerismo ceremonies in her home was severely burned in a fire as a child and was also saved from drowning; both events, she believed, were signs that she was chosen to serve the saints (Prorok 2000). A client exhibiting the behavior associated with ataques de nervios may be told that she or he is in fact a medium who has not developed the faculties for communicating with spirits, particularly if she or he is inordinately sensitive to others or has obsessive ideas or dreams. Such a person will receive a recommendation to become an apprentice medium to a more developed and experienced one.

Typical of the "initiatory illness" experience, an alteration of everyday consciousness "is the "deathlike state" or experience of death and rebirth observed in religious healing in many cultural contexts. It is the initial step to personal transformation and a sense of mission to help other sufferers. The "wounded" healer heals herself while helping others (Koss-Chioino 1992: 37):

> Anna was twenty-two years old when the spirits literally "threw her to the floor." Her family described these as "convulsive attacks" that did not appear to be epilepsy. As a result, Anna began to frequent Spiritist *centros* and often "transformed into other people." She said she actually took on the personalities of other people. . . . After a while, she stopped going to the *centros* because she "did not like the way they worked."
>
> Later, Anna again took the healer role in a *centro* in Puerto Rico, one that conformed more to Kardecian practice. She was observed having the same sort of "convulsive attacks," but they did not lead to possession by spirit beings. During these attacks, the other mediums merely left her alone unless she became aggressive which sometimes occurred, and then they would exert come control over her through their *guías*. At other times, she became possessed in the accepted way; spirits spoke through her with "great clarity." (Koss-Chioino 1992: 35)

Most researchers have noted that the outcome of Spiritist healing intervention has been approximately the same as that of patients treated by mainstream psychologists, but with a difference—Spiritist practice prefers the idea of "healing" (*sanar*) rather than "curing." "'Healing' means accepting and living with wounds as well as changing the perceptions of distress" (Koss-Chioino 1992: 199).[31] Not a single treatment for disease or distress, Spiritism is an ongoing process toward personal transformation and evolution of the self.

> Both psychological and traditional healers intend to work with elements of self beyond those that are conscious and visible, beyond verbal expressions and behavior: psychiatrists use "psyche" or "personality," psychologists use the "unconscious" . . . and Spiritists work with "spirits." All of these are culturally constituted constructs about human "beings" that structure individuals' awareness about themselves (Koss-Chioino 1992: 200).

In Brazil, Spiritist medicine rivals that of the medical profession. Hess has observed that a substitution of "unconscious" for imperfect spirits would lead to the realization of how close Kardec's nineteenth-century discourse on spirits and spirit possession is to that of modern psychiatry; Spiritism occupied an "interstitial space" between the popular healing practices and the medical orthodoxies of the time. Hess's comments regarding Brazil, a South American country that is "one of the world's richest laboratories of religious syncretism" (1991: 2), are also applicable in the Caribbean context:

> "Interstitial" seems to be the appropriate term for Spiritist doctrine in general. Spiritism occupies the space between existing institutional and ideological boundaries, between popular healing and orthodox medicine, between Catholicism and Protestantism, and among the various reformist and utopian movements of the day. If one were to skip ahead to Brazil, the word "syncretic" would perhaps be a more appropriate adjective. Indeed, the ideological multiplicity and flexibility of Spiritist doctrine was clearly a factor behind its enormous success in this Afro-Latin country. (Hess 1991: 79)

Women and Espiritismo

It has been observed that in general women are more actively involved as mediums and as participants in Espiritista centros (although not necessarily in leadership positions) and adhere for a longer period to Spiritualist solutions than men. "Thus men as Spiritist healers (although there are fewer of them than women) are usually leaders and organizers of *centros*, while women carry out most of the healing work by taking spirits into their bodies" (Koss-Chioino 1992: 33). Harwood notes that in a Spiritist Puerto Rican family the wife/mother's responsibilities are to the spiritual as well as the material needs of the home. Her spiritual duties include a periodic spiritual cleansing with smoke or sahumerio followed by a washing or riego to prevent or dispel evil influences; the use of incense, flowers, or candles to attract the spirits; and the maintenance of a home altar similar to those seen in Espiritismo centers. Glasses of water are regularly replaced on the altar and in other parts of the home (1977: 144–145).

And in a manner analogous to other possession cults, Espiritismo confers a special status on mediums in the community. When Harwood's book was published in 1977, he noted that this status transformation most directly affected Puerto Rican women who, given their subordinate position in Puerto Rican patriarchal society, had fewer outlets than men to achieve formal leadership roles in other Hispanic religious organizations. Harwood suggested that the importance of mediumship as a path to prestige would decline among Puerto Rican women as they progressively achieved a higher status in the occupational sphere (1977: 183).

In Puerto Rico the experienced Espiritista healer is much sought after; one such healer was influential in the research path of Mario Núñez-Molina. Raised in a family and community of strong Espiritista believers in Lares, Puerto Rico, as a boy Núñez-Molina suffered from a serious condition that doctors claimed would require surgery.[32] In desperation his parents turned to an Espiritista healer named Gumersindo:

> The first thing he did was to put a cup of water on a table. Then he laid his hand on my head and stomach, performing several *pases* (spiritual cleansings). After this, he took the cup of water and said to me: "Drink it, thinking you will be cured." I drank the water as he told me, believing it to be the medicine I needed to be healed. The last thing I remember from this experience was my parents asking Gumersindo, "How much do we owe you?" He responded: "It is free. The healing power has come from God and the good spirits. I am not responsible for it. Your child has been cured." He was right: from that moment my health problems completely disappeared. This pivotal healing experience motivated me to study the therapeutic dimensions of Espiritismo. It also contributed significantly to the development of my experiential approach to the study of this healing system. (2001: 122)

Typically there was no charge for Espiritista healing services: it was considered a God-given gift. As a student conducting fieldwork, Núñez-Molina sought out the work of Doña Gela, a Puerto Rican Espiritista healer renowned in her community for her "spiritual injections." Although skeptical at first, the researcher soon discovered for himself the authenticity of her unusual therapeutic approach. While Núñez-Molina observed the Espiritista-client relationship at the Center, Doña Gela noted that he appeared tired and began to massage his back and stomach, administering one of her spiritual injections. Attempting to maintain his objectivity as a researcher, he nevertheless reacted to them. "It was somewhat painful. I told Doña Gela: 'These injections are too strong.' Everybody in the room began to laugh, and Doña Gela smiled at me, continuing her massage. When she finished, I looked at my stomach and arm and saw three red dots at the places in my body where I had been 'injected'" (2001: 123).

Women such as Doña Gela are also protagonists in Puerto Rican and Cuban fictional writing on the island and in the Diaspora. While the theme of Espiritismo may have inspired fewer artistic works than Santería and Vodou,[33] those that exist are just as revealing of cultural norms. This is exemplified by the novel, autobiographical narratives, and short stories of U.S. Puerto Rican author Judith Ortiz Cofer and *Botánica* (1990), a play by the Cuban-American dramatist Dolores Prida.[34]

Ortiz Cofer's novel *The Line of the Sun* (1989) and Dolores Prida's *Botánica* reflect these trends in the female characters. In the novel, the rebellious healer/witch "La Cabra" is the town's most sought after medium, practicing an Espiritismo combined with Santería, one of the "new ways" she had learned in New York (1989: 25). La Cabra's sexual fascination for the males is matched by the envy and fear she produces in the female population of the small Puerto Rican town (leading to her rejection and expulsion from the community). The novel's narrator-protagonist's mother Ramona transports her family's Espiritista beliefs to their immigrant home in New Jersey, with disastrous results. In *Silent Dancing: A Partial Remembrance of a Puerto Rican Childhood* (1990), the narrative "Talking to the Dead" tells of Ortiz Cofer's grandfather who is a Mesa Blanca Spiritist. The incident in the novel in which the Espiritista father uses trance to ascertain the whereabouts of a son lost and abused in the United States is also based on autobiographical facts narrated in the same essay and recalls the origins of the Cuban Espiritismo de Cordón described above in which family members invoked the spirits to discover the whereabouts of distant relatives fighting in combat against Spanish colonial forces.

In Prida's play the protagonist Doña Geno, owner of a New York botánica that blends Espiritismo and Santería, cures a variety of ills with healing modalities that combine Espiritismo, Santería, traditional and New Age herbalism, folk psychology, and a hefty dose of common sense. In the following excerpt, written with Prida's characteristic blend of humor and wit, the protagonist greets a familiar female client who enters the botánica in search of a remedy for her husband's indifference, an attitude that the client attributes to fading attractiveness:

LUISA: My hair. In the last few months it's been falling out, it's become dull, flat. And I had such a beautiful head of hair! . . . What would you recommend, Doña Geno?

GENO: *Sábila.* The *americanos* call it "aloe vera." I have it in liquid, gelatin, and capsules. . . . Child, it's been proven that aloe vera has medicinal properties for the treatment of arthritis, high blood pressure, asthma, vaginitis, bedwetting, warts, hemorrhoids, athlete's foot, boils, colitis, diarrhea, constipation, flu, apoplexy, dandruff, toothache and . . . baldness! But that's not all. Aloe vera is also a cleansing, refreshing and moisturizing nutrient for the skin. It stimulates the pancreas, repels insects, and eliminates foot odor; it helps you lose weight, it's a hair conditioner, and a powerful sexual stimulant.

LUISA: Heavens! Give me six bottles of the liquid, six jars of the gelatin and four bottles of capsules!

GENO: Just in case, I suggest that you burn this "Perpetual Help" incense several times a day, and put a few drops of this "Come with Me" essence in your bath water. I prepare it myself. Also, jot down this spiritual prescription to bring good luck to your home. Listen carefully. Take an egg, tie a piece of white and a piece of blue ribbon around it, put a few drops of your regular lotion . . . place the egg on a dish and light up a red candle. Say three Lord's Prayers and blow the candle out. Place the egg at the foot of your bed all night. Next day, pick it up and throw it into the river.[35]

From the perspective of language the two works share important characteristics. The authors of *The Line of the Sun* (in English but with Espiritista terminology in Spanish) and *Botánica* (presented in Spanish with English words and phrases interspersed throughout) both feel confident that their reader/audience does not require religious terms associated with either Espiritismo or Santería to be translated. These generally remain unexplained: a Latino public knows either firsthand or indirectly of the unusual spiritual spells or cures referred to in the works. Indeed, it is unusual to encounter anyone from the Caribbean (and increasingly from the wider U.S. culture) who has not heard of such practices.

A botánica in Boston and its proprietor, Steve Quintana. Photo courtesy of the artist Héctor Delgado.

Women and Folk Healing: The Curandera

Beyond the novel and the play's compassionate vision of ethnic identity and generational conflicts of the type frequently found in U.S. Latino writing, poignant gender issues are also an important theme in their works: the spiritual leaders in these unorthodox practices as well as the nontraditional healers in both works are women. The fact that the proprietor and unofficial "therapist" of Prida's folk pharmacy-cum-store-cum-temple is female, as are many of those who enter in search of such medical and/or spiritual advice and "ritual therapy" (men, of course, are not entirely absent), is authentic representation. Having played an important role in folk and spiritual healing for centuries, it is not unusual to encounter women managing or presiding over such establishments or in comparable healing venues.

Unfortunately, as portrayed in Ortiz Cofer's novel, they have endured an unequal share of the vilification and victimization traditionally associated with such practices. The women in these works are healers in the above-mentioned *curanderismo* tradition, which is in fact a complex cultural healing system with common roots in healing modalities found throughout the Caribbean and Latin America. It combines Hippocratic humoral (hot-cold) theories of disease with Spanish traditions based on Moorish influences, Amerindian herbal medicine, and diverse spiritual traditions ranging from

African-based systems to the Spiritist philosophy of Allan Kardec which inspired the creation of spiritual healing centers throughout the Caribbean, Mexico, and Brazil, among other countries in Latin America—the "integrative" medical resource of the people.[36]

Unorthodox medicine, like its religious counterpart, has been more accessible to women; there they can claim an authority denied them in mainstream institutions and are more at liberty to utilize female traditions of care taking to alleviate their suffering communities. Koss-Chioino observes that spirit possession is "largely a feminine activity" with three to four women Espiritistas to every male and fewer men than women undergoing possession. Some describe the experience as a soothing and tranquil "coolness," although during healing work an intranquil spirit can be distressful and harsh. Others have described possession in sexualized terms, as a "penetration" of their bodies, being filled up with heat or fluid, expressing feelings akin to being "dominated, oppressed by a foreign force personified (for the sake of description) as an external being" (1992: 82). This has led some Puerto Rican feminists to be ambivalent toward the traditional healer role for women, which they believe reinforces the female subordinate role and lack of entitlement (1992: 43). Koss-Chioino and others consider that the spirits' guides—the *Madamas*[37] and gypsies, for example—serve the function of expressing repressed conflicts and represent a type of psychic resolution for women living in patriarchal cultures where most women cannot go beyond a constricted public space. This type of female spirit guide represents marginalized women, the sorceresses and witches feared and rejected by men and women, but they are also a symbol of repressed feminine strength. They frequently express in possession the explicit sexual desires of women and repressed and unexpressed grievances. "These *guías* are talked about as if they were eternally supportive and powerful, much like an inner wish for an ideal mother" (Koss-Chioino 1992: 43).

The fact that so many believers in Espiritismo are women is undoubtedly due to the spiritual possibilities it affords them that they cannot find in mainstream religions. The spiritual hierarchy is egalitarian; spiritual categories are not linked to age, race, class, or sex, and ascending in the spiritual pyramid is open to all. Female empowerment in the leadership role of Espiritismo, the position of a respected and admired medium-healer, is attainable if one has the strength of purpose to study the spirit world and strive to realize its moral and spiritual principles. The status women can attain as healers does not require formal education or rigid training. Furthermore, the wide autonomy afforded for personal interpretation and approach to ritual practice as well as the absence of a centralized organizational authority (as we have seen in other Caribbean religious practices) gives women a sanctioned space in an ideology in which "not only is each man [and woman] his [her] own priest but each *centro* leader aspires to be his own (and others') bishop!" (Koss 1977: 39).[38]

In U.S. Mexican and Mexican American communities the curandera has also historically played an important healing role, similar to the one described above in the example of Puerto Rican espiritistas. In the urban areas of the United States with large Mexican American populations, the botánica is also a site for spiritual, emotional, and physical healing; they are community-based centers where the local Latino population finds culturally compatible approaches to healing and accessible treatment. In *Medicine Women,* Curanderas, *and Women Doctors,* we learn that the healing techniques of the Hispanic women healers known as curanderas, whether from areas like northern New Mexico or the large urban centers of New York City or East Los Angeles, are as varied as the cultures of the groups themselves. All have inherited their healing techniques, in varying degrees, from the curanderismo tradition described above, a synthesis of folk Catholicism, Spanish/Moorish medicine, and Indoamerican healing systems: "a religious and medical nexus articulated in colonialism" (León 2008: 300). The most respected of the Mexican American folk healers, earning the title of a "*curandera total,*" have earned the designation due to a command of various subspecialties like midwifery and massage and the knowledge of the power of each plant's essence and its healing properties that vary with celestial, lunar, and seasonal cycles. Curanderas use "ritualism and symbolism in their art and are able to move in and out of dimensions not bound to earth—the spiritual and the mystical" (Perrone et al. 1989: 90).

Curanderas fill a need in areas of the United States where people continue to rely on a heritage of herbs, spiritual healing, and folk practices; in some remote rural communities of New Mexico, for example, folk medicine is still the only kind of treatment available. An increasing number of people, however, choose to see a folk healer for the remedies of the ancestors and medical theories based on balance and harmony to treat their spiritual health while simultaneously receiving conventional medical treatment. Women have long been relegated the task of preserving cultural traditions from generation to generation, among them the ancient curative practices, and have preserved effective nontraditional methods as a viable alternative. Their services have been undervalued and even dangerously maligned, however, as attested by the persecution of women throughout the centuries, often based on malicious charges of witchcraft, persecuted for practicing their traditional skills. (The figure of the maligned curandera has also entered Chicano literary culture, representing an affirmation of Mexican American cultural and spiritual identity, as we will see below.)

In his work examining the profound shifts in U.S. identity being forged by the ever growing Latino communities of the country, *Defining a New American Identity in the Spanish-Speaking United States,* Héctor Tobar describes the divisions he observed as a child in South-Central Los Angeles between the "rational world of Yankee democracy" and the "antirational universe of catholic saints, of ointments and murmured prayers."

> When I was young, I thought this world was mine alone, but now I see that the latino supernatural hovers over most of the city. [. . .] Over there, mystique is something created by makeup artists and special effects gurus. [. . .] But on my side of the city we are ruled by the baroque, by angels who cure the sick, who relieve the suffering of wives with wayward husbands, and who sometimes take the souls of innocent children. My side of the metropolis is a round-the-clock Mass. (2005: 17)

The Sagrado Corazón botánica that Luis D. León examines in "Borderlands Bodies and Souls: Mexican Religious Healing Practices in East Los Angeles," is one such space of faith and healing, a site encoded by "multiple and multivocal religious symbols drawn from Mexican Catholicism, Aztec, and Native North American traditions, literally creating a hybrid religious text for which the exact meaning is left to the interpretive faculties of the viewer" (298). Here the curandera he refers to as "Hortencia," who refers to herself as an *espiritualista,* offers hope and guidance to those who enter the storefront establishment. The remedies, baths, and candles on the shelves have the intriguing names and promised rewards of the type described above in Epiritismo centros, and share shelf space in the store with the spiritual entities Chango and Elegua of Santería, Hindu deities, and other spiritual icons, including folk "saints" of the type not recognized or sanctioned by the Catholic Church—San Simón, María Lionza, El Niño Fidencio—who are popular legendary healers for many in Latin America. Although Hortencia may be considered the "priestess" of the botánica, León reminds us that this, like others of its type, is a *commercial* enterprise owned by investors with several other such establishments in East Los Angeles that hire curanderas to manage and operate the sites.

The charisma of blessings and gift so central to religious narratives is giving way to the rationale of capitalist ideology. As a result, religious expectations are blended with financial means, and religious spaces serve multiple purposes. Sagrado Corazón, for example, is at once a medical clinic
of sorts, a religious articles store, a sacred place of magic and devotion,
an extension of devotional images and practices fostered by the Catholic
Church, and a store that is in business for profit. As such, it is the epitome
of a postmodern religious place, whose success is found precisely in its
ability consistently to transform religious irony and indeterminacy into
efficacious social functionality. (318)[39]

The Spirits in Literature and the Arts

Hortencia's literary counterpart is found in Ultima, the fictional curandera
of the famous novel *Bless Me, Ultima* by celebrated Chicano author Rudolfo
Anaya who, like many other artists, has drawn creative inspiration from the
spiritual practices examined throughout this book. "Literary creolization" has
produced what we refer to as "spirited" cultural identities and, in many cases,
an "initiated" readership, understood here as one with a familiarity and affinity with the magical realism of Creole spirituality from the point of view of an
"insider." The initiated reader has an awareness and appreciation of the spiritual
layers in an artistic work by a "spirited" writer/artist who has attained a certain
degree or level of spiritual/religious understanding, from the most basic linguistic and cultural appreciation to the more committed level of practitioners
or adepts who have undergone ritual initiation. The living dynamic of these
religious traditions has led to their continued creolization in the islands of the
Caribbean and in the diaspora and, consequently, in diasporic Creole literature, as in the writing of Lydia Cabrera. In the case of such Mexican American
authors as Rudolfo Anaya and Gloria Anzaldúa, their spirited identity derives
from the syncretized indigenous and Roman Catholic *mestizo*[40] practices and
beliefs that permeate their works, as we will briefly examine here.

Lydia Cabrera's monumental ethnographic work *El monte* was essential in
the creation of the field of the Afro-Cuban religious and cultural ethnography (see chapter 3 in this book); *El monte* was the work of an ethnographer
who was also a creative writer, interests that are clearly evident in Cabrera's
fiction written prior to the publication of her ethnographic book. Cabrera's
short stories introduced the religions to a larger audience while maintaining
the integrity of the spiritual practices. Published in 1934, *Cuentos negros de*

Cuba (Afro-Cuban Tales) was her first short story collection and is frequently read solely in terms of local folkloric traditions and the author's skillful use of African languages; the stories should be recognized, however, as an example of the incorporation of religious, cultural, and spiritual traditions into the body of Cuban and Cuban American twentieth-century literature in order to more accurately reflect Cuban identity since, as the author herself noted, "No se comprenderá a nuestro pueblo sin conocer al negro" (Our people cannot be understood without an understanding of our blacks). In her study *Lydia Cabrera and the Construction of an Afro-Cuban Cultural Identity*, Edna Rodrí-guez-Mangual observes that Cabrera offers an "alternative to the standard, homogeneous interpretations of Cuban identity . . . the black cosmogony re-created in her work becomes a place of enunciation of an alternative identity that exposes the limits of official discourse" (Rodríguez-Mangual 2004: 20).

The story "El sapo guardiero" ("The Watchful Toad") from *Cuentos negros* is one example of the author's foregrounding of a spirited identity within Cuban national culture. While it can be read as a mythical tale of twins "the size of bird feed" who are lost in the dark forest of an evil witch, the domain of which is guarded by a toad who "protected the woods and their secret," sleeps in a puddle of "dead water," and has not seen the light in many centuries, the "initiated" reader, aware of the ritual-specific language used in the story, will know that they are in a Palo Monte *monte*, a sacred wild of religious spirits and rituals. The monte is for Afro-Cubans and for those familiar with the symbolic universe of the culture the residence of the deities, the spirits of the ancestors, and supernatural beings.

> "Cocuyero, give me eyes so that I may see!
> Horror of dreams, let all tremble! I knock over la Seiba[41]
>   angulo, the *seven Rays*, Mamma Louisa . . .
> *Sarabanda*! Jump, wooden horse! Lightning Tornado!
>   *Evil wind*, carry it off, carry it off!"
> The woods were pressing against his back on tiptoes and watching him anxiously. From the dead branches, ears were hanging, listening to his heartbeat. Millions of invisible eyes, with sharp, furtive glances, pierced the compact darkness. And behind everything lay silence's inexorable claw.
> The guardian toad left the twins lying on the ground.
> "No matter who suffers, Sampunga wants some blood!
> No matter who suffers, Sampunga wants some blood!" (Italics added, Cabrera 2004: 167)

The forest is further described with ritualized expressions and language suggestive of the contents and rituals for the making of an *nganga* cauldron of the Palo Monte religion in Cuba.

> In the muddy stomach.
> Dust of the crossroads.
> *Earth from the cemetery, dug at night.*
> Black earth from an anthill, because ants have worked doggedly,
> thinking neither of pain nor pleasure, since the beginning of time. The
> *Bibijaguas,*[42] industrious and wise.
>
> Stomach of Mama Téngue. She learned her mysterious work in the
> roots of the Grandmother Seiba, in the earth's womb for seven days.
> For seven days she learned the work of silence among the fish in the
> river's depths, Mama Téngue drank the moon.
>
> With the hairy spider and the scorpion, the rotten rooster head and
> with owl-eye, eye of immovable night, blood yoke, the Word of the
> Shadows shone, "Evil Spirit! Evil Spirit! Mouth of darkness, worm's
> mouth, consuming life! Allá Kiriki, allai bosaikombo, allá kiriki!"
>
> Flat on her stomach, the old woman spat alcohol along with dust
> and Chinese pepper into the enchanted saucepan.
>
> On the ground, *she drew arrows with ashes* and sleeping serpents
> with smoke. She made the seashells speak. (Italics added, Cabrera
> 2004: 167–168)

For the uninitiated reader the story is a delightful example of folklore, similar to the naïve readings of Cuban poet Nicolas Guillen's well-known poem "Sensemayá" which ignored the ritualized language of the verses, labeling them examples of *jitanjáforas*, invented poetic words created for their suggestive sounds rather than their meanings. For the initiated or privileged reader, however, the references to "Evil Wind" in the Cabrera story and especially to "Sarabanda" (Zarabanda) are a clue to another—spiritual—reality: the Congo religious traditions in Cuba.

The nganga theme is also found outside Cuban literature in Creole U.S. Latino writing. It is the basis of the short story "The Cauldron," by U.S. Latina author Lyn Di Iorio Sandín. In the story a cauldron left behind in an abandoned hacienda, "made of iron blackened by fire and years of exposure, stands in the center of the ruins under the ceibas. Malodorous soil, flavored with blood and a human skull, is a sign that the cauldron is the prison of a fuiri, a dead one." The author substitutes the word *fuiri* for the more commonly used words *nkisi* or *mpungo* for the Congo spirits as a more "poetic and evocative" choice of language, following the use of the word by the well-known writer of Santería literature Migene González-Wippler.[43] History and spirituality converge in the story, along with the avenging of past injustices with regard to the enslaved Africans in Puerto Rico.

> La Margarita's owner was a *sinverguenza*, an upstart Corsican. He had a concubine, a slave who, according to the historical sources, had been a priestess among the Congos. The oral tradition tells us a little more about this woman. It says she got the man his property with her magic. After he had glutted himself on all the land he could get, he decided to marry the mayor's daughter and live happily after. The Congo woman killed herself out of grief. Or maybe the Corsican killed her. No one really knows. The rumor was that he learned her magic. He imprisoned her spirit in that cauldron you've been hearing so much about. It was after her death that strange things began to happen in the town [. . .] (Dí Iorio Sandín 1998: 159–160)[44]

Rudolfo Anaya's fictional character Ultima, the magical curandera/bruja (folk healer/witch) of his 1972 novel *Bless Me, Ultima* is, for many U.S. students from schools that now include the novel on their standard reading lists, their introduction to Chicano culture. Anaya often depicts the spirits of the ancestors and the local New Mexican magical traditions in his fiction and essays in order to express the "truth" of his *Nuevo Mexicano* culture, elements which may make some uncomfortable, but which are part of the "mundo mental," the psychic world of the Nuevo Mexicano people. In the words of his fellow New Mexican José Armas, the mix of the mystical, spiritual, and magical is particular to New Mexican writing; Anaya's success was in capturing that culture.

> It is much more than a style. It is a form, a dimension of literature which captures an underground manifestation in the culture of Chicanos in *Nuevo Mexico.* . . . There is magic and there is witchcraft. Both are unexplainable and unacceptable in rational terms to Western thinking or religious doctrine, yet they are very much alive, very real. . . Superstition, witchcraft and spirits are alive and active in the lives of the New Mexico writer. They are not so outrageous to accept. (1986: 42–43) [45]

In *Bless Me, Ultima* and in his numerous works following, Rudolfo Anaya creates what he calls New World characters with a unique New World nature derived from the people and earth of the Americas.

The definition of Chicano culture must come from a multicultural perspective. Many streams of history define us and will continue to define us, for we are the synthesis that is the Americas.

Christ and Quetzalcoatl are not opposing spiritual figures; they fulfill the humanistic yearning toward harmonious resolution. Harmony within, harmony with neighbors, harmony with the cosmos. The Virgin of Spanish Catholicism and the Aztec Tonantzin culminate in the powerful and all-loving Virgen de Guadalupe. And los santos of the Catholic Church, and those more personal saints of my mother's altar, merge and share the sacred space of the kachinas of the Indian pueblos.

This metaphor, "Los santos son las kachinas," the saints are the kachinas, has become a guiding metaphor of synthesis for me. The Old World and the New World have become one in me. Perhaps it is this syncretic sensibility of harmony that is the ideal of the New World character. (1995: 363–364)

Anaya's New World identity responds to the religious syncretism discussed in the Introduction to this book, the result of an ongoing process that integrates traditional beliefs with new religious practices, a dynamic pattern of continuity and change. In the Americas, when the Europeans imposed their religions on the indigenous peoples, they merged their original beliefs with those of the Christian religion to form a syncretized, New World spirituality. In some cases, the native peoples and others were forced to accept a foreign belief system and went underground to avoid persecution. The maintenance of traditional beliefs is the result of their *defiance* and *resistance*. The ceremonies of the church remained in the open, but the deeper beliefs and folk remedies went underground. Folk medicine is not presented in Anaya's novels as simply a time-proven curative practice: within its cultural context, it is another affirmation of cultural identity.

Almas Afines (Kindred Spirits)

The artistic influence of the Afro-Diasporic religious traditions extends beyond the Caribbean and its Diaspora: artist devotees of the Santería/Regla de Ocha orishas comprise a diverse group from many cultural and religious traditions, among them Mexican American muralists and writers who consider themselves "daughters of Yemayá," the deity associated with the oceans, the moon, fertility, and motherhood (see chapter 2). The orisha of dreams and female secrets, ancient wisdom, and the collective unconscious, little wonder at her appeal to female creative artists.[46]

Among the best known of these devotees is Chicana author and scholar Gloria Anzaldúa, a self-defined "spiritual activist" for whom mestiza consciousness comprises inclusionary politics, a "tolerance for ambiguity," and real and symbolic boundary transgression. Widely studied for her theoretical contributions in the reinterpretation of postcolonial realities, Anzaldúa's politics of spirit, equally radical in its focus, is less well-known and, at times, marginalized from serious intellectual discourse as a nostalgic anachronism or fanciful New Age superstition: "[T]here is a tacit understanding that no self-respecting postmodernist would want to align herself (at least in public) with a category such as the spiritual, which appears so fixed, so unchanging, so redolent of tradition."[47] Anzaldúa's spiritual activism defies scholarly and academic prejudice, and questions reductionist Western scientific epistemology. Spiritual activism for Anzaldúa begins with a reclaiming of the power of inner transformation of spirit in order to create the consciousness that will lead to a transformation of unjust social structures, as noted by AnaLouise Keating in her study of Anzaldúa's activist spirituality. "Although revisionist mythmaking does play a role in her spiritual activism, Anzaldúa does not try to resurrect 'old gods,' reclaim an 'authentic' precolonial spirituality or religion, or in other ways nostalgically reinvigorate pseudo-ancient traditions or beliefs. Instead, she investigates a variety of indigenous and post-indigenous histories and traditions in order to learn from them, and she applies what she learns to our contemporary situation" (2008: 55–56).

For Luis D. León, Anzaldúa's consciousness and "religious poetics" emerges from "a lifetime of struggle, from experiencing injustice and subsequently transforming pain into tactical maneuvers. In the borderlands, the tragic soul of a poet is nurtured" (2008: 319). In a symbolic spiritual border crossing in the years prior to her untimely death, and with an inclusive perspective and "radical interconnectedness," Gloria Anzaldúa embraced the spiritual energies represented by the Yoruba orisha Yemayá. Thus, we conclude this book as we began in the Introduction, with Anzaldúa's poem petitioning the orisha's protection.

> Yemayá
> I come to you, Yemayá,
> ocean mother, sister of the fishes.
> I stop at the edge of your lip
> where you exhale your breath on the beach—
> into a million tiny geysers.
> With your white froth I anoint my brow and cheeks,
> wait for your white-veined breasts to wash through me.

Yemayá, your tongues lick me,
your green mouths nibble my feet.
With your brine I inhale the beginnings of life.
Your silver tongues hiss then retreat
leaving hieroglyphs and silence on the sand.

Take me with you, Yemayá.
Let me ride your flaking tortoise shell,
dance with your serpents and your seals.
Let me roar down the marble cliffs of your shoulders
varooming into waterfalls—
chipping into a million emeralds!

Beached at the edge of your lilac skirt,
you lay driftwood, a feather, a shell at my feet.
Your silver tongues hiss then retreat.
I wipe the salt spray from my face,
Yemayá, ocean mother,
I take you home in a bottle.
Tonight I will sleep on your rolling breasts.
Esta noche sueño contigo.[48]

Glossary

Abakuá: Cuban secret male societies of Carabalí origin.

aché or **ashé,** or **asé, se, áse, ase:** The "word" or "power" that created the universe in Regla de Ocha/Santería, originating from the supreme god, Olodumare.

ahijados: "Godchildren," or protégés, in the practice of Santería/Regla de Ocha.

alaña: Owner of a set of consecrated batá drums in Santería/Regla de Ocha. Also Oluañá.

Añá: The force or power inhabiting the sacred batá drums.

anaforuana: The pictographic writing system of the Abakuá.

ange: See **lwa.**

Arará: In Cuba, the name given to traditions and persons from the area of Dahomey.

asiento: The culminating initiation ceremony in Regla de Ocha/Santería. To "make the saint."

ason: A sacred beaded gourd rattle belonging to Vodou priests and priestesses and used in Rada ceremonies.

babalao or **babalocha** (male) and **iyalocha** (female): A priest (priestess) who occupies a central place in the hierarchy of Santería/Regla de Ocha, guides the initiate's development, and is in charge of specific liturgies, among them divination. The babalao is a high priest in charge of the divination system known as Ifá.

Babalú Ayé: One of the divinities whose worship has taken deepest root in Cuba; the orisha of illness, miraculous yet severe and implacable toward those who do not obey him or forget to fulfill their promises.

bagi: In Vodou, the sanctuary room containing the altar to the lwa, an elaborately furnished habitation, where the lwa can find on display its special things; not only are these pieces of property tokens of devotion, preserved by the houngan, but they make up the lineaments and capture the idiosyncrasies of the lwa.

bain démarré: In the French Caribbean, a special bath given to wash away the effects of the evil eye and bad luck. There are also *bains de la chance,* or good luck baths, which can be taken in the ocean or at home with sea, river, or rainwater and various herbs.

batá drums: Consecrated drums used for sacred ceremonies. These drums are offered food because they bear within them a spirit or semigod who possesses a magic secret, añá, which the drums' players and builders refuse to reveal.

bembé: Name given to religious Regla de Ocha/Santería drum celebrations to invoke the orishas (also **tambor** and **güemilere**).

bête a man ibé: In Guadeloupe, a sorceress who wanders at night with one human foot and one horse or donkey hoof, shrieking and dragging a long iron chain around her waist.

Bizango: One of the most important of the secret societies of Vodou, an important arbiter of social life among the peasantry; protects community resources, particularly land, by setting power boundaries within the village and inflicting punishment on those who violate its codes.

bocor, bokor, or **boco:** A houngan who can use his supernatural powers for evil.

botánica: A store that sells the religious paraphernalia used by practitioners of Regla de Ocha and Espiritismo.

brujería: Spanish word for witchcraft or sorcery.

brûler zin: Initiation ceremony of the "boiling pots," during which the initiate who knows how to "tie fire" is elevated to the status of kanzo.

cabildo: Mutual-aid confraternities of enslaved Africans and free blacks belonging to the same ethnic group during the colonial period; later the name given to house-temples in Santería/Regla de Ocha.

camino: Road; one of the aspects, sometimes contradictory, of the orishas (also avatar); one of the groups of prosified verses used in Santería divination.

causa: In Espiritismo, a spirit that creates problems or misfortune for the living.

caye-mystére: House of the lwa, containing one or more altars to the gods. Each god has his or her own altar, which contains a mélange of objects, flowers, plates of food and drink, *cruches* or *govis,* the earthenware jars or bottles belonging to the spirits of the dead, and *pots-de-tête,* which contain the hairs or nail parings of the initiates to keep them safe.

Centro Espiritista: Spiritist center, temple, or meeting place.

Changó or **Shango:** A virile hero and warrior, one of the most venerated of the tutelary orishas of Cuban Santería/Regla de Ocha; a womanizer and drinker, quarrelsome, courageous, and daring; the orisha of music, master of the sacred batá drums, god of thunder and lightning.

cheval or **horse:** Person "mounted" or possessed by an orisha or lwa.

collares: Sacred bead necklaces used in Santería rituals and in other practices influenced by Santería.

Congo: In Cuba, the name given to slaves and practices of Bantú origin.

criado: Literally "servant," in Regla de Palo the name given to initiates ritually prepared to become possessed (also called *perros*).

crise de lwa: That moment when a lwa inhabits the head of his or her servitor, articulating the reciprocal and mutual abiding of human and god.

curandero, curandera: Faith or folk healer, often combining herbalism and spiritual work.

derecho: A small offering of money made by an initiate of Santería to Eleguá, the trickster, who must be propitiated so that the message of divination meets with no obstacle or distortion.

despojo: A spiritual purification.

déssounin (dégradation in the north of Haiti): The major death ceremony in Haitian Vodou.

dilogún: One of the three systems of divination in Santería/Regla de Ocha; utilizes cowry shells.

djab (djablesse if a woman): Devil spirit who seduces and tricks men.

drapo Vodou: Richly sequined and beaded banners unfurled and danced about during ceremonies to signal the spirits represented by the vèvè (ritual designs) or by the images of corresponding Catholic saints sewn on them; their reflective brilliance is said to attract the spirits into the human gathering.

Duppy: Ghosts or spirits in Obeah.

ebó: In Regla de Ocha/Santería, a ceremony of offering or sacrifice.

egún: In Cuba, the spirits of the dead, the ancestors.

ekuelé, opele, okpuele, or **okuelé:** Chain or necklace of Ifá used by babalaos in Regla de Ocha divination.

Eleguá or **Esú-Eleguá, Legba:** In Santería/Regla de Ocha and in Vodou, a deity who is ruler of the roads in worship; he opens or closes paths, indicates the crossroads, and is master, in some sense, of the future, the hereafter. A trickster spirit and messenger.

fundamento: Stones and tools enclosed in the altar containers serving as residence for the orishas.

Gagá: A socioreligious practice followed by Haitians and their descendants in the sugarcane regions of the Dominican Republic; it has roots in rará, Haitian traveling groups who dance, play music, and display their rituals and traditions in neighboring villages during the Christian Holy Week before Easter Sunday.

gros bon ange or **ombre-cadavre:** One of the three parts of individual identity in Haitian Vodou, the double of the material body—something like *spiritus* but understood as the shadow cast by the body on the mind.

Guédé: The spirits of the underworld and death as well as of eroticism, sensuality, and fertility.

hounfort or **ounfò:** The temple, surroundings, and ceremonial altar of Haitian Vodou; includes a central dwelling of one or more rooms, circumscribed by the **peristyle** (or tonnelle), in the middle of which is the *poteau-mitan* (potomitan), or center post, that reflects the traffic between heaven and earth.

houngan, gangan, or **oungan:** In Vodou, a religious leader who initiates new hounsi and facilitates the community's contact with the deities and ancestral spirits.

hounsi or **spirit wives:** The Vodou servitors, most often women, who have been initiated into the mysteries and have passed the trial by fire (the brûler zin); they are born anew as *hounsi kanzo,* as opposed to *hounsi bossale* (from the Spanish *bozal,* wild or untamed).

Ifá: See Orula.

ilé orisha: House-temple in Santería/Regla de Ocha.

l'invisible: See **lwa.**

itútu: Funeral ceremony in Santería.

iyalocha: Priestess in Santería/Regla de Ocha. Name given to a female initiate in Santería.

iyawo: Young or recent initiate of Santería.

juego: Name (along with *potencia, tierra, plante,* and *partido*) used to refer to the lodge or confraternity of the Abakuás or ñáñigos.

kanzo: Vodou initiation.

Kariocha: Regla de Ocha/Santería initiation rite "to place the orisha on the head"; also asiento.

konesans (connaissance): A basic stage of participation in Vodou; knowledge of special lore, which gives power to the houngan or mambo.

kouche: Vodou initiation rite, "to be laid on the floor."

Kumina, Pukumina, or **Pocomania:** Religious practice of Jamaica, derived from indentured servants from the Kongo region, which syncretized with Protestant fundamentalism.

laplas (laplace): Ritual assistant in Vodou.

lave tèt: Ritual cleansing, "washing head," in Vodou initiation.

Legba: See **Eleguá**.

libretas sagradas: In Santería/Regla de Ocha, notebooks and handwritten manuscripts containing personal treasuries of sacred literature.

Lucumí: In Cuba, slaves and traditions of Yoruba origin.

lwa or **lwa** or **mystère, ange, saint, invisible:** Supernatural being in Vodou; usually translated as god or divinity, but more akin to a genie or spirit. The *lwa héritage* or *lwa racine* is either connected to the family land or inherited directly from parents or ancestors. Either inherited lwa that come with the land, those lwa "in your blood," or the lwa *maît-tête* (master of the head) received in initiation, they are always distinguished from the bad gods who cannot be trusted, the *lwa volé* or *lwa acheté*; these bad gods are paid or enticed into service by a bocor or ritual specialist who might have more money or other tempting "goods" than the houngan.

madrina: See **padrino**.

maman-ventre: Placenta; in Guadeloupan tradition it is entrusted to the father, who buries it under a young mango or breadfruit tree, which becomes the child's "landmark," or *point de repére*.

mambo or **manbo:** Vodou priestess (see **houngan**).

manger-lwa: One of the most important ceremonies in Vodou, at which a lwa is fed his or her preferred food; any variation in the expected offering can result in the lwa's desertion or revenge.

mayombero: A **palero**, practitioner of the Cuban Regla de Palo of Congo origin.

mpungu: The spirits that inhabit the nganga cauldron of a palero.

Myal: Jamaican African-derived religious practice akin to Obeah but incorporating ritual dancing, drumming, and spirit possession.

mystère: See **lwa**.

mystic marriage: Marriage with a lwa in Vodou.

nación: Enslaved Africans who shared the same ethnic or geographic origin.

ñáñigo: Member of the Abakuá society.

nganga: The spirit of the dead, as well as the recipient or cauldron in which the spirit resides, in the Regla de Palo. (Also *prenda, macuto, nkisi*.)

Obatalá: An androgynous orisha in Santería/Regla de Ocha, the god of purity and justice; he also represents truth, the immaculate, peace—hence his representation at times as a white dove and wisdom.

Obeah, Obi, or **Obea:** A belief system divided into two broad categories. The first involves the casting of spells for various purposes, both good and evil: protecting oneself, one's property, family, or loved ones; harming real or perceived enemies; bringing fortune in love, employment, personal or business pursuits. The second involves healing through the application of knowledge of herbal and animal medicinal properties. Obeah, thus conceived, is not a religion as such but a system of beliefs grounded in spirituality and an acknowledgment of the supernatural and involving aspects of witchcraft, sorcery, magic, spells, and healing.

obi: Coconut.

ocha: Saint. Santería is also called Regla de Ocha or the worship of the saints.

Ochosi: An old orisha in Santería/Regla de Ocha, a warrior and hunter, the protector and saint of prisons; Ochosi, Eleguá, and Ogún form the triumvirate of the warrior orishas.

Ochún (Oshún): A Santería orisha, possessor of all the attributes valued in women: coquettish, beautiful, fawning, affectionate, docile, and industrious; defined as a *mulata* orisha, mistress of the river, fresh water, gold, and honey.

Ogún or Ogou: One of the oldest orishas of the Yoruba pantheon; superior warrior, rival of Changó, a symbol of primitive force and terrestrial energy; himself a forger of metals, he is the protector of blacksmiths. Ogún, Ochosi, and Eleguá form the triumvirate of the warrior orishas.

Olofi: Also Olodumare and Olorun. In Santería/Regla de Ocha, the creator of the world, which was initially populated solely by orishas; later he distributed his powers among them so that he need not interfere at all in human fate.

ombre-cadavre: See **gros bon ange**.

omiero: A sacred herbal liquid used in Santería/Regla de Ocha rituals.

omo: Child of orisha, devotee.

opele, okpuele, or **okuele chain:** Commonly cast by the babalao during a divination ritual, its pattern is read to determine the fate of a newborn, the rightness of a marriage, or the measures to be taken for carrying out a funeral. When cast in the correct manner, it indicates a series of eight vertical markings, set in two columns of four, which constitute the configuration called an *odù* or *orgún*.

ori: Head. One's personal orisha.

oriaté: Master of dilogún, deemed worthy of the highest respect, an individual to whom the specialists of Santería submit themselves, particularly in any matter related to the deciphering of some mystery or prophecy. An obá oriaté is a santero with expertise in divination.

orishas (orichas) or **santos:** Deities of Santería, spirits of Yoruban ancestors or divinities often identified in new correlations with Catholic saints. An orisha is pure form, immaterial ashé, and can become perceptible to humans only when he is incorporated in them through possession.

oro (oru): Liturgical rhythms and chants for the orishas.

Orula or Orúnla, Orúmila, or **Ifá:** Tutelary divinity in the pantheon of Cuban Santería/Regla de Ocha, master of the Table of Ifá and of divination.

Osain: Santería's mysterious herb healer, master of the secrets of the bush.

otanes: The sacred stones of Santería/Regla de Ocha.

ounfó: See **hounfort**.

oungan: See **houngan**.

Oyá: A severe divinity in Santería/Regla de Ocha, related directly to the phenomenon of death, mistress of lightning and of the wind, and gatekeeper of the cemetery.

padrino or madrina: The godfather or godmother, head of the ilé, or religious community; becomes mother or father to a family of children, forming a group popularly known as a *línea de santo,* a line or lineage of initiates.

palero: Priest of the Regla de Palo religion in Cuba who specializes in working with the spirits of the dead. Also **mayombero**.

Palo or Palo Monte: Literally means "stick." Of Congo origin, it is one of the Central African-based Cuban religions.

pases: A type of spiritual healing in Espiritismo.

patakí or **caminos:** A group of prosified verses used in Santería divination.

perispirit: In Spiritism, the semi-material body composed of vital fluids or energies that surrounds the spirit; the link which unites the soul and the body, a principal intermediary between matter and spirit. Upon death the perispirit becomes the spiritual body of the "discarnate" spirit. Also referred to as the "astral" body.

peristyle or **tonnelle:** A structure, part of the hounfort, in the middle of which is the *poteau-mitan,* or center post, which reflects the traffic between heaven and earth.

petit bon ange: In Haitian Vodou, one of the three parts of individual identity, the source of consciousness and affect; depends on the lwa for protection, for keeping it steady and bound to the person.

Petro (Petwo): Family of Creole lwas originating in Haiti but owing greatly to traditional Kongo religion; born in the mountains of Haiti, nurtured in secret; repositories of the moral strength of the escaped slaves who led the Haitian Revolution.

quimboiseurs or **kenbwazé:** Sorcerers in Guadeloupe's Quimbois; they can be good or evil and fall in several categories: those who read the past, present, and future in the flames of candles or the designs made by melting wax on candles; healers, who practice white magic and utilize "good" herbs; *gadé zaffés* (*gadédzafé*) who work with secrets such as conjuring.

Rada: Pantheon of lwas in Haitian Vodou, of Dahomean or Yoruban origin.

registro: In Santería/Regla de Ocha, consultation that relies on a reading of the configurations determined by a specific procedure of casting palm nuts or the ekuele chain.

regla: Religion, order, or rule, based on the *reglamientos* or regulations of cabildo life after independence in 1898. A word used in Cuba to describe the African-based religions, sects, and practices, Regla de Ocha and Regla de Palo.

rogación: Purification ritual in Regla de Ocha/Santería.

Santería: "Way of the Saints." A popular term for the Regla de Ocha religion in Cuba.

Santerismo: A merging of Espiritismo and Santería.

santero and **santera:** An initiate in Santería/Regla de Ocha; unconditionally dedicated, rigorously disciplined, and committed to a particular orisha for life.

santos: See **orishas.**

shaman: A figure who distinguishes himself or herself by the nature and intensity of an ecstatic experience that gives access to levels of transcendence higher than those other members of the community can reach.

Shango: See **Changó.**

siete potencias africanas: Seven African Powers of Cuban Santería/Regla de Ocha: Eleguá, Ogún, Changó, Yemayá, Obatalá, Ochún, and Orula.

Sikán or **Sikanecua:** In Abakuá origin myth, the woman who discovered the secret embodied in the sacred fish Tanze.

sopera: Tureen in which the sacred **otanes** or stones of Santería/Regla de Ocha, the fundamento, are kept.

tambor: See bembé.

Tata-Nganga: Male priest and head of a house-temple of the Regla de Palo.

Vèvè: A mystical design representing the attributes of a lwa traced on the ground with maize flour, ash, coffee grounds, or brick dust.

Vodou, or Voodoo, Vodoun, Vaudon: From the word used by the Fon tribe of southern Dahomey to mean spirit, god, or image; a religious system whose beliefs and rituals center on the worship of the lwas, which can have multiple emanations depending on locale, on a particular ritual, on the composition of the hounfort, or on their association with particular individuals or family groups. The reciprocal abiding of human and god, which is the cornerstone of Vodou practice, is articulated through the phenomenon of possession, or the **crise de lwa.**

wanga: In Vodou, charms or spells.

Yemayá: In Santería/Regla de Ocha, the universal mother, queen of the sea and of salt water, the orisha of intelligence, of rationality; sometimes tempestuous and wild, sometimes calm and sensual. A harmonious personality characterizes her children.

zombi, zombie, or zonbi: A living corpse, a person whose soul is believed to have been extracted by a sorcerer and who has been thus reduced to slavery.

Notes

PREFACE

Aisha Khan (July–December 2007: 191).

INTRODUCTION

1. The spelling of Vodou (also Voodoo, Vodoun, and Vaudon) is, like many other terms of African origin used to describe various practices and beliefs, a constant source of debate among scholars and believers. The text reflects our preferences; citations naturally maintain the individual preference of those cited.

2. See Charles Stewart, ed., *Creolization: History, Ethnography, Theory*, "Introduction," for an excellent historical overview of the use of the term (2007: 1–25). In the same volume, "Creole Colonial Spanish America," by Jorge Cañizares-Esguerra, examines the political use of the term by Latin Americans who contrasted their Creole status as a tactic against Spanish "Peninsulars" in the struggle for independence (26–45).

3. Aisha Khan, "Creolization Moments" (2007: 237–238).

4. Stewart 2007: 5.

5. For an interesting discussion on the global preoccupations of Caribbean authors and the issue of postcolonial cultural identity, see Patricia Krüs, "Myth and Revolution in the Caribbean Postmodern" (2006: 149–167).

6. Torres-Saillant notes that when Benítez Rojo was questioned during a lecture at Syracuse University in 2001 by Puerto Rican author Mayra Santos-Febres as to why he relied on Chaos Theory, "given the availability of similar paradigms in the cosmology of Santeria in his own native Cuban culture, he immediately agreed with her and proceeded to explain his choice in terms of what he thought would be preferred in the U.S. academy." (Torres-Saillant 2006: 87)

7. *Créolité*, as we note in our discussion, is a French Antillean literary term for Creole identity. *Métissage* (French) and *mestizaje* (Spanish) both relate to the mixture of race and/ or culture.

8. Desmangles (1992: 172). In "Trans-Caribbean Identity and the Fictional World of Mayra Montero," Fernández Olmos argues for yet another category of religious syncretism, exemplified by the *Gagá* cult in the Dominican Republic. Gagá is a Vodou-derived practice brought by emigrating Haitian sugarcane workers to the Dominican Republic, where it was transformed and reinterpreted by local folk practices and beliefs. It is "an interesting example of nontraditional Caribbean syncretism: instead of a hybridity between the European and the colonized, Gagá exemplifies a secondary type of syncretism, one between (ex)colonized peoples" (1997: 273).

9. "[T]he concept of syncretism has been used in many different ways since Plutarch wrote the history of the Cretans. During the period of expansion of European colonialism, for instance, when ethnography was deployed to describe colonized peoples, syncretism defined a stage of evolution (progress), serving to explain the ways "uncivilized" societies "assimilated" more "advanced" cultures. . . . [W]e propose a reinscription of the contact between, for example, European and African symbolic systems in syncretic articulations, not as contradictory but as *antagonistic,* i.e., in relations which are animated by the partial presence of the other within the self, such that the differential identity of each term is at once enabled and prevented from full constitution. These relations, which, depending on the configurations of power in contingent historical conditions, may or may not crystallize into oppositionalities, exist both horizontally (in equivalential alignments among diverse groups united in struggle, as in the Cretan example) as well as vertically (in dominant/subaltern confrontations, as in colonialism). Antagonistic relations, then, indicate the limits of absolutist conceptions of culture based upon a closed system of unalloyed, hetero-topic differences, and thereby expand the logics of struggle" (Becquer and Gatti 1991: 70–72).

10. Patrick Bellegarde-Smith believes that the syncretic process in Haitian Vodou deviates from that of other "Neo-African" religious expressions in the Americas for historical reasons: "Vodou is a heteroclite compendium of many African cults 'rendered' in a Haitian historical and sociological context. It appears perhaps as the most creolized of African-derived systems in the Americas. Its liturgical language is Haitian (Creole), not Fon, Ewe, Yoruba, or Lingala. Cut off from the source of 'fresh' Africans, paradoxically because of its early independence, and abandoned to itself, Vodou has become the least 'pure' of the new religions, neigher Nago or Kongo, yet African in its essence. Early contacts with islamicized Africans—and these had transformed Islam—had long ended. Government- and church-sponsored endemic persecutions tended to reinforce the conflation between *lwa*/orisha and Roman Catholic saints, but these functional equivalencies remained tenuous. Deities, after all, are cosmic energy, archetypes, and moral principles. Saints, however, are dead (white) people whose edifying life stories remain in darkness for almost all Haitians. . . . [F]ew of the adepts [have] any knowledge of the lives of the saints whose images they revere as representations of their gods. The saints have disembodied spirits, as the person who is 'mounted' by the spirit does in the ritual. Each *lwa*/orisha has multliple aspects, represented by *different* saints (unconnected to each other in time and space), a situation so complicated that only one with the patience of a saint could hope to unravel it, but they would not succeed. Camouflage was *one* consideration" (2005: 62–63).

11. In *Voice of the Leopard: African Secret Societies and Cuba,* Ivor L. Miller notes that the nineteenth-century Afro-Cuban religious leader Andrés Petit introduced the Christian crucifix into the Abakuá lodges to meet a need at that historical moment—to defend the practices from official repression. This "illustrates the intentional fusion of distinct practices by innovators with a community-based tradition, who are often criticized by the traditionalists. . . . Church purists have consistently characterized non-Christian practices as 'syncretic,' therefore false. The various traditions emerging from this activity evidence why traditions like Abakuá, Santería (Ocha), and Palo Mayombe cannot be contained within a ritual recipe book, because their ceremonies are never stagnant reproductions, but ritual theater and artistic enterprises that develop according to the mastery of those present" (2009: 116).

12. For a discussion of legitimacy and religious syncretism in Latin America, as well as power and empowerment via the articulation of syncretic elements, see Benavides (1995).

13. In his study of the Abakuá Society in Cuba, David H. Brown (2003) notes that, although Creole sycretisms are typically believed to result from the encounter of African and Catholic belief systems, those interpretations preclude individual idiosyncratic agency in the creation of religious cultural meaning and the significant influence of popular and mass culture in the transformation of religious symbols. Altars serve as an excellent example: "Abakuá objects and signifying practices, no less than those of any other group, are produced as the ongoing outcomes of struggles and exceed the 'results' of any imagined initial 'encounter' of 'Europe' and Africa'. . . . Altars are examples of 'synthetic' knowledge production and aesthetic creativity par excellence, assemblages from fragments or streams of multiple cultures as opposed to direct representation of nature" (6).

14. Based primarily on Castellanos and Castellanos, *Cultura afrocubana* (1992, 3: 16–18). Just as the insights regarding the creolization process described above have crossed the boundaries of the geographic region—Brazil and other Latin American countries, and even such U.S. cities as New York and Miami reveal the type of cultural amalgamation characteristic of the region—it should be noted that Creole religious beliefs have gone beyond geographic, racial, and class boundaries as well. Their devotees are found throughout South America—including areas of Brazil with Italian, Polish, and German immigrants and in countries like Uruguay and Argentina with an insignificant number of persons of African descent—and in the United States outside the Cuban and Latino communities (Barnes 1989: 10).

15. See Cros Sandoval (1995), and Fernández Olmos and Paravisini-Gebert (2001).

16. Juana Elbein Dos Santos and Deoscoredes M. Dos Santos (1984: 78).

17. African-derived practices are often described in the scholarly literature as "spiritist" religions due to the element of possession of followers by the spirits. In this book only Espiritismo is referred to as "Spiritism" or spiritist, as identified in the Caribbean. Of course, to some degree all religions that believe in the spirits can be identified as spiritist; the Christian Pentecostal rituals that attempt to achieve a direct experience of possession by the Holy Ghost are one example of a Christian spiritist practice, albeit one with a more "mainstream" spirit.

18. Spirit possession exists throughout the world in one form or another and can be defined as an "altered state of consciousness indigenously interpreted in terms of the influence of an alien spirit" (Crapanzano and Garrison 1977: Introduction, 7).

19. Joan D. Koss has written of the creativity of Caribbean cult rituals and the "transformation of the mundane through the use of possession-trance" (1979: 376). When ritual participants are possessed by the *dramatis personae* of a particular belief system, rather than follow the limited stereotypical patterns associated with the supernatural character incarnated, numerous variations (the multiple avatars of the *orisha* and the *lwa,* for example, and the portrayal of the more typical spirit guides in *Espiritismo*) allow for individual variation of their characterization in possession. A successful cult leader, she claims, must be flexible and creative in combining meaning and aesthetics to the cult ritual "performance." Koss cites Métraux (1972: 64), who describes the ideal *hungan* as "at one and the same time priest, healer, soothsayer, exorcizer, organizer of public entertainment and choirmaster:"

Ritual as a creative forum is most clearly seen, in my opinion, in these cult cases. Two important attributes of cult activity provide for this condition: first, cult rituals, as distinct from those of most established religions, attract their participants through the offer of direct contact with supernatural beings. Even though this contact may be achieved initially only through a third party, the cult adept, priest, or spirit medium, there is a process of democratization of the "power" to communicate with the supernatural world which is both ideal and actual—that is, that any believer can become an adept, even though not all develop sufficient powers to do so. Second, cult ideologies in the Caribbean are, in terms of their basic patterns, deceptively simple. They consist of good and bad *loa, orisha,* spirits or powers who "work" according to the dictates of their human communicants but can as often manifest their own characterological attributes to disturb the behavior of those who lack the knowledge and power to deal with them. Those who become adepts and can organize their own groups acquire their leadership status by successfully dealing with the multiple, variable expressions of the personal disturbances of their followers. Their manipulative techniques of divining, healing, and advice-giving cannot possibly respond to set and detailed formulas, pedantically derived by arduous interpretation over years of discussion. To be a successful cult leader or adept, creative ability is requisite (376–377).

20. Following in the path of Edward Tylor, one of the earliest anthropologists who developed an evolutionary theory of religion in his *Primitive Culture* (1871), Frazer's work (1922; 1966) was influential in its time, viewing magic as part of a progressive development of societies on the developmental path to religion and ultimately to science. However, Frazer's unilinear evolutionary approach, his clear bias against religion, and his ethnocentric methods and use of ethnographic sources have been criticized and are viewed as problematic today and of little value to scholars of religion.

21. Magic is also a means to a political and social end, as we see in the Haitian Revolution that famously began with a Vodou ceremony and a solemn oath or pact to gain liberation. African slaves were convinced that they would overcome their French oppressors due to the power afforded them by Vodou's ritual magic and the protection they would receive from the African deities, the *lwas*. The belief that persons can assume an animal form to escape the bullets of the enemy, lycanthropy, is a type of metamorphosis or magico-ecstatic transformation accomplished through the use of ritual possession, ointments, or charms: "El propósito del Pacto Solemne que figura en *El reino de este mundo* de Carpentier es precisamente poner a los esclavos bajo la protección de las divinidades africanas. . . En general los hechos relacionados con el vodú se saben ya que hasta ahora lo mencionado en la obra de Carpentier se realiza cada día en las campañas de Haíti; quiero hablar del poder licantrópico, de personas que no pueden ser alcanzadas por las balas etc. Todo esto es moneda corriente hoy día en Haíti." (Personal correspondence with Haitian Joseph Pierre-Antoine.)

In "Romantic Voodoo: Obeah and British Culture, 1797–1807," Alan Richardson (1997) describes a similar role of Obeah in slave revolts in the British West Indies regarding oaths of secrecy and fetishes that promised invulnerability. Yvonne P. Chireau (2003) observes that spiritual oaths were administered by priests and other appointed religious functionaries for various motives. In the well-known historical event, the New York Conspiracy of 1712, an insurrection of a diverse group of "American-born blacks, native American Indians (or mestizos), and Africans of the 'Nations of Caramantee and Pappa,'" the participants had sworn an oath and used an enchanted powder to ensure their invulnerability, "The conspirators were bound together by the act, having sealed a covenant between themselves and the invisible forces of the supernatural world." Nearly all were apprehended, tried, condemned, and executed (2003: 61).

22. *Working the Spirit: Ceremonies of the African Diaspora* (1994: 6–7). See our *Sacred Possessions: Vodou, Santería, Obeah, and the Caribbean* (1997: 3).

23. Also of interest in the area of African American expressions of religious pluralism, globalization, and sexual diversity is Monica A. Coleman, *Making a Way Out of No Way: A Womanist Theology* (2008).

24. Some Mexican Americans refer to themselves as Chicano/a, usually considered a more politically identified term, popularized as a result of the Mexican American social justice movements of the 1960s.

25. Duke University Press (2009). Also see Gloria Anzaldúa, *Interviews = Entrevistas /* (2000).

CHAPTER 1

1. Long (1774, 2: 451–452, 473). Quoted by Alan Richardson in "Romantic Voodoo" (1997).

2. Figures from Knight (1970: 10) based on Aimes (1907) and von Humboldt (1969). See also Curtin (1969). The slave trade continued illegally in Cuba until the mid-1860s. Abolition was formally decreed in 1880 with an eight-year "apprenticeship" of freed slaves which ended in 1886. On abolition, see Knight (1970: chapters 7–8).

3. For a description of the conditions of life in the sugar mill, see Moreno Fraginals (1976: 142–153). On Cuban slavery, see H. Thomas (1971: chapter 13).

4. Estimates on the number of slaves imported to Cuba vary. Curtin (1969) describes the difficulty of arriving at an accurate number and offers the following estimates: to 1773 (based on Aimes 1907) 13,100; 1774–1807, 119,000; 1808–1865, 568,500 (Curtin 1969: 44); for the entire period of the slave trade in Spanish America, 702,000 (Curtin 1969: 46). Manuel Moreno Fraginals (1976) places the number at over one million but many agree that Curtin's figures underestimate the count (Castellanos and Castellanos 1988, 1: 25).

5. For defense and concealment purposes, maroon communities took advantage of the harshness of their natural environment. Many of their villages were surrounded by palisades or, in Spanish, *palenques*; hence the generic name.

6. For a more general discussion of maroon societies in the Americas, see Price (1973), especially the Introduction, 1–30.

CHAPTER 2

1. The terms will be used interchangeably here as they are with many practitioners.

2. Palmié believes that the African-derived practices formed throughout the nineteenth and twentieth centuries and that grew to be the Afro-Cuban and Afro-Brazilian religious formations seen today in Cuba and Brazil were "resultants of erratic shifts in the larger Atlantic matrix that temporarily linked places like Havana or Salvador da Bahia with specific African source origins. And it was this matrix that generated what, at times, must have been stunningly diverse patterns of circulation of heterogeneous African cultural forms in single New World localities" (2002: 142).

3. *Regla* translates as religion, order, or rule, based on the *reglamientos* or regulations of Afro-Cuban religious life after independence in 1898. In Cuba, *regla* is used to describe the various African-based religions, sects, and practices.

4. The term Lucumí has several different explanations. References in early maps and writings on Africa mention the kingdom of Ulcami, Ulcuma, Ulcumí, or Oulcoumi in the area of "Yorubaland" in southwestern Nigeria and parts of Benin and Togo. The designation "Yoruba" to describe the Yoruba-speaking subgroups, including the Oyo, Ijebu, and Egba, did not come into general usage until a later period; those originating from those areas were called Lucumí in Cuba, perhaps based on their own preferred form of identification or, some speculate, on a Yoruba greeting, "Olucumí," meaning "my friend."

5. It is believed that six principal African cultural groups (with many subgroups) predominate among the Cuban slave population. In very brief summary they are: the Lucumí, Yoruba peoples of southwest Nigeria, Dahomey, Togo, and Benin; the Carabalí from the Cross River area on the border of eastern Nigeria and Cameroon (the ancient Calabar); the Arará from Dahomey and western Nigeria (their name is based on the kingdom of Ardra—Benin—which is home to the Ewe and Fon peoples); the Congos from the Congo Basin, referred to in Cuba as Congos or Bantus; the Mandinga from the upper Niger and the Senegal and Gambia valleys; the Gangás from the coast and interior of Sierra Leone and northern Liberia (Castellanos and Castellanos 1988, 1: 28–44; Bolívar Aróstegui 1997: 20–21; Matibag 1996: 18–19).

6. [M]asters began to refuse to send slaves on Sundays to mass, and sought first permission to build chapels at their mills in order to avoid interference of the parish, and finally to cease any pretense at religious instruction for slaves. . . . The new slave code of 1789, the Spanish Code Noir, high-minded though it was in intention, was largely a dead-letter: instruction in the Catholic religion and attendance of priests on feast days; the proportion of men to women and hours and years of work; the punishment and the health provisions—all these were ignored. (H. Thomas 1971: 74) And Moreno Fraginals remarks, "The Church had very substantial sugar interests," and monasteries and seminaries also received significant profits from sugarmills (1976: 58).

7. Richard Robert Madden, *The Island of Cuba,* quoted in Louis A. Pérez, Jr. (1992: 157). Madden, a surgeon and a writer, served as the English Superintendent of Freed Slaves in Havana from 1836 to 1840.

8. Moreno Fraginals (1976: 51–59).

9. Murphy (1993: chapters 10 and 11).

10. In Spanish *cabildo* usually means an administrative town council; in Cuba the fraternities or societies themselves would assume that name.

11. Scholars have noted the existence of cofradías of Africans in Spain prior to their existence in the New World (Cros Sandoval 1995: 83–84).

12. For a comprehensive description of this impressive celebration in Cuba, "one of the most picturesque scenes of colonial life," see Fernando Ortiz (1920). See also a personal description by the North American physician who traveled to the island in the nineteenth century, J. G. F. Wurdemann (1971: 83–84).

13. Palmié observes the processes by which, analogous to the Brazilian situation studied by Bastide, elements of African cultures that reached Cuba had begun to recombine into New World complexes and local practices: " Time, in the long run, would erode all [African-derived] traditions, however firmly [they came to be] anchored in the new

habitat. But the slave trade continuously renewed the sources of life by establishing continuous contact between old slaves, or their sons, and the new arrivals, who sometimes included priests and medicine men. In this way, throughout the whole period of slavery, religious values were continuously rejuvenated at the same time that they were being eroded. . . . [W]e should certainly give up the notion of cult centers surviving through the centuries down to the present day (something that slavery precluded) and think of a chaotic proliferation of cults or cult fragments arising only to die out and give way to others with each new wave of arrivals" (2002: 141–142).

14. According to the authors, cabildos were important sites of transformation that were decisive in the formation of Cuban national culture in general.

Precisely because they preserved the African legacy, they became cultural depositories, from which elements passed on to the white world that were later integrated into a new Afro-Cuban mixture. Dances and music that were conserved behind cabildo doors originally had a religious or ritual character but slowly went into the public domain and combined with the music and dance of European origin to produce Cuban music and Cuban dances, which are not white or black, African nor European, but Afro-Hispanic—mulatto. (Castellanos and Castellanos 1988, 1: 114)

All translations, unless otherwise indicated, are our own.

15. In 1955 Nicolas Angarica published his *Manual de Orihate: Religión Lucumí* that stressed the need to codify and systematize ritual practices, given the enormous divergence existing at the time; variations still remain, however: see D. Brown (1989: 11, 94–96) and Brandon (1993: chapter 4). Brandon regards this period as a transformative phase of Santería, "in which the religion assumes the form of a predominantly Yoruba-spiritist-Catholic amalgam," including the development of "Santerismo" and alternative branches of Santería in the twentieth century within Cuba and in the Diaspora (1993: 5).

16. In Puerto Rico (and in the U.S. southwest, especially New Mexico), *santero* has a different meaning, referring to traditional artisans who carve three-dimensional representations of *santos* (saints) from wood for personal or public devotion.

17. It has been claimed that the Yoruba have had the greatest influence of all the African cultures on the development of New World religions: Yoruba divinities "constitute the driving force behind new religions known as Candomblé and Macumba in Brazil, Shangó in Trinidad and Tobago, Grenada, and Barbados, Kele in Saint Lucia, and Santería in Cuba, Venezuela, the United States, and other countries. Yoruba influence is also evident in other New World 'Africanisms' such as the Voodoo of Haiti and Òrìsa-Voodoo of Òyótúnjí, South Carolina" (Lawal 1996: 3).

18. Castellanos and Castellanos feel that, though Regla de Ocha is not strictly monotheistic, it can be considered a variety of the concept, explaining the syncretism in Cuba of Olodumare with the concept of God the Father and the Holy Spirit in Catholicism, while the orishas identified with the Virgin Mary and the saints. The cult of the orishas affirms the power of the Supreme Being (1992, 3: 21–23).

19. Many scholars underscore the predominance of Lucumí religion over other African-based religions in Cuba due to its popularity and its structural influence over other traditions. While Yoruba culture appears to dominate the other transplanted cultures in Cuba, Eugenio Matibag advises that we not forget that the Lucumí system was created as a result of the "crossing and mixing" of components of other systems that brought all Afro-Cuban practices into being: "The Lucumí predominance has obscured the vital

contribution of other West African religious traditions transported into its architectonics, especially the Bantu-Congo, the Calibar-Abakuá, the Dahomeyan-Arará" (1996: 39).

20. The "Oricha tradition" is the approach used by many scholars in order to widen the perspective regarding Yoruba religion and Yoruba-based syncretic practices in the Americas (Santería/Regla de Ocha in Cuba, Shango and the Oricha religion in Trinidad, Candomblé in Brazil).

21. For excellent profiles of the orishas in English, see Matibag (1996), Gonzalez-Wippler (1989), and Ramos (1996).

22. Antonio Benítez Rojo goes further in observing more than simply the African and Hispano-Catholic origins of orishas. He identifies a process of "supersyncretisms" in Cuban culture in the intercultural signification whereby the patron saint of Cuba, the Virgen de la Caridad del Cobre, for example, has her origins in the Spanish Virgen of Illescas (a saint with Byzantine origins), the native American taino deity Atabey or Atabex, and the Yoruba orisha Ochún (Benítez Rojo 1996: 12–16).

23. Bastide notes a similar phenomenon in the Yoruba-based practice of Candomblé in Brazil:

Orixás are not confined to a single form. There are at least twenty-one Exús, not just one. There are twelve different forms of Shangô, sixteen different forms of Oxun. It is therefore likely that each form (or at least the principal ones) will have its Catholic equivalent. . . . Saint Jerome is not the counterpart of Shangô in general but of Shangô Ogodo, so that this correspondence does not prevent or contradict the identification of Shangô with Saint Anthony, Saint John, or even Saint Bárbara, these saints being linked with other forms of the same god. (1978: 270)

The Orisha religion in Trinidad exhibits a similar pattern:

The process of syncretism in the Orisha and other Afro-American religions involving Catholic saints and African gods has been largely haphazard and inconsistent, another indication that the initial blending was done under duress. . . . [I]n Trinidad Shango is also a general name used to denote more than one spirit. . . . [W] orshipers use seven different names for this group of spirits: Saint John the divine, Saint John the Revelator, and Saint John the Baptist identify one spirit; Saint John the Shepherd and Saint John of the Cross refer to another, Saint John of Lightning and Thunder and Saint John and the Harbinger identify one spirit each—resulting in a total of four distinct spirits. (Houk 1995: 183, 185–186)

The Orisha religion is also referred to as the Shango cult in Trinidad. See Simpson (1965).

24. Hybridity and improvisation have been the hallmarks of the fluid and dynamic Creole ethos that reflects what Joel James Figarola has called "the principle of multiple representation" or the tendency to signify the same referent by varied names, objects, forms, and symbols. Different and seemingly disparate modalities and representations nevertheless operate and are organized under a unitary principle: in Regla de Ocha, for example, the multiple avatars or manifestations of the orishas, the 256 possible combinations of the signs or *letras* of the divination systems, and the "plural crystallizations" of a deity or force in the mind of the believer (the orisha as manifest in a likeness or representative figure or statue, in the devotee in possession, etc.); in Regla Conga the nganga cauldron is magical in its totality and/or its components, the "mother" nganga from which "daughter" ngangas are derived represent and affect each other, the nganga represents the dead person from which it was constructed as the dead also represents the

nganga, the ngangas and the *palero* or *ngangulero* who created it are considered one and the same, and so on (James Figarola 1999b: 13–17). James Figarola notes that the principle of multiple representation is not limited to Creole religious practices: in Christianity some of the more well-known examples are the concept of the Divine Trinity (God the Father, the Son, and the Holy Spirit), the cult of the saints, and the Marian cult in which the Virgin Mary has thousands of diverse and varied representations (James Figarola 1999b: 99–100).

25. While there is general agreement on attributes and symbolic colors, numbers, and the like, there is also some discrepancy. Some of the more representative views are expressed here.

26. Several powerful orishas such as Orula—who is only received in an exclusive and distinct initiation ceremony reserved for Orula's children, the *babalao* priests, Babalú Ayé, Ochosi, and Osain—although also included below, are among the orishas not usually "seated" on the heads of priests and priestesses (see section on Initiation, below). They are "received" in ceremonies particular to them but are not the principal deities to claim the initiate as their "child" because of the nature of their power (Osain, as "owner" of the forests and that which is wild in nature would be too vast and overwhelming to be spiritually crowned on an individual's head, for example).

27. Based on Barnet (1997: 88–99), and Canizares (1993: chapter 6). Barnet lists Osain among the orishas relegated to secondary importance in Cuba: Oba, Orisha Oke, Naná Burukú, the Ibbeyi (twins), Inle, Aggayú Solá, and Yegguá (1997: 88). "The syncretic process still taking place in Cuba is complex. . . . [S]ome divinities gain prominence through transculturation and others lose it or grow weaker. . . . A hierarchical ordering of these divinities in relation to their powers and attributes is never definitive but is dependent on historical stages and the needs of the believers" (1997: 97).

28. While there is usually agreement among practitioners, tracing and defining the orisha family tree is often a matter of local tradition.

29. See Barnes (1997) for a fascinating discussion of Ogún's diverse and evolving representations in Africa and the Americas.

30. According to Bascom, in Trinidad, northern Brazil, and Grenada Shango is the name given to a cult in which the Yoruba gods or "powers" are worshiped and in which a similar syncretism with Catholic saints exists (1972: 10–12).

31. David H. Brown makes the interesting observation that the representation of orishas in Lucumí ritual are a significant example of borrowing/loan translations, signs from the Cuban secular historical experience: the otanes or stones repose in "borrowed," mass-produced eighteenth-century European tureens . . . the oricha "comes down" speaking the Lucumí ritual tongue, wears Spanish-derived royal cabildo costume, and will repose beneath a colonial-era royal "throne." . . . The orichas of Cuban houses remain the image of cabildo kings and queens described by nineteenth-century observers of the comparsas. . . . Ochún's image as a flirtatious, vain, cinnamon-skinned woman who carries a fan, whose Afro-Cuban avatar is the peacock (pavo real), is borrowed from the stereotyped, distinctly colonial mulata. (1989: 104–106).

32. Among Babalú Ayé's avatars is Chapkuana, the original god of smallpox among the Yoruba.

33. Desi Arnaz made the name famous when he sang "Babalú" on the TV comedy show, "I Love Lucy."

34. At times Saint Lazarus is identified with the New Testament parable, at others with Lazarus, brother of Mary and Martha, brought back from the dead by Jesus Christ, and on yet other occasions with the medieval Saint Lazarus.

35. See I. Castellanos (1996: 47).

36. *Monte* in this context combines several meanings: forest, countryside, brushland, or an uncultivated or virgin landscape, a "sacred wild." By way of extension, parks, backyards, and vacant lots can substitute (D. Brown 1989: 355).

37. Priests and priestesses rarely make a living from the predetermined fees charged for ritual work. The Ilé serves as a support system for many of its members who cannot rely on other sources; an important service provided by the santero or santera is health care, particularly involving traditional remedies. See Murphy (1994: 87–88), Fernández Olmos and Paravisini-Gebert (2001), and Cros Sandoval (1979).

38. Women are well represented in the Regla de Ocha sacred leadership.

39. A description of the initiation of a babalao can be found in Canizares (1993: 35–37).

40. Based on Castellanos and Castellanos (1992: 3).

41. Although the initiation for santos which live "in the house" is conducted within the igbodu, the initiations of santos such as Eleguá, Ogún, and Ochosi, who live in the "monte" or mountains, are often conducted outside the house-temple under a *trono de patio* or patio throne constructed of leaves and draped in front with a white sheet to set the space apart.

42. See D. Brown (1989) for an excellent description of Regla de Ocha's ceremonial artistry.

43. After the initiation the iyawó spends one year under the supervision of his or her padrino and madrina. The iyawo must dress in white, cover his or her head in public, eat from a white plate with a spoon, refrain from shaking anyone's hand, and, if eating with other santeros, sit on the floor. A woman cannot use cosmetics nor look at herself in the mirror for the first three months following initiation. During the year the novitiate will receive sacred instruction on how to pray and honor the orishas and will begin to learn the secrets of divinations with coconut and cowry shells as well as instruction in the Yoruba or Lucumí language. According to Vega, "I understood that these changes in my lifestyle symbolized the process of shedding unconscious habits, spiritually centering while analyzing my daily behavior. . . . These restrictions assist you in concentrating on your new path" (Vega 2000: 238).

44. The *libreta* is a true work of oral popular literature. It contains "myths and fables, lists of proverbs, Yoruba-Spanish vocabulary words, ritual formulas, recipes for spells and sacred foods, stories about the orichas and details concerning their avatars, songs, the secrets of divination systems, the names of herbs of the gods and their uses in the rites and popular pharmacopoeia, etc. In other words, all of the wisdom of the ancient Yoruba and their culture that refuses to die" (Martínez Furé 1979: 211–212).

45. See an interview with santero Steve Quintana on the use of dolls in Santería houses, in Wexler (2001).

46. For a more complete presentation, see Matibag (1996: 73–85).

47. See González-Wippler (1989: 142–144) for the complex formula and also Brandon (1991).

48. Based on Gonzalez-Wippler (1989: 130–131) and Cabrera (1980: 189–191). The spellings and pronunciations of the odu names vary among authors.

49. Based on Cros Sandoval (1975: 86–87).

50. Matibag (1997).

51. Based on Canizares (1993: 70–72) and Vélez (2000: 120–128).

52. Several works explore the growing evidence of a significant lesbian, gay, bisexual and transgender presence in the Creole Religions. See Connor (2004) and Vidal-Ortiz (2005).

53. There is some indication that female babalaos exist in Nigeria but that is not the case in the Americas (Murphy 1994: 89). However, González-Wippler offers a personal testimonial of the unusual and controversial case of a North American Jewish woman, Patri Dhaifa, who was initiated into the mysteries of Ifá in 1985 by an African priest (1989: 110–120).Hagedorn reflects on the controversy surrounding women *batá* players and her study of the drums in Cuba. Clark challenges traditional notions regarding the category of gender in Orisha traditions suggesting, among other ideas, that Santería is a female-based religion and that gender crossing "is integral to the practice of Santería" (2005: 84).

54. Antonio Benítez Rojo presents an intriguing argument concerning the "narrative practice" of the "Peoples of the Sea," that is, non-Western peoples, and Caribbean culture with respect to rhythm, communication—"Rhythm-Word"—and the "talking" African drums: "the African languages are so rhythmic and sonorous that they can be imitated by the dun-dun, the talking drum, whose skins . . . make communication possible between one village and another, with the mediation of any alphabetical code. . . . [I]t can be said that African culture's genres have been codified according to the possibilities of percussion" (1996: 169).

55. David H. Brown (2003) offers a similar "insider" perspective on the thorny issues regarding the Cuban Revolutionary government's embrace of "folklore" as an emblem of the island's popular culture with respect to the Abakuá Secret Society.

56. D. Brown (1989: 109–120) and Gregory (1999).

57. On the written mode of transmission of the religion and transformations that have occurred as a result, see Isabel Castellanos (1996: 47–48).

58. D. Brown (1989: 106–109) and Gregory (1999: 30–35). Palmié's "Against Syncretism: 'Africanizing' and 'Cubanizing' Discourses in North American *òrìsà* Worship" presents an illuminating analysis and comparison of Cuban American and African American perceptions of the tradition of Afro-Cuban religious practices.

59. In *Making the Gods in New York: The Yoruba Religion in the African American Community*, Mary Cuthrell Curry states that Santería jars the sensitivities of African Americans who prefer to embrace the Yoruba religion excluding the Catholic influences found in the Cuban practice (1997: 134).

60. Cros Sandoval (1979).

61. The legal battles of Santero Ernesto Pichardo in Florida are an example. His Babalu-Aye Temple in Hialeah, Florida, was shut down in 1987 due to community complaints regarding animal sacrifice, but was permitted to reopen in 1993 after a Supreme Court ruling stated that laws banning the ritual sacrifice of animals violated the free exercise of religion clause of the First Amendment.

CHAPTER 3

1. The Regla Conga . . . most likely resulted from the union forged in the belly of slave ships from three different African cultural forms: the cult of fire and of metal objects of the iron guilds—composed solely of males, prohibited from transmitting their secrets—, widely disseminated among the western Kikongo; the healing

rituals of the *quimbandeiros* [healing sorcerers], strongly linked to the mysteries of the jungle; and the preeminence of the sorcerer or *nganguleros* [makers of magic charms or *ngangas*] of the villages in the interior zones of the Congo Basin. . . . All of this that is mixed together due to the slave trade and contact in the slave barracks gives rise in the Caribbean to a new product without necessarily in this case—and I emphasize this aspect—a clash with Christianity as an indispensable condition. (James Figarola 1999a: 134)

2. Matibag (1996: chapter 5); Castellanos and Castellanos (1992, 3: chapter 2).

3. Matibag (1996: 156); Barnet (1983: 203–207).

4. González-Wippler (1989: chapter 19); Matibag (1996: chapter 5); Castellanos and Castellanos (1992, 3: chapter 2).

5. Based on correspondence with the author.

6. The novel reflects an unfortunate stereotype in Cuban popular culture regarding the Chinese. In the mid-nineteenth century a significant number of Chinese indentured laborers were brought into the country to work alongside or replace the African and Creole black slaves in the cane fields.

7. For similar practices in the United States, see Zora Neale Hurston's (1931) account of her research.

8. For a personal testimony of the initiation, see González Bueno (1993).

9. "The BaKongo, or people of Kongo culture, had a traditional reaction to takeovers which makes their impact on neo-African mythologies and literatures much more difficult to study. They rejected the foreign codes by feeding the outsider with only part of their system of signification or with makeshift subsystems which could easily adjust to the will of the colonizer" (Piedra 1997: 132).

10. A similar idea exists in the Cuban Regla de Palo: control of a person's "shade" means control of the person's life force and removing it, "quitar la sombra," will lead to his or her death.

11. David H. Brown offers a fascinating analysis of the military metaphors that inform Palo work, comparing it to the historical tradition of Cuban cimarron society (1989: 371–375).

12. According to Palmié, there is also a gender component to the distinctions between Regla de Ocha and Regla de Palo. "To a certain extent, this opposition between refinement and crudeness, civilization and wildness, has a gendered dimension. Although women fulfill ritual roles in both types of cult, palo tends to be represented as a 'cosa de hombre.' In contrast to regal ocha, which contains a large number of homosexual adherents (sometimes euphemistically referred to as *overly refined*), palo groups are characterized by a pronounced homophobic atmosphere, and many women have told me that they dislike the machismo that pervades social relations within a 'casa de palo'" (2002: 164).

13. Quiñones paraphrases Fernando Ortiz (1954: 70–71).

14. A. J. H. Latham, *Old Calabar, 1600–1891* (Oxford: Clarendon Press, 1973).

15. A creolization of *abakpa*, a term used to describe the Ejagham peoples of Calabar.

16. Members of the organization must "prove" themselves manly enough to belong. Hence the stipulation that no homosexuals can be ñáñigos, who must be "hombres probados" (proven men).The definition of "real men," however, is complicated; men could have relationships with other men but, if taking the "active" *macho* role (*bugarrones*) they would not consider themselves "homosexuals" (D. Brown 2003: 28–29).

17. Palmié's definition of the cabildo takes into account the creolization process, referring to them as "intentional communities based not on ascriptions of origin, but on autonomous constructions of collective identity and allegiance. Viewed in this light, the existence of 'cabildos' of any one named Afro-Cuban 'nation' becomes an indicator less of the mere numerical strength of particular African population segments in the Cuban diaspora, than of the capacity of groups of Africans (however constituted) to forge common patterns of identification under certain New World conditions—whether the resulting collective identities were based on factual Old World ethnic commonalities, or on New World allegiances translated into an ethnic idiom" (2007: 285).

18. See D. Brown (2003), Palmié and Pérez (2005), Palmié (2007), and Miller (2009).

19. For an excellent analysis of Abakuá ideographs and ritual costume, see Thompson (1984: chapter 5).

20. For a more comprehensive analysis of the Abakuá society, see Cabrera (1970), Castellanos and Castellanos (1992, 3: chapter 3), D. Brown (2003), and Miller (2009).

21. Sosa Rodríguez observes in the alternative name of "chalice" for the drum (given its shape and its sacred contents) and other similar terms used by the Ñáñigos a further example of syncretism with Roman Catholicism (1982: 180).

22. Cuban popular music has been influenced by Abakuá, as it has by the other Afro-Cuban religions, whether by the many Cuban musicians who are members of the religion or by those outside Cuba who admire its rhythms and movements (Miller 2009).

23. Castellanos and Castellanos (1992, 3: 220–222).

24. See Ortiz's study of the Havana underworld at the beginning of the twentieth century, *Hampa Afro-Cubana* (1916; reprinted in 1987), and David H. Brown's (2003) valuable research concerning the Abakuá and their evolving relationship with Cuban governmental authorities from colonial times to the contemporary period.

25. In "Ecué's Atlantic: An Essay in Methodology," Stephan Palmié disagrees with Miller's premise and presents an interesting debate, arguing that "the apparent dispersion of Cross-River-type secret societies ought not to be seen as a pattern of diffusion from a (temporarily prior) point of inception to (temporarily later) sites of recreation, but as a total pattern of simultaneous 'Atlantic' eventuation and cultural production" (2007: 275).

26. Cabrera (1983); Laguerre (1987). The ideas regarding healing practices expressed here are based on Fernández Olmos, "*La Botánica Cultural*" (2001).

27. Hurston (1931).

28. Translation in Fernández Olmos, "Black Arts" (2001).

CHAPTER 4

1. The Catholic Church broke off relations with the Dessalines government in 1805 and ordered its priests out of the country. Between 1805 and the Concordat of 1860 (which was an agreement between the Vatican and the government of General Geffard), there were only a handful of Catholic priests in the country.

2. For more on this role of the oungan and manbo, see Paravisini-Gebert's "'He of the Trees': Nature, the Environment, and Creole Religiosities in Caribbean Literature" (2005).

3. For a detailed description of what happens to *serviteurs* during possession, see Katherine Dunham's *Island Possessed* (1969).

CHAPTER 5

1. See Claudette A. Anderson's "Judge, Jury or Obeahman? Power Dynamics in the Jamaican House O'law" (2008).

2. Guyanese Comfa is a comparable practice. Comfa, as Michelle Asantewa describes it, is "the generic term used to define the manifestation of spirits. Anyone who becomes spiritually possessed on hearing the beating of drums is said to 'ketch Comfa'" (2008: 1). The practice, she explains, is linked to "Okomfa"—the traditional /"fetish" priests and the dance of Akom in Ghana, West Africa, which in Guyana was associated with the worship of the "watermamma" spirit brought to Guyana by African slaves:

> Comfa ceremonies were held when there was a misfortune in the village or in a family when information was needed to give account of certain inexplicable travesties. The "Watermamma" spirit was invoked to provide solutions to problems or to remove evil manifesting in an individual, family or community. The main feature of a Comfa ceremony which was held to honour the "Watermamma" was a dance sometimes called "cabango," "cumfo" or "catamarrha." (2008: 1)

3. Interestingly, Cobb, the young apprentice learning the craft from "Mr. Murray, indicated in an interview that he intended to set up his practice in an affluent neighborhood: His destination is uptown, among the more well-to-do Jamaicans. 'I am going to set up in Eastwood Park Gardens. This is where the calling says that I must go,' discloses Cobb with a wide grin" (Luton 2009).

4. George Blyth, *Reminiscences of Missionary Life. With Suggestions to Churches and Missionaries* (Edinburgh: William Oliphant & Sons, 1851), 172–175. Quoted by Diane Stewart (1997).

5. The name Zambi is also used by practitioners of the Cuban Congo religion, Regla de Palo, who share similar practices and traditions.

6. The Obeah practiced in Dominica, with its emphasis on gaddé zaffés and belief in soucouyants, is very close to Martinican and Guadeloupean beliefs. Jeffrey Mantz, in his work on accusations of Obeah practice in Dominica, has found an interesting link between reports that individuals practice some form of witchcraft and accusations of homosexuality. In these instances, the condemnation of Obeah practitioners is transferred to individuals who may or may not be homosexual, in a manifestation of the persistent homophobia that characterizes Dominican society:

> Homosexuality does not replace Obeah as a 'modern' or digital age object of scorn; rather it complements it as something that indexes newly emergent cultural fears and anxieties. As a complementary discourse, *mépwi* about homosexuality follows many of the same structural patterns as that about Obeah, focusing on behavioral practices and a predisposition for intentional malice, rejecting any possible assertion that the practices might be innate, inborn, or otherwise out of the control of the accused. (Mantz 2008: 10)

CHAPTER 6

1. Rastafarian notions of an ancestral homeland is based on a complex set of notions known as Ethiopianism, an ideology derived from biblical references to all black peoples as Ethiopians. These references underscore the African peoples' proud cultural heritage, shown to predate European civilization. Ethiopianism has been used to express the

political, cultural, and spiritual aspirations of blacks throughout the Diaspora since the eighteenth century. As a unifying metaphor for African brotherhood, it has provided the basis for shared notions of destiny and identification between African peoples.

2. Haile Selassie (1892–1975), Emperor of Ethiopia from 1930 to 1974, was born Tafari Makonnen, son of a chief advisor to Emperor Menilek II. He is best known for his efforts to modernize Ethiopia. After a successful early career as a reform-minded provincial administrator, he had come to represent the most progressive elements of the Ethiopian elite. His marriage in 1911 to Wayzaro Menen, a great-granddaughter of Menilek II, brought him into the royal family. Tafari became the rallying point for the Christian resistance against Melinek II's successor, Lij Yasu, whose close ties to Islam were resented by the primarily Christian population. In 1916, after Lij Yasu was ousted and replaced by Zauditu, Melinek II's daughter, Ras (Prince) Tafari was named regent and heir apparent to the throne. In 1930, at Zauditu's death, he was crowned emperor, taking the name of Haile Selassie ("Might of the Trinity").

The early years of Haile Selassie's reign were marked by progressive reforms in education, the justice system, the burdensome system of feudal taxation, and the centralization of the government. He was forced into exile in 1936, after Italy invaded Ethiopia, and did not resume his throne until British and Ethiopian forces invaded the country in 1941 and recaptured Addis Ababa. Opposition to Haile Selassie's autocratic rule, however, began to surface in the 1950s, as he failed to heed increasingly strident calls for democracy. A new constitution granted in 1955 failed to limit his powers. Overt opposition surfaced in 1960, when a dissident wing of the army secured control of Addis Ababa, and was dislodged only after a sharp engagement with loyalist elements. Haile Selassie ruled Ethiopia until 1974, when widespread famine, ruinous levels of unemployment, and the government's perceived inability to improve conditions prompted the army to mutiny. He was replaced by a provisional Marxist military government and was kept under house arrest in his palace, where he died a year later. He was said to have died of natural causes, but it was later revealed that he was strangled on the orders of the military government.

3. Haile Selassie, a devout Christian, was not himself a Rastafarian, and what he thought of his deification in the faraway land of Jamaica has never been entirely clear. He is said to have refused to see a group of Jamaican Rastas who went to Ethiopia to honor him and who found themselves turned away at the palace gates. Many Rastafarians refused to believe the reports of his death, regarding it as a trick of the media to challenge their faith. They believe that Haile Selassie has moved on to a state of perfect flesh, and sits on the highest point of Mount Zion, awaiting judgment.

4. Disillusioned by this failure, Edwards and his followers founded the Bobos, a Rasta group of believers in black supremacy who live in an organized commune in Jamaica and have been recognized by the United Nations as an independent flag-bearing nation (D. Stewart 1997: 144). The Bobo Rastas, known for their radical adherence to the principles of black nationalism, live in ascetic contemplation of Rastafarian principles, closely observing a series of taboos (see below) that they believe will lead to a pure and selfless community.

5. The term Nyabinghi also describes an Afro-Jamaican drumming style.

6. The Nyabinghi struggle against the British in Uganda, led by their valiant Queen Muhumusa, raged for twenty years from 1917 to 1937 and was followed closely by the press in Jamaica, particularly after rumors had spread in 1935 that Haile Selassie had taken over the leadership of the Nyabinghi movement.

7. The idea that salt repels the spirits is found in other Caribbean Creole practices, particularly with regard to food offerings to certain spirits.

8. For a literary treatment of Rastafarianism, see Jamaican novelist Erna Brodber's *Jane and Louisa Will Soon Come Home* (1981) and *Myal* (1988).

CHAPTER 7

1. The Catholic Church in the 1860s considered Spiritism a form of demonology or superstition for its support of the belief in reincarnation and communication with the dead. The bishop of Barcelona ordered an auto-da-fé for Spiritist books in 1861. "The auto-da-fé undoubtedly stirred up French nationalism—one of the burned books was *L'Histoire de Jeanne d'Arc* [The History of Joan of Arc], dictated by the saint through a French medium—and it helped to create a following in both France and Spain. Kardec's popularity could only have increased when the bishop died nine months after the auto-da-fé and his repentant spirit appeared through French mediums and begged for Kardec's forgiveness, which the Spiritist leader graciously granted" (Hess 1991: 67–69).

2. James Figarola considers Espiritismo de Cordón one of the four major magicoreligious systems of Cuba along with Regla de Ocha, Regla de Palo, and the Cuban variant of Vodou. In his view all these are original and historical religions born in Cuba (1999a, 1999b).

3. The use of such terms as "commissions" to refer to spirits who have the authority to represent and protect humans in the spirit world, and an earlier reference to the division of spirits into *cuadros espirituales* or spiritual "cadres" in Cuban and Puerto Rican variants of Espiritismo are an indication of the influence of militarism in nineteenth-century Caribbean societies, particularly in Cuba and Puerto Rico, the two islands still under strict Spanish military control. Suárez Rosado observes that the principle of the spirit guides as warriors that protect human beings in life's struggles is "intimately tied to the popular iconography of Catholic religious images, the mystics, martyrs and warriors" (1992: 128).

Interestingly, in the Venezuelan Spiritist cult of María Lionza which has developed since the 1960s, a cult with roots in Kardecism, Amerindian shamanism, folk Catholicism, and Afro-American religions, the spiritual protector entities worshiped and invoked belong to different *cortes* (courts)—the Indian Court, African Court, Court of doctors, and so on—and include important Venezuelan historical figures (Pollak-Eltz 1999–2000).

4. Koss (1977) notes that the concepts of a "universal fluid" continuous with all objects in the universe which could be used to cure nervous disorders and other ailments if attracted and transmitted through magnets and hand gestures or "passes" was first introduced by Franz Mesmer (1734–1815), considered by some the "historical godfather of psychoanalysis" (Koss 1977: 25–26). According to his biogrqphers, Kardec was intimately familiar with Mesmerism and Magnetism.

5. Bastide (1971) continues in the essay to compare the *cordoneros* to "Umbanda spiritualism" in Brazil.

6. Brandon (1993) discusses the Spiritist *Misa Espiritual* for the dead in relation to the *Misa Africana* (African Mass), a separate African funeral rite called *Itutu* (discussed briefly in chapter 2 on Santería/Regla de Ocha) which involves divination of the will of the dead through cowrie shells, or the Ifá priest's divining chain.

By the time Espiritismo assumed prominence among santeros, the practice of having the African Itutu funeral rite done parallel with the two Catholic masses [one performed nine days after death and the second at the first-year anniversary] had become orthodoxy and tradition. After Espiritismo appeared on the scene there arose differences of opinion among the mass of Santería devotees and priests concerning the status of the spiritual mass as a death rite (1993: 179).

Discrepancies—although by no means a rupture—arose between the Espiritista-oriented santeros and those who felt that the Spiritist trance state could not replace Santería divination devices (1993: 175–180).

7. It is believed that the growth of Kardecism in Cuba coincided with the decline of the Yoruba/Lukumi *egungun* ritual: the presence of egungun specialists at funerals was indispensable as they had the ability to become possessed by the spirit of the dead. The lack of such specialists among the Yoruba transported to Cuba, and the complicated nature of the rituals led to its demise by the mid-nineteenth century. Espiritismo practice served to replace the egungun to contact the spirit of one's ancestors.

8. Núñez-Molina (1987, 2001), and Koss (1977).

9. Néstor Rodríguez Escudero, cited in Hess (1991: 206).

10. "The differences in Brazil between 'evangelical' and 'scientific' Spiritists seem in Puerto Rico to collapse into a single category of 'scientific Spiritism.' In turn, scientific spiritism is defined in opposition to Puerto Rican 'popular Spiritism,' which may be compared with what is sometimes called Spiritist-line Umbanda in Brazil" (Hess 1991: 209).

11. Hess notes the observations of Néstor Rodríguez Escudero, a Puerto Rican historian of Espiritismo, who commented in the 1980s that all variants of Spiritism were in decline in Puerto Rico, substituted by Pentecostalism, which was winning converts from both Spiritism and Catholicism. "Thus," Hess remarks, "the ultimate expression of the centrifugal tendency within Spiritism may not be a form of Spiritism at all, but Pentecostalism" (1991: 208).

12. Morales-Dorta calls Espiritism a "native religion" of Puerto Rico (1976: 14).

13. Other researchers have made the same claim. For Vega (1999), however, the indigenous form of Puerto Rican Espiritismo is not a legacy of the Yoruba tradition, which is the foundation of Cuban Santería, but rather that of the ancestor worship of African Kongo cultures brought to the island by enslaved Africans during the nineteenth century, which marks the later phase of the slave trade in Puerto Rico (slavery was abolished on the island in 1873). Her ideas on the subject reflect interesting parallels with those of James Figarola with regard to Cuban Congo influences in the emergence of the Cuban Espiritismo variant, Espiritismo de Cordón (1999a, 1999b).

And Stanley Fisch describes an Espiritista session that took place in 1967 in a U.S. Puerto Rican community in which the rituals were clearly influenced not only by Santería but also by Cuban Espiritismo de Cordón: "Finally, José told the group to stand and form a chain. We linked hands by hooking middle fingers and raised our hands over our heads. Immediately, Antonia, Pedro, and Lisa began shaking. Lisa stopped after a few seconds, and Pedro began flamenco-type dancing into the center of the circle. Antonia came out of her possession as Pedro danced back to his place, and in a full, clear voice, summoned all the evil influences ('malas influencias') to leave the *centro*" (Fisch 1968: 385).

14. According to Pérez y Mena, the "sorcery" of the Afro-Cuban Palo Monte religion is having an impact on Puerto Rican Spiritualism, whose historical equivalent, he believes,

is Brazilian Umbanda. In fact, he refers to Puerto Rican Spiritualism as "Puerto Rican Umbanda" (1991: 237).

15. A term found in Brandon (1993).

16. Pérez y Mena (1991: chapter 2).

17. Koss refers to botánicas as "Spiritist pharmacies" (1979: 382).

18. González-Wippler enumerates several categories of mediums (*mediunidades*) in Espiritismo: *mediunidades videntes* (mediums who can see the spirits), *mediunidades clarividentes* (mediums who can see the future), *mediunidades auditivas* (mediums who can hear the spirits speak in their ears), *mediunidades de comunicación* (mediums who become possessed by spirits), *mediunidades de arrastre* (mediums who can take on evil spirits and banish them), and *mediunidades de transporte* (mediums who are able to project their consciousness to other places, including the realm of the spirits) (1989: 277).

19. As Koss-Chioino reminds us, "*Espiritistas* diagnose the causes of illness and other problems but do not directly 'heal.' Healing can occur when the spirit medium assists the sufferer to come into harmony with the spirit world so as to change his or her physical condition, emotions, way of life, or destiny" (Koss-Chioino 1992: 13).

20. Fernández Olmos, "*La Botánica Cultural*: Ars Medica, Ars Poetica" (2001: 1).

21. Based upon the observations of Harwood (1977) and Pérez y Mena (1991).

22. Prorok (2000) details an elaborate and complex Santerismo altar, a "feminized" ritual space, of an Espiritista in New York City.

23. Koss (1979: 388). The use of dolls in Spiritist and Santería practices is extensively explored in Wexler's interview with Steve Quintana (Wexler 2001).

24. In popular representations of the Seven African Powers, the African orisha are portrayed as Roman Catholic saints within a medallion but identified with the names of the orisha associated with each saint above; the medallions encircle a crucified Christ labeled as "Olofi." See note 26 below.

25. See chapter 2 on Santería/Regla de Ocha for a discussion of the attributes of the orishas/saints.

26. Brandon (1993) notes the popular representation of the Seven African Powers in chromolithographs, on glass votive candles (found in botánicas and grocery stores in Hispanic neighborhoods), and in commercially printed prayers and posters, using Catholic imagery but referred to by Lukumí names. The orisha are portrayed as a set of medallions linked by a chain embellished with metal weapons associated with Ogún, the orisha of warfare and iron—a hammer, axe, hook, arrow, spear, hatchet, and cutlass—surrounding a crucified Christ (Olofi). "These syncretized orisha are brought over as a group and set into the ideological system of Espiritismo" (Brandon 1993: 110). Practitioners of either or both religious systems—Santería and Espiritismo—can access the power and blessings of each in a form of "religious appropriation."

27. According to Koss-Chionio:

Although all the *Espiritistas* I know disavow spirit work that would harm rather than heal, a widespread underlying fear of their special kind of power lends itself to thoughts about, and direct accusations of their being, witches (*brujas*). Stories of going to spirit workers to prepare a harmful "work," or charm (*trabajo malo, hechizo, magia negra, daño*) are not uncommon. Some *Espiritistas* are reputed to be able to "revoke" the harmful "work," which can include turning it back onto its originator. . . . Although it is recognized that a few spirit mediums do arrange evil spells, they are excluded from the informal fraternity of *Espiritistas* and are generally regarded as misguided, unwise individuals who do not really intend evil . . . "ignorant, superstitious persons" who do not follow the sacred mandate to align oneself only with forces of "light." (1992: 76–77) For another perspective on brujería, see Raquel Romberg, *Witchcraft and Welfare: Spiritual Capital and the Business of Magic in Modern Puerto Rico* (2003).

28. Koss-Chioino remarks on the culturally congruent patterns of some psychological behavior in Spiritism:

In cultures such as that of Puerto Rico, it is difficult to distinguish between psychotic expressions—hallucination and delusions—and vision and experiences of spirits, because the latter are a very real part of the culturally constituted environment of many people. . . . From the psychological viewpoint, the images of Spiritist believers are extremely elaborate but so are those of some schizophrenics, especially with regard to social roles and interactions. Although they *appear* to be similar, there is one great difference: Visions and experiences of spirits are all framed by real and complex relationships—between medium-healers and their clients, between healers and spirits, and between clients and spirits. In contrast, the schizophrenic person usually withdraws from social interaction, and his imaginings are typically aspects of an internal dialogue. . . . Spiritist visions, on the other hand, although possessing a large variety of detail, actually conform to rather narrowly defined patterns. . . . When the content of a vision does not conform to expected patterns, it is rejected as a "true" experience of spirits. (1992: 140)

For a detailed discussion of the relationship between Spiritism and psychology, see Koss-Chioino (1992) and Garrison (1977).

29. "Culture inevitably structures pathologies of interpreting and feeling, as well as supplying idioms of distress, illness concepts, categories, and models for responding to the inner experiences of emotional chaos and disordered perception" (Koss-Chioino 1992: 169). See also Fernández Olmos, "*La Botánica Cultural*" (2001).

30. There are numerous examples of this in the research literature. Anna Wexler's essay, an interview with Steve Quintana, is an excellent personal account (2001).

31. Whereas "development" is considered a lifelong condition—more difficult at its inception than later—other types of spirit-causing distress (such as difficulty with a spirit coming from a past incarnation, problems with one's own spirit, or being *encadenada* [tied to a chain of disturbed spirits and unable to break free of this entanglement]), usually require only short-term attention and are generally worked on in one or perhaps a few sessions. (Koss-Chioino 1992: 59)

32. Núñez-Molina (2001).

33. Espiritismo has inspired plastic artists in the form of paintings and installations of Espiritismo altars and artifacts.

34. *The House on Mango Street* (1984) by the Mexican American author Sandra Cisneros includes another example of the incorporation of Espiritista themes in U.S. Latino writing.

35. Our translation.

36. In *Sacred Leaves of Candomblé: African Magic, Medicine, and Religion in Brazil*, Robert A. Voeks observes the following regarding the hot-cold approach:

This ancient concept is at the heart of early European and Asian health and healing theories, and it is a dominant organizing principle in many Latin American and African American folk medical systems as well. Although the presence of a hot-and-cold etiology among Hispanic Americans can be attributed to diffusion from Old World sources, the existence of this concept among Mesoamerica's pre-Hispanic civilizations—the Mayas, Aztecs, and Zapotecs—as well as among the isolated indigenous South American societies argues for the independent evolution of the hot-and-cold paradigm in the New World. (1997: 131)

37. The *Madama* is "a 'dark feminine' image . . . of woman" (Koss-Chioino 1992: 204).

38. A sentiment that brings to mind the comments of one of Cabrera's informants in *El monte* (1983), regarding the absence of a centralized organizational authority in Santería/ Regla de Ocha: "We have no Pope!"

39. See Romberg (2003) and C. Long (2001) for an illuminating discussion of the business of magic and religion.

40. Mestizo/a refers to a person of mixed racial heritage, usually of mixed Spanish and Amerindian blood. In general, the terms mestizo and mestizaje refer to racial or cultural mixture.

41. The tropical *seiba* (also written *ceiba*) trees are considered magical in many Caribbean cultures.

42. Large ants.

43. Based on personal correspondence with the author.

44. The above-mentioned ideas are based on Fernández Olmos (2007), 63–92.

45. In fact, the category that has most disturbed some readers of *Bless Me Ultima*, even going so far as to consider the novel dangerous for young readers, is precisely that of magic. The novel enjoys the dubious distinction of appearing on the list of the 100 Most Challenged Books on the Banned Books List of the decade in the ten years prior to 2000, published by the American Library Association's Office for Intellectual Freedom. For an analysis of Anaya's novels, see Fernández Olmos (1999).

46. In addition to fomenting criticism of the received, the legacy of countercultural and civil rights struggles has led to the search for more useful social, political, and spiritual models. Chicana artists have looked to the distant past, to Mesoamerican and North American Indigenous female deities, to those of African diasporic and Buddhist pantheons, and to the goddesses of ancient Europe and the Mediterranean, in part, in order to imagine a future beyond patriarchal cultures. They have variously assimilated goddesses-spiritualities . . . . [O]thers have studied and incorporated aspects of African-diaspora *santería* in their lives and/or their art practices. (Laura E. Pérez 2007: 299)

47. Alexander (2005). Cited in Keating (2008: 55).

48. We are grateful to AnaLouise Keating for her generosity in sharing this poem from her book, *The Gloria Anzaldúa Reader* (2009: 242).

Works Cited

Aimes, Hubert H. S. *A History of Slavery in Cuba, 1511–1868.* New York: G. P. Putnam, 1907.

Ajisafe, A. K. *The Laws and Customs of the Yoruba People.* Lagos: Kash and Klare, 1946.

Alexander, M. Jacqui. *Pedagogies of Crossing: Meditations on Feminism, Sexual Politics, Memory, and the Sacred.* Durham: Duke University Press, 2005.

Anaya, Rudolfo A. *Bless Me, Ultima.* Berkeley, Calif.: Quinto Sol Publications, 1972. New York: Warner Books, 1994.

———. "The New World Man." In *The Anaya Reader.* Rudolfo A. Anaya, ed. New York: Warner Books, 1995, 353–365.

Anderson, Claudette A. "Judge, Jury or Obeahman? Power Dynamics in the Jamaican House O'law." Paper presented at the Conference on "Obeah and Other Powers: The Politics of Caribbean Religion and Healing," July 16–18, 2008.

Anzaldúa, Gloria. *Borderlands : The New Mestiza = La frontera /.* San Francisco: Aunt Lute, 1987.

———. *Interviews = Entrevistas /.* AnaLouise Keating, ed. New York: Routledge, 2000.

Apter, Andrew. "Herskovits's Heritage: Rethinking Syncretism in the African Diaspora." *Diaspora: A Journal of Transnational Studies* 1.3 (1991): 235–260.

Argüelles Mederos, Aníbal, and Ileana Hodge Limonta, eds. *Los llamados cultos sincréticos y el espiritismo: Estudio monográfico social en la sociedad cubana contemporánea.* Havana: Editorial Academia, 1991.

Armas, José. "Chicano Writing: The New Mexico Narrative." In *Contemporary Chicano Fiction: A Critical Survey.* Vernon E. Lattin, ed. Binghamton, N.Y.: Bilingual Press/Editorial Bilingüe, 1986, 32–45.

Arthur, Charles, and Michael Dash, eds. *Liberté: A Haitian Anthology.* Kingston: Ian Randle: 1999.

Asantewa, Michelle. "Comfa as 'Arts of Imagination.'" Paper presented at the Conference on "Obeah and Other Powers: The Politics of Caribbean Religion and Healing," July 16–18, 2008.

Balutansky, Kathleen M., and Marie-Agnès Sourieau, eds. *Caribbean Creolization: Reflections on the Cultural Dynamics of Language, Literature, and Identity.* Gainesville: University Press of Florida, 1998.

Banbury, R. Thomas. *Jamaica Superstitions, or the Obeah Book.* Kingston: De Souza, 1895.

Banton, Michael. *Anthropological Approaches to the Study of Religion.* New York: Frederick A. Praeger, 1966.

Barnes, Sandra T., ed. *Africa's Ogun: Old World and New.* Bloomington: Indiana University Press, 1997.

Barnet, Miguel. *La fuente viva.* Havana: Editorial Letras Cubanas, 1983.

————, ed. *Biography of a Runaway Slave: A Novel*. W. Nick Hill, trans. Willimantic, Conn.: Curbstone Press, 1994.

————. "La Regla de Ocha: The Religious System of Santería." In *Sacred Possessions: Vodou, Santería, Obeah, and the Caribbean*. Lizabeth Paravisini-Gebert, trans. New Brunswick: Rutgers University Press, 1997, 79–100.

Barret, Leonard. *The Rastafarians: The Dreadlocks of Jamaica*. London: Heinemann, 1977.

Bascom, William R. "The Focus of Cuban Santeria." *Southwest Journal of Anthropology* 6.1 (1950): 64–68.

————. "Two Forms of Afro-Cuban Divination." In *Acculturation in the Americas*. Sol Tax, ed. Chicago: University of Chicago Press, 1952.

————. *Shango in the New World*. Austin: African and Afro-American Research Institute, University of Texas at Austin, 1972.

Bastide, Roger. *African Civilizations in the New World*. Peter Green, trans. London: C. Hurst and Company, 1971.

————. *The African Religions of Brazil: Toward a Sociology of the Interpenetration of Civilizations*. Helen Sebba, trans. Baltimore: Johns Hopkins University Press, 1978.

Beckwith, Martha Warren. *Black Roadways: A Study of Jamaican Folk Life*. Chapel Hill: University of North Carolina Press, 1929.

Becquer, Marcos, and Jose Gatti. "Elements of Vogue." *Third Text* 16–17 (Winter 1991): 65–81.

Bell, Hesketh. *Obeah and Witchcraft in the West Indies*. London: Sampson Low, Marston & Co., 1893.

Bellegarde-Smith, Patrick, ed. *Fragments of Bone: Neo-African Religions in a New World*. Urbana: University of Illinois Press, 2005.

Benavides, Gustavo. "Syncretism and Legitimacy in Latin American Religion." In *Enigmatic Powers: Syncretism with African and Indigenous Peoples' Religions among Latinos*. Anthony M. Stevens and Andrés I. Pérez y Mena, eds. New York: Bildner Center for Western Hemisphere Studies, 1995, 19–46.

Benítez Rojo, Antonio. *The Repeating Island: The Caribbean and the Postmodern Perspective*. James E. Maraniss, trans. Durham: Duke University Press, 1996.

————. "Three Words toward Creolization." In *Caribbean Creolization: Reflections on the Cultural Dynamics of Language, Literature, and Identity*. Kathleen M. Balutansky and Marie-Agnés Sourieau, eds. Gainesville: University Press of Florida, 1998, 53–61.

Benson, LeGrace. "Kiskeya-Lan Guinée-Eden: The Utopian Vision in Haitian Painting." *Callaloo* 15:3 (Summer 1992): 726–734.

Bernabé, Jean, Patrick Chamoiseau, and Raphaël Confiant. *Eloge de la Créolité*. Paris: Gallimard, 1989.

Betto, Frei. *Fidel and Religion: Castro Talks on Revolution and Religion with Frei Betto*. New York: Simon and Schuster, 1987.

Bilby, Kenneth. "An (Un)Natural Mystic in the Air: Images of Obeah in Caribbean Song." Paper presented at the Conference on "Obeah and Other Powers: The Politics of Caribbean Religion and Healing," July 16–18, 2008.

Binder, Wolfgang, ed. *Slavery in the Americas*. Würzburg: Königshauser & Neumann, 1993.

Blier, Suzanne Preston. *African Vodun: Art, Psychology and Power*. Chicago: University of Chicago Press, 1995.

Blyth, George. *Reminiscences of Missionary Life. With Suggestions to Churches and Missionaries*. Edinburgh: William Oliphant and Sons, 1851.

Bolívar Aróstegui, Natalia. *Los orishas en Cuba*. Havana: Ediciones Unión, 1990.

——. *Cuba: Imágenes y relatos de un mundo mágico*. Havana: Ediciones Unión, 1997.

Bolívar Aróstegui, Natalia, and Carmen González Díaz de Villegas. *Mitos y leyendas de la comida afrocubana*. Havana: Editorial de Ciencias Sciales, 1993.

Brandon, George. "The Uses of Plants in Healing in an Afro-Cuban Religion, Santeria." *Journal of Black Studies* 22.1 (1991): 55–76.

——. *Santería from Africa to the New World: The Dead Sell Memories*. Bloomington: Indiana University Press, 1993.

Brathwaite, Edward. *Folk Cultures of the Slaves in Jamaica*. London: New Beacon Books, 1970. Reprint 1974.

Brathwaite, Edward Kamau. "The African Presence in Caribbean Literature." *Daedalus* 103.2 (Spring 1974): 73–109.

Brodber, Erna. *Jane and Louisa Will Soon Come Home*. London: New Beacon Books, 1981.

——. *Myal*. London: Beacon Books, 1988.

Brown, David Hilary. "Garden in the Machine: Afro-Cuban Sacred Art and Performance in Urban New Jersey and New York." Vols. 1 and 2. Ph.D. dissertation, Yale University, 1989.

——. "Toward an Ethnoaesthetics of Santería Ritual Arts." In *Santería Aesthetics in Contemporary Latin American Art*. Arturo Lindsay, ed. Washington, D.C.: Smithsonian Institution Press, 1996, 77–145.

——. *The Light Inside: Abakuá Society Arts and Cuban Cultural History*. Washington, D.C.: Smithsonian Institution Press, 2003.

Brown, Karen McCarthy. *Mama Lola: A Vodou Priestess in Brooklyn*. Rev. ed. Berkeley: University of California Press, 2001.

——. "Writing about the Other." *Chronicle of Higher Education*, 15 April 1992, A56.

Buchner, J. H. *The Moravians in Jamaica*. London: Longman & Co., 1854.

Buisseret, David, and Steven G. Reinhardt, eds. *Creolization in the Americas*. "Introduction" by David Buisseret. College Station, Tex.: University of Texas Press, 2000.

Butler, Melvin L. "The Weapons of Our Warfare: Music, Positionality, and Transcendence among Haitian Pentecostals." *Caribbean Studies* 36:2 (2008): 23–64.

Cabrera, Lydia. *La sociedad secreta abakuá: narrada por viejos adeptos*. Miami: Colección del Chicherukú, 1970.

——. *La Regla Kimbisa del Santo Cristo del Buen Viaje*. Miami: Colección del Chicherukú en el exilio, 1977.

——. *Yemayá y Ochún: Kariocha, Iyalorichas y Olorichas*. New York: Colección del Chicherukú en el exilio, 1980.

——. *El monte. Igbo, finda, ewe orisha, vititi nfinda (Notas sobre las religiones, la magia, las supersticiones y el folklore de los negros criollos y el pueblo de Cuba)*. Miami: Ediciones Universal, 1983. [1954]

——. *Reglas de Congo: Palo Monte Mayombe*. Miami: Ediciones Universal, 1986.

——. *Afro-Cuban Tales. Cuentos negros de Cuba*. Alberto Hernández-Chiroldes and Lauren Poder, trans. and ed. Lincoln, Nebr.: University of Nebraska Press, 2004.

Campbell, Horace. *Rasta and Resistance: From Marcus Garvey to Walter Rodney*. Trenton, N.J.: Africa World Press, 1987.

Campbell, John. *Obeah: Yes or No? A Study of Obeah and Spiritualism in Guyana*. 1976.

Canizares, Raul. *Walking with the Night: The Afro-Cuban World of Santería*. Rochester, Vt.: Destiny Books, 1993.

Cañizares-Esguerra, Jorge. "Creole Colonial Spanish America." In *Creolization: History, Ethnography, Theory.* Charles Stewart, ed. Walnut Creek, Calif.: Left Coast Press, 2007, 26–45.

Castellanos, Isabel. "The Use of Language in Afro-Cuban Religion." Ph.D. dissertation, Georgetown University, 1976.

———. "From Ulkumí to Lucumí: A Historical Overview of Religious Acculturation in Cuba." In *Santería Aesthetics in Contemporary Latin American Art.* Arturo Lindsay, ed. Washington, D.C.: Smithsonian Institution Press, 1996, 39–50.

Castellanos, Isabel, and Josefina Inclán. *En torno a Lydia Cabrera.* Miami: Ediciones Universal, 1987.

Castellanos, Jorge, and Isabel Castellanos. *Cultura afrocubana 1 (El negro en Cuba, 1492–1944).* Miami: Ediciones Universal, 1988.

———. *Cultura afrocubana 3 (Las religiones y las lenguas).* Miami: Ediciones Universal, 1992.

Castro Flores, María Margarita. "Religions of African Origin in Cuba: A Gender Perspective." In *Nation Dance: Religion, Identity, and Cultural Difference in the Caribbean.* Patrick Taylor, ed. Bloomington: Indiana University Press, 2001, 54–62.

Chevannes, Barry. *Rastafari: Roots and Ideology.* Syracuse: Syracuse University Press, 1994.

———, ed. *Rastafari and Other African-Caribbean Worldviews.* New Brunswick: Rutgers University Press, 1998.

Chireau, Yvonne P. *Black Magic: Religion and the African American Conjuring Tradition.* Berkeley: University of California Press, 2003.

Christian, William A. *Local Religion in Sixteenth-Century Spain.* Princeton: Princeton University Press, 1981.

Cisneros, Sandra. *The House on Mango Street.* Houston: Arte Público Press, 1984.

Clark, Mary Ann. *Where Men Are Wives and Mothers Rule: Santería Ritual Practices and Their Gender Implications.* Gainesville: University Press of Florida, 2005.

Coleman, Monica A. *Making a Way Out of No Way: A Womanist Theology.* Minneapolis: Fortress Press, 2008.

Collier, Gordon, and Ulrich Fleischmann, eds. *A Pepper-Pot of Cultures: Aspects of Creolization in the Caribbean.* Amsterdam-New York: Rodopi, 2003. (Matatu [Journal] 27–28.)

Connor, Randy P. *Queering Creole Spiritual Traditions: Lesbian, Gay, Bisexual, and Transgender Participation in African-Inspired Traditions in the Americas.* New York: Harrington Park Press, 2004.

Conway, Frederick, 1978. "Pentecostalism in the Context of Haitian Religion and Health Practice." Ph.D. dissertation, American University, Washington, D.C.

Crapanzano, Vincent, and Vivian Garrison, eds. *Case Studies in Spirit Possession.* New York: John Wiley, 1977.

Cros Sandoval, Mercedes. *La religion afrocubana.* Madrid: Playor, 1975.

———. "Santería as a Mental Health Care System: An Historical Overview." *Social Science and Medicine* 13B (1979): 137–151.

———. "Afro-Cuban Religion in Perspective." In *Enigmatic Powers: Syncretism with African and Indigenous Peoples' Religions among Latinos.* Anthony M. Stevens and Andrés I. Pérez y Mena, eds. New York: Bildner Center for Western Hemisphere Studies, 1995, 81–98.

Cuervo Hewitt, Julia. "Yoruba Presence: From Nigerian Oral Literature to Contemporary Cuban Narrative." In *Voices from Under: Black Narrative in Latin America and the Caribbean*. William Luis, ed. Westport, Conn.: Greenwood Press, 1984, 65–85.

———. *Aché, presencia africana: tradiciones yoruba-lucumí en la narrativa cubana*. New York: Peter Lang, 1988.

Curtin, Philip D. *Two Jamaicas: The Role of Ideas in a Tropical Colony, 1830–1865*. Cambridge: Harvard University Press, 1955.

———. *The Atlantic Slave Trade: A Census*. Madison: University of Wisconsin Press, 1969.

Cuthrell Curry, Mary. *Making the Gods in New York: The Yoruba Religion in the African American Community*. New York: Garland, 1997.

Davis, Wade. *The Serpent and the Rainbow*. New York: Warner Books, 1985.

———. *Passage of Darkness: The Ethnobiology of the Haitian Zombie*. Chapel Hill: University of North Carolina Press, 1988.

Danticat, Edwidge. *Krik? Krak!* New York: Soho Press, 1995.

Dayan, Joan. "Erzulie: A Women's History of Haiti." *Research in African Literatures* 2 (Summer 1994): 5–31. (Reprinted in *Postcolonial Subjects: Francophone Women Writers*. Minneapolis: University of Minnesota Press, 1996.)

———. "*Haiti, History, and the Gods*. Berkeley: University of California Press, 1998.

———. "Vodoun, or the Voice of the Gods." In *Sacred Possessions: Vodou, Santería, Obeah, and the Caribbean*. Margarite Fernández Olmos and Lizabeth Paravisini-Gebert, eds. New Brunswick: Rutgers University Press, 1997, 13–36.

Deerr, Noel. *The History of Sugar*. 2 vols. London: Chapman and Hall, 1950.

Deive, Carlos Esteban. *Vodú y magia en Santo Domingo*. Santo Domingo: Museo del Hombre Dominicano, 1975.

De La Cancela, Victor, Peter J. Guarnaccia, and Emilio Carrillo. "Psychosocial Distress among Latinos: A Critical Analysis of *Ataques de Nervios*." *Humanity and Society* 10.4 (November 1986): 431–437.

Depestre, René. *Change*, Violence II, No. 9, Paris: Seuil, 1971.

Deren, Maya. *Divine Horsemen: The Living Gods of Haiti*. London: Thames and Hudson, 1953.

Desmangles, Leslie G. *The Faces of the Gods: Vodou and Roman Catholicism in Haiti*. Chapel Hill: University of North Carolina Press, 1992.

Dhaen, Theo, and Pieter Vermeulen, eds. *Cultural Identity and Postmodern Writing*. Amsterdam-New York: Rodopi, 2006.

Diamond, Jared. *Collapse: How Societies Choose to Fail or Succeed*. New York: Viking, 2005.

Di Iorio Sandín, Lyn. "The Cauldron." *The Bilingual Review Revista Bilingüe*. 23.2 (May–August 1998): 157–165.

Di Iorio Sandín, Lyn, and Richard Perez, eds. *Contemporary U.S. Latino/a Literary Criticism*. New York: Palgrave Macmillan, 2007.

Dos Santos, Juana Elbein, and Deoscoredes M. Dos Santos. "Religion and Black Culture." In *Africa in Latin America: Essays on History, Culture, and Socialization*. Leonor Blum, trans., Manuel Moreno Fraginals, ed. New York: Holmes and Meier, 1984, 61–82.

Droogers, André. "Syncretism: The Problem of Definition, the Definition of a Problem." In *Dialogue and Syncretism: An Interdisciplinary Approach*. Jerald Gort et al., eds. Grand Rapids, Mich.: William B. Eerdmans, 1989, 7–25.

Dunham, Katherine. *Island Possessed*. Chicago: University of Chicago Press, 1969.

Ebroïn, Ary. *Quimbois, magie noire, et sorcellerie aux Antilles*. Paris: Jacques Gran-cher, 1977.

Edwards, Albert. "Maroon Warfare: The Jamaica Model." In *Maroon Heritage: Archaeological, Ethnographic and Historical Perspectives*. E. Kofi Agorsah, ed. Kingston, Jamaica: Canoe Press/UWI, 1994, 158–159.

Edwards, Bryan. *The History, Civil, and Commercial, of the British Colonies in the West Indies*. London: John Stockdale, 1807.

Ellis, A. B. "On Vodu Worship." *Popular Science Monthly* 38 (1891): 649–653.

Fardon, Richard, ed. *Counterworks: Managing Diverse Knowledge*. London: Routledge, 1995.

Fernández, Damián J., ed. *Cuba Transnational*. Gainesville: University Press of Florida, 2005.

Fernández Olmos, Margarite. "Trans-Caribbean Identity and the Fictional World of Mayra Montero." In *Sacred Possessions: Vodou, Santería, Obeah, and the Caribbean*. Margarite Fernández Olmos and Lizabeth Paravisini-Gebert, eds. New Brunswick: Rutgers University Press, 1997, 267–282.

———. *Rudolfo A. Anaya: A Critical Companion*. Westport, Conn.: Greenwood Press, 1999.

———. "Black Arts: African Folk Wisdom and Popular Medicine in Cuba." In *Healing Cultures: Art and Religion as Curative Practices in the Caribbean and Its Diaspora*. Margarite Fernández Olmos and Lizabeth Paravisini-Gebert, eds., New York: Palgrave–St. Martin's Press, 2001, 29–42.

———. "*La Botánica Cultural*: Ars Medica, Ars Poetica." In *Healing Cultures: Art and Religion as Curative Practices in the Caribbean and Its Diaspora*. Margarite Fernández Olmos and Lizabeth Paravisini-Gebert, eds., New York: Palgrave–St. Martin's Press, 2001, 1–15.

———. "Spirited Identities: Creole Religions, Creole/U.S. Latina Literature, and the Initiated Reader." In *Contemporary U.S. Latino/a Literary Criticism*. Lyn Di Iorio Sandín and Richard Perez, eds. New York: Palgrave Macmillan, 2007, 63–92.

Fernández Olmos, Margarite, and Lizabeth Paravisini-Gebert, eds. *Sacred Possessions: Vodou, Santería, Obeah, and the Caribbean*. New Brunswick: Rutgers University Press, 1997.

———. *Healing Cultures: Art and Religion as Curative Practices in the Caribbean and Its Diaspora*. New York: Palgrave–St. Martin's Press, 2001.

Fisch, Stanley. "Botanicas and Spiritualism in a Metropolis." *Milbank Memorial Fund Quarterly* 46 (1968): 377–388.

Fleurant, Gerdes. "The Ethnomusicology of Yanvalou: A Study of the Rada Rite of Haiti." Ph.D. dissertation, Tufts University, 1987.

Foner, Philip S. *A History of Cuba and Its Relations with the United States*, 2 vols. New York: International Publishers, 1962.

Forde, Maarit. "The Moral Economy of Rituals in Early 20th Century Trinidad." Paper presented at the Conference on "Obeah and Other Powers: The Politics of Caribbean Religion and Healing," July 16–18, 2008.

Fowles, L. B. *The Land of the Pink Pearl: Life in the Bahamas*. London: Marston and Co., 1999.

Frazer, Sir James George. *The Golden Bough*. Abridged edition. New York: St. Martin's Press, 1966. (First abridged edition published 1922.)

Frye, Karla. "Obeah and Hybrid Identities." In Elizabeth Nunez Harrell's *When Rocks Dance*." In *Sacred Possessions: Vodou, Santería, Obeah, and the Caribbean*. Margarite Fernández Olmos and Lizabeth Paravisini-Gebert, eds. New Brunswick: Rutgers University Press, 1997, 195–215.

Garrison, Vivian. "The 'Puerto Rican Syndrome' in Psychiatry and *Espiritismo*." In *Case Studies in Spirit Possession*. Vincent Crapanzano and Vivian Garrison, eds. New York: John Wiley and Sons, 1977, 383–449.

Garvey, Amy Jacques, ed. *Philosophy and Opinions of Marcus Garvey*. New York: Arno Press, 1968.

Geertz, Clifford. "Religion as a Cultural System." In *Anthropological Approaches to the Study of Religion*. Michael Banton, ed. New York: Frederick A. Praeger, 1966, 1–46.

Genovese, Eugene D. *Roll, Jordan, Roll: The World the Slaves Made*. New York: Vintage Books, 1976.

Gilroy, Paul. *The Black Atlantic: Modernity and Double Consciousness*. Cambridge: Harvard University Press, 1993.

Glick-Schiller, Nina, and Georges Fouron. "Ti Manno and the Emergence of a Haitian Transnational Identity." *American Ethnologist* 17:2 (1990): 329–347.

Glissant, Edouard. *Caribbean Discourse: Selected Essays*. J. Michael Dash, trans. Charlottesville: University Press of Virginia, 1989.

———. "The Cultural 'Creolization' of the World: Interview with Edouard Glissant." *Label France* 38 (January 2000). http://www.france.diplomatie.fr/label_france/ENGLISH/DOSSIER/2000/15creolisation.html

González Bueno, Gladys. "An Initiation Ceremony in Regla de Palo." In *Afrocuba: An Anthology of Cuban Writing on Race, Politics and Culture*. Pedro Pérez Sarduy and Jean Stubbs, eds. Melbourne: Ocean Press, 1993, 117–120.

González-Wippler, Migene. *Santería: The Religion*. New York: Harmony Books, 1989.

Gregory, Steven. *Santería in New York City: A Study in Cultural Resistance*. New York: Garland, 1999.

Griffin, Glenn A. Elmer. "Come, We Go Burn Down Babylon: A Report on the Cathedral Murders and the Force of Rastafari in the Eastern Caribbean." *small axe* 21 (October 2006): 1–18.

Guabo, Emanuela. "Revival Zion: An Afro-Christian Religion in Jamaica." *Anthropos* 89:4/6 (1994): 33–47.

Guillen, Nicolás. *Sóngoro Cosongo*. Buenos Aires: Editorial Losada, 1952.

Hagedorn, Katherine J. *Divine Utterances: The Performance of Afro-Cuban Santería*. Washington, D.C.: Smithsonian Institution Press, 2001.

Hall, Gwendolyn Midlo. *Social Control in Slave Plantation Societies: A Comparison of St. Domingue and Cuba*. Baltimore: Johns Hopkins University Press, 1971.

Hannerz, Ulf. "The World in Creolisation." *Africa* 57 (1987): 546–559.

Hart, Richard. *Slaves Who Abolished Slavery*. Kingston, Jamaica: Institute of Social and Economic Research, 1985.

Harwood, Alan. *Rx: Spiritist As Needed: A Study of a Puerto Rican Community Mental Health Resource*. New York: John Wiley and Sons, 1977.

Hedrick, Basil C., and Jeanette E. Stephens. *It's a Natural Fact: Obeah in the Bahamas*. Colorado: Museum of Anthropology, University of Northern Colorado, 1977.

Herskovits, Melville. *The Myth of the Negro Past*. Boston: Beacon Press, 1958 [1941].

Hess, David J. *Spirits and Scientists: Ideology, Spiritism, and Brazilian Culture*. University Park: Pennsylvania State University Press, 1991.

Hoetink, H. "'Race' and Color in the Caribbean." In *Caribbean Contours*. Sidney W. Mintz and Sally Price, eds. Baltimore: Johns Hopkins University Press, 1985, 55–84.

Homiak, John P. "Dub History: Soundings on Rastafari Livity and Language." In *Rastafari and Other African-Caribbean Worldviews*. Barry Chevannes, ed. New Brunswick: Rutgers University Press, 1998, 127–181.

Houk, James T. *Spirits, Blood, and Drums*. Philadelphia: Temple University Press, 1995.

Hurbon, Laënnec. *Le Barbare imaginaire*. Paris: Les Editions du Cerf, 1988.

Hurston, Zora Neale. "Hoodoo in America." *Journal of American Folklore* 44.174 (October–December 1931): 317–417.

———. *Tell My Horse: Voodoo and Life in Haiti and Jamaica*. New York: Harper and Row, 1990 [1938].

James Figarola, Joel. *Sobre muertos y dioses*. Santiago de Cuba: Ediciones Caserón, 1989.

———. *La muerte en Cuba*. La Habana: Ediciones UNION, 1999a.

———. *Los sistemas mágico-religiosos cubanos: principios rectores*. Caracas: UNESCO, 1999b.

Jameson, Robert Francis. *Letters from the Havana, during the Year 1820*. London: John Miller, 1821.

Kardec, Allan. *Spiritualist Philosophy: The Spirits' Book*. Anna Blackwell, trans. New York: Arno Press, 1976, reprint. (Original edition, Boston: Colby and Rich, Publishers, 1875.)

Keating, AnaLouise. "'I'm a Citizen of the Universe': Gloria Anzaldúa's Spiritual Activism as Catalyst for Social Change." *Feminist Studies* 34.1/2 (Spring/Summer 2008): 53–69.

———, ed. *The Gloria Anzaldúa Reader*. Durham: Duke University Press, 2009.

Kebede, Alemseghed, and J. David Knotterus. "Beyond the Pales of Babylon: The Ideational Components and Social Psychological Foundations of Rastafari." *Sociological Perspectives* H1.3 (1998): 499–517.

Kennedy, J. "Haitian Art Inspired by Vodun." *American Visions* 6: 3 (1991): 14.

Khan, Aisha. "Creolization Moments." In *Creolization: History, Ethnography, Theory*. Charles Stewart, ed. Walnut Creek, Calif.: Left Coast Press, 2007, 237–253.

———. "Small Places Writ Large: Globalization and the Caribbean," *Caribbean Studies* 35.2 (July–December 2007): 183–192.

Kincaid, Jamaica. *At the Bottom of the River*. New York: Farrar, Straus, Giroux, 1983.

Kissoon, Carolyn. "A Trip to the Obeahman." *Trinidad Express*, May 10, 2009. http://www.trinidadexpress.com/index.pl/article_news?id=161475488. Accessed on September 3, 2009.

Kitzinger, Sheila. "Protest and Mysticisim: The Rastafari Cult of Jamaica." *Journal for the Scientific Study of Religion* 8:2 (1969): 240–262.

Klein, Herbert S. *Slavery in the Americas: A Comparative Study of Cuba and Virginia*. Chicago: University of Chicago Press, 1967.

———. *African Slavery in Latin America and the Caribbean*. New York: Oxford University Press, 1986.

Knepper, Wendy. "Colonization, Creolization, and Globalization: The Art and Ruses of Bricolage." *Small axe* 11.1 (2006): 70-86.

Knight, Franklin W. *Slave Society in Cuba during the Nineteenth Century*. Madison: University of Wisconsin Press, 1970.

———. *The Caribbean: The Genesis of a Fragmented Nationalism*. New York: Oxford University Press, 1978.

Koss, Joan D. "Religion and Science Divinely Related: A Case History of Spiritism in Puerto Rico." *Caribbean Studies* 16.1 (1977): 22–43.

———. "Artistic Expression and Creative Process in Caribbean Possession Cult Rituals." In *The Visual Arts: Graphic and Plastic*. Justine M. Cordwell, ed. The Hague: Mouton, 1979.

————. "Expectations and Outcomes for Patients Given Mental Health Care or Spiritist Healing in Puerto Rico." *American Journal of Psychiatry* 144.1 (January 1987): 56–61.

Koss-Chioino, Joan. *Women as Healers, Women as Patients: Mental Health Care and Traditional Healing in Puerto Rico.* Boulder: Westview Press, 1992.

Krüs, Patricia. "Myth and Revolution in the Caribbean Postmodern." In *Cultural Identity and Postmodern Writing.* Theo Dhaen and Pieter Vermeulen, eds. Amsterdam-New York: Rodopi, 2006, 149–167.

Lachatañeré, Rómulo. *Manual de Santería.* Havana: Editorial de Ciencias Sociales, 1995 [1942].

Laguerre, Michel S. *Afro-Caribbean Folk Medicine.* South Hadley, Mass.: Bergin and Garvey Publishers, 1987.

————. *American Odyssey: Haitians in New York City.* Ithaca: Cornell University Press, 1984.

————. *Voodoo and Politics in Haiti.* New York: St. Martins, 1989.

Landius, Jan, and Mat Lundahl. *Peasants and Religion: A Socioeconomic Study of Dios Olivorio and the Palma Sola Movement in the Dominican Republic.* London: Routledge, 2000.

Laroche, Maximilien. "The Myth of the Zombi." In *Exile and Tradition: Studies in African and Caribbean Literature.* Rowland Smith, ed. London: Longman, 1976, 44–61.

Latham, A. J. H. *Old Calabar, 1600–1891.* Oxford: Clarendon Press, 1973.

Lawal, Babatunde. "From Africa to the Americas: Art in Yoruba Religion." In *Santería Aesthetics in Contemporary Latin American Art.* Arturo Lindsay, ed. Washington, D.C.: Smithsonian Institution Press, 1996, 3–37.

Leach, MacEdward. "Jamaican Duppy Lore." *Journal of American Folklore* 74 (1961): 207–215.

Leon, Luis D. "Borderlands Bodies and Souls: Mexican Healing Practices in East Lost Angeles." In *Mexican American Religions: Spirituality, Activism, and Culture.* Gaston Espinosa and Mario T. Garia, eds. Durham: Duke University Press, 2008, 296–320.

Levi-Strauss, Claude. *The Savage Mind.* Chicago: University of Chicago Press, 1966.

Lewis, I. M. *Ecstatic Religion: A Study of Shamanism and Spirit Possession.* Harmonsworth, England: Penguin Books, 1971.

Long, Carolyn Morrow. *Spiritual Merchants: Religion, Magic and Commerce.* Knoxville: University of Tennessee Press, 2001.

Long, Edward. *The History of Jamaica,* 3 vols. London: T. Lowndes, 1774.

Luton, Daraine. "Learning Obeah: Kingstonian Studies 'High Science' in Portland Hills." *Jamaica Gleaner,* March 29, 2009. http://www.jamaica-gleaner.com/gleaner/20090329/news/news6.html. Accessed on August 10, 2009.

Mantz, Jeffrey W. "Sexual Scapegoating: Dominica's Political Economy of Witchcraft and Erotic Accusation." Paper presented at the Conference on "Obeah and Other Powers: The Politics of Caribbean Religion and Healing," July 16–18, 2008.

Martin, F. David. "What Is Christian Painting?" *Leonardo* 10:1 (1977): 23–29.

Martínez Furé, Rogelio. *Diálogos imaginarios.* Havana: Editorial Arte y Literatura, 1979.

Matibag, Eugenio. *Afro-Cuban Religious Experience: Cultural Reflections in Narrative.* Gainesville: University Press of Florida, 1996.

————. "Ifá and Interpretation: An Afro-Cuban Literary Practice." In *Sacred Possessions: Vodou, Santería, Obeah, and the Caribbean.* Margarite Fernández Olmos and Lizabeth Paravisini-Gebert, eds. New Brunswick: Rutgers University Press, 1997, 151–170.

McCartney, Timothy. *Ten, Ten the Bible Ten: Obeah in the Bahamas*. Nassau, Bahamas: Timpaul Publishing, 1976.

McDaniel, Lorna. "Memory Spirituals of the Ex-Slave American Soldiers in Trinidad's 'Company Villages.'" *Black Music Research Journal* 14:2 (1994): 119–143.

Métraux, Alfred. *Voodoo in Haiti*. Hugo Charteris, trans. New York: Schocken, 1972.

Miller, Ivor L. *Voice of the Leopard: African Secret Societies and Cuba*. Jackson: University Press of Mississippi, 2009.

Millet, José. *El espiritismo. Variantes cubanas*. Santiago de Cuba: Editorial Oriente, 1996.

Mintz, Sidney W. *Caribbean Transformations*. Baltimore: Johns Hopkins University Press, 1974.

Mintz, Sidney W., and Sally Price, eds. *Caribbean Contours*. Baltimore: Johns Hopkins University Press, 1985.

Missick, Rupert. *No Cure for Sure: Obeah Stories of the Bahamas as Told by Rupert Missick*. Nassau: Missick-Francis Press, 1975.

Mitchem, Stephanie Y. *African American Folk Healing*. New York: New York University Press, 2007.

Mohammed, Patricia. "The Sign of the Loa." *small axe* (September 2005): 124–149.

Moral, Paul. *Le Paysan Haïtien: Etude sur la vie rurale en Haiti*. Port-au-Prince: Editions Fardin, 1978.

Morales, Beatriz. "Afro-Cuban Religious Transformation: A Comparative Study of Lucumí Religion and the Tradition of Spirit Belief." Ph.D. dissertation, City University of New York, 1990.

Morales-Dorta, José. *Puerto Rican Espiritismo: Religion and Psychotherapy*. New York: Vantage Press, 1976.

Moreau de St. Méry, Louis-Élie. *Description Topographique, Physique, Civile, Politique, et Historique de las Partie Française de l'Isle de St. Dominque*. Paris: Libraire Larose, 1958 [1797].

Moreno Fraginals, Manuel. *The Sugarmill: The Socioeconomic Complex of Sugar in Cuba, 1760–1860*. Cedric Belfrage, trans. New York: Monthly Review Press, 1976.

Moreno Fraginals, Manuel, ed. *Africa in Latin America: Essays on History, Culture, and Socialization*. Leonor Blum, trans. New York: Holmes and Meier, 1984.

Morrish, Ivor. *Obeah, Christ and Rastaman: Jamaica and Its Religions*. Cambridge, England: James Clark, 1982.

Mosquera, Gerardo. "Africa in the Art of Latin America." *Art Journal* 5.4 (Winter 1992): 30–38.

———. "Elegguá at the (Post?)Modern Crossroads: The Presence of Africa in the Visual Art of Cuba." In *Santería Aesthetics in Contemporary Latin American Art*. Arturo Lindsay, ed. Washington, D.C.: Smithsonian Institution Press, 1996, 225–258.

Murphy, Joseph M. "Lydia Cabrera and *la Regla de Ocha* in the United States." In *En Torno a Lydia Cabrera*. Isabel Castellanos and Josefina Inclán, eds. Miami: Ediciones Universal, 1987, 246–254.

———. *Santería: African Spirits in America*. Boston: Beacon Press, 1993.

———. *Working the Spirit: Ceremonies of the African Diaspora*. Boston: Beacon Press, 1994.

New York Times. "Haile Selassie Is Mobbed by Jamaica Cult Adherents." April 22, 1966: 8.

Nuñez-Molina, Mario A. "'Desarrollo del medium': The Process of Becoming a Healer in Puerto Rican 'Espiritismo.'" Ph.D. dissertation, Harvard University, 1987.

———. "Community Healing among Puerto Ricans: *Espiritismo* as a Therapy for the Soul." In *Healing Cultures: Art and Religion as Curative Practices in the Caribbean and Its Diaspora*. Margarite Fernández Olmos and Lizabeth Paravisini-Gebert, eds. New York: Palgrave–St. Martin's Press, 2001, 115–129.

O'Brien, Derek, and Vaughan Carter. "Chant down Babylon: Freedom of Religion and the Rastafarian Challenge to Majoritarianism." *Journal of Law and Religion* 18:1 (2002–2003): 219–248.

Ortiz, Fernando. *Hampa Afro-Cubana: Los negros esclavos*. Havana: Revista Bimestre Cubana, 1916. (Reprint, *Los negros esclavos*. Havana: Editorial de Ciencias Sociales, 1987.)

———. "La fiesta afro-cubana del 'día de reyes,'" *Revista bimestre cubana* [Havana] 15.1 (1920): 5–26.

———. "Los cabildos afro-cubanos," *Ensayos etnográficos*. Miguel Barnet and Angel L. Fernández, eds. Havana: Editorial de Ciencias Sociales, 1984, 11–40.

———. *Los instrumentos de la música afrocubana*, Vol II. Havana: Publicaciones de la Dirección de la Cultura del Ministerio de la Educación, 1954.

Ortiz Cofer, Judith. *The Line of the Sun*. Athens: University of Georgia Press, 1989.

———. "Talking to the Dead." In *Silent Dancing: A Partial Remembrance of a Puerto Rican Childhood*. Houston: Arte Publico Press, 1990.

Padura Fuentes, Leonardo. *Adiós Hemingway y La cola de la serpiente*. Havana: Ediciones Unión, 2001.

Palmié, Stephan. "Ethnogenetic Processes and Cultural Transfer in Caribbean Slave Populations." In *Slavery in the Americas.*Wolfgang Binder, ed. Würzburg: Königshauser & Neumann, 1993, 337–364.

———. "Against Syncretism: 'Africanizing' and 'Cubanizing' Discourses in North American òrìsà Worship." In *Counterworks: Managing Diverse Knowledge*. Richard Fardon, ed. London: Routledge, 1995, 73–104.

———. *Wizards & Scientists: Explorations in Afro-Cuban Modernity & Tradition*. Durham: Duke University Press, 2002.

———. "Creolization and its Discontents." *Annual Review of Anthropology* 35 (2006): 433–456.

———. "Ecué's Atlantic: An Essay in Methodology." *Journal of Religion in Africa* 37.2 (2007): 275–315.

Palmié, Stephan, and Elizabeth Pérez. "An All Too Present Absence: Fernando Ortiz's Work on Abakuá in its Sociocultural Context. *New West Indian Guide / Nieuwe West-Indische Gids* 79. 3 & 4 (2005): 219–227.

Paravisini-Gebert, Lizabeth. *Phyllis Shand Allfrey: A Caribbean Life*. New Brunswick: Rutgers University Press, 1996.

———. "Women Possessed: Eroticism and Exoticism in the Representation of Woman as Zombie." In *Sacred Possessions: Vodou, Santería, Obeah, and the Caribbean*. Margarite Fernández Olmos and Lizabeth Paravisini-Gebert, eds. New Brunswick: Rutgers University Press, 1997, 37–58.

———. "'He of the Trees': Nature, the Environment, and Creole Religiosities in Caribbean Literature." In *Caribbean Literatures and the Environment*. Elizabeth DeLoughrey et al., eds. Charlottesville: University Press of Virginia, 2005, 182–196.

———. "Sacred Forms: Ritual, Representation, and the Body in Haitian Painting." In *Bodies Beautiful: Aesthetic Dimensions of Religion in the African Diaspora*. Anthony Pinn, ed. New York: Palgrave Macmillan, 2009, 91–112.

Paton, Diana. "Obeah Acts: Producing and Policing the Boundaries of Religion in the Caribbean." *small axe* 28 (2009): 1–18.

Patterson, Orlando. *The Sociology of Slavery: An Analysis of the Origins, Development and Structure of Negro Slave Society in Jamaica*. London: Macgibon and Kee, 1967.

Payne-Jackson, Arvilla, and Mervyn C. Alleyne. *Jamaican Folk Medicine: A Source of Healing*.Kingston: University of the West Indies Press, 2004.

Penrose, Clement A. "Sanitary Conditions in the Bahamas Islands." In *The Bahama Islands*. George Burbank Shattuck, ed. New York: Johns Hopkins Press (Geographical Society of Baltimore), 1905.

Pérez, Laura E. *Chicana Art: The Politics of Spiritual and Aesthetic Altarities*. Durham: Duke University Press, 2007.

———. "Hybrid Spiritualities and Chicana Altar-Based Art: The Work of Amalia Aesa-Bains." In *Mexican American Religions: Spirituality, Activism, and Culture*. Gaston Espinosa and Mario T. Garcia, eds. Durham: Duke University Press, 2008, 338–358.

Pérez, Lisandro. "The Catholic Church in Cuba: A Weak Institution." In *Puerto Rican and Cuban Catholics in the U.S., 1900–1965*. Jay P. Dolan and Jamie R. Vidal, eds. Notre Dame: University of Notre Dame Press, 1994, 147–157.

Pérez, Jr., Louis A. *Slaves, Sugar, and Colonial Society: Travel Accounts of Cuba, 1801–1899*. Wilmington, Del.: Scholarly Resources, 1992.

Pérez Sarduy, Pedro, and Jean Stubbs, eds. *Afrocuba: An Anthology of Cuban Writing on Race, Politics and Culture*. Melbourne: Ocean Press, 1993.

Pérez y Mena, Andrés Isidoro. *Speaking with the Dead: Development of Afro-Latin Religion among Puerto Ricans in the United States*. New York: AMS Press, 1991.

Perrone, Bobette, H. Henrietta Stockel, and Victoria Krueger. *Medicine Women, Curanderas, and Women Doctors*. Norman: University of Oklahoma Press, 1989.

Philalethes, Demoticus [pseud.]. "Hunting the Maroons with Dogs in Cuba." In *Maroon Societies: Rebel Slave Communities in the Americas*. Richard Price, ed. Garden City: Anchor Press/Doubleday, 1973, 60–63.

Phillippo, James. *Jamaica: Its Past and Present State*. London: J. Snow, 1843.

Piedra, José. "From Monkey Tales to Cuban Songs: On Signification." In *Sacred Possessions: Vodou, Santería, Obeah, and the Caribbean*. Margarite Fernández Olmos and Lizabeth Paravisini-Gebert, eds. New Brunswick: Rutgers University Press, 1997, 122–150.

Pollak-Eltz, Angelina. "The Worship of Historical Personalities in the Cult of Maria Lionza in Venezuela." *Anales del Caribe: Centro de Estudios del Caribe* 19–20 (1999–2000): 187–191.

Poupeye, Veerle. *Caribbean Art*. New York: Thames and Hudson, 1998.

Pollard, Velma. *Dread Talk: The Language of Rastafari*. 2nd ed. Montreal & Kingston: McGill-Queen's University Press, 2000.

Pradel, Lucie. *African Beliefs in the New World*. Catherine Bernard, trans. Trenton, N.J.: Africa World Press, 2000.

Prahlad, Anand. *Reggae Wisdom: Proverbs in Jamaican Music*. Jackson: University Press of Mississippi, 2001.

Price, Charles, Donald Nonini, and Erich Fox Tree. "Grounded Utopian Movements: Subjects of Neglect." *Anthropological Quarterly* 81:1 (Winter 2008): 127–159.

Price, Richard, ed. *Maroon Societies: Rebel Slave Communities in the Americas*. Garden City: Anchor Press/Doubleday, 1973.

Prida, Dolores. *Botánica*. In *Beautiful Señoritas and Other Plays*. Houston: Arte Publico Press, 1991.

Prorok, Carolyn V. "Boundaries Are Made for Crossing: The Feminized Spatiality of Puerto Rican *Espiritismo* in New York City." *Gender, Place and Culture: A Journal of Feminist Geography* 7.1 (March 2000): 57–79.

Pullen-Burry, Bessie. *Jamaica as It Is, 1903*. London: T. F. Unwin, 1903.

Putnam, Lara. "Rites of Power and Rumours of Race: The Circulation of Supernatural Knowledge and Sacrifice Tales in the Greater Caribbean, 1890–1940." Paper presented at the Conference on "Obeah and Other Powers: The Politics of Caribbean Religion and Healing," July 16–18, 2008.

Pye, Michael. "Syncretism and Ambiguity." *Numen* 18 (1971): 83–93.

Quiñones, Tato. *Ecorie abakuá: cuatro ensayos sobre los ñáñagigos cubanos*. Havana: Ediciones Unión, 1994.

Ramos, Miguel "Willie." "Afro-Cuban Orisha Worship." In *Santería Aesthetics in Contemporary Latin American Art*. Arturo Lindsay, ed. Washington, D.C.: Smithsonian Institution Press, 1996, 51–75.

Rampini, Charles. "Letters from Jamaica." In *After Africa*. Roger D. Abrahams and John F. Szwed, eds. New Haven: Yale University Press, 1983.

Report of the Lords of the Committee of the Council Appointed for the Consideration of All Matters Relating to Trade and Foreign Plantations. London, 1789.

Richardson, Alan. "Romantic Voodoo: Obeah and British Culture, 1797–1807." In *Sacred Possessions: Vodou, Santería, Obeah, and the Caribbean*. Margarite Fernández Olmos and Lizabeth Paravisini-Gebert, eds. New Brunswick: Rutgers University Press, 1997, 171–194.

Richman, Karen E. "A More Powerful Sorcerer: Conversion, Capital, and Haitian Transnational Migration." Paper presented at the Conference on "Obeah and Other Powers: The Politics of Caribbean Religion and Healing," July 16–18, 2008.

Rigaud, Milo. *La Tradition voudoo et le voudoo haïten*. Paris: Editions Niclaus, 1953.

——. *Secrets of Voodoo*. New York: Arco, 1969.

Rodman, Selmen. *Where Art Is Joy—Haitian Art: The First Forty Years*. New York: Ruggles de Latour, 1988.

Rodney, Walter. *Groundings with My Brothers*. London: Bogle-L'Ouverture, 1969.

Rodríguez, Escudero, Néstor A. *Historia del Espiritismo en Puerto Rico*. Puerto Rico: Author, 1991.

Rodríguez-Mangual, Edna. *Lydia Cabrera and the Construction of an Afro-Cuban Cultural Identity*. Chapel Hill: University of North Carolina Press, 2004.

Rodney, Walter. *Groundings with My Brothers*. London: Bogle-L'Ouverture, 1969.

Rodríguez, Escudero, Néstor A. *Historia del Espiritismo en Puerto Rico*. Puerto Rico: Author, 1991.

Romberg, Raquel. *Witchcraft and Welfare: Spiritual Capital and the Business of Magic in Modern Puerto Rico*. Austin: University of Texas Press, 2003.

——. "Global Spirituality: Consumerism and Heritage in a Puerto Rican Afro-Latin Folk Religion." In *Contemporary Caribbean Cultures and Societies in a Global Context*. Franklin W. Knight and Teresita Martínez-Vergne, eds. Chapel Hill: University of North Carolina Press, 2005, 131–155.

Romero Cesareo, Ivette. "Sorcerers, She-Devils, Shipwrecked Women: Writing Religion in French-Caribbean Literature." In *Sacred Possessions: Vodou, Santería, Obeah, and the Caribbean*. Margarite Fernández Olmos and Lizabeth Paravisini-Gebert, eds. New Brunswick: Rutgers University Press, 1997, 248–266.

Rosenberg, June. *El gagá: Religión y sociedad de un culto dominicano.* Santo Domingo: Editora de la UASD, 1979.

Sanders, Rory. "From the Root of King David: A Rastafarian Primer." In *Reggae International.* Stephen Davis and Peter Simon, eds. New York: R&B, 1982, 59–71.

Schuler, Monica. "Myalism and the African Tradition." *Savacou* (June 1970): 8–31.

Schwieger Hiepko, Andrea. "Creolization as a Poetics of Culture: Édouard Glissant's 'Archipelic' Thinking." In *A Pepper-Pot of Cultures: Aspects of Creolization in the Caribbean.* Gordon Collier and Ulrich Fleischmann, eds. Amsterdam-New York: (Rodopi, 2003. 237–259. (Matatu [Journal] 27–28.)

Seabrook, William B. *The Magic Island.* New York: Harcourt, Brace, 1929.

Seaga, Edward. "Revival Cults in Jamaica." *Jamaica Journal* 3:2 (June 1969): 1–12.

Seda, Eduardo. *Social Change and Personality in a Puerto Rican Agrarian Reform Community.* Evanston: Northwestern University Press, 1973.

Sharp, Lynn L. "Fighting for the Afterlife: Spiritists, Catholics, and Popular Religion in Nineteenth-Century France." *Journal of Religious History* 23.3 (October 1999): 282–295.

Sides, Hampton. "The Calibration of Belief." *New York Times Magazine,* Sec. 6 (December 7, 1997): 92–95.

Simpson, George Eaton. *The Shango Cult in Trinidad.* Rio Piedras, P.R.: Institute of Caribbean Studies, University of Puerto Rico, 1965.

———. *Black Religion in the New World.* New York: Columbia University Press, 1978.

Sosa Rodríguez, Enrique. *Los ñáñigos.* Havana: Casa de las Américas, 1982.

Stevens, Anthony M., and Ana María Díaz-Stevens, eds. *An Enduring Flame: Studies on Latino Popular Religiosity.* New York: Bildner Center for Western Hemisphere Studies, 1994.

Stevens, Anthony M., and Andrés I. Pérez y Mena. *Enigmatic Powers: Syncretism with African and Indigenous Peoples' Religions among Latinos.* New York: Bildner Center for Western Hemisphere Studies, 1995.

Stewart, Charles, ed. "Introduction." *Creolization: History, Ethnography, Theory.* Walnut Creek, Calif.: Left Coast Press, 2007.

Stewart, Charles, and Rosalind Shaw, eds. *Syncretism/Anti-Syncretism: The Politics of Religious Synthesis.* New York: Routledge, 1994.

Stewart, Dianne Maria Burrowes. "The Evolution of African-Derived Religions in Jamaica." Ph.D. dissertation, Union Theological Seminary, New York, 1997.

Suárez Rosado, Angel. "Ese constante sabor por comunicainos con el más allá." In *La tercera raíz: presencia africana en Puerto Rico.* San Juan: Centro de Estudios de la Realidad Puertorriqueña, Instituto de Cultura Puertorriqueña, 1992.

Taussig, Michael. *Shamanism, Colonialism, and the Wild Man.* Chicago: University of Chicago Press, 1987.

Taylor, Patrick, ed. *Nation Dance: Religion, Identity, and Cultural Difference in the Caribbean.* Bloomington: Indiana University Press, 2001.

Thomas, Hugh. *Cuba: The Pursuit of Freedom.* New York: Harper and Row, 1971.

Thomas, Keith. *Religion and the Decline of Magic.* New York: Charles Scribner's and Sons, 1971.

Thompson, Robert Farris. *Flash of the Spirit: African and Afro-American Art and Philosophy.* New York: Vintage, 1984.

———. "From the Isle beneath the Sea: Haiti's Africanizing Vodou Art." In *Sacred Arts of Haitian Vodou*. Donald Cosentino, ed. Los Angeles: UCLA Fowler Museum of Cultural History, 1995, 91–119.

Thumma, Scott, and Edward R. Gray, eds. *Gay Religion*. Walnut Creek, Calif.: AltaMira Press, 2005.

Tobar, Héctor. *Defining a New American Identity in the Spanish-Speaking United States*. New York: Riverhead Books, 2005.

Torres-Saillant, Silvio. *An Intellectual History of the Caribbean*. New York: Palgrave Macmillan, 2006.

Torrey, E. Fuller. *Witchdoctors and Psychiatrists: The Common Roots of Psychotherapy and Its Future*. Rev. ed. New York: Harper and Row, 1986.

Turner, Mary. *Slaves and Missionaries: The Disintegration of Jamaican Slave Society, 1787–1834*. Chicago: University of Illinois Press, 1982.

Turner, Victor. *The Ritual Process: Structure and Anti-Structure*. Ithaca: Cornell University Press, 1969.

———, ed. *Celebration: Studies in Festivity and Ritual*. Washington, D.C.: Smithsonian Institution Press, 1982.

Tylor, Edward Burnett. *Primitive Culture: Researches into the Development of Mythology, Philosophy, Religion, Art, and Custom*. London: J. Murray, 1871.

Udal, J. S. "Obeah in the West Indies." *Folklore* 26 (1915): 255–295.

Vega, Marta Moreno. "Espiritismo in the Puerto Rican Community." *Journal of Black Studies* 19.3 (January 1999): 325–354.

———. *The Altar of My Soul: The Living Traditions of Santería*. New York: Ballantine Publishing, 2000.

———. *When the Spirits Dance Mambo: Growing Up Nuyorican in El Barrio*. New York: Three Rivers Press, 2004.

Vélez, María Teresa. *Drumming for the Gods: The Life and Times of Felipe García Villamil, Santero, Palero, and Abakuá*. Philadelphia: Temple University Press, 2000.

Vidal-Ortiz, Salvador. "Sexuality and Gender in Santería: LGBT Identities at the Crossroads of Santería Religious Practices and Beliefs." In *Gay Religion*. Scott Thumma and Edward R. Gray, eds. Walnut Creek, Calif.: AltaMira Press, 2005, 115–137.

Voeks, Robert A. *Sacred Leaves of Candomblé: African Magic, Medicine, and Religion in Brazil*. Austin: University of Texas Press, 1997.

von Humboldt, Alexander. *The Island of Cuba*. Translated into English with notes and preliminary essay by J. S. Thrasher. New York: Derby and Jackson, 1856. (Reprint, New York: Negro Universities Press, 1969.)

West-Duran, Alan. "Rap's Diasporic Dialogues: Cuba's Redefinition of Blackness." In *Cuba Transnational*. Damián J. Fernández, ed. Gainesville: University Press of Florida, 2005, 121–150.

Wexler, Anna. "'I Am Going to See Where My Oungan Is': The Artistry of a Haitian Vodou Flagmaker." In *Sacred Possessions: Vodou, Santería, Obeah, and the Caribbean*. Margarite Fernández Olmos and Lizabeth Paravisini-Gebert, eds. New Brunswick: Rutgers University Press, 1997, 59–78.

———. "Dolls and Healing in a Santería House." In *Healing Cultures: Art and Religion as Curative Practices in the Caribbean and Its Diaspora*. Margarite Fernández Olmos and Lizabeth Paravisini-Gebert, eds., 2001, 89–113.

Williams, Joseph J. *Voodoos and Obeahs: Phrases of West Indian Witchcraft*. New York: Dial, 1932.

Wurdemann, J. G. F. *Notes on Cuba*. Boston: Munroe, 1844. (Reprint, New York: Arno Press, 1971.)

Yawney, Carole D. *Lions in Babylon: The Rastafarians of Jamaica as a Visionary Movement*. Ottawa: National Library of Canada, 1980.

DISCOGRAPHY

Afro-Cuba: A Musical Anthology. Rounder CD 1088. Examples of Arará, Yesá, Matanzas batá, and güiro.

Alan Lomax in Haiti. Various artists. Harte Recordings B002FOQY7C, 2009.

Havana, Cuba, c. 1957: Rhythms and Songs for the Orishas. Smithsonian Folkways CD 40489. Examples of Regla de Ocha ritual batá drum music recorded by Lydia Cabrera and Josefina Tarafa. Annotated by Morton Marks.

Sacred Rhythms of Cuban Santería. Smithsonian Folkways CD 40419.

Síntesis. *Ancestros*. Qba-Disc 9001.

Index

About the Authors

MARGARITE FERNÁNDEZ OLMOS is a professor of Spanish and Latin American literatures at Brooklyn College of the City University of New York. She is the author or coeditor of many books, including *U.S. Latino Literature: A Critical Guide for Students and Teachers* and *The Latino Reader: An American Literary Tradition from 1542 to the Present*.

LIZABETH PARAVISINI-GEBERT is a professor in the department of Hispanic studies on the Randolph Distinguished Professor Chair and Director of the Environmental Studies Program at Vassar College. She is the author of many books and is coeditor with Fernández Olmos of *Healing Cultures: Art and Religion as Curative Practices in the Caribbean and Its Diaspora* and *Sacred Possessions: Vodou, Santería, Obeah, and the Caribbean*.